VENTRILOQUIZED
BODIES

Francis Picabia. Title page. Littérature no. 10, 1 May 1923.

VENTRILOQUIZED

BODIES

Narratives of Hysteria
in Nineteenth-Century France

JANET BEIZER

CORNELL UNIVERSITY PRESS
ITHACA AND LONDON

FRONTISPIECE: Francis Picabia. Title page. *Littérature* no. 10, 1 May 1923. (© 1993 ARS, N.Y./A.D.A.G.P./SPADEM, Paris; photo Pauline Page.)

Passages from Gustave Flaubert, *Correspondance*, Pléiade edition edited by Jean Bruneau. Copyright © Editions GALLIMARD 1973, 1980, 1991. Reprinted by permission of Editions Gallimard.
Excerpts from *La Servante* by Louise Colet. Reprinted from *Femmes de lettres au XIXe siècle: Autour de Louise Colet*, edited by Roger Bellet. Reproduced by permission of Presses Universitaires de Lyon.
Excerpts from *Madame Bovary* by Gustave Flaubert, edited and translated by Paul de Man. Copyright © 1965 by W. W. Norton and Company, Inc.
Passages from *Nana* by Emile Zola, translated by George Holden. Copyright © George Holden, 1972. Reproduced with permission of Penguin Books Ltd.
Passages from *Monsieur Vénus*, by Rachilde. Copyright © Flammarion, 1977. Reproduced by permission of Flammarion. Passages from *Monsieur Vénus*, by Rachilde, translated by Madeleine Boyd. Copyright © Covici, Friede, 1929. Reprinted by permission of Flammarion.

Chapter 1 appeared in French translation as "Femme-texte et roman hystérique" in *Revue internationale de psychopathologie* 4 (1991).
Chapter 3 appeared in *Compar(a)ison* 1 (1993).
Chapter 4 appeared in French translation as "Les Lettres de Flaubert à Louise Colet: Une physiologie du style" in *L'Oeuvre de l'oeuvre: Etudes sur la correspondance de Flaubert*, edited by Raymonde Debray Genette, Presses Universitaires de Vincennes, 1993.
A portion of Chapter 6 appeared in *Home and Its Dislocations in Nineteenth-Century France*, edited by Suzanne Nash, State University of New York Press, 1993.
Parts of Chapter 7 appeared in *L'Esprit Créateur* 29 (Spring 1989); 25 (Winter 1985); and 25 (Summer 1985) under the respective titles: "The Body in Question: Textuality, Anatomy, and Fetishism in Zola"; Remembering and Repeating the *Rougon-Macquart*: Clotilde's Story"; and "Uncovering *Nana*: The Courtesan's New Clothes."

First published 1994 by Cornell University Press.

International Standard Book Number 0-8014-2914-5 (cloth)
International Standard Book Number 0-8014-8142-2 (paper)
Library of Congress Catalog Card Number 93-41379
Librarians: Library of Congress cataloging information appears on the last page of the book.

Design: Christine Taylor
Composition: Wilsted & Taylor

Printed in the United States of America

♾ The paper in this book meets the minimum requirements of the American National Standard for Information Sciences—Permanence of Paper for Printed Library Materials, ANSI Z39.48-1984.

To my parents

CONTENTS

ILLUSTRATIONS

ACKNOWLEDGMENTS

As I was returning from San Francisco when this book was about two-thirds written, my plane lost one of its two engines as it began to climb. Craning my neck to look through the window behind me, I could see flames leaping; straining my ear, I could hear a flight attendant's tremulous voice crack while telling the passengers to stay calm. As the plane limped back over the Bay to an uncertain landing, I indulged in a few last telepathic good-byes and, Huck Finn–like, attended my own funeral. No eye at this scene of mourning was dry—least of all my own—when *Ventriloquized Bodies* was rescued from a death by incompletion, through the efforts of two friends who vowed to continue my thoughts and finish my words. I trust Jessica Feldman and Farzaneh Milani to extricate from the presumptuousness of this fantasy the sense of intellectual and spiritual kinship that produced it. As close colleagues and critical friends, they read, challenged, and stoked my writing through all of its phases.

I am deeply grateful to Kaveh Safa, who always made time to give my work in progress the benefit of his insight and his erudition. In the midst of many de-

ACKNOWLEDGMENTS

xii
•
mands, Martha Noel Evans commented on much of the book, which has profited from her expertise in the theory of hysteria. Nelly Furman responded to the manuscript with a sensitivity to detail that helped shape my revisions. Francine du Plessix Gray read and critiqued the Flaubert-Colet chapters with a connoisseur's eye. I had the good fortune to meet Evelyne Ender and Jacqueline Carroy in the later stages of my work, and to gain from their knowledge of hysteria and the hospitable contexts they offered in Geneva and Paris, respectively, for our exchanges. In Paris, Claude Lazard has for the past twenty years provided an intellectual home, and with the other Lazards often a more literal roof. Michèle and Claude Joigny have given spiritual and earthly nourishment, over the years, in Paris and Bergerac. Catherine Girard opened the first window onto Paris for me, long ago, and has joined me in many other explorations since. And I continue to learn from Josette Pacaly and to be inspired by her intellect and her integrity.

Nancy Armstrong, Deborah Baker, Charles Bernheimer, Scott Bryson, Lionel Duisit, Jan Goldstein, Janet Horne, Marie-Hélène Huet, Dianne Hunter, Elisabeth Ladenson, Deborah McDowell, Mary McKinley, Jann Matlock, D. A. Miller, and Margaret Waller have all graciously commented on portions of the manuscript. Their suggestions have been invaluable. Other friends and colleagues have engaged in conversation—sometimes bridging miles or disciplines—that indirectly worked its way into my text. Tiina Allik, Deborah Lesko Baker, Peter Brooks, Ross Chambers, Françoise Gaillard, Joan Holladay, Laura Rivkin, and Michelle Safa provided sustaining wisdom and encouragement. I had the opportunity to articulate the first stages of this research in a graduate seminar on hysteria and the novel. I am indebted to my students for engaging me in an ongoing process of rethinking and reformulating my ideas. Without the counsel and kind acts of Paul Barolsky, Jenny Clay, Kandioura Dramé, Asti Hustvedt, James Leith, and Janet Timberlake, it would have been difficult to bring this project to a close.

My venture into the nineteenth-century medical record took me into labyrinthine contexts often strange to my experience. I was fortunate to be guided by the medical expertise of Ochine Karapetian and Kenneth Greer, who advised me on dermographism; Christopher Perry, who assured me that a specialist in the field did not find my reading of nineteenth-century hysteria treatises aberrant; Ruth Weeks, who led me to the physiological phantasms of J. P. Möbius and beyond; and Steven Seidner, who taught me, among other things, all I needed to know about borborygmi.

Time and travel necessary to my research and writing were made possible by the generosity of the American Council for Learned Societies, the National Endowment for the Humanities, the American Philosophical Society, and the University of Virginia. Their support is gratefully acknowledged. Research took me between libraries in Paris and Charlottesville, with a foray to Avignon. I would like to give

special thanks to Véronique Leroux-Hugon of the Charcot Library at the Salpêtrière Hospital in Paris, to Christie Stephenson and Jack Robertson of the Fiske
Kimball Fine Arts Library at the University of Virginia, and to Bryson Clevenger
of the Alderman Library at the University of Virginia. I am grateful to Pauline
Page for her careful reproduction of many of my illustrations, to Virginia Ger-
mino, Jean-Luc DeSalvo, and Sarah Skrainka for their skillful help in preparing
the manuscript, and to Gail Moore and Judy Birckhead, for their expert technical
assistance. And at Cornell University Press, I wish to thank Teresa Jesionowski for
her gracious guidance, her sense of humor, and her time, and Bernhard Kendler,
who supported this project well before it was a book.

To my family, a gratitude that can only be obliquely evoked. My father touched
my childhood with a passion for words and a sense of their power, and my mother,
with a love of novels that runs in the blood, and her own childhood copy of Bram
Stoker's *Dracula*, from which I wrote the last pages in this book. Laura Beizer has
in defiance of geography been a constant presence in my life, shifting effortlessly
and synchronously with me between the trivial and the weighty, the real and the
imaginary, and laughing with me when the opposition disappears. And Anne
Sandburg, who danced always to the drummer she heard without ever striving to
be different, taught me a great deal by her example.

Finally, a special note of thanks to all the friends, colleagues, and passersby who
swallowed the often hefty portions of vampire soup that I doled out freely during
the last mad days of immersion in *Dracula*. They know who they are.

JANET BEIZER
Charlottesville, Virginia

VENTRILOQUIZED
BODIES

INTRODUCTION

This is a book that both is and is not about hysteria, for it shed its original skin somewhere along a sinuous course toward the light. It began with Tante Dide, the hysterical founding mother of Emile Zola's *Rougon-Macquart* dynasty, as a reflection on the paradoxical identification of her convulsed, inarticulate woman's body as narrative source. It took preliminary shape as an extended musing on the recurrent figuration, in Zola's text, of an incoherent, unconscious, incapacitated, or otherwise mute woman's body that nevertheless produces the stuff of stories. Dide's heirs in the *Rougon-Macquart*, lesser hysterics they, also display bodies that are the site of gestures and throbbings that a male narrator then translates into words, in a reversal of what Freud would later call *conversion hysteria*. As my conceptualization of literary hysteria crystallized in the image of women's bodies in textual poses—saying nothing, signifying all—hysteria's body escaped the confines of Zola's corpus. I recognized its form in a great number of male-authored nineteenth-century texts, which seemed to exist in a tense relationship with the as-

INTRODUCTION

2
•

siduously demarcated hysterical Other upon whom they depended for their very lives.

At that point in the mid 1980s when I came to this project, the hysteric was being rediscovered by literary and cultural critics on both sides of the Atlantic and was often recovered in feminism's name as a figure emblematic of revolt against the patriarchy: as a cult figure.[1] A certain late twentieth-century feminism ironically repeated the surrealists' embrace of fin de siècle hysteria as poetic liberation: "la plus grande découverte poétique de la fin du XIXe siècle" ["the greatest poetic discovery of the late nineteenth century"], in the words of Louis Aragon and André Breton.[2] They doubtless found in the hysteric's aphasic murmurings and inarticulate cries a delivery from syntax, a subversion of social and cultural codes, a transgressive poetics, as they discovered in the well-photographed postures and convulsions of the generally female hysterical body an alternative theater, a living erotic art.[3]

Although I too was fascinated by the link between hysteria and expression, I was troubled by the surrealist salute to hysterics as fellow artists, for such a perspective seemed to romanticize a condition in fact suffered as expressive blockage and constraint. My own approach shifts their emphasis on the immediacy of hysterical expression ("un moyen suprême d'expression" ["a supreme expressive medium"]) toward the mediated expression of hysteria.[4] I was less interested in what hysterics themselves expressed than in the ways in which they served the expressive powers of others and the reasons for which the nineteenth-century concept of hysteria was metaphorically useful and even necessary to that era's narrative discourse. For long before the surrealists' recuperation of hysteria as a protopoetics, a varied series of writers (novelists, journalists, historians) had discovered this potential and tapped it: metaphorized it, converted its maiming force into narrative power.

To better comprehend the hysteric's seductiveness for nineteenth-century literati, I set out to take the measure of clinical hysteria. I read every history of the disease I could find and spent several months in the Salpêtrière Hospital's Charcot Library immersed in the reading of nineteenth-century medical texts. Background

[1] See, for example, Hélène Cixous's comments in her dialogue with Catherine Clément, "L'Intenable," in Cixous and Clément, *La Jeune Née* (Paris: 10/18, 1975), 271–96; and Dianne Hunter, "Hysteria, Psychoanalysis, and Feminism: The Case of Anna O.," in *The (M)other Tongue: Essays in Feminist Psychoanalytic Interpretation*, ed. Shirley Nelson Garner, Claire Kahane, Madelon Sprengnether (Ithaca: Cornell University Press, 1985), 89–115.
[2] Louis Aragon and André Breton, "Le Cinquantenaire de l'hystérie," *La Révolution Surréaliste* 4 (15 March 1928): 20. All translations throughout the book are my own unless otherwise stated in the notes.
[3] For a study of hysteria at the Salpêtrière under Charcot from the perspective of image (with an emphasis on the spectacle of hysteria as a reflection of the processes used to set it up, such as photography and staging), see Georges Didi-Huberman's *Invention de l'hystérie: Charcot et l'iconographie photographique de la Salpêtrière* (Paris: Macula, 1982).
[4] Aragon and Breton, "Le Cinquantenaire," 22.

reading. But as the days passed and the pages turned, distinctions between background and foreground, medical and literary, scientific and fictional, truth and myth began to slip and slide and then to blur. In the course of these months, *hysteria* virtually disappeared. In its place was a discourse made in the image of all that was feared, desired, and repudiated by nineteenth-century rational men.

The move from a consideration of hysteria as diagnosis of a female malady to a reconsideration of the female malady as a broader-based cultural symptom describes the path of this book. Though I state it baldly here in the cavalier tones of all retrospective introductions, my thinking did not follow a smooth linear development; it evolved bit by bit in the process of reading and writing, and even, on a smaller scale, within each individual chapter. Because it may be useful to follow a process rather than confront a conclusion, and because it is in any case impossible to eliminate the traces of an evolution, I have made little effort to purge these traces.

In fact the evolutionary record is everywhere inscribed as a split in my own narrative and my own discourse, for it is difficult to speak of hysteria without reifying or essentializing or naturalizing, *by that act of naming*, the very idea I have instead come to construe and want to present as discourse, process, and construct. Given that we write behind the bars of discourse and that coherent writing does not allow for a self-reflective deconstructive pause at every turn, my narrative of hysteria will of necessity be doubly positioned. Nowhere perhaps will this split be more in evidence than in the pages immediately following, where I introduce hysteria with a brief history of what has been called by that name for well over two thousand years and designated by a consistent configuration of symptoms for almost twice as long. Such a history can only be a fiction, for there has never been a second of that time when hysteria existed as an entity outside a web of contexts (misogyny, pathology, death, religion, and the supernatural, among others), and each of those contexts has a history as well, which includes other contexts—and so on. I take this historical ground as my departure point, knowing that I tread on quicksand.

Despite its eruption as the nineteenth-century equivalent of a media event, hysteria was not born with that century. Anyone attempting to trace the medical record of the disease must traverse all of medical history and encounter a proliferation of texts at every step along the way. Although the search is further complicated by the very mystification of the disease (commentators repeatedly warn that hysteria defies definition), some general constants emerge.

From Egyptian antiquity until the seventeenth century, hysteria was conceptualized virtually without contestation as a female disease, a uterine disorder.[5]

[5] The texts I have found most useful in preparing the following summary (in addition to the nineteenth-century primary sources listed in the bibliography) are Paul Bercherie, *Genèse des concepts freudiens*

4
•

Though specific details varied slightly, general etiological and symptomatological features remained constant over a little-interrupted span of some thirty-eight centuries. Medical writers largely agreed that the malady was causally related to sexual abstinence and amenorrhea (its most frequent victims being virgins, widows, and nuns), and their writings generally emphasized the physical manifestations of the hysterical seizure: suffocation, vomiting, palpitations, convulsions, fainting, the voiding of large quantities of urine, and speech disturbances.

The earliest extant medical record, the Egyptian *Kahun Papyrus* (dating roughly from 1900 B.C.), set the etiological and therapeutic patterns that were to remain fixed for centuries. This document attributed various behavioral anomalies to the workings of a mobile uterus, which roamed around the body crowding other organs, or alternatively, to "starvation" of the uterus. The task of the physician therefore involved alternatively chasing or luring the strayed organ back to its rightful position, or else nourishing it. The patient was given repulsive substances to inhale or ingest, or her genital organs were fumigated with enticing aromatic substances. These fragrant odors were sometimes incorporated in a waxen image of the male deity Thoth, which was then used as a vulvar fumigating device to draw the womb back to its place.

Greek and Roman contributions to the theory of hysteria were predominantly derivative. Greek representations of the wandering womb find their most apt expression in Plato's *Timaeus*: "The womb is an animal which longs to generate children. When it remains barren too long after puberty, it is distressed and sorely disturbed, and straying about in the body and cutting off passages of the breath, it impedes respiration and brings the sufferer into the extremest anguish and provokes all manner of diseases besides."[6]

Hippocrates (460–377 B.C.) was the first to use the term *hysteria*, derived from the Greek *hystera*, "uterus." He explained why the disease could be caused by sexual continence: the abstemious uterus dried up, lost weight, and consequently was able to migrate in search of moisture. The pressure of the dislocated womb, along with its obstruction of other organs and passages, produced the symptoms that the Egyptians had first recorded. The remedies prescribed by Hippocrates and followed by physicians well into the nineteenth century placed marriage and pregnancy in prime position.

Galen (130–201 A.D.) recognized the stationary and fixed position of the womb but nevertheless believed it was responsible for hysteria. A major proponent of hu-

---

(Paris: Navarin, 1983); Jean-Marie Bruttin, *Différentes Théories sur l'hystérie dans la première moitié du XIXe siècle* (Zurich: Juris Druck, 1969); and Ilza Veith, *Hysteria: The History of a Disease* (Chicago: University of Chicago Press, 1965).
[6] Plato, *Timaeus*, 91c. Quoted by Veith, *Hysteria*, 7–8.

morism, he taught that continence caused retention of the seminal humor in the
womb, and that this in turn corrupted the blood and irritated the nerves. Alterna-   •
tively, retention of the menses had the same effect.

During the Middle Ages, medicine, largely dominated by the church, was confronted with the difficult task of reconciling the state of the art with the Christian
ethic. It was troubling to think that sexual continence, ostensibly a virtue, could
generate disease. Hysteria therefore ceased to be considered a malady related to abstinence and became a sign of sexuality, a sexual curse that bore witness to a pact
with the devil. The disease became a heresy and was accordingly treated with organized persecution from about the ninth century to the seventeenth. The most
noteworthy text of this period was the *Malleus Maleficarum* (*Witches' Hammer*) of
1494, a manual of persecution commissioned by the pope and written by monks
for use by inquisitors. It ascribed any kind of sexual pleasure to the devil's work.
Woman's gratification was an obvious sign of demonic interference, and man's
pleasure could be derived only from a satanically influenced female partner. Any
lust present in either sex was therefore a female (that is, demonic) contribution.

Although during the Renaissance a few voices (notably those of Jean de Wier
and Paracelsus) were raised to dispute the association between hysteria and sorcery,
it died hard. Despite a dawning interest on the part of physicians in the observation
of patients and a limited turning back to the Hippocratic tradition, it was only in
1680 that a royal edict outlawed the execution of witches in France.

We can trace the first clear expression of hysteria as a cerebral disease affecting
both sexes to Charles Lepois in 1618. The theory went largely unheeded, however,
for some fifty years until it was re-presented by Thomas Willis in 1667 and then by
Thomas Sydenham (the "English Hippocrates") in 1681. Even then, one could
hardly say it took the world by storm. The uterine theory continued to have numerous and staunch supporters until well into the nineteenth century, and the battle between the uterine and the cerebral or neurological schools of thought was
waged for more than three centuries.

Despite the fact that proponents of these new theories ostensibly sought to displace the womb theory upward and, correlatively, to bisexualize hysteria, they retained implications that hysteria was a female province. Sydenham and others
shifted the traditional descriptive focus from the hysterical fit and its physical
symptoms to a wide range of nervous symptoms, including emotional responses
but also behavioral traits such as capriciousness and exaggeration (features of the
sort that were to dominate nineteenth-century diagnoses of the malady). They also
began to emphasize an affective rather than a somatic etiology, tracing the disease
to moral causes, or passions. But this meant that women were more prone to hysteria than men were, for their nature was more delicate and impressionable, their

6
•   responses more emotional—and necessarily so, for their maternal destiny so commanded. Denied a literal etiological role, the womb nevertheless returned as a metaphoric agent of hysteria.

When hysteria was attributed to men, it retained its identity as a female complaint. As a male affliction, it was usually ascribed to the effeminacy of the victim or of his life-style. Sydenham, for example, declares: "As to females, if we except those who lead a hard and hardy life, there is rarely one who is free from [hysterical complaints]. . . . Then, again, such male subjects as lead a sedentary or studious life, and grow pale over their books and papers, are similarly afflicted."[7]

Eighteenth-century views of hysteria continued to be fraught with ambiguity. Many scientists who espoused so-called neurological theory did not absolutely abandon uterine theory; they retained causal notions of abstinence, amenorrhea, and uterine disorder but claimed that these factors acted upon the nerves. William Cullen is a case in point. Although he classified hysteria (in 1775) as a neurological disease, he traced it to the traditional uterine disorder, whose definition he amplified, however, to include the ovaries. Nymphomaniacs were especially vulnerable. The century closed with Philippe Pinel (perhaps best known as the figure who symbolically unchains the female insane in the painting by Tony Robert-Fleury).[8] Pinel essentially followed Cullen but offered a modified etiological perspective that synthesized—appropriately, on the eve of the nineteenth century—traditional somatic causes (amenorrhea, leukorrhea, continence) and the modern affective or behavioral causes that were to become increasingly frequent in the new century: "Une grande sensibilité physique ou morale, l'abus des plaisirs, des émotions vives et fréquentes, des conversations et des lectures voluptueuses"[9] ["Great physical or moral sensitivity, abuse of pleasures, vivid and recurrent emotions, voluptuous conversation and reading"].

In the course of the nineteenth century, the theory of hysteria changed radically in appearance while maintaining an essential conservatism. If we move from the early part of the century, and theorists such as Jean-Baptiste Louyer-Villermay, to the 1870s and 1880s (the "golden age of hysteria") and the neurologist Jean-Martin Charcot, there appears to be a change of emphasis from the uterus to the brain. It

[7] Thomas Sydenham, cited by Veith, *Hysteria*, 141.

[8] "Pinel libérant les aliénés," a mural hanging outside the Charcot Library at the Salpêtrière Hospital, was painted in 1878; the actual event occurred in 1795 and was preceded by a symbolic unchaining at Bicêtre, the corresponding male institution. For an analysis of this event as myth and a commentary on the significance of the painted representation of the female unchaining, see Jacques Postel, "Philippe Pinel et le mythe fondateur de la psychiatrie française," *Psychanalyse à l'université* 4 (March 1979): 197–244; and Elaine Showalter, *The Female Malady: Women, Madness, and English Culture, 1830–1980* (New York: Pantheon, 1985), 1–3.

[9] Philippe Pinel, quoted by Bercherie, *Genèse*, 28–29.

would be incorrect, however, to speak of a linear passage from a gynecological to a neurological concept of hysteria. First, the uterine theory was in fact still well represented at least as late as the 1880s.[10] But more significantly, the notion of passage does not account for the pervasive overlapping of these two seemingly incompatible theories. We might instead more accurately speak of their coexistence—not only as represented by different authors within the same period, but as presented within the texts of individual authors.

As nineteenth-century explanations of hysteria evolve and ostensibly leave the womb, they inevitably return to its image. When the association with female anatomy is explicitly denied, it is implicitly retained in the notion of a biologically necessary and predetermined feminine character and role.[11] Although one of Charcot's better-known efforts involved ridding hysteria of its uterine etiology and female identification, he himself was never fully able to effect this change, as a careful reading of his work will attest. Hysterogenic zones around the ovaries and the mammary glands and ovarian compressors to stop or prevent hysterical seizures are only the most concrete examples of the many vestiges of genital theory in his work.[12] It has been convincingly argued that Charcot's specimen male hysterics actually supported the genital theory they were meant to disprove.[13] Workers, vagabonds, and déclassés, these men were not only marginal (and therefore assimilable to women) but were also, as if in echo to the most ancient of uterine theories, virtual incarnations of mobility.

The persistence of uterine theory in the face of scientific advances, its tenacity in the midst of medical texts that ostensibly know better, its insistence as metaphor—all bear witness to the fact that hysteria transcends the medical domain. Charcot's ultimate inability to break away from traditional explanations of the disease may be explained as a failure on two counts to understand this nonreducibility of hysteria. The successful (if impossible) theoretical revolution would have called for a rupture neither with etymology, as he demanded, nor with anatomy, as he implied, but with ideology. As Gérard Wajeman has noted in response to Charcot's call for a break with etymology, the important issue is less the power of a word (hysteria, *hystera*, "uterus") to hide or distort a medical reality (the site of the disease)

[10] The persistence of gynecological theories is concretely attested to by the practice of treating hysteria by ovariectomy or clitoridectomy. See Veith, *Hysteria*, 210; Gérard Wajeman, "Psyché de la femme: Note sur l'hystérique au XIXe siècle," *Romantisme* 13–14 (1976): 65, n. 6; Showalter, *The Female Malady*, 75–78.

[11] On the "modernization" of genital theories of hysteria, see François Laplassotte, "Sexualité et névrose avant Freud: Une mise au point," *Psychanalyse à l'université* 3 (1978): 205.

[12] See Gladys Swain, "L'Ame, la femme, le sexe et le corps: Les métamorphoses de l'hystérie à la fin du XIXe siècle," *Le Débat* 24 (1983): 111; and Veith, *Hysteria*, 232.

[13] See Wajeman, "Psyché," 64; and Michèle Ouerd, Introduction to Jean-Martin Charcot, *Leçons sur l'hystérie virile* (Paris: Le Sycomore, 1984), 11–30.

8

•

than the power of a discourse, building over centuries, to construct and convey an image of woman.[14]

When we read the medical discourse on hysteria as part of a more encompassing cultural discourse on women, Charcot's contribution to the theory of hysteria becomes less a point of departure than a continuation, less a focal point than part of a sociocultural pattern. His importance as a popularizer of this pattern cannot be denied.[15] But the surge of interest in hysteria during the nineteenth century preceded Charcot. The medical spotlight fixed on the disease in the last third of the century was a consequence and not a cause of a more generalized attention.

For almost forty centuries, from ancient Egypt through nineteenth-century France, the discourse of hysteria manifested an essential continuity in its association of the disease with femininity, sexuality, mobility, fluidity, and aphasia. If the nineteenth century marked a rupture, it was less with theory than with praxis: with the uses or exploitation of hysteria. From about the second third of the century onward, with gathering force in the 1860s, the disease figured prominently in literature, newspapers, journals, salons, and eventually, the street. By the 1880s it had spread through the novel in near epidemic proportions. Appropriated by the intelligentsia and later by the general public, the medical term became an aesthetic and then a more general sociocultural category. Figure of femininity, label of disorder and difference, hysteria was available for a wide and often contradictory range of aesthetic and political purposes: instrument of misogyny, agent of differentiation, magnet diagnosis of society's multiple ills, emblem of creative frenzy, identification of the writing self as Other, designation of the century's marginalized symbolic center.

To apprehend the phenomenon that I call the hystericization of culture, we must focus here on a historical moment experienced as anchorless and uncentered: a moment of crisis related to the razing of political and social structures and, more significantly, the demolishing of a symbolic system. The body of the hysteric—mobile, capricious, convulsive—is both metaphor and myth of an epoch:

[14] See Wajeman, "Psyché," 58.

[15] Noted in the annals of medical history for transforming hysteria from an anatomical (i.e., female) malady to a neurological (and therefore theoretically not sex-dependent) disease, for applying hypnotic techniques to the study of hysteria, for imposing nosographic order on a hitherto protean disease, and (not least of all) for training Freud, Charcot was more commonly recognized in his day as a scientific showman, teacher-cum-ringmaster of the *leçons du mardi*, weekly lecture-demonstrations during which the star Salpêtrière hysterics were displayed, hypnotized, and put through a series of paces. Renowned and sought after by the *Tout-Paris* of his day, surrounded by an inner circle of acolytes (familiarly referred to as the *charcoterie*), Charcot has been compared to Jacques Lacan, and his *leçons* to Lacan's *séminaires*. Charcot in his prime drew crowds including eminent political figures, visiting royalty, artists, actors, art and literary critics, journalists, and writers. See Jacqueline Carroy-Thirard, "Hystérie, théâtre, littérature au XIXe siècle," *Psychanalyse à l'université* 7 (March 1982): 299–317.

emblem of whirling chaos and cathartic channeling of it. Fashioned in the image
of the times, the hysteric offers surface glitter and inner disarray. Fastened onto the
hysteric's almost totemic form is the anxiety of an age.

This is not to deny the existential reality of a disease whose symptoms, phases,
and postures are well documented, but rather to dislocate the pathologist's perspective, to shift the emphasis from content to context, from product to production: to
talk less about hysteria as entity than of hystericization as process. To transfer our
gaze to the proliferation of the conditions in which such a malady thrives is to in-
quire into its cultural uses and usefulness. In other words, it is to tease out the relationship between hysteria and the stories nineteenth-century French culture
used to represent itself.

I make the allusion to storytelling advisedly, for although hysteria figured also
in theater and poetry, there is a particularly good fit between the work that narrative seeks to do and the raw material offered by hysteria. Narrative is a great arti-
ficer: it imposes temporal and formal order on the inchoate flow of experience,
and signification in the interstices of meaning. The silences and incoherences of
hysteria were perceived as an invitation to narrate: it is precisely because the hysteric cannot tell her story that this story, in the form of a blank to be filled in, is so
readily accessible as narrative matter. But also, it is because the hysteric's story is
not *only* hers—it is a more inclusive cultural story that, repressed, can be spoken
only in the Other's name—that the hysteric is so readily appropriated as narrative
screen.

The growing belief, in the nineteenth century, in the superiority of impersonal
or objective styles of narration finds a support in the hysteric's semiotic body,
which relays language to gesture and physical symptom. The hysteric becomes a
useful device for authors who strive to hide words behind matter and to disguise
telling as showing. The sleight of hand is easily revealed. Female bodily discourse,
an illusionist's work, turns out to be a ventriloquist's hoax. As my title suggests,
ventriloquy is the image that is everywhere implicitly operative in my conception
of the narrative staging of hysteria. By what may be more than a curious coincidence, the term figures repeatedly in nineteenth-century medical texts where, as I
discuss in Chapter 2, it is used in apparent innocence to describe the sounds made
by hysterics. Though my invocation of ventriloquy arguably gains a certain metonymic reinforcement from that era's medical usage, I intend it as a metaphor to
evoke the narrative process whereby woman's speech is repressed in order to be expressed as inarticulate body language, which must then be dubbed by a male
narrator.

That hysteria, beginning with Freud, came to be associated with discourse, and
more specifically with narrative, is by now a commonplace, as is the contrasting of

Freud and Charcot in terms of speech as opposed to spectacle, listening as opposed to viewing. (As Stephen Heath has succinctly put it, "Charcot sees, Freud hears.")[16] But my concern is to show that before Freud, before the "talking cure," before the patient's entry into discourse, hysteria was already discursive. Michel Foucault's observation that the production of discourse is in every society "à la fois contrôlée, sélectionnée, organisée et redistribuée par un certain nombre de procédures qui ont pour rôle d'en conjurer les pouvoirs et les dangers" ["simultaneously controlled, selected, organized, and redistributed by a number of procedures whose role is to exorcise the forces dangerous to that society"] serves as a reminder that discourse in the large sense is not only what is spoken but what is silenced, and what is then imposed in its place.[17]

I approached this book with a curiosity about hysteria in narrative, and arrived at a plexus of aesthetic and cultural issues: the association of reading, women, and spatial relations; the use of vaporization as narrative strategy; the structural and functional resemblances of the fetish, irony, and hysteria; the projection of femininity and, correlatively, of voice as fluidity; the work of gender dichotomization in the grounding of signifying systems; the politics of pathology; the shifting imaginary order in postrevolutionary France. These concerns that emerge from within the context of nineteenth-century narratives of hysteria are of course provoked by my situation as a late twentieth-century feminist critic reading from the standpoint of narratology, cultural history, and psychoanalysis. To the extent that I live within culture and speak within language, I am myself already ventriloquized, and my reading of nineteenth-century hysteria inevitably repeats the ventriloquizing process that is its object.

Though ventriloquy is everywhere implicit as metaphor in this book, it is more directly present—as allegory, referent, and theoretical construct, respectively—in the three chapters of Part I. These opening chapters are essentially devoted to the medical literature of hysteria, to the interactions of clinical and literary descriptions of the disease, and—before I turn to hysteria's place in the novel—to the role of the novel in the medical text of hysteria. The path from Part I to Parts II and III is marked by a move from medicine to literature, but the separation of genres manifests a more striking continuity, for hysteria's text has no center, no locus, no bounds, and little definition. It is not a place but a mobile discursive practice that defies containment in space or time. The lesson to be learned from the continuity of scientific, historical, literary, popular, and epistolary texts is that they all merge in the vaster, vaguer cultural text. For this reason I sought to explore a panoply of

16 Stephen Heath, "Difference," *Screen* 19 (Fall 1978): 58.
17 Michel Foucault, *L'Ordre du discours* (Paris: Gallimard, 1970), 10–11.

genres and a diversity of literary "classes." Long-forgotten penny dreadfuls, canonized novels, and proselytizing political narratives are juxtaposed in the following pages, as are prose passages that bring exquisite pleasure to my soul and doggerel that brings a shudder to my spirit. I read these vastly assorted texts as cultural artifacts.[18]

With the exception of Part I, which traverses the entire century, the chapters follow the chronology of the texts studied. In Part II, I turn to the literary uses of hysteria in the 1850s, well before Charcot's wide-scale popularization of medical teachings, in order to show that fin de siècle scientific categories were in fact already well-ensconced cultural idioms. In a series of three chapters focused, respectively, on the Gustave Flaubert–Louise Colet correspondence, Colet's *La Servante*, and Flaubert's *Madame Bovary*, I contend that *Madame Bovary* and *La Servante* should be read as part and parcel of the correspondence: two more letters in a vitriolic epistolary dialogue about the gendering of texts, the fluidity of style, and the (dis)embodiment of voice. Hysteria, ostensibly a point of gender demarcation, turns out to be the turning point at which the dichotomous categories constitutive of the diagnosis (feminine/masculine, body/mind, fragmentation/cohesion) can no longer hold.

In Part III, I move on to narratives that are coincident with hysteria's heyday and that, at the same time, self-consciously exploit hysteria as historical figure. The first of three chapters is a reading of selections from Zola's *Rougon-Macquart* cycle, whose central metaphor is that of hysteria as hereditary degeneration—but also as source of narrative energy. I go on to consider Maxime Du Camp's nonfictional chronicle of the Paris Commune, *Les Convulsions de Paris*, and the incursion of the hysteria metaphor into the political-historical arena. I find signs of a crisis of representation woven into the text of Du Camp's narrative, and suggestions that the imaginary of the new regime is founded upon the hystericized body of woman. In the last chapter I turn to Rachilde's *Monsieur Vénus*, which I read as a woman's ironizing citation of nineteenth-century commonplaces about hysteria, sexuality, masculinity, femininity, and representational art.

Rachilde and Louise Colet use hysteria in ways both continuous with and disruptive of the master discourse. As women taking up the pen in a patriarchal society, they inevitably take on the discourse with the power even as they contest it. To speak more generally, hysteria seems to have had limited appeal as muse to nineteenth-century women writers. The hysteric was not, I think, a very attractive

[18] For a cogent introduction to the problematics of high art/mass culture oppositions and the ideological bases of quality distinctions—issues beyond the scope of this book—see Andreas Huyssen, *After the Great Divide* (Bloomington: Indiana University Press, 1986); and Peter Stallybrass and Allon White, *The Politics and Poetics of Transgression* (Ithaca: Cornell University Press, 1986).

12

•

or inspirational subject for women who wrote, given that her body was defined by the absence of its woman's voice. Writing about these devocalized bodies today, I cannot hope to reintegrate the nineteenth-century hysterical body with its voice; I can only mouth the voicelessness and strive to expose the discourse that spoke in its place.

PART ONE

MEDICAL STORIES

1 THE TEXTUAL WOMAN AND THE HYSTERICAL NOVEL

To Open the Question

In dreams, a writing tablet signifies a woman,
since it receives the imprint of all kinds of letters.
ARTEMIDORUS, *ONEIROCRITICA*

● In 1881, the journalist Jules Claretie published *Les Amours d'un interne*, a love story set in the hysteria wards of the Salpêtrière Hospital. Claretie had documented his novel in the best naturalist fashion, having long been among the faithful at Charcot's *leçons du mardi*, the *soirées du mardi*, and the *leçons du vendredi* as well. Accordingly, in his prefatorial claim to have pioneered the novelistic exploration of hysteria, the author gave priority to his medical confreres and subordinated his novel to a medical model:

> On trouvera, étudiée dans ce volume,—et pour la première fois par un romancier,—une des formes les plus étranges de la grande maladie du siècle. . . . Il appartenait . . . au romancier d'étudier, *après les savants*, ces manifestations inquiétantes, attirantes aussi, et ces cas bizarres.[1]

---

[1] Jules Claretie, *Les Amours d'un interne* (Paris: Dentu, 1881), i–ii; my emphasis. All references to the novel will be to this edition, and will be provided in the text. Claretie was a novelist, playwright, and essayist as well as a journalist; he also became administrative director of the Comédie-Française in 1885.

*One will discover in this volume the study—and for the first time by a novelist—of
one of the strangest forms of the great* maladie du siècle. . . . *It was the novelist's
turn to study, after the scientists, these foreboding but also seductive displays, and
these bizarre cases.*

But an unexpected element intrudes upon this neat schema, a supplement that
eludes both science and its pretended literary double: that "quelque chose d'*au
delà*" ["otherworldliness"] to which Claretie alludes briefly in his preface (ii)—an
apparition that contradicts the naturalist observation of material reality yet
emerges from it—and to which we will have occasion to return.

In 1880, while Claretie would have been writing his novel, Dr. Charles Richet,
one of Charcot's associates (and, incidentally, a closet novelist), published a medical expert's account of hysteria designed to redress popular misconceptions about
the disease—misconceptions propagated in part, the author charged, by novelists.[2]
The article, which appeared in the literary *Revue des deux mondes*, explicitly derives its authority from medical advances at the Salpêtrière. Rather unexpectedly,
however, the doctor ends up deferring to the novelists, enhancing his clinician's
perspective with examples culled from novels of the preceding quarter century.
For there, Richet explains, one encounters "des descriptions exactes qui complé-
teront ce que nous venons de dire de l'état psychique des femmes nerveuses" (346)
["precise descriptions that complete what we have just said of the psychic condition of nervous women"]. As the novelist's and the doctor's approaches to hysteria
intersect—that is, as they meet but also cross each other—they provide a glimpse
of the complex interplay between literary and medical representations of the
disease.

THE NOVELIST AND THE DOCTOR

Together Claretie and Richet confirm the fact, too often overlooked, that the late
nineteenth-century heyday of hysteria in France was not confined to the domain
of pathology but was a literary phenomenon as well. Together the two presenta-
tions of hysteria bear witness to the popularization of a medical category: by 1880,
the term had become not only familiar to a lay public, but fascinating, captivating.
The ambiguous allure of Claretie's adjectives ("strange," "bizarre," "foreboding,"
"seductive") and Richet's stated effort to correct popular (novelistic) misrepresen-

[2]Charles Richet, "Les Démoniaques d'aujourd'hui," *Revue des deux mondes* 37 (15 January 1880):
341. Further references will be provided in the text. Under the pen name Charles Epheyre, Richet was
a prolific novelist, publishing, among other works, *Possession* (Paris: Ollendorff, 1887) and *Soeur
Marthe* (*Revue des deux mondes* 93 [15 May 1889]: 384–431), both of which leaned heavily on hysteria, hypnotism, and hallucination. Epheyre reenters my text in Chapter 3.

tations of the disease suggest that the diagnostic category had in fact become a vehicle for the imagination.

But here the coincidence ends. Claretie and Richet contradict each other in ways that preclude a clear-cut relationship between literary and medical discourses of hysteria. While the novelist draws his authority from the clinic, specifically from the much-publicized troupe of hysterics and their attendant doctors at the Salpêtrière, the clinician turns to the novel in order to corroborate medical research. While the writer in 1881 sees himself as a literary experimenter injecting an exotic pathological strain into the novel, the physician, at roughly the same time, finds considerable traces of hysteria in the novel well before the disease was in clinical vogue.

The *chassé-croisé* of scientific and literary positions in these samples is indicative of hysteria's elusiveness in the stories told about it: when one is about to locate it, to assign it to a time, place, or discipline, it turns out to have already been, elsewhere; and so the examining focus must be deferred or displaced. The disease is framed as conceptually recalcitrant as well; in literary and medical texts alike, it is represented as resisting circumscription.[3] Claretie and Richet once again furnish exemplary testimony.

The literary inability to define hysteria in direct, nonmetaphorical terms is explicit. Claretie's young physician-protagonist explains:

> Une définition, c'est toujours difficile. Je vous dirai plutôt ce que l'hystérie n'est point. . . . Ça peut être érotique—pour donner raison au vulgaire,—ça peut être sombre, ça peut être mystique, ça peut être religieux, ça peut être tout. C'est, si vous voulez, l'exagération de tout. L'hystérique . . . est en dehors de la règle commune, et le monde et le demi-monde, le théâtre, les salons, tout Paris est plein d'hystériques. . . . C'est même la grande maladie moderne, l'hystérie! La société souffre d'une névrose ou d'une névrite gigantesque. (124)

> A *definition is always difficult. I can more easily tell you what hysteria is not.* . . . *It can be erotic—to echo common opinion—it can be dark, it can be mystical, it can be religious, it can be everything. It is, if you wish, the exaggeration of everything. The hysteric is outside common norms, and both the world and the* demi-monde, *the theater, salons, all of Paris is full of hysterics.* . . . *In fact, it is the great modern ailment! Society suffers from a gigantic neurosis or neuritis.*

[3] I want to emphasize that it is not hysteria itself that is elusive, resistant, recalcitrant, and so on; a disease is after all not a person. If it appears to be vague or evasive, it is because it has been defined as such. And the fact that hysteria and women have overlapping attributes (the "characteristics" of hysteria are often borrowed from commonplaces about female nature so that the disease "behaves" like a woman) is one more indication of the metaphoric nature of the diagnosis.

While this definition is less than precise, it does at least indicate two features of hysteria. The one, exaggeration, is clearly labeled. The other, contagion, is never named as such, but is evidenced by the spread of the disease from the clinic to high society, to the margins of society, to the theater and to salons, to all Paris and indeed to all of modern society. Even Claretie's style seems to have caught the disease, for it is noticeably afflicted with the only named symptom, exaggeration. Although his definition rapidly moves from the literal to the figurative, it is not evident, in this particular passage, to what metaphoric end the disease is being appropriated. Elsewhere in the novel, however, the metaphor is elucidated.

Les Amours d'un interne might more accurately be called (pastiching Balzac's Comment aiment les filles), Comment aiment les internes, for it is all about the ill-fated love choices of the young Salpêtrière doctors and their associates. To the question suggested by my substituted title—how do interns love?—the answer must be "badly," although Claretie implies that they could not do much better. It is not that they all love or lust after their patients (although some do), but rather that the boundaries between the Salpêtrière wards and the salons of Paris are extremely tenuous. While Combette's sexual exploitation of a young woman sets off her nascent hysteria, sending her straight to the Salpêtrière, where Mongobert then loves her as a patient, Combette eventually marries a high-strung heiress described as "cette petite hystérique du monde" (430) ["this little society hysteric"], and Pédro's infatuation for a beautiful if nervous young Russian ends in the debilitating discovery of this woman's particular brand of hysteria: Olga is a skoptzy, a religious fanatic who has had herself sexually mutilated. The protagonist, Pierre, speaks indirectly for Pédro (and for all the other interns as well) when, dually prompted by an inmate's attack on a colleague and his own unrequited love, he exclaims: "Tu vois, les femmes, ça vous déchire toujours quelque chose, la peau du front ou les muscles du coeur!" (291) ["You see, women always tear some part of you, the skin of your brow or your heart muscles!"].

In the course of the novel, "les femmes" and "les hystériques" become virtually interchangeable categories—so much so that the religious hysteric Olga is apostrophized as "cette idéale créature, plus femme que toutes les autres femmes" (379) ["that ideal creature, more of a woman than all other women"]. Despite its veneer of journalistic objectivity, Les Amours d'un interne clearly appropriates hysteria as a figure of woman.

It would be naive, however, to turn to the clinician's text as a likely source for an antidote to Claretie's metaphoricity. It is true that the opening of Richet's "Les Démoniaques d'aujourd'hui" promises to demystify hysteria, to make known "les faits positifs élucidés par les savans contemporains" (341) ["positive facts elucidated by contemporary scientists"], suggesting that the scientist will deliver the letter behind the figure. But the few concrete details he delivers about the affliction work essentially to reinforce age-old stereotypes about femininity. The hysteric, according to Richet, has a mobile and impressionable nature, lacks willpower, and is able to contain neither secrets nor secretions. Dominated by her passions, she is overly emotional, subject to frequent and unmotivated fits of crying, capricious, egotistical, fickle, and prone to exaggeration. She is excessively imaginative, histrionic, and dishonest. In fact, Richet insists, she is not only, like a child, insincere and deceitful; she is a forger of fictions and a lover of lies. Leaving nothing to chance, Richet goes on to interpret his data for us: "On peut même dire que les hystériques sont femmes plus que les autres femmes" (346) ["One can even say that hysterics are women more than other women"].

This is a startling definition for many reasons; most immediately because it almost exactly replicates Claretie's characterization of the hysteric Olga: "more of a woman than all other women." From novelist to clinician, we have come full circle. In vain do we move from literature to medicine in search of a scientific basis, a concrete or proper sense, a degree zero of hysteria. For when we begin to unravel the medical texts (and although he is writing for a largely literary audience, Richet is perfectly representative of the spirit if not the technical detail of such texts), when we comb through medical representations of hysteria, we find that the disease is in every case already a metaphor. Medical and narrative discourses each individually use hysteria as a metaphor that transcends them both, revealing glimpses of the imaginary of the period in which both are enmeshed.

I do not mean to contest the rapid and widespread diffusion of hysteria as medical term during the Charcot years at the Salpêtrière: neither the epidemic spread nor the wide-scale popularization nor the rapid narrative circulation of hysteria at this time can be denied.[4] But I do want to avoid attributing to the clinic the invention of a cultural concept that does not originate there, that is only belatedly taken over and disseminated by the clinic under the name of hysteria. Because Richet presumes that the lay public has a prior empirical if not technical knowledge of the subject, he can make accessible the arcana of medicine by mere allusion to colloquial conceptions: "Tout ce qu'on a coutume d'attribuer au tempérament nerveux de la femme rentre dans le domaine de l'hystérie" (343) ["All that is customarily attributed to woman's nervous temperament falls in the domain of hysteria"].

Contagions, rhetorical as well as literal, do not begin at plague levels. The medical term must be understood in relation to a more global sociocultural and aesthetic category. Figure of femininity correlatively associated (by way of traditional misogyny) with disorder, duplicity, and alterity, hysteria easily lends itself, in this fin de siècle society subject to convulsive upheavals, to a multiplicity of meta-

[4]For an excellent survey of the diffusion of hysteria from the clinic to literature, newspapers, salons, and the streets, see Jacqueline Carroy-Thirard's "Hystérie, théâtre, littérature au XIXe siècle," *Psychanalyse à l'université* 7 (March 1982): 299–317.

phoric uses: diagnosis of the assorted wounds of contemporary civilization, emblem of marginality, sign of expressivity and even of poetic furor. It is this last phenomenon—which we might more generally qualify as a poetics of hysteria or as the hystericization of aesthetics—that I want to approach in the second part of this chapter, in the form of a reflection on an excerpt from Claretie's novel.

Les Amours d'un interne stages that fascinating and perturbing practice known as dermographism, which appears here and there on the hysterical body in the pages of *L'Iconographie photographique de la Salpêtrière* as well as in other medical publications of the period. It consists of imprinting graffiti-like markings on the anesthetic but otherwise impressionable skin of the hysteric, following the vagaries of the doctor's will: doctor's signature, patient's name, diagnosis, invocation of the devil, ornamental design, and so on.[5] Neither a physiological explanation (malfunction of the vasomotor system) nor a potential therapeutic justification (which in any case was not offered) nor photographic documents (which do exist) succeed in exhausting the meaning of this experimental writing.

INSCRIBING THE BODY

The following tableau is excerpted from a chapter of *Les Amours d'un interne*. We are in the hysteria ward along with a group of attendant interns gathered around Mathilde Mignon, a young and beautiful hysteric. She is in a comatose sleep after a night of delirium. Dr. Fargeas, the novel's eminent specialist in nervous disorders, uses Mathilde's supine body for a demonstration of dermographism.

> Mathilde était totalement anesthésique et il suffisait de tracer, sur sa peau
> blanche, d'une douceur pareille à une peau d'enfant, les caractères qu'on
> voulait pour qu'aussitôt, à la place touchée par l'ongle ou le crayon du
> docteur, une saillie rouge apparût, d'une proéminence telle qu'en tâtant

---

[5] See Georges Didi-Huberman, "Une Notion de 'corps-cliché' au XIXe siècle," *Parachute* 35 (1984): 8–14. Dermographism, as medical science understands it today, is a form of physical urticaria (an irritated, patchy condition of the skin) whose outbreaks are provoked by a release of histamines when the skin is stroked, rubbed, or scratched. There is a wheal-and-flare reaction sometimes accompanied by itching and burning at the site of such physical stimulation. The reaction may last forty-eight hours, but usually fades more quickly. While nineteenth-century doctors believed that hysterics were more prone to dermographism than others, because they were more "impressionable," late twentieth-century medicine finds the condition in approximately 5 percent of the general population. It is not sex-linked and is not correlated with any psychological disorder. When I spoke to doctors about dermographism today I discovered one element of continuity amid the changes that one hundred years have brought about: a fascination (which I share) with the ability of the human body to bear meaning. Doctors today continue to use the dermographic patient as writing pad, inscribing names, signs, and messages upon the skin. Two of the three doctors I talked with spoke of their collections of dermographic photographs.

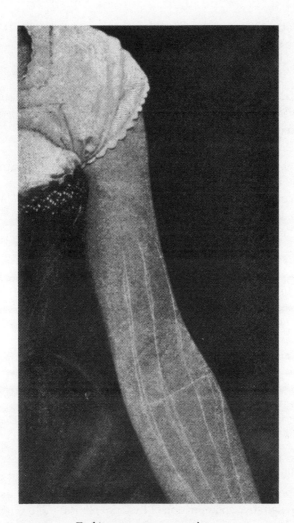

FIGURE 1. *Etchings on young woman's arm.*
Women—especially hysterics—were said to be
more impressionable *than men; consequently*
they were thought to be more often subject to
dermographism, the immune reaction that
doctors appropriated as skin-writing or
skin-drawing, and sometimes referred to as
autography or lithography.
(Published in T. Barthélémy, Etude sur le
dermographisme ou dermoneurose toxivasomotrice,
1893; photo Bibliothèque Interuniversitaire de
Médecine, Université René Descartes, Paris.)

ces caractères, on pût reconnaître la lettre que venait d'écrire là
[le docteur].

"Trouble trophique et qui durera plusieurs heures," disait le chef.
"Le cas est assez fréquent." . . .

Et, pendant quelques heures, en effet, les caractères tracés sur cette
peau blanche demeuraient visibles, comme une inscription parfaitement
déchiffrable.

"Un aveugle pourrait la lire!" disait Pédro.

"C'est la *femme lithographique*, cette Mathilde," ajoutait le petit
Finet. . . .

"Toi qui as inventé l'hystérie, Pauline," lui disait Pédro, "tu n'as pas ça,
toi, la possibilité de servir de papier à lettres vivant!"   (312)

*Mathilde was completely anesthetic; and when the desired characters were traced
on her white skin, soft as a child's skin, immediately at the spot touched by the
doctor's nail or pencil, a red welt appeared so prominently that by touching the
characters, one could recognize the letter that [the doctor] had just written there.*

*"A trophic disorder that will last several hours," said the head doctor. "It is a
rather frequent phenomenon." . . .*

*And for several hours, the characters traced on this white skin remained visible,
like a perfectly decipherable inscription.*

"A blind man could read it!" said Pédro.

"This Mathilde is a lithographic woman," added Finet. . . .

*"Even you who invented hysteria, Pauline," said Pédro, "you don't have that—
the ability to serve as living writing paper!"*

As Mathilde's hysterical body becomes a text to be deciphered by the attendant spectators, Claretie's text becomes an inscription on a woman's body, an allegory of the narrative appropriation of hysteria. Here as more generally, the expressive faculties of the hysterical body are overdetermined. Mathilde is not only
a textual woman but "a lithographic woman." And her status as text and visual art
object is further compounded by the narrative context, which turns the medical
demonstration into a staged spectacle and Mathilde's displayed body into living
theater.

In the hysteric's hyperfemale, hyperexpressive body, sex and text are joined.
Mathilde's "peau blanche, d'une douceur pareille à une peau d'enfant" ["white
skin, soft as a child's skin"] is at once a sexual and a textual marker: a sign of femininity, her white skin should also be read as a writing surface, a blank parchment
or tabula rasa. Each time the sensual aspect recurs (in the repetition of "peau
blanche," in the implied scratch of the doctor's nail, and in the verbs "toucher"

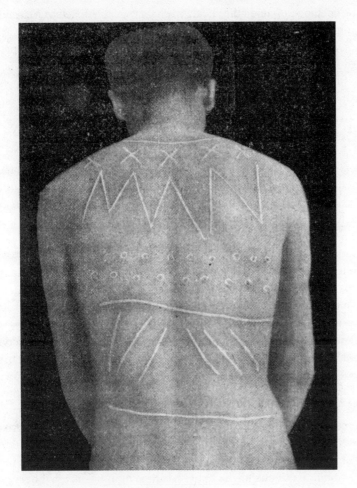

FIGURE 2. *Although neither woman nor hysteric, this patient is described by his doctors as very nervous, excessively emotional, and deplorably impressionable—and so predisposed to dermographic manifestations. (Published in F. Allard and H. Meige,* Archives générales de médecine *2, 1898; photo B.I.M., Université René Descartes, Paris.)*

and "tâter"), it is in the service of writing; for what is being touched, handled, or scratched into being is the flesh made word.

As the doctor writes upon the "living writing paper" presented by Mathilde's literally impressionable flesh, her woman's hysterical body *underwrites* Claretie's text; it gives form and authority to the writing, reading, and interpretive processes involved in textual production.[6] The inscription on Mathilde's skin, a text in the text of the novel, emblematizes the semiotic valorization of the nineteenth-century hysterical body, which writers perceived as a system of signs, an alphabet of gestures to be pressed into narrative service.

And yet, even while implying the crucial role played by the hysterical body in the nineteenth-century novel, Claretie's text does its utmost to complicate it—that is, to suggest that this body is never simply semiotic. It emits messages, but it also receives them. Let me elaborate by considering this body-text as production rather than product. When the doctor puts his mark onto Mathilde's flesh, the raised red letter that appears evokes a brand, a sign burned into the flesh. The allusion to branding within this allegory of the hysterical flesh made naturalist word points to an important connection between language and power, discourse and possession.[7] It reminds us once again—*pace* Aragon and Breton, who eulogized hysteria as a "supreme means of expression"—that when we are given the hysterical body to "read" in place of language, we are always in fact reading someone else's superimposed text.[8]

The interplay of hysteric discursivity and mechanisms of control is everywhere implied in this passage. Hysteria becomes discursive when the doctor imprints his message on the blank pad of Mathilde's body. This scenario, which apposes writing and blankness, pencil and paper, speech and speechlessness, male mastery and childlike submission (the child explicitly connoted by the woman's "peau d'enfant") is congruent with the traditional heterosexual oppositions of Western metaphysics: male/female, active/passive, subject/object, technè/physis, mind/body, and so on.[9] Although Mathilde crosses over into discursivity, any claim for a deconstruction of traditional dichotomies resulting from the fact that her body be-

[6] Although I am speaking of an authority that derives from the clinical domain, it is to be taken in sharp counterdistinction to the scientific or medical authority which Jean Starobinski, among others, refers to in his preface to Victor Segalen, *Les Cliniciens ès lettres* (Paris: Fata Morgana, 1980), 17. The authority of the hysterical body is a *counterauthority*, a source of truth whose power derives from its hidden value, its implicit contestation of received truths.

[7] See Elaine Scarry's fascinating analysis of the dynamics of power contained in the relationship between the body and language, in *The Body in Pain: The Making and Unmaking of the World* (Oxford: Oxford University Press, 1985).

[8] Louis Aragon and André Breton, "Le Cinquantenaire de l'hystérie," *La Révolution surréaliste* 4 (15 March 1928): 20.

[9] For an elaboration on this dichotomy, see Hélène Cixous and Catherine Clément, *La Jeune Née* (Paris: 10/18, 1975), 115–20.

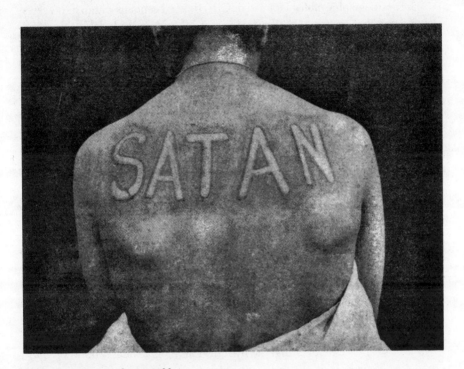

FIGURE 3. *Doctors fascinated by
dermographism often used the sign of
the devil in their writing experiments.
The clarity of this photograph suggests
that it may have been retouched.*
(Published in T. Barthélémy, Etude sur le
dermographisme; *photo B.I.M.,
Université René Descartes, Paris.)*

comes intelligible strikes me as specious, for the potential scandal of the speaking body is neutralized by virtue of its production by an external agent. In fact the body does not speak; it is spoken, ventriloquized by the master text that makes it signify. The woman becomes a text, but she is a text within a text, a text *framed* as signifying source by another, mediating text.

The dermographic tableau framed by Claretie's text contains within it, however, a blind spot that opens a possibility for the semiotic process to elude authorial control, subverting classic paradigms and metaphoric structures. For although the text speaks insistently of the visibility, legibility, and transparency of the letters on Mathilde's skin, it simultaneously occults them. The message is never seen, read, or deciphered for us. Mathilde's signifying body, inhabiting the unexamined gap between Claretie's novel and the doctor's "perfectly decipherable inscription" then constitutes an element of excess, an inarticulate, unreadable space—a textual symptom. We might speak of *Les Amours d'un interne* as a hysterical novel because the hysteria thematized there eventually attacks the narrative, propagating its silences, its excesses, its incoherences.

The phantom letters carried by Mathilde's body do not need to be read to make known the threat they bear, a threat dimmed by the emphatic paleness of her skin but that can be articulated in the form of a question: what would happen if the hysterical body no longer allowed itself to be signed, labeled, diagnosed, but if, insubordinate, itself become a creator, a producer of meaning, this body assumed its own power and went on to deliver an unexpected, even fatal message? What would this message be—this message that uncannily recalls the "quelque chose d'*au delà*" that separated from "literal reality" to insinuate itself into the preface of the novel—and why does it inspire such fear?

It is critical to remember that the hysterical dermographic inscription is a text that must be replaced in the vaster context of the body-text, a concept or perhaps more accurately an intuition whose sources are lost in the mists of time and that manifests itself in such varied domains as popular wisdom and science, by such diverse notions as palm reading and the genetic code. But the best illustration of the body-text (the one that is both most graphic and most revealing) would be the apparatus that figures in Kafka's "In the Penal Colony": writing implement and torture implement simultaneously, whose macabre function is to inscribe in the flesh the sentence that the prisoner can read only when dying of the wounds inflicted by the inscription.[10] This sentence, both phrase and condemnation, is a violent figuration of the sentence every body bears. In other words, the body (which is to say, the material condition of life) *is* this sentence: its scars, its graying hairs, its wrinkles are the lexicon; its shiverings, its tremors, its death throes are the punctuation.

[10] Franz Kafka, "In the Penal Colony," in *The Complete Stories*, trans. Willa and Edwin Muir, ed. Nahum N. Glazer (New York: Schocken, 1976), 140–67.

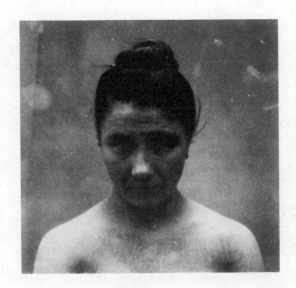

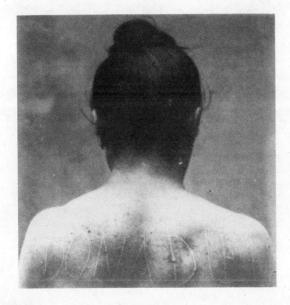

FIGURE 4. *A dermographic woman who has
been inscribed, recto/verso, with her first and
last names: Angéline Donadieu.*
*(Published in M. Lannois, Nouvelle Iconographie
de la Salpêtrière 14, 1901; photo B.I.M., Université
René Descartes, Paris.)*

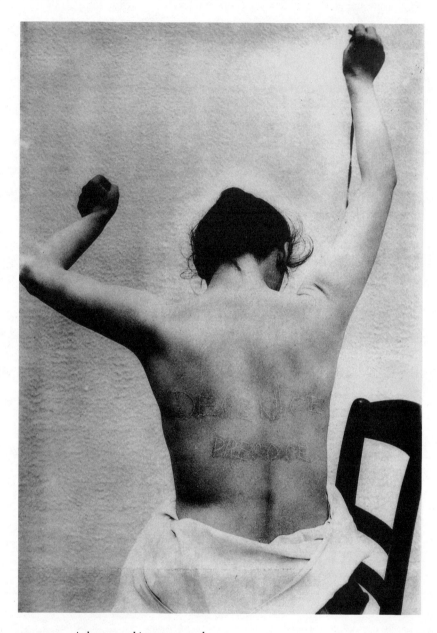

FIGURE 5. *A dermographic woman made
to bear the imprint of her own diagnosis:*
démence précoce.
(Published in L. Trepsat, Nouvelle Iconographie de
la Salpêtrière 17, 1904; *photo Pauline Page.)*

In the case of hysterical dermographism, the inscription is double; one is confronted with an inscription that covers another one—a palimpsest of sorts—a superimposed text that attempts to suppress the sentence, that originary (and doubtless final) text. For the message of a body semiotic in and by itself—whatever the sex—is death. Whence dermographism or invitation to a duel, struggle to the death with death played out on the field of the hysterical body. If the hysterical body is the chosen ground for this battle, it is because this paradigmatic woman's body is, as everyone knows, changeable, malleable, and impressionable. In the anticipatory words of Andreas Cappellanus, who spoke them some seven centuries earlier: "A woman is just like melting wax, which is always ready to take a new form and to receive the impress of anyone's seal."[11]

But the soft white skin is only apparently a tabula rasa, an unmarked pad. It bears a sentence, always already etched and always already repressed, which unpredictably returns from beyond the pale. That is why it is so necessary to efface the letters, reinscribe the body, prove that it could be the bearer of another message, that it could be the work not of God, but of men. By means of an eminently Promethean gesture, clinicians and writers alike struggle to steal God's word, labor to inscribe on the hysterical body a new gospel, which would say: "And the flesh will be made word; it will become the word of Men."

[11] Andreas Cappellanus, *The Art of Courtly Love* , ed. Frederick W. Locke, trans. John Jay Parry (New York: Frederick Ungar, 1957), 50. (Written ca. 1186.)

2 THE DOCTORS' TALE

Nineteenth-Century Medical Narratives of Hysteria

L'homme, tel qu'il soit, est le maître; *nous sommes l'intermédiaire entre lui et la bête, que Proudhon classait ainsi: ménagère ou courtisane. Je l'avoue, avec peine toujours, nous sommes la caste à part, rendue telle à travers les âges. Quand nous avons du courage, c'est un cas pathologique; quand nous nous assimilons facilement certaines connaissances, c'est un cas pathologique.*

LOUISE MICHEL, *MÉMOIRES*

● As readers of nineteenth-century fiction, especially realist and naturalist novels, we are all familiar with authorial prefaces that explain each author's representation of hysteria by documenting it: that is, by referring to contemporary medical treatises and by evaluating the novelistic portrayal of hysterics according to the standards of contemporary diagnostic paradigms. Jean Starobinski has suggested that the nineteenth-century novel turned to hysteria (among other pathological models) to borrow the sanction of medical discourse in the face of a crisis of traditional authority:

> De quelle autorité la littérature pouvait-elle encore se prévaloir, vers le milieu du XIXe siècle, lorsque la vérité passa sous la juridiction du physiologiste, du chimiste, du clinicien? . . . La petite foule qui décide du climat intellectuel se donnait rendez-vous . . . aux démonstrations de Charcot. . . . Que restait-il à la littérature, une fois les anciens paradigmes esthétiques et moraux devenus caducs?[1]

[1] Jean Starobinski, preface to Victor Segalen, *Les Cliniciens ès lettres* (Paris: Fata Morgana, 1980), 17.

What authority could literature still exercise, toward the middle of the nineteenth century, when truth moved into the jurisdiction of the physiologist, the chemist, the clinician? The intellectual trendsetters were gathering at Charcot's demonstrations. Where could literature turn, once the old aesthetic and moral paradigms were worn out?

Starobinski's account of the literary appropriation of clinical hysteria is an accurate historical description of the privileged role medicine played in the hierarchic behavior of two discourses.[2] We see this not only in literary borrowings from the clinic, but in the response of the medical establishment, which appropriated literature—or more accurately, reappropriated pathology—in a current of writing intended to appraise and correct literary deviation from medical knowledge. Using a variety of channels including medical theses, treatises, and the bimonthly *Chronique médicale*, medical surveillance of literary ventures into pathology became a burgeoning intergenre that knew few bounds. Moving from contemporary to antecedent literature, the doctors alternately approved and disqualified the expertise of their literary confreres and forebears.[3] In so doing, they reasserted their own authority in matters of pathology.

Our contemporary critical accounts of nineteenth-century fictional hysterics often tacitly imitate that century's model of scientific truth and literary copy.[4] Implicit in such a model is the assumption that hysteria has an objective existence and even essence, a hidden reality that one might locate somewhere (in some medical lair) and put on display.[5] Now, if we echo the doctors in this way, treating lit-

[2] I would argue, however, that in the overwhelming majority of cases, narrative energy was invested in the hysteric far more often than in her attendant physician. In practice, literature was far less tempted by the ostensibly compelling authority of medical discourse than it was by medicine's discursive unconscious: by hysteria as a disruptive force that medicine both mastered and indulged.

[3] See Starobinski's preface to Segalen's *Les Cliniciens ès lettres*, 20–21.

[4] The continuity is not surprising in view of the fact that positivism and the myth of objectivity have become institutions of scientific writing in the twentieth century. See Emily Martin's *The Woman in the Body: A Cultural Analysis of Reproduction* (Boston: Beacon Press, 1987) for an excellent discussion of the power of metaphor to construct "scientific truths" about bodies.

[5] I use the metaphor advisedly—not only because hysteria is traditionally conceptualized as an animal/womb roving in its body/cage, but because it is difficult to forget the following rhetorical flourish delivered by Charcot in one of his lessons on male hysteria: "Où l'hystérie va-t-elle se nicher? Je vous l'ai montrée bien souvent, dans ces derniers temps dans la classe ouvrière, chez les artisans manuels, et je vous ai dit qu'il fallait la chercher encore sous les haillons chez les déclassées, les mendiants, les vagabonds; dans les dépôts de mendicité, les pénitenciers, les bagnes peut-être?" ["Where will hysteria make its nest? I have often showed it to you of late in the working class, in craftsmen, and I have told you that it is to be found under the rags of déclassés, of beggars, of vagabonds, in workhouses, penitentiaries, perhaps prisons?"] Hysteria here becomes a nesting bird that can be lured out of its shady hiding place. Jean-Martin Charcot, *Leçons sur l'hystérie virile*, ed. Michèle Ouerd (Paris: Le Sycomore, 1984), 237. For an astute presentation of the mystification of hysteria throughout the theory that constructs it, see Martha Noel Evans, *Fits and Starts: A Genealogy of Hysteria in Modern France* (Ithaca: Cornell University Press, 1991), 1–8.

erature as simple handmaiden to medicine, passive bearer of a mirror held up to reflect or refract a master discourse that could potentially deliver the disease as an objective reality, we then ignore medicine's own differences from itself: the ways in which the medical discourse of hysteria is, not unlike narrative discourse, already literary, a tissue of letters that always means more than it says, says more than it means to say, and eludes its own apparent mastery.

What follows is an attempt to reexamine the relationship between medical and literary discourses of hysteria, to destabilize the distinctions between them, and to erode the complementary notion that the disease has an objective albeit elusive identity. I want to decenter the focus on the Salpêtrière, Charcot, and the scientific as "real" in order to trace hysteria's spread in both clinic and novel as a metaphor participating in the imaginary in which science and literature are equally engaged.[6] This initial glance at hysteria's recurrent figurations in the medical writings will open the way for an understanding of why the disease was such a compelling resource for narrative in general.

I will be reading a medley of nineteenth-century medical texts on hysteria from the perspective of a literary critic, superimposing texts, seeking pattern in the repetition and modulation of their internal inconsistencies. My texts span the nineteenth century. They include J.-B. Louyer-Villermay's *Traité des maladies nerveuses ou vapeurs, et particulièrement de l'hystérie et de l'hypochondrie* of 1816 and his 1818 entry "Hystérie" in the *Dictionnaire des sciences médicales*; H. Landouzy's *Traité complet de l'hystérie*, dating from 1846; J. L. Brachet's 1847 *Traité de l'hystérie*; P. Briquet's 1859 *Traité clinique et thérapeutique de l'hystérie*; the 1874 entry "Hystérie" by G. Bernutz in the *Dictionnaire de médecine et de chirurgie pratique*; Charles Richet's 1880 *Démoniaques d'aujourd'hui*; J. Grasset's entry "Hystérie" in the 1889 *Dictionnaire encyclopédique des sciences médicales*; and selections from Charcot's *Leçons*, dating from 1888–89.[7]

The organization of my observations corresponds not to the ritual medical cat-

[6] As Sander L. Gilman has pointed out, "Medical iconography . . . borrows from and contributes to the general pool of images found in a culture." Gilman, *Difference and Pathology: Stereotypes of Sexuality, Race, and Madness* (Ithaca: Cornell University Press, 1985), 28.

[7] G. Bernutz, "Hystérie," in *Dictionnaire de médecine et de chirurgie pratique*, ed. Jaccoud (Paris: Baillière, 1874), vol. 18; J. L. Brachet, *Traité de l'hystérie* (Paris: Baillière, 1847); P. Briquet, *Traité clinique et thérapeutique de l'hystérie* (Paris: Baillière, 1859); Jean-Martin Charcot, *L'Hystérie*, ed. E. Trillat (Toulouse: Privat, 1971), hereafter abbreviated as *H*; Charcot, *Leçons sur l'hystérie virile*, hereafter abbreviated as *LHV*; Joseph Grasset, "Hystérie," in *Dictionnaire encyclopédique des sciences médicales*, ed. A. Dechambre and L. Lereboullet (Paris: Asselin & Houzeau/Masson, 1889), vol. 15; H. Landouzy, *Traité complet de l'hystérie* (Paris: Baillière, 1846); J.-B. Louyer-Villermay, "Hystérie," in *Dictionnaire des sciences médicales* (Paris: Panckoucke, 1818), vol. 23, hereafter abbreviated as *DSM*; J.-B. Louyer-Villermay, *Traité des maladies nerveuses ou vapeurs, et particulièrement de l'hystérie et de l'hypochondrie*, 2 vols. (Paris: Méquignon, 1816); hereafter abbreviated as *TMN*; Charles Richet, "Les Démoniaques d'aujourd'hui," *Revue des deux mondes* 37 (15 January 1880). Page references to these medical texts will appear parenthetically in the body of my text.

egories used by the clinicians I am reading and citing (symptoms, physical causes, moral causes, treatment, etc.), but to a nexus of cultural myths about woman that cut across these divisions and let us glimpse the process by which gender identities are discursively constructed. Specifically, I will track across the medical texts three phases of a tripartite effort to *fix* woman's hysteria-producing difference: to determine or to define it, to regulate or.to stabilize it, and to repair or to amend it. Along the way, we bear witness to the production of a metaphorical body that completely replaces the real body of the hysteric. In fact the increasing metaphoricity of this body paradoxically corresponds to the materializing efforts of the doctors' descriptions of it.

But before continuing, I must recognize my own inevitable implication in the process of gender construction that I work to expose in these pages. The fact that I set out to show how gender is constructed does not stop me—try as I will—from endlessly speaking from within its constructs and ceaselessly reconstructing it. The metaphoricity of this chapter—in small part a deliberate echo of the clinicians' rhetoric, in greater part unwilled—reproduces at points too numerous to detail the linguistic hegemony of the gendered body of thought I ostensibly deconstruct.[8] Vanity leads me to suggest that the gendering of my own discourse is more subtle than that of the one I set out to expose; reason tells me that even if this were the case, subtlety is no cause for celebration for those of us who would like to unbind thought from gender. I insist on this problem because it should affect a reading of this chapter and of the gendered body (of thought, of language) that it unveils. Writ large on this body is the story of an Other century, but it is implicitly our own body, our own story, as well.

This story is one that I have preferred to "stage" rather than write, which is to say that I have tried to let the clinicians speak, limiting my interventions as much as possible to the choice, organization, and framing of their texts. It goes without saying that my presentation of these texts is not innocent, as will be evident in the play between this and subsequent chapters, which revoice and modulate and speculate about the features of hysteria introduced here.

DEFINING HYSTERIA

On a regular basis throughout the nineteenth century, medical writers prefaced their remarks on hysteria with a caveat concerning the impossibility of the enterprise. At mid-century, Brachet cautioned: "Avant de chercher ce qu'est l'hystérie,

---

[8] Consider, for example, the case of literature acting as "handmaiden to science, passively holding up a mirror to reflect or refract the master discourse" (32, *supra*) or that of literature "far less tempted" by the authority of medical discourse (31, *supra*, note 2)—a single case, in effect, for both examples define literature in the feminine terms of subordination to or seduction by a male master.

essayons de dire ce qu'elle n'est pas: cela nous serait plus facile" (346) ["Before seek-ing what hysteria is, let us say what it isn't; that is an easier task"]. Even as late as 1889, and taking into account Charcot's work of ordering and classifying the dis-ease, Joseph Grasset echoed Thomas Sydenham's seventeenth-century opinion that "l'hystérie est un véritable protée qui se présente sous autant de couleurs que le caméléon" (241) ["hysteria is a veritable Proteus that shows as many different colors as a chameleon"], and he complained that the hysteria entry was "l'article de ce Dictionnaire le plus difficile à faire *clair* et *court*" (240) ["the most difficult arti-cle in this Dictionary to write *clearly* and *concisely*"].

A selection from one doctor's summary of causes is indicative of the persistent classification of the disease as generally overdetermined (and therefore amor-phous). According to Louyer-Villermay, hysteria could be attributed to any one of the following:

> Un système utérin ardent et lascif . . . le dérangement du tribut périodique, la continence volontaire ou forcée, quelquefois l'onanisme . . . une imagination brûlante . . . un coeur trop tendre ou facile à enflammer . . . une température excessive, et surtout en chaud, une exposition méridionale, un sol aride, des vents brûlans, l'action prolongée de rayons solaires, l'impression du froid . . . les émanations marécageuses et méphitiques . . . un trop long séjour au lit . . . l'abus des parfums . . . les truffes . . . les moules . . . la vanille, la canelle, peut-être les fraises, les framboises . . . des lavemens composés avec des plantes drastiques, irritantes, vénéneuses . . . le dérangement de nos sécrétions ou excrétions . . . la lecture des romans.   (DSM 231–35)

> *An ardent and lascivious uterine system . . . an unruly periodic tribute, voluntary or forced continence, sometimes onanism . . . a burning imagination . . . an overly tender or excitable heart . . . extreme temperatures, especially heat, a southern exposure, arid soil, stinging winds, prolonged exposure to the sun's rays, exposure to cold . . . swampy and noxious smells . . . too long a stay in bed . . . overuse of perfumes . . . truffles . . . mussels . . . vanilla, cinnamon, maybe strawberries and raspberries . . . enemas containing purgative, irritating, or poisonous extracts . . . irregular secretions and excretions . . . the reading of novels.*

A disease whose essential defining characteristic was time and again given as in-definability, whose causes and symptoms were too numerous to be circumscribed, and whose methods of treatment were limited only by the imagination, hysteria in the nineteenth century was an accommodating vehicle for just about any idea or

entity one wished to contain or displace. It was, in the words of one of its special-
ists, Dr. Charles Lasègue, "la corbeille à papier de la médecine où l'on jette les
symptômes inemployés" ["the wastepaper basket of medicine where otherwise un-
employed symptoms are thrown"]. As Susan Sontag has more generally remarked
a century later, "Any important disease whose causality is murky, and for which
treatment is ineffectual, tends to be awash in significance."[9] Because of its associations with an infinite universe of physical and moral causes, with open-
endedness, with malleability, hysteria was a ready vessel for medical and literary
authors alike, a crucible that received the fears and desires of a culture and melded
them into myth.[10]

As the very representative quotation from Louyer-Villermay suggests, hysteria,
for the nineteenth-century imagination, had inherent affinities with the body and
soul of woman and could, therefore, under the various rubrics of causes, symptoms, predisposing conditions, prevention, and treatment, accommodate an ever-
increasing range of sexually related fantasies and anxieties. Doctors were not inclined to dissolve the time-honored bond between hysteria and female anatomy
and physiology, although the association became increasingly figurative as the
century wore on. In 1818 Louyer-Villermay frames his investigation by this question: "Si nous démontrons qu'il existe une maladie dont l'utérus est le siége [sic], et
qui est bien distincte de tous les désordres qui peuvent exister dans les organes gén-
itaux de l'homme; ne sera-t-il pas évident que cette affection est exclusive chez la
femme?" (DSM 228) ["If we demonstrate that a malady exists whose seat is the
uterus, and which is quite distinct from any disorders of the male genital organs,
will it not be obvious that this is an exclusively female ailment?"]. And in 1846
Landouzy's treatise builds to the following rapturous conclusion:

> Nous arrivons à regarder l'appareil génital [de la femme] comme siége
> unique de l'hystérie; et, chose remarquable! la conclusion à laquelle nous
> conduit l'analyse raisonnée des observations enregistrées pendant plus de
> vingt siècles, se trouve être la même que celle d'Hippocrate et des
> premiers pathologistes.   (211)

> *We come to view the [female] genital apparatus as the unique seat of hysteria, and
> wonder of wonders! the conclusion to which we are led by analysis of the recorded
> observations of more than twenty centuries turns out to be the same as that of
> Hippocrates and the earliest pathologists.*

[9] Susan Sontag, *Illness as Metaphor* (New York: Farrar, Straus & Giroux, 1977), 58; Charles Lasègue,
cited in Henri Cesbron, *Histoire critique de l'hystérie* (Paris: Asselin & Houzeau, 1909), 198.
[10] Hysteria was constructed in the stereotypical image of woman and then reified as capricious and elusive, escaping or evading definition. As Evans has so beautifully shown, the causality of hysteria was
"murky" because it was constructed that way (*Fits and Starts*, 2–3).

It was Hippocrates, of course, who indelibly marked the disease with its uterine connotation by naming it. Hysteria: the age-old appellation and the etymology were not easily repudiated by a century adrift, cut loose from its heritage and consequently obsessively respectful of derivations, of origins. On this basis, Louyer-Villermay argued that so-called hysterical symptoms observed in male patients could not possibly be authentic:

> Car le mot hystérie implique la non-existence de cette maladie chez l'homme. Or, l'impropriété des termes étant, dans les sciences, la première entorse donnée à la raison, ce mot ne saurait être conservé, s'il ne nous représentait une idée exacte, celle d'une maladie propre à la femme. (*DSM* 230–31)

> *For the word hysteria implies the nonexistence of this malady in man. Now, because incorrect terminology in the sciences fundamentally distorts truth, this word could not be retained if it did not represent a true idea, that of a malady proper to woman.*

And in the latter years of the century, we find Charcot still attesting to the force of etymology as he makes it the emblem of his battle against uterine theory: "Rompre avec l'étymologie!"[11] ["Let us break with etymology!"].

The nineteenth century did, however, move away from a strict construction of etymology. Brachet explains:

> Ce n'est pas seulement parce qu'elle a un utérus qu'elle y est sujette [à l'hystérie], c'est parce qu'elle a des nerfs anatomiquement et physiologiquement disposés à cette forme d'affection pathologique. . . . Voilà pourquoi l'homme efféminé . . . sera exposé à avoir l'hystérie. (98)

> *It is not only because she has a uterus that she is subject to [hysteria]; it is because she has nerves anatomically and physiologically prone to this kind of pathological condition. . . . That is why the effeminate male . . . may become hysterical.*

G. Bernutz, in the *Dictionnaire de médecine et de chirurgie pratique*, attempts to update uterine theory:

> Comme le veut la science moderne . . . la femme est femme par toutes les parties de son être et ne l'est pas uniquement par l'utérus. . . .

[11] Charcot, cited by Gérard Wajeman in "Psyché de la femme: Note sur l'hystérique au XIXe siècle," *Romantisme* 13–14 (1976): 58.

L'économie est subordonnée dans les deux sexes au rôle qui est départi à chacun d'eux. . . . L'homme . . . s'est fait le roi de la terre, et il a plus ou moins civilisé le monde. Le rôle plus modeste de peupler l'univers, qui est départi à la femme, domine . . . toute son économie, qui est tout appropriée à la pénible fonction de la maternité. Aussi l'ancien adage gynécologique: *mulier id est quod est propter solum uterum*, n'est-il vrai qu'à la condition de ne pas le prendre dans le sens restreint que lui donnaient nos prédécesseurs, mais de lui attribuer une signification plus générale, et de le faire servir à exprimer que la femme est toute maternité, que son économie est toute imprégnée de maternité. (184)

As modern science holds . . . woman is woman by every part of her being and not uniquely by her uterus. . . . The economy of both sexes is subordinated to the role dealt to each of them. . . . Man . . . has become king of the earth, and he has more or less civilized the world. The more modest role of populating the universe, which has been given to woman, dominates . . . her entire economy, which is entirely adapted to the arduous function of maternity. Thus the old gynecological adage, mulier id est quod est propter solum uterum, *[woman is that which she is because of her uterus alone] is true only on the condition that we do not take it in the restricted sense our predecessors did, but that we attribute to it a more general sense, and have it mean that woman is all maternity, that her economy is entirely impregnated with maternity.*

The modernized, apparently enlightened view of hysteria as a maternal rather than a uterine malady does not fool us for long; the metonymic move from uterus to maternity after all echoes traditional metonymic substitutions for the womb: in French, hysteria was also called *mal de mère* [mothersickness], and in English *fits of the mother* and *rising of the mother*. In fact, the ostensibly less restrictive translation of the adage as "woman is maternity" turns out to be more restrictive, because by replacing "uterus" with "maternity," it converts female biology into social destiny, imprisoning woman in an anatomical and physiological cage securely barred by redundancy: "woman is all maternity . . . her economy is entirely impregnated with maternity." The metaphor of impregnation is all the more "pregnant," to echo the redundancy, because it suggests that the maternalization of woman, like impregnation, is not a simple testimony to nature's way, but records the work of a man.

As the doctors shift from uterus to maternity, from female structure to function and, correlatively, social role, their attempts to delimit hysteria as a female but not necessarily uterine complaint repeatedly turn into attempts to define femininity and female sexuality and to find ultimate distinctions between male and female

38
•
sexuality and roles. Behind the explicit question "Why does hysteria belong to women?" are the deeper, unasked, but implicit questions, "What is a woman?" and "What is sexual difference?"[12]

In an essentializing introduction to a chapter he calls "Etudes du physique et du moral de la femme" ["Studies of the physical and moral nature of woman"], Brachet announces his intent to present "une idée de la femme, de son physique, de ses facultés et de son caractère" ["an idea of woman, of her physique, her faculties, and her character"] and to point out "les caractères essentiels qui lui sont propres, qui servent à la faire distinguer, à la faire ce qu'elle est" (63) ["the essential traits that belong to her, that serve to distinguish her, that make her what she is"]. His prose building to a mawkish pitch, Brachet writes a curious ode to difference (between the sexes) that is simultaneously a portrait of woman as monolith:

> Toutes les parties de son corps présentent les mêmes différences: toutes respirent la femme; le front, le nez, les yeux, la bouche, les oreilles, le menton, les joues. . . . Si nous portons nos regards à l'intérieur, et qu'à l'aide du scalpel nous mettions à découvert les organes, les tissus, les fibres, nous rencontrons partout . . . la même différence. . . . Aussi les femmes semblent jetées dans un moule commun: on rencontre chez elles beaucoup moins de variétés de constitution que chez l'homme. Les exceptions sont une méprise de la nature. (64)

> *All parts of her body present the same differences: all exude woman; the brow, the nose, the eyes, the mouth, the ears, the chin, the cheeks. . . . If we look on the inside, and, with the help of the scalpel, bare the organs, the tissues, the fibers, everywhere we encounter . . . the same difference. . . . Thus women seem cast in a common mold: we find much less constitutional variety in them than in men. Any exceptions are a mistake of nature.*

The tactic of making all women one and the same, through and through, in order to create an essential woman radically different from men is a common feature of these treatises; the construction of a very overstated distinction *between* men and

---

[12] Clearly these questions are not confined to the doctors' texts; they are among the dominant concerns of the century. Their philosophers were Nietzsche, Proudhon, and Schopenhauer; their sociologist, Lombroso; their essayist, Michelet; their novelists, too numerous to detail. In any case these names are merely representative. Michel Foucault has written a few lapidary pages on the ubiquitous nineteenth-century obsession with sexual identity in his introduction to the English edition of the memoirs of a young hermaphrodite, *Herculine Barbin: Being the Recently Discovered Memoirs of a Nineteenth-Century French Hermaphrodite*, trans. Richard McDougall, ed. Michel Foucault (New York: Pantheon, 1980), vii–xvii.

woman serves to mask the possibility of an uncontrollable variability *within* the category of woman—and, correlatively, within the category of men.[13] Moreover, the recurrent and methodical attribution of woman's frightening difference to her maternal destiny serves to circumscribe and contain—if at times only barely— what is otherwise marked as pathological. Brachet continues:

> Nous ne devons pas le dissimuler, la différence est beaucoup plus grande pendant l'âge de la puberté, pendant l'âge des amours. La femme, chargée de la plus grande et de la plus laborieuse tâche de la génération, semble alors ne vivre que pour cet acte et son produit. Tout en elle par conséquent doit présenter une organisation qui s'y rapporte.   (65–66)

> *We must not hide it; difference is much greater during the years of puberty and the years of love. Woman, charged with the greatest and most arduous task of generation, seems then only to live for this act and its product. Therefore, everything about her must be organized accordingly.*

Female difference, maternity, and pathology are allied in a close and unstable relationship. Where maternity no longer divides female sexuality from pleasure, the never entirely reliable buffer between difference and pathology disappears. Louyer-Villermay lists a wide range of experiences that can lead to hysteria, presumably because of their titillating effect on a woman. Among them are the following:

> Un grand nombre de couvertures imprimant aux organes générateurs une sorte d'éréthisme . . . l'action des sinapismes, de l'urtication . . . et surtout . . . l'action des cantharides . . . les vêtemens très-étroits . . . les bains tièdes . . . l'excès ou l'habitude des alimens aphrodisiaques ou doués d'une excitation spéciale sur l'appareil génital.   (DSM 232)

> *A great number of covers excessively stimulating the reproductive organs . . . the effects of mustard plasters, of being whipped with nettles . . . and above all the effects of Spanish fly . . . tight clothing . . . lukewarm baths, excessive or habitual consumption of foods that are aphrodisiacs or have an especially exciting effect on the genital area.*

[13] As Barbara Johnson has more generally remarked, "The differences *between* entities (prose and poetry, man and woman, literature and theory, guilt and innocence) are shown to be based on a repression of differences *within* entities, ways in which an entity differs from itself." *The Critical Difference: Essays in the Contemporary Rhetoric of Reading* (Baltimore: Johns Hopkins University Press, 1980), x–xi.

Brachet gives a more dramatic example of the risks of female sexual pleasure. In a clinical observation he tells of a woman whose hysterical fit was brought on by sexual climax. By way of conclusion he registers his astonishment that this is not a more frequent occurrence. Although he does not agree with those authors who regard hysteria as a moment of orgasm, he finds it hard to dispute the fact that "les jouissances de l'amour . . . portent beaucoup sur les nerfs, et . . . prédisposent aux affections nerveuses et à l'hystérie" (173) ["sexual pleasure . . . weighs heavy on the nerves . . . and creates a predisposition toward nervous states and hysteria"].

REGULATING HYSTERIA: SECRETIONS AND EXCRETIONS

Woman is predisposed toward hysteria by every sex-specific aspect of her physiology. The doctors generally concur that puberty, menstruation, pregnancy, childbirth, lactation, and menopause are particularly risk-ridden, along with coitus—but also continence.[14] Medical experts consistently stress the special importance of surveying menstruation, monitoring its regularity, and attending promptly to disor amenorrhea, to which they attribute a temporary hysteria that almost always disappears, Bernutz assures, "avec l'établissement régulier de la menstruation" (280) ["when menstruation is regulated"]. This emphasis on regulating menstruation is especially interesting in the original French texts because the most commonly used expression for menstruating, être réglée, also means "to be well ordered, steady, stable, fixed." Paradoxically, it is from the very moment a woman begins to menstruate, becomes réglée, regulated, fixed in her (female) role, that her entire being is open to dérangement—that is, most immediately, to menstrual disturbances, but also to the vaguer, more general unruliness translated by hysteria. It then seems clear that the specific preoccupation with menstrual disorders hides a more fundamental anxiety about menstruation as disorder, or the essential disorder of the female condition.

The concern about menstrual dysfunction extends to embrace the potential disturbance of woman's every secretion and excretion. Louyer-Villermay lists the following, in addition to menstrual irregularities, as prime causes of hysteria:

> Le dérangement de nos sécrétions ou excrétions, de la transpiration . . .
> les leucorrhées, leur acreté, leur extrême abondance ou leur

[14] There is a running debate in the clinical texts about whether nuns or prostitutes are more susceptible to hysteria. For more on nineteenth-century constructions of that other phantasmatic figure, the prostitute, which often intersect with constructions of hysterics, see Charles Bernheimer, *Figures of Ill Repute: Representing Prostitution in Nineteenth-Century France* (Cambridge: Harvard University Press, 1989).

interruption, les catarrhes du vagin . . . peut-être aussi la rétention d'une
liqueur *spermatique* ou *spermatiforme* . . . l'omission d'une saignée
habituelle, la tendance vers un flux hémorrhoïdal ou sa suppression,
enfin des hémorrhagies spontanées ou artificielles trop abondantes . . .
une surabondance de bile ou de sucs intestinaux.   (*DSM* 232–33)

The derangement of our secretions, excretions, or perspirations . . . leukorrhea, its
acridity, its overabundance or interruption, vaginal catarrhs . . . maybe also the
retention of a spermatic *or* spermatiform *liquid . . . the omission of a regular*
bloodletting, the tendency toward hemorrhoidal discharge or its suppression,
finally, overabundant spontaneous or artificially-induced hemorrhages . . .
excessive bile or intestinal juices.

These bodily fluids combine with others in patterns of drips and flow that serve as
harbingers or aftereffects of the hysterical fit. The crisis is announced, according to
Louyer-Villermay, by various effluvia:

Une urine abondante, les excrétions utéro-vaginales, accompagnées
parfois d'une sensation voluptueuse . . . les retours du flux menstrual
. . . une effusion de larmes considérable . . . les clous, les furoncles, les
abcès, les sueurs, les diarrhées, la salivation.   (*DSM* 249)

Abundant urine, utero-vaginal excretions sometimes accompanied by a
voluptuous sensation . . . recurrences of menstrual flow . . . heavy flow of
tears . . . carbuncles, boils, abcesses, sweat, diarrhea, salivation.

Similar signs announce the attack's conclusion:

[Une] effusion de larmes, envies fréquentes d'uriner, émission abondante
d'une urine claire et limpide, écoulemens muqueux ou spermatiques
fournis par le vagin ou l'utérus, accompagnés parfois d'une sensation
voluptueuse.   (*DSM* 258)

[An] outpouring of tears, frequent desire to urinate, abundant emission of clear
and limpid urine, mucus or spermatic discharges from the vagina or the uterus,
sometimes accompanied by a voluptuous sensation.

The doctors repeatedly paint woman as incontinent slave to her secretions, unable to control her dripping, flowing, spurting, oozing bodily fluids. The phantasmatic nature of the portrait becomes especially clear when the medical narratives

diverge from the habitual configurations to expand on more unusual forms of the general pattern. Thus Grasset reports on the weekly attacks of a particular hysteric:"Chaque fois elle avait une centaine d'éternuements; l'écoulement qui tombait des narines suffisait à tremper un mouchoir" (305) ["Each time she sneezed a hundred sneezes; the dripping from her nose was enough to soak a hand-kerchief"]. And with undisguised fascination along with a dose of sensationalism, Briquet tells of a case of galactorrhea, or hypersecretion of milk:

> Au moindre mouvement, le lait s'en échappait [du sein] comme d'un arrosoir. . . . La pression en fait darder le lait en jets multiples, et dès que la pression vient à cesser, le lait coule constamment goutte à goutte, aussi la malade le recueille au moyen d'un vase qu'elle suspend à sa ceinture. . . . Quand la malade se lève ou quand elle s'assied sur son lit, les gouttes de lait font place à des jets nombreux. (482–83)

> *At the slightest movement, milk spurted [from her breast] as from a watering can. . . . Pressure makes the milk shoot out in multiple streams, and as soon as the pressure lets up, the milk flows constantly drop by drop; therefore, the patient collects it in a container that she hangs at the waist. . . . When she gets up or when she sits on her bed, the drops of milk give way to numerous cascades.*

I want to emphasize at this point that we are talking not only about hysterics but also about female traits that predispose toward hysteria, and finally about general female characteristics. We must consider them as constituting a sliding scale be-cause they exist, in these medical writings, on a continuum with no clear breaks, as Grasset reminds us: "Sans vouloir manquer ici de galanterie, je ferai remarquer que la plupart des traits de ce caractère des hystériques ne sont que l'exagération du caractère de la femme. On arrive ainsi à concevoir l'hystérie comme l'exagération du tempérament féminin" (331) ["Although I don't want to be ungallant, I must point out here that most traits of the hysterical character are only an exaggeration of woman's character. We then come to conceive of hysteria as the exaggeration of the feminine personality"]. So we find that it is an almost imperceptible step from woman's secretory abnormalities to the pathology of normal female secretions. Brachet points the way, in a summary of female secretory difference:

> Tout le monde sait avec quelle facilité les larmes coulent chez la femme, combien la transpiration et la perspiration cutanée sont faciles et abondantes, combien la digestion est rapide, à cause de la formation plus prompte du suc gastrique et de la sécrétion plus prompte aussi de la bile; combien enfin les urines sécrétées semblent se presser de s'amasser dans la vessie pour être plus tôt évacuées. (67)

Everyone knows how easily woman's tears flow, how ready and abundant are
woman's transpiration and perspiration, how quick is her digestion because of her
more rapid formation of gastric juice and her more rapid secretion of bile; finally,
how urine, once secreted, seems in a hurry to collect in the bladder in order to be
more quickly eliminated.

These excesses are not confined to the secretory and excretory systems; they find their analogue in a series of moral characteristics that the medical men persistently treat as an incontrovertible eternal feminine. The link between the physiological and moral levels is to be found in woman's ready and abundant tears, simultaneous testimony to the uncontrollable flow of her secretions and the constant overflow of her emotions and her imagination.

REGULATING HYSTERIA: LOGORRHEA

One of the most insistent aspects of female effusiveness is verbal incontinence. Hysterics are, not unexpectedly, hyperbolically loquacious: they deliver an irrepressible flow of words and noises that sometimes takes the structured form of fictions and lies. Richet describes the overpowering urge hysterics have to tell tales: "Rien ne leur plaît plus que . . . de raconter des histoires absolument fausses, . . . d'énumérer tout ce qu'elles n'ont pas fait, tout ce qu'elles ont fait, avec un luxe incroyable de faux détails" (344) ["Nothing pleases them more than to tell utterly false stories, to enumerate all they haven't done, all they have, with an incredible excess of false detail"]. Bernutz notes the use, by hysterics, of another kind of socially unacceptable speech: "L'interposition involontaire dans la conversation . . . de mots grossiers ou de blasphèmes, qui reviennent à chaque instant sans qu'elles puissent, si bien élevées qu'elles soient, s'en défendre" (246) ["The involuntary interposition in conversation . . . of dirty words or profanity, which constantly reappear, leaving {the hysterics} unable to offer any resistance, however well brought up they may be"].

The doctors represent hysterical voice as remarkable not only for its effusiveness but for its incoherence. Charcot tersely summarizes an era of medical opinion that sees hysterical discourse as notable for its absence, on the one hand (aphonia, aphasia), and for its insignificant (if irrepressible) presence, on the other: "Vous voyez comment crient les hystériques. On peut dire que c'est beaucoup de bruit pour rien" (H 119) ["You see how hysterics shout; one might say it is a lot of noise for nothing"]. Hysterics laugh or cry indiscriminately, sing or speak nonsense words, make animal noises, and give free rein to unseemly body sounds: hiccups and borborygmi (stomach rumblings) are most frequently cited. Louyer-Villermay remarks: "Les malades pleurent involontairement ou jettent des éclats

44

•

de rire; quelquefois elles chantent ou tiennent . . . des propos incohérents" (*TMN* 57) ["Patients cry involuntarily or burst into gales of laughter; sometimes they sing or speak . . . incoherently"]. Landouzy observes in some patients incessant loquacity, which in other patients less articulately appears as uncontrollable barking, hiccups, or sharp cries (327ff.). Bernutz, too, reports barking and also entire epidemics of meowing (246).

The doctors' representation of hysterical voice is a caricature of culturally accepted perceptions of female voice, for if human voice is situated between mind and matter—"between body and language," in the words of Guy Rosolato—woman's voice is skewed so far to the side of corporeality as to all but deny the other end of the connection.[15] The voice of hysteria that sings and cries to the medical men, laughs and burps, meows and barks, grunts and babbles, is the negative double of accepted patriarchal speech: devoid of the control and signifying clarity of adult language, it is replete with the affective and sonorous properties that the doctors renounced when they entered linguistic manhood. Kaja Silverman's words about the cinematic production of female voice—words that are equally pertinent to the clinical production of hysterical voice—will help me to elaborate: "The child 'finds' its 'own' voice by introjecting the mother's voice, [and through a symmetrical gesture] the male subject subsequently 'refines' his 'own' voice by projecting onto the mother's voice all that is unassimilable to the paternal position. . . . What must be jettisoned is the vocal and auditory 'afterbirth' which threatens to contaminate the order and system of 'proper' speech."[16] As Silverman suggests, and as the medical texts confirm, female voice is constructed as a kind of depository for the human vocal properties repudiated (but obscurely desired) by men.[17] But what especially fascinates me in this commentary is the choice of "afterbirth" as a metaphor for a certain vocality. Literally, the afterbirth is, of course, the ensemble of placenta and fetal membranes expelled from the uterus after birth. That which was prior to life, and then nourished it, changes place: it leaves last, and it leaves as waste material. Waste is the flip side of creating; the afterbirth, by any other name, is the placenta. The analogy with maternal language, disintegrated into its component sounds, is clear. So, too, I will argue, is an analogy with hysteria (understood as a metonymy for the uterus, for the mother, and, more generally, for woman as these texts construct her). The path from voice to uterus is prepared by the clinicians, who repeatedly signal affinities between the female vocal and sex organs. Louyer-Villermay speaks of "les rapports sympathiques qui existent entre

[15] Guy Rosolato, "La Voix: Entre corps et langage," *Revue française de psychanalyse* 37 (1974): 75–94. See Chapter 5 for a fuller discussion of female voice.
[16] Kaja Silverman, *The Acoustic Mirror: The Female Voice in Psychoanalysis and Cinema* (Bloomington: Indiana University Press, 1988), 81.
[17] Silverman more pejoratively calls female voice a "dumping ground for disowned desires, as well as for the remnants of verbal incompetence." *Acoustic Mirror*, 81.

l'utérus et le larynx" (*TMN*, 107) ["the close relationship that exists between the uterus and the larynx"], and yet more strongly states: "L'utérus a une grande influence sur le larynx" (*TMN*, 204) ["The uterus has a strong influence on the larynx"]. Metaphoric connections between the voicebox/throat/neck and vagina/uterus/cervix are retained from antiquity well into the nineteenth century.[18]

Before I go on, let me mention an etymological detail that I borrow from Martha Noel Evans. The neuter plural of *hystera* (the Greek word for uterus, from which the English *hysteria* derives), *hysteria*, literally "things of the uterus," "signifies the placenta, *or more precisely, the afterbirth*."[19] The etymological connections among the words *hysteria*, *uterus*, *placenta*, and *afterbirth* suggest to me an uncanny record, in language, of a well-preserved cultural construction. Briefly stated, the production of hysteria follows the evolution of the afterbirth. Nurturing is discarded; the idol falls. Hysteria is a formation that answers to both reverence and disgust: like the afterbirth/placenta, it depends upon contradiction and paradox. Hysteria always comes back to such structures of ambiguous and ambivalent thought. I too shall return to them.

Before moving too far beyond the range of babble and noise, I want to say one more word about animal sounds. Rather, I shall let Bernutz and Briquet say it for me, for both of these doctors link meowing to ventriloquy, in a curious move that constitutes the dark underside of their texts: the textual unconscious making a fleeting appearance in the text. Bernutz breaks off a discussion of hysterical barking and meowing to offer the following suggestion: "On devrait, suivant Briquet, rapprocher de ces miaulements, qui se propagent par contagion, une autre espèce de bruits, consistant dans une sorte de ventriloquie" (246) ["Following Briquet, one should link these meowings, which spread by contagion, to another kind of noise, which consists of a sort of ventriloquy"]. When we follow his reference to Briquet, we find an attempt to explain in scientific terms (specifically, that the noises are produced by convulsions of the respiratory muscles) the ventriloqual phenomenon (also—synonymously—called "engastrimisme") that, he continues, was mistakenly understood during the "so-called" possession at Loudun as the devil's voice: "C'est l'engastrimisme . . . qui a fait croire que le diable parlait dans leurs corps" (320) ["It was ventriloquy . . . that led to the belief that the devil was speaking in their bodies"]. And Briquet closes his commentary by again associating cat noises with ventriloquy and subsuming both to scientific explanation: "Dans ces cas, le jeu anormal des muscles respirateurs produisait fortuitement, ce que les engastrimistes ne font qu'après une certaine étude; l'art de la ventriloquie se lie,

---

[18] See Thomas Laqueur, *Making Sex: Body and Gender from the Greeks to Freud* (Cambridge: Harvard University Press, 1990), 36. I am grateful to Wayne Koestenbaum for sharing an unpublished paper about voice and sexuality.
[19] Evans, *Fits and Starts*, 4; my emphasis.

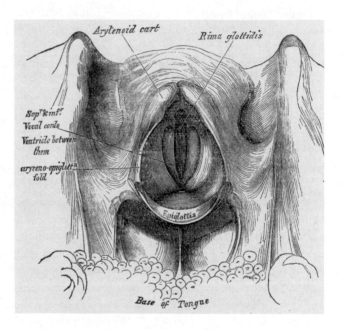

FIGURE 6. *This nineteenth-century
illustration of the opening of the larynx could
easily be taken for a view of the external female
genitals. Assimilations of female vocal and
sexual organs were not uncommon.*
(Published in Max Müller, Lectures on the Science
of Language *2, 1865; photo Pauline Page.)*

comme on le sait, à l'art d'imiter les cris des animaux: du miaulement à la ventriloquie il n'y a qu'un pas" (320–21) ["In such cases, the abnormal action of the respiratory muscles fortuitously produces what ventriloquists produce only after considerable study; the art of ventriloquy is linked, as we know, to the art of imitating
animal sounds: from meowing to ventriloquy is only a step"].

Now, although scientific explanation explicitly triumphs in the cited passages
by Bernutz and Briquet, the excursus through possession, mewing women, and
bodies ventriloquized by the devil gives us a great deal to reflect upon along the
way. The passages work together to conflate ancient and modern concepts of ventriloquy. The older, literal sense of the term refers to the practice of speaking from
the belly, or appearing to do so. By extension, the ventriloquist would be one who
has an evil spirit speaking from within. The modern sense of the term—which was
already current in the early nineteenth century—separates subject and object of
ventriloquy, making the ventriloquizing agent external to the body from which
speech appears to emanate. If the doctors' comparison of hysterical animal noises
to ventriloquy is to confirm their physiological explanation of such sounds (convulsions of the respiratory muscles), then ventriloquy must be understood in its archaic sense, in which subject and object coincide. But if we consider the comparison in the context of the doctors' references to ventriloquy as an "art" requiring
"considerable study," we are instead within the context of the more current sense
of ventriloquy as performance. In this case we make a distinction between subject
and object of speech. If hysterical meowing is like the art of ventriloquy, we may
well wonder what diabolical or medical performer is at work.

The curious intersection of science, sorcery, and ventriloquy in these excerpts
reveals a flicker of uncertainty in the predominantly positivistic discourse of hysteria. Bodies are spoken, science behaves like art, and pathology is not clearly distinguishable from possession. Science and its arcane double engage in a contest of
voices that has no clear issue. If, as retrospective medicine asserted, hysteria was
the devil's ventriloquist at Loudun and at other scenes of ostensible possession,
then conversely, the devil could give hysteria voice, and the doctors, devil's advocates, might then speak not only for their conscious rational selves, but for and
from an alien point of view.

Such moments of self-implication are exceedingly rare; far more typical is the
presentation of hysterical voice as an unrestrained interiorized force that must be
stopped. Unable to hold her tongue, helpless to contain the flood of fictions,
words, yaps, and cries endlessly welling up within her and spilling out, the
nineteenth-century hysteric presents an extreme version of the image of "leaking
vessel" traditionally associated with the verbally and sexually excessive woman.[20]
Small wonder, then, that Richet compares the hysterical attack to a dripping pipe
to be turned on or off with the aid of a faucetlike ovarian compressor:

[20] Patricia Meyer Spacks, *Gossip* (Chicago: University of Chicago Press, 1986), 39–40.

Pour prendre une comparaison grossière, mais intelligible, il semble que la compression de l'ovaire soit à l'attaque d'hystérie comme un robinet est à l'écoulement d'un tuyau rempli d'eau. Si on tourne le robinet, l'écoulement cesse pour reprendre dès qu'on a de nouveau remis le robinet dans la position primitive. (356)

To make a gross but understandable comparison, it seems that ovarian compression is to the hysterical attack as a faucet is to a dripping, water-filled pipe. If one turns the faucet, the dripping stops, only to begin again once one has turned the faucet back to its original position.

REGULATING HYSTERIA: MOBILITY

The feminine or hysterical personality (either term will do) is not only excessive and incontinent, like female physiology, but—again analogously—inconstant and volatile, in need of regulation. "Voyez en effet combien la sensibilité et la mobilité sont différentes chez la femme," says Brachet, "elle change d'idées, de sentiments, d'impressions, avec une rapidité inconcevable" (68, 71) ["Look at how different woman's sensitivity and mobility are. . . . Her ideas, her feelings, her impressions change with inconceivable rapidity"]. Fixed by medical opinion (that is, determined) as a mobile creature, woman needs still more fixing (regulating, stabilizing) to approach the male norm. In the words of Bernutz, "l'organisme féminin . . . jouit d'une mobilité très-remarquable, qui contraste avec la fixité et la stabilité, qui caractérise l'organisme masculin" (185) ["the feminine organism . . . is endowed with quite a remarkable mobility, which contrasts with the fixity and stability that characterize the male organism"].

Woman's mobile personality, her fickleness, is in the hysteric of course only exaggerated, Bernutz continues, becoming "une impressionnabilité *excessive* . . . une mobilité intellectuelle *anormale*" (227; my emphasis) ["an *excessive* impressionability . . . an abnormal intellectual mobility"]. The mobility that the doctors persistently cite as female property, cause and symptom of hysteria, is, on the one hand, a medical recoding, a scientific sanctioning of an age-old adage ("la donna è mobile"), and, on the other hand, an updated replay of the traditional attribution of hysteria to a wandering womb. But there is much more at stake here; the focus on the vagaries of woman's mind and the travels of her uterus serves to occult political issues related to the fear that woman will not stay in her place within the home, the family, and society, and the threat that, moving outside these traditional structures, she will dislocate ostensibly fixed social boundaries and values.

When we recall that public secondary education for girls in France was almost nonexistent until the Camille Sée Law of 1880,[21] and that throughout the century the rallying cry for advocates of women's rights was better education, literacy, and the opening of the liberal professions to women, we can understand the medical establishment's repeated attribution of hysteria to excessive education—and, correlatively, to the reading of novels—as a defensive gesture, an attempt to keep existing social boundaries in place. Brachet advises against "l'éducation qu'on fait donner aux jeunes personnes [qui] . . . leur inspir[e] des sentiments souvent bien différents de ceux qu'elles devraient avoir dans leur position sociale" (88) ["the education given to young women {that} . . . inspires feelings often quite different from those befitting their social position"] and traces a particular case to just such deplorable origins: "éducation recherchée, beaucoup trop recherchée pour la fille d'un honnête artisan, qui ne devait pas aspirer à un rang trop au-dessus du sien" (103) ["fine education, much too fine for the daughter of an ordinary artisan, who should not aspire to rise above her own station in life"]. And Richet more broadly states: "A Paris . . . où les jeunes filles des classes inférieures et de la petite bourgeoisie reçoivent une éducation supérieure à leur état social, l'hystérie est très fréquente" (346) ["In Paris . . . where young ladies of the lower classes and the petite bourgeoisie are educated beyond their social standing, hysteria is very frequent"].

That the pathology issue is also a sex issue is of course patent; what now begins to be clear is that it is a class issue as well. Grasset exhorts: "Ne faisons pas de déclassés, formons les enfants à regarder toujours au-dessous d'eux pour plaindre et aider, au lieu de regarder toujours au-dessus pour soupirer et envier . . . et nous diminuerons le nombre des hystériques" (334) ["Let's not make déclassés; let's mold our children to look below themselves to pity and to help, instead of looking above to sigh and to desire, and we will reduce the number of hysterics"]. This transmutation of sexual pathology into class pathology is nowhere as clear as in Charcot's lessons on male hysteria, where, as Michèle Ouerd has observed, lower-class marginality replaces female eccentricity:

> Les hommes hystériques eux, puisqu'ils ne sont pas des femmes, ne peuvent avoir cette mobilité de caractère. Ils seront donc des instables sociaux, tel ce malade qui a exercé une vingtaine de métiers, tels ces vagabonds qui sont condamnés à errance toute leur vie. . . . Finalement, la classe ouvrière est imaginée dans le grand corps social de la République fin de siécle comme l'utérus migrateur de l'hystérique traditionnelle.[22]

21 Claire Goldberg Moses, *French Feminism in the Nineteenth Century* (Albany: State University of New York Press, 1984), 174–78.
22 Michèle Ouerd in her introduction to Jean-Martin Charcot, *LHV*, 26–27.

Male hysterics, not being female, cannot possess that mobility of character. They will, therefore, be socially unstable, like the patient who exercised some twenty occupations, or the vagabonds condemned to wander all their lives. . . . Finally, the working class is imagined, in the great social body of the fin de siècle Republic, like the migrating uterus of traditional hysteria.

The language in which Charcot describes his male hysterics is by now familiar; "déclassés, mendiants, vagabonds, dégénérés, déséquilibrés" ["déclassés, mendicants, vagabonds, degenerates, unbalanced people"] are recurring terms that all have to do with displacement or instability. Like hysterics of the more traditional female variety, Charcot's men are in perpetual motion, have no fixed center: "Ils n'ont pas de domicile fixe. . . . Il mène une vie errante. . . . Il vit de la profession de chanteur des rues, dans la banlieue de Paris . . . couchant par-ci par-là" (*LHV* 237–44) ["They have no fixed abode. . . . He lives a wandering life. . . . He makes his living as a street singer, on the outskirts of Paris . . . sleeping here and there"].

This, of course, is another case of social conservatism that is being practiced in the name of pathology or power that is masquerading as diagnosis.[23] When the clinicians separate the normal from the abnormal, they also designate a fixed, stable center of society as distinct from a devalued periphery; society's unacceptable elements are exiled as mobile, deviant, eccentric. By the latter part of the century the hysteria label was an attempt to pin down or arrest the upwardly mobile desires of various social outcasts. These marginalized elements come to include not only those perceived as inferior by sex or by class, but by race as well. Charcot among others comes to associate hysteria with Judaism. Here is his description of one of his patients: "Il est mû, constammant, par un besoin irrésistible de se déplacer, de voyager, sans pouvoir se fixer nulle part. . . . Il est Israëlite, remarquez-le bien"[24] ["He is constantly moved by an irresistible need to move about, to travel, without being able to settle down anywhere. . . . He is Jewish, note it well"]. Typed as unsettled, undisciplined, and unstable, the unempowered classes and races are effeminized, and hystericized by analogy to woman.

Throughout the century, however, the prototypical female hysteric continues to be the consuming center of medical attention; ill-defined and unstable, she presents a persistent challenge to medical men, who often find themselves called upon in the line of duty to double as repairmen. Having followed efforts to define and then to regulate feminine difference, I would like to turn briefly now to attempts at repair.

[23] It is probably true that power always takes on other trappings—at least when it works most effectively—and, correlatively, that diagnosis always vehiculates power. My deferred feminist perspective makes this example of the medicalization of power particularly blatant for me.
[24] Charcot, *LHV*, 231, 236; see also Briquet, *Traité*, 103; Grasset, "Hystérie," 264.

REPAIRING HYSTERIA

Landouzy, in his historical overview of cures for hysteria, offers the following:

> Il faut lire les anciens auteurs pour se faire une idée des innombrables
> recettes inventées contre l'hystérie. L'une des plus infaillibles consistait
> en un petit sachet contenant des testicules de renard pulvérisés. Placé au
> cou, ce sachet triomphait à l'instant de toute affection hystérique. . . . Il
> n'est pas jusqu'au pénis humain, qui, desséché et pris en poudre, n'ait été
> proclamé souverain contre cette maladie.   (294)

> *One must read the ancient authors to get an idea of the innumerable prescriptions
> invented to cure hysteria. One of the most infallible consisted of a small bag
> containing pulverized fox testicles. Hung around the neck, this bag instantly
> routed any hysterical condition. . . . Even the human penis, dried and powdered,
> has been declared a powerful cure for this malady.*

Although Landouzy and his contemporaries do not themselves subscribe to such
primitive cures, they do collectively continue to endorse what might be understood as another version of the same thing. In Louyer-Villermay's words, "[l'hys-
térie] cède presque toujours à l'union des sexes" ["{hysteria} almost always yields to
sexual union"]. Or, in the words used to describe a particular but common case:
"Elle choisit un mari jeune et très-amoureux, devint bientôt enceinte, et se rétablit
parfaitement" (*DSM* 260, 244) ["She chose a young and very loving husband,
soon became pregnant, and was completely cured"].

The practice of prescribing husband and/or baby to treat or ward off the hysterical state speaks not only to the belief that woman needs to be fixed in her place
(confined to the home) but also to the belief in a female place that needs to be
fixed, a female part that is damaged or missing. In a revealing choice of words,
Brachet traces woman's tendency toward hysteria to "une modification spéciale
physiologique de son système nerveux" (97) ["a special physiological modification
of her nervous system"]. The difference *between* the sexes is interpreted as a female
"modification" or alteration of the male model, female difference or deviation
from a male standard. Well before Freud translated sexual difference as female castration, clinicians were in fact if not in name engaged in similar interpretive strategies, and were reading hysteria as the dramatic outward sign of an otherwise
veiled female loss.

The implicit association of hysteria and what would later be labeled "female
castration" recurs, in varying forms, throughout nineteenth-century clinical writings on the disease. In the *Dictionnaire des sciences médicales*, the "proof" of hys-

teria's female exclusivity yields castration as an inevitable corollary. Louyer-Villermay gives the following lesson in comparative anatomy in explanation of woman's predisposition to the malady: "Les organes de la génération ne peuvent être retranchés dans le sexe, tandis que l'appareil génital, tout extérieur chez l'homme, et chargé de fonctions plus limitées, semble former un système comme isolé, et qui peut être enlevé facilement" (*DSM* 229) ["The female reproductive organs cannot be cut off, while the male genital apparatus, entirely external and charged with more limited functions, seems to form an isolated system that can easily be removed"]. Although woman's reproductive organs have the dual advantage of being less vulnerable and more important than man's, their role, the author continues, is short-lived, while man's procreative aptitudes go on indefinitely, *"comme si la nature avait voulu établir une compensation"* [*"as if nature had wanted to establish a compensation"*]. The assigning of hysteria to women must evidently be viewed as an attempt to equilibrate the lot of the two sexes—or, more accurately, to indemnify men for a perceived imbalance. If prolonged fertility is nature's compensation to men for the less complicated role played by their genital organs, then, in analogous fashion, the assigning of hysteria to women is nature's compensation to men for incurring the greater risk of loss. Hysteria, then, is an alternative form of castration visited upon women by men: "nature's compensation," or male revenge for the unfair protection of the female reproductive organs.

In another curious passage, Louyer-Villermay associates hysteria with castration via the effects of this disease on the voice. Voice modifications brought about by hysteria (and other uterine disturbances) are testimony, the doctor says, to the close and exclusive relationship between the female genital organs and voice organs. He adds: "L'influence qu'exerce sur la voix de l'homme une opération barbare ne peut infirmer cette opinion; ces changements sont le résultat d'une violence extérieure, tandis que ceux que nous avons notés . . . sont le produit de phénomènes naturels"[25] ["The influence exerted on man's voice by a barbarous operation cannot invalidate this opinion; these changes are the result of external violence, while those we have noted . . . are the product of natural phenomena"]. The doctor's efforts to distinguish between voice change in men and women in effect work to assimilate the two; the mere mention of the voice-modifying consequences of castration in this context suggests that the uterine alteration responsible for female vocal change is analogous to castration, the difference here being that male castration is an "external violence" while female castration is a "natural phenomenon," the ordinary—if pathological—condition of woman, a kind of congenital defect.[26] It is a phenomenon whose violence and brutality are named but

[25] Louyer-Villermay, *TMN*, 209; see also 204, 107.
[26] In one very unusual case reported by Brachet, male hysteria is associated with castration. Apparently female castration can be "carried" by male hysterics:

denied and in which it is difficult to avoid reading a projection of the production of the castrato's voice—female voice bearing the mark of difference as castration. When pondering these representations of hysterical voice, it is again useful to invoke the metaphor of the afterbirth: a shared blood sign of the unbearable reversibility of life after birth is reassigned as the Other's bleeding lack.

The myth of hysteria here feeds into and fuses with the larger story the nineteenth century was telling itself about sexual difference; it provided one means of neutralizing the threat of female alterity. However, the effort to fix feminine identity cannot avoid also fixing masculine identity, for the process whereby woman is constructed as alien to man simultaneously encloses men in an inflexible mold that lacks everything that defines women. To remedy these lacks, without admitting them, their incorporation in/as women must be alternately enshrined and degraded.

Paradoxically, then, it is precisely the representation of woman as sexually disfigured Other (as hysteric) that enables her to be transfigured as oracular voice or mantic text. The apparent interiority, mutability, alterity of female nature constitutes an absence that can easily be reformulated as potential presence, a lack that can be transformed into promised supplement—a blank that can be filled in as sign. Thus Brachet associates hysterical delirium with "des exaltations singulières, bizarres, éloquentes, et même poétiques de l'imagination" (285–86) ["singular, bizarre, eloquent, and indeed poetic states of exaltation"], and Landouzy notes the following:

> Dans l'hystérie . . . on a quelquefois remarqué des attaques surprenantes par l'élocution comme inspirée, et par le grandiose des pensées de

---

Entre autres faits d'hystérie chez les hommes, je ne puis oublier celui dont j'ai été le témoin dans l'infirmerie d'un établissement auquel j'étais attaché. . . . Le malade pouvait avoir 30 ans. Il prenait des crises extraordinairement violentes et il perdait connaissance. Plusieurs hommes ne pouvaient pas le contenir. . . . Dans une de ses crises, le malade en se débattant, appliqua involontairement un coup violent sur le testicule droit de l'infirmier. Cette glande fut pendant 24 heures, le siége d'une douleur atroce que rien ne put calmer. Alors la douleur s'apaisa. Mais en même temps le testicule avait disparu, il avait été absorbé, je ne trouvai plus que le cordon et quelques fragments de l'épididyme. (Brachet, 192–93)

Among other manifestations of hysteria in men, I cannot forget the one I witnessed in the infirmary of an establishment I was affiliated with. . . . The patient was about thirty. He was overcome by extraordinarily violent fits and he lost consciousness. Several men could not restrain him. . . . During one of his fits, the patient, as he struggled, involuntarily struck the attendant's right testicle with great force. For twenty-four hours this gland was the site of intense pain that nothing could assuage. Then the pain subsided. But at the same time the testicle had disappeared; it had been absorbed; I could only find the spermatic cord and some fragments of the epididymus.

certaines malades; ce qui faisait dire à Diderot, que dans le délire
hystérique, la femme revient sur le passé, qu'elle lit dans l'avenir et que
tous les temps lui sont présents. Rien qui se touche de plus près . . . que
l'extase, les visions, les prophéties, les révélations, la poésie fougueuse et
l'hystéricisme.   (84–85)

*Sometimes hysterical attacks . . . are noteworthy due to an elocution that seems
inspired, and the grandiose nature of patients' thoughts; this is what led Diderot to
say that in hysterical delirium, woman returns to the past, reads the future, and
sees all times at once. Nothing is as interrelated . . . as ecstasy, vision, prophecy,
revelation, inspired poetry, and hystericism.*

By means of a fetishistic reversal, the nineteenth century recuperates its hystericized margins: indefinability is endowed with the portent of meaning, secretions carry secrets, emotional overflow suggests lyrical flow, delirium is the troubled voice of revelation, and speech loss opens the space of an incommunicable sublime.

But it is worth emphasizing that hysteria's voice can be valorized as signifying source only when it has been negatively introduced within the phallic order: that is, once it has been fetishized. This means that to associate the hysteric with expressivity or communication is to deny recognition of another language, another voice whose lack or loss can only be refigured as primal plenitude. In other words, the process I have called the transfiguration of hysteria is always a mediated process: the conversion of hysterical symptom into literary sign always involves the mediation of a controlling discourse whose own story is at stake in the conversion process. This knowledge I think obliges us to approach the poetics of hysteria with heightened critical vigilance. When hysteria is diagnosed (by doctors, surrealists, or others) as a "supreme means of expression,"[27] we must reply, "Whose expression?" When letters of blood or ink appear on otherwise mute hysterical bodies, we must seek the nail or pen that inscribed them. And—to speak finally in the doctors' tongue—when leaking pipes are transfigured as lyrical vessels, we must bear witness to the hand that turns the faucet.[28]

[27] Louis Aragon and André Breton, "La Cinquantenaire de l'hystérie," *La Révolution surréaliste* 4 (15 March 1928): 22.
[28] This is admittedly not an easy hand to find. Does it represent language? Culture? Power? Are all three the same thing?

3 READING WOMEN

The Novel in the Text of Hysteria

> *My recent reading has caused me for some reason to*
> *remember myself as I was when a young girl, reading*
> *high Romances and seeing myself simultaneously*
> *as the object of all knights' devotion—an unspotted*
> *Guenevere—and as the author of the Tale. I wanted to*
> *be a Poet and a Poem, and now am neither. . . .*
> *I hit on something I believe when I wrote that*
> *I meant to be a Poet and a Poem. It may be that this*
> *is the desire of all reading women.*
>
> A. S. BYATT, *POSSESSION*

● Virtually every nineteenth-century medical text on hysteria offers a pro-phylactic to the (implicitly male) reader seeking to protect his wife, daughter, or woman patient from the ravages of the female condition. The barrier that physi-cians recommend almost unanimously is illiteracy. To be sure, the ban on letters ranges with medical opinion from greater to lesser inclusivity (the written word is categorically anathema in some quarters, but in others newspapers and pious texts, for example, are acceptable exceptions). Opinion converges, however, where the novel is concerned: a common thread links the nineteenth-century hysteria texts to the work of a certain Samuel-Auguste Tissot, an eighteenth-century Swiss phy-sician who declared that any daughter exposed to a novel at a tender age would come down with hysteria several years later. Every doctor cites Tissot, but there is a revealing variance from text to text in the matter of framing the incubation pe-riod and even naming the specificity of the disease: some treatises give the critical ages as ten and fifteen, others as fifteen and twenty, still others as ten and twenty; some predict hysteria, some nervosity, some the vapors. Clearly his warning had by the early nineteenth century become a medical axiom so familiar that it needed only to be roughly paraphrased rather than quoted verbatim.[1] In fact Tissot's thread leads not only throughout but outside the clinical literature, losing itself in the vaster social fabric where we find reading, women, and hysteria knotted into the texture of the time.

IL NE FAUT PAS QUE LES FEMMES SACHENT LIRE: SUBVERSION AND THE NOVEL

A half-century before *Madame Bovary's* 1856 staging of popular conceptions of the fine madness that afflicts female readers and the special hell to which they are doomed, Sylvain Maréchal's 1801 tract, *Projet d'une loi portant défense d'apprendre à lire aux femmes* [*Plan for a law forbidding women to learn to read*] (reprinted posthumously in 1853 as *Il ne faut pas que les femmes sachent lire* [*Women must not learn how to read*]) compiled a culture's received ideas about women, books, and the dreaded consequences of their union.[2] The association is not new to the nineteenth century; it is at least partly rooted in the time-honored theological precept that equates ignorance and innocence, book knowledge and carnal knowledge, and in the equally long theological and secular tradition of misogyny.[3] Building upon these traditions is a well-established strain of novel criticism that reaches a crescendo in the eighteenth-century *querelle du roman*, resounding summarily in Rousseau's prefatory pronouncement in *La Nouvelle Héloïse*: "Jamais fille chaste n'a lu de roman" ["A chaste girl has never read a novel"].[4]

It is, however, the more immediate ideological subtext that gives the nineteenth-century nexus of women and novels its notable virulence. In view of feminist claims throughout the century for education, literacy, and the opening of the liberal professions to women, we need to reevaluate the increasing attribution of hysteria to excessive education—and, correlatively, to the reading of novels—as a defensive gesture, an attempt to keep rapidly eroding social boundaries in place. The specter of democracy looms ominously in nineteenth-century France precisely because the new order might allow no specters, not a ghost of an erstwhile system of distinctions. In this light gender difference appears as one of the

---

[1] In fact I have not been able to locate the source of the quotation. In addition to *De la santé des gens de lettres* and *Traité des nerfs et de leurs maladies*, which are the likeliest places for such a warning to appear, Tissot's works include *L'Onanisme: Dissertation sur les maladies produites par la masturbation* and *Traité de l'épilepsie*.
[2] Sylvain Maréchal, *Projet d'une loi portant défense d'apprendre à lire aux femmes* (Paris: Massé, 1801).
[3] See Michael Danahy, *The Feminization of the Novel* (Gainesville: University of Florida Press, 1991).
[4] For an excellent presentation of the *querelle du roman*, see Georges May, *Le Dilemme du roman au XVIIIe siècle* (New Haven: Yale University Press, 1963).

last bastions against chaos remaining,[5] though the increasing vigilance with which the boundaries of gender-aligned public and private spheres are maintained after the revolution speaks to their fragility and the feared interpenetrability of purportedly separate spheres.[6] The thoroughness of cultural border policing can be evaluated by its institutionalization in postrevolutionary France as a discourse (in the Foucauldian sense) not so much descriptive as constitutive of the social order. Arthur Schopenhauer's influential "Essai sur les femmes," widely disseminated in French literary circles once it was translated in 1880, taught a lesson ("Il ne devrait y avoir au monde que des femmes d'intérieur" ["There should only be housewives in the world"]) that was arguably so well received as theory because it was already everywhere in place as practice, meshed within the fabric of societal mores.[7] We hear it anticipated, for example, in another essay "Sur les femmes," this one written by the moralist Madame Guizot and reproduced in an 1866 conduct book for girls—a book written by women evidently inculcated with the doctrine of dichotomous spheres and the concomitant rhetoric of female interiority:

> L'imagination d'un homme s'élance sur tous les points où il peut atteindre; l'imagination d'une femme se concentre sur ce qui peut la toucher; elle connaît parfaitement tout ce qui est en dedans et aux environs d'elle-même, elle voit peu et mal ce qui s'en éloigne. . . . Il est bien des secrets de morale que la bonté seule apprend à la vertu; il en est mille que la sensibilité révèle seule à la bonté, c'est là le domaine des femmes, qu'elles le cultivent: c'est là, c'est dans leur propre manoir qu'est pour elles la source inépuisable de richesses, elles ne feront que perdre ailleurs ce qu'elles y ont amassé, il est si rare qu'une femme gagne quelque chose à sortir de chez elle![8]

> A *man's imagination leaps toward all points he can reach; a woman's imagination concentrates on what touches her; she knows well what is within and around*

[5] Geneviève Fraisse quotes this curious formulation of a qualified will to equality from Gracchus Babeuf's 1796 *Manifeste des égaux*—edited by Maréchal: "Qu'il ne soit plus d'autre différence parmi les hommes que celle de l'âge et du sexe" ["Let there be no other difference between men than that of age and sex"]. Fraisse, *Muse de la raison: La démocratie exclusive et la différence des sexes* (Paris: Alinéa, 1989), 23.
[6] For an informative discussion of the maintenance of separate spheres, see Lynn Hunt, "The Unstable Boundaries of the French Revolution," in *A History of Private Life*, trans. Arthur Goldhammer, ed. Michelle Perrot, vol. 4 (Cambridge: Harvard University Press, Belknap Press, 1990) and Claire Goldberg Moses, *French Feminism in the Nineteenth Century* (Albany: State University of New York Press, 1984).
[7] Arthur Schopenhauer, *Essai sur les femmes*, trans. Jean Bourdeau, ed. Didier Raymond (Paris: Alcan, 1884; reprint, Paris: Actes Sud, 1987), 33.
[8] Madame Guizot in Madame A. Tastu, *Lectures pour les jeunes filles* (Paris: Didier, 1866), 148.

*herself, she ill perceives whatever is at a distance from her. . . . There are many
moral secrets that goodness alone teaches to virtue; there are thousands that
sensitivity reveals solely to goodness; let women cultivate that sphere, which
belongs to them; it is there in their own abode that they will find the inexhaustible
source of riches; they will only lose elsewhere what they have amassed there. It is so
seldom that a woman has anything to gain by leaving the house!*

Medical warnings about the subversive potential of reading women must then
initially be read against a political agenda of stability and containment that often
has recourse to a scare rhetoric of errancy and transgression.[9] It is perfectly in keeping with such a discourse that Dr. Landouzy qualifies novels as "toutes ces dévia-
tions littéraires . . . qui impriment presque nécessairement une direction vicieuse
à l'esprit, à la sensibilité et aux affections des jeunes filles" ["all those literary devia-
tions . . . that almost necessarily imprint a vicious direction on the mind, the sensitivity, and the feelings of young girls"][10] and that Dr. Brachet warns against an education unsuited to women's subordinate social position, which will encourage
"ce faible de l'esprit humain pour grandir et s'élever, pour sortir de sa sphère" ["this
foible that leads the human spirit to grow, rise up, and leave its sphere"].[11]

The age-old association of hysteria with the mobility of women's bodies and
spirits (the wandering womb, capriciousness, inconstancy) is not so much redefined in the nineteenth century as deliteralized, conceptually refined now in sociopolitical terms (upward and outward mobility, domestic restlessness, roving
thoughts, driving ambition, and the potential displacement of gender, class, and
family structures). The hysteria doctors, in accordance with this refining and recasting of female mobility, no longer seek to reaffix the vagrant womb to its point
of origination, but to enwomb woman, to confine her once more within the domestic sphere by binding not her feet, but her mind. For hysteria is caused, in the
progressive terms of nineteenth-century medicine, by "la réalité inférieure au
rêve" ["reality that falls short of dreaming"], as if in echo to Flaubert's elliptical
etiology of Emma Bovary's malady: "[l]es rêves trop hauts, . . . [l]a maison trop
étroite" ["her overexalted dreams, her too cramped home"].[12] Reality's house could
then very well split apart at the beams, unless measures be taken to impede the expansion of its inhabitant dreams.

[9] For some astute comments on vagabondage as a social disease, see Kristin Ross, *The Emergence of
Social Space: Rimbaud and the Paris Commune* (Minneapolis: University of Minnesota Press, 1988),
55–59.
[10] H. Landouzy, *Traité complet de l'hystérie* (Paris: Baillière, 1846), 264.
[11] J. L. Brachet, *Traité de l'hystérie* (Paris: Baillière, 1847), 88.
[12] Charles Richet, "Les Démoniaques d'aujourd'hui," *Revue des deux mondes* 37 (15 January 1880):
356; Gustave Flaubert, *Madame Bovary*, ed. Jacques Suffel (Paris: Garnier Flammarion, 1979), 141;
trans. Paul de Man (New York: Norton, 1965), 77.

There is a telling irony in perceiving reading as the emblematic escape weapon with which the iconoclastic female menace hacks her way out of the house of culture, for as Nancy Armstrong has argued, the novel was one of the primary instruments used to carve out the domestic order and to delimit it as woman's domain. The novel then becomes a two-edged sword, a force of domesticity and privatism so effective in its work of isolating and separating home from the heartless world that the intended haven becomes an inscrutable lair. Privacy breeds secrecy; as the domestic sphere is more and more withdrawn from the public, ever interiorized the better to establish discipline and control, it couches the growing possibility of an other, inner world that eludes surveillance.[13]

So we might say of the novel—and of the woman who reads it—what Freud said about the word *heimlich*, specifically, that it "is not unambiguous, but belongs to two sets of ideas, which . . . are . . . very different: on the one hand, it means what is familiar and agreeable, and on the other, what is concealed and kept out of sight."[14] We can think of that locus classicus of nineteenth-century painting, the woman reading before a window, as a graphic illustration of the ambiguous role attributed to the novel; for the hidden world enclosed in the book (or perhaps in the woman reading the book) is projected outward, reflected by the landscape represented on the other side of the window: *a world that ought perhaps to have remained secret, and yet comes to light.* Or we could more specifically think about Manet's *Gare Saint-Lazare*, which evokes the reader's secret world through an iron grill that bars her from her own scene of reading, immobilizes her at the very site of travel, locked in a moment of inner journey. The ambiguities inherent in such scenes are well summarized in *Madame Bovary* by Léon's manipulative mirroring of Emma's own response to reading: "On se promène immobile dans des pays que l'on croit voir" ["Without having to move, we walk through the countries

---

[13] Nina Baym's contention, which I adopt but displace here, is that the novel (in America) supports the ideology of home as fortress against the world by domesticating pleasure, but simultaneously jeopardizes this ideology by fostering individualism and solitude. Baym, *Novels, Readers, and Reviewers: Responses to Fiction in Antebellum America* (Ithaca: Cornell University Press, 1984), 50–51. I am arguing here for an element that escapes, or threatens to elude, the institutionalization of power that Nancy Armstrong so well describes. See Nancy Armstrong, *Desire and Domestic Fiction* (Oxford: Oxford University Press, 1987).

For contemporary accounts of male reactions to women reading which are analogous to nineteenth-century representations of reading as otherworldly, see Janice Radway's *Reading the Romance: Women, Patriarchy, and Popular Literature* (Chapel Hill: University of North Carolina Press, 1984). One of Radway's informants offers the following commentary on her husband's reactions to her activities: "For a while Dan was not thrilled that I was reading a lot. Because I think men do feel threatened. They want their wife to be in the room with them. And I think my body is in the room but the rest of me is not" (89).

[14] Sigmund Freud, "The 'Uncanny,'" in *The Standard Edition of the Complete Works of Sigmund Freud*, trans. James Strachey, Anna Freud, Alix Strachey, and Alan Tyson, ed. James Strachey, 24 vols. (London: Hogarth Press, 1955), 17:224–25.

FIGURE 7. *Edouard Manet.*
Gare Saint-Lazare. 1873.
(Photo © 1993, National Gallery of Art,
Washington. Gift of Horace Havemeyer in
memory of his mother, Louisine W. Havemeyer.)

of our imagination"].[15] If the ambiguities in such representations of reading initially correspond to the uncertain power of novels in women's lives, they more fundamentally express the ambivalence of the cultural imaginary that produced them: an ambivalence about a genre and a gender once constructed as constitutive of home and hearth but that somehow developed—much like the meaning of *heimlich*, which came to coincide with its opposite, *unheimlich*—in such a way as to augur the destruction of that cultural home.

LES LIAISONS ILLICITES: SEDUCTION AND THE NOVEL

The crux of my argument until this point has been that the identification of female derangement with books can be explained as a projection of male fears regarding the potential power of a literate sisterhood. This argument makes sense, but it does not explain enough. It does not sufficiently absorb the insistent presence of the novel in the text of hysteria, and it does not explain a curious turnabout: the novel plays the same seductive role in clinical hysteria that hysteria plays in the novel. While novelists consistently conflate hysteria and eroticism, equating hysterics and seductresses—a practice doctors are quick to discredit—clinicians eroticize the novel and the act of reading with a vehemence and persistence bordering on the obsessive. Doctors trace the tendency of novels to induce disease directly to their power to seduce. As Dr. Bernutz plainly states in 1874, "Il est malheureusement certain que ces livres ont une influence sur le moral, et qu'on peut leur attribuer un certain nombre des liaisons illicites, qui, comme nous l'avons vu plus haut, engendrent un si grand nombre de cas d'hystérie" ["Unfortunately, it is certain that these books influence morality, and we can attribute to them a good number of illicit affairs, which, as we have seen, engender so many cases of hysteria"].[16]

Paradoxically, however, some of the very doctors who protest the novel's seductive wiles and denounce its role in the etiology of hysteria actively contribute to its production. Doctors H. Beaunis, A. Binet, Charles Richet, and Charcot himself were all closet novelists; their published fiction appeared pseudonymously.[17] How are we to interpret this professional and moral doubling? Is this simply a case of hypocrisy? If so, is the bad faith situated in the doctor as writer or in the writer as doctor? Is it possible that the doctors turned novelists in a Frankensteinian attempt to create new experimental subjects? In an entrepreneurial attempt to stimulate busi-

[15] Flaubert, *Madame Bovary*, 117; trans. de Man, 59.

[16] G. Bernutz, "Hystérie," in *Dictionnaire de médecine et de chirurgie pratique*, ed. Jaccoud (Paris: Baillière, 1874), 281–82.

[17] Charcot's fiction has not, to the best of my knowledge, been published; manuscripts exist at the Charcot Library at the Salpêtrière Hospital. For a provocative case study of the phenomenon of doctor/writer doubling, see Jacqueline Carroy, "Dédoublements: L'énigmatique récit d'un docteur inconnu," *Nouvelle revue de psychanalyse* 42 (Fall 1990): 151–71.

ness? In a Don Juanesque move to seduce ready victims? Or instead, did the novelists know better than to believe what they as doctors professed about the inevitable path leading women from novels to seduction and hysteria? I have no answers
to these questions, which in their very irresolution invite speculation about the
gender of the novel-reading public and about the workings of the author-reader seduction model.

Recent research about the nineteenth-century reading public in fact challenges
traditional assumptions linking novels to a predominantly female audience. James
Smith Allen presents statistical evidence that literacy rates for women lagged behind those for men until well into the nineteenth century, and he cautions even
then against confusing the history of literacy with the history of reading, while Michael Danahy and Lise Queffelec separately offer cogent arguments suggesting
that the feminization of the novel's public is a phantasmatic projection of the gendered partitioning of culture rather than a reflection of real readership.[18] There is
a slippage from the consideration of woman as the novel's sole reader to that of
woman as its privileged reader and then on to woman as the privileged image of its
reader, so that the general reading public is very easily and subtly subsumed under
the sign of the feminine. In this way the verifiably male component of the novel's
public is not so much denied as such, but feminized.

If the novel reader is not necessarily a woman, but is rather only phantasmatically feminine, what happens to the traditional seduction scenario that we have
grown accustomed to accepting as the novel's implicit contract with its reader?[19] I
would like to address this question obliquely by way of a detour through a short
novel by Charles Epheyre, *Soeur Marthe*.[20] Epheyre, who was more commonly
known, and whom we have already met, as Dr. Charles Richet, was one of Charcot's interns at the Salpêtrière and in the late 1870s introduced him to hypnotism.[21] Richet also wrote, under his own name, various treatises and articles on
somnambulism, hysteria, and general psychology. *Soeur Marthe*, one of several
novels by Epheyre/Richet (whose other literary ventures included poetry, fables,
and theater), appeared in 1889 in the *Revue des deux mondes*.

Soeur Marthe tells a multilayered story about doubling and dividing. The epon-

[18] James Smith Allen, *In the Public Eye: A History of Reading in Modern France, 1800–1940* (Princeton: Princeton University Press, 1991), 55–82. See Danahy, *Feminization of the Novel*, and Lise Queffelec, "Le Lecteur du roman comme lectrice: Stratégies romanesques et stratégies critiques sous la
Monarchie de Juillet," *Romantisme* 53 (1986): 9–10.
[19] Ross Chambers and Sarah Kofman have written provocative pages on seduction and the novel. See
Chambers, *Story and Situation: Narrative Seduction and the Power of Fiction* (Minneapolis: University
of Minnesota Press, 1984) and Kofman, "Séductions, essai sur *La Religieuse* de Diderot," in *Séductions: De Sartre à Héraclite* (Paris: Galilée, 1990).
[20] Charles Epheyre [Charles Richet], *Soeur Marthe, Revue des deux mondes* 93 (15 May 1889):
384–431.
[21] Carroy, "Dédoublements," 151–71.

ymous Marthe is the saintly half of a split personality, the other side of which is a temptress named Angèle who emerges when the nun is hypnotized. The text plays with name associations by calling its angel in the house of the Lord "Marthe" (alluding antithetically to the worldly sister of the biblical story), while giving the angel's name to the seductress. This rather obvious transposition is the cover for the textual inversion of male and female lead roles: although the female object of the plot is most obviously split, the male subject is in fact an inherently divided figure as well (as are the narrator and the author). Laurent, the doctor protagonist, at several points evokes his own dualistic nature ("nous sommes tous, plus ou moins, ressemblans à ces somnambules" ["we all more or less resemble somnambulists"])[22] and becomes quite clearly a divided soul when striving to resist the disarming appeal of the passionate nun. Torn between a kind of oceanic feeling that overcomes him when he is with Marthe/Angèle and a (not entirely plausible) fear of legal reprisals should he elope with her, he orders Angèle (to whom Marthe has ceded in a somnambulist trance) never to reappear.

Now, while Laurent's motivation for repudiating Angèle is explicitly given as fear—a fear we are invited to place under the paternal sign of the Law ("l'idée de la cour d'assises . . . l'épouvant[ait]. . . . Toutes les sévérités de la loi retomberaient sur lui" ["the idea of the assize court filled him with dread. . . . The harshest penalties of the law would fall upon him"])—everything else suggests that he flees Angèle/Marthe as the embodiment of an engulfing maternal presence.[23] It is her music that initially and repeatedly sweeps over Laurent, overwhelms him. Laurent listens to her at the organ "avec ravissement" ["with rapture"]—and the narrator emphatically specifies her ravishing repertoire: Gounod's *Ave Maria* and Rossini's *Stabat Mater*.[24] Laurent is a man of science whose ambivalent attraction to the mysterious depths of the human spirit and passions is expressed early in the novel: "Il se sentait attiré, en même temps qu'effrayé, par ces profondeurs inouïes, abîmes sans fin où tout est inconnu" ["He was simultaneously attracted by and afraid of these unheard-of depths, bottomless abysses where all is unknown"]. He reacts to the young woman's music with a similar ambivalence: "Il s'abandonnait au charme de cette musique délicieuse. . . . Il craignait de montrer à quel point il avait été ému" ["He abandoned himself to the charm of this delicious music. . . . He was afraid to show how much he had been moved"].[25] The narrative, itself divided, offers two different orders of explanation for Laurent's fear, orders that we might anachronistically name Oedipal and pre-Oedipal, and that are similarly at

[22] Epheyre, *Soeur Marthe*, 395.
[23] Ibid., 405–6.
[24] Ibid., 387, 403. Later, when he regrets having banished Angèle and tries desperately (and unsuccessfully) to summon her, Laurent plays Mozart's *Requiem*, shortly before declaring, "Elle est morte, morte!" ["She is dead, dead!"] (419, 421).
[25] Ibid., 385, 387.

work in determining Laurent's ambivalent sexual and aesthetic responses. The doubled, divided structure has still another repercussion; Laurent's internal split (he is a skeptical man of science but also a passionate adventurer) is externally replicated by the couple Laurent/George, where George the steady married friend serves as a foil to his friend's more dominant adventurous tendencies.

But these multiple divisions hide behind the focal Marthe/Angèle split, which cries out for attention. Given that this minor variation on the angel/whore scenario replicates one of the most hackneyed of male fantasies, we cannot but wonder about the dangerous seductive lure that doctors such as Richet/Epheyre attributed to novels (such as this one?) left in the hands of nubile young women. I would argue that only a woman "read[ing] in drag," to borrow Susan Winnett's phrase, could possibly be seduced by such male fantasies, in which woman is "neither an independent subjectivity nor a desiring agent but, rather, an enabling position" sustaining an a priori state of affairs "between men."[26] This bypassing of women is nowhere clearer than in Sylvain Maréchal's *Projet d'une loi portant défense d'apprendre à lire aux femmes* [Plan for a law forbidding women to learn to read], which explicitly addresses itself "Aux Chefs de maison; Aux Pères de Famille; et aux Maris" ["To Heads of Households; to Fathers; and to Husbands"], continuing, "vous tiendrez donc la main à ce Règlement; il vous intéresse plus peut-être encore que les femmes qui en sont l'objet principal" ["you reach out in support of this Ruling; it is quite possibly of greater interest to you than to women who are its principal object"].[27] If the novel-reading public is phantasmatically feminized, reading desire may nonetheless be construed as generically male.

As we begin to confront the strange hybrid reader that emerges from these clinical forays into women and the novel, the question of what we can expect to learn here about gender and reading needs to be very carefully framed. I want therefore to digress briefly in order to frame an approach that will orient the pages to follow.

A child of eleven or twelve seeking moral compensation for the task of babysitting for a slightly younger sister presumed the right to supervise the younger girl's television curriculum. This meant, most fundamentally, banishing her from the room with an admonitory "this is not for you" whenever, in the course of a movie, a dimming of lights promised a sex scene or a quickening of music announced violence. While the younger girl obediently repaired to an adjoining room, her older sister would remain before the screen, transfixed by an emotional current whose element of unease I strongly suspect and whose component of fascination I quite clearly remember—for I was that child. I reveled in my uncertain power.

[26] Susan Winnett, "Coming Unstrung: Women, Men, Narrative, and Principles of Pleasure," *PMLA* 105 (May 1990): 507.
[27] Maréchal, *Projet d'une loi*, i–ii.

To the question of what these childhood episodes told about my sister's interest in, readiness for, or responses to televised sex and violence, I would have to answer today (with the insight of two decades of hindsight) "not a thing." On the contrary, I would have to admit that the scenarios I was directing for myself and my sister (my self and my alter ego)—"you leave, I stay"—were compromises whose formation revealed the ambivalent intensities of my own prepubescent fantasies: the fear of what is desired and the seductiveness of what is condemned.

I suspect much adult censorship bears a strong resemblance to this very simple child's pattern. The mechanism that allows desire and fear to be denied, projected, and thereby mastered—but also simultaneously indulged—helps to explain the doctors' fascinated prohibition of the novel. The anecdote elucidates, too, the futility of any attempt to analyze aesthetic reception (be it television viewing or novel reading) when the only evidence available concerns censorship of this experience—unless the focus shifts to the censor's own relationship to the censored aesthetic object or experience. This is where the syntactic oscillation of my chapter title becomes important, shifting our reading of subject and object positions in "Reading Women." For if nineteenth-century diatribes against women and reading don't much advance our understanding of women's ways of reading, they do move us by leaps and bounds into questions of how men read women, and also how men read reading.

As I begin to speculate on these questions, I want, however, to supplement the taboo conjunction of women and reading with a third term that has been implicit in my argument until this point: space. In what follows I want to suggest that the fantasized coupling of women and reading (expressed hyperbolically by hysteria and the novel) wraps around a participatory body of anxiety about spatial processes and relationships: presence and absence, mobility and immobility, distance and fusion, interior and exterior, boundaries, conquest, possession, separation, and loss. I will be looking at two conceptual traditions that, I will argue, are not separate: on the one hand, the perception of space as a feminine (and particularly maternal) province as opposed to a vision of time as the father's domain; and on the other hand, the conception of reading as an activity oriented in space. (I am not alluding here to representations by different formalisms of the novel's structure as alternately space or time bound, but rather to the spatial structure of the reading process.)

Consider the following citations as pretext for some comments on the interweavings of women, reading, and space. I selected my corpus by a kind of cross-reading—a reading across gender, genre, and time—in the belief that only by reading across categories, in between the lines, as it were, can we begin to understand what has been women's place in textual space, and think about what it might mean to read otherwise.

UNE CARTOGRAPHIE DES COÏTS: SPACE AND THE NOVEL

"'Father's time, mother's species,' as Joyce put it; and indeed, when evoking the name and destiny of women, one thinks more of the *space* generating and forming the human species than of *time*, becoming or history." So speaks Julia Kristeva, framing Joyce.[28] Dr. Louyer-Villermay contrasts the female and male reproductive systems in terms of a similar spatiotemporal dichotomy in his 1818 entry "Hystérie" in the *Dictionnaire des sciences médicales*. He describes the uterus, in comparison to its male counterpart, as "situé beaucoup plus profondément" ["situated much more deeply"] and ascribes to it "[une] influence extraordinaire, [une] sorte d'empire" ["{an} extraordinary influence, {a} kind of empire"], which spatial advantage he hastily counterbalances as he celebrates male reproductive longevity: "Après quarante ans, la femme n'est plus apte à devenir mère, tandis que l'aptitude à procréer se prolonge chez l'homme presque indéfiniment, comme si la nature avait voulu établir une compensation" ["After age forty, woman can no longer become a mother, while the ability to procreate is prolonged in man almost indefinitely, as if nature had wanted to grant compensation"].[29]

John Donne more aggressively spatializes—indeed, territorializes—female anatomy in his elegy "To His Mistris Going to Bed":

> O my America! my new-found-land,
> My kingdome, safeliest when with one man man'd,
> My Myne of precious stones, My Emperie,
> How blest am I in this discovering thee![30]

In the novel *Femmes*, Philippe Sollers's narrator—he too a trailblazer—relates one of his conquests. As he explores what he calls "le four abstrait de la jouissance incurvée" ["the abstract kiln of curved delight"], he muses: "Il y a longtemps que je pense qu'une véritable cartographie des coïts serait souhaitable" ["I've always thought a cartography of coitus would be a good idea"]—and the context makes clear that on this cartographer's map, "coitus" is a synecdochic label for inner female space.[31] And Sean Connery, about to betray his native England in *The Russia*

[28] Julia Kristeva, "Women's Time," trans. Alice Jardine and Harry Blake, *Signs* 7 (Autumn 1981): 15.
[29] J.-B. Louyer-Villermay, "Hystérie," in *Dictionnaire des sciences médicales*, vol. 23 (Paris: Panckoucke, 1818), 228–29.
[30] John Donne, Elegie XIX, "To His Mistris Going to Bed," in *John Donne: Poetry and Prose*, ed. Frank J. Warnke (New York: Random House, Modern Library, 1967), 96.
[31] Philippe Sollers, *Femmes* (Paris: Gallimard, 1983), 29; trans. Barbara Bray, under the title *Women* (New York: Columbia University Press, 1990), 19.

House, turns to Michelle Pfeiffer playing his Russian girlfriend and begins to make love to her with these words: "*You're* my only country now."[32]

Gaston Bachelard, in *La Poétique de l'espace*, domesticates female geographies, writing that before being cast into the world, "l'homme est déposé dans le berceau de la maison. Et toujours, en nos rêveries, la maison est un grand berceau" ["man is deposited in the cradle of the house. And always in our dreams, the house is a great cradle"]. He elaborates: "Quand on rêve à la maison natale, dans l'extrême profondeur de la rêverie, on participe à cette chaleur première, à cette matière bien tempérée du paradis matériel" ["When we dream of our house of birth, in the deepest reverie, we partake of that first warmth, of that well-tempered matter that is part of material paradise"].[33] While home is explicitly and repeatedly designated as the locus of dreaming, the metaphorical fashioning of home as womb throughout the essay places dream and dreamer more pointedly within maternal space. This particular slippage comes as no surprise for readers of Freud, who earlier discovered an "*unheimlich* place" coinciding with "the entrance to the former *heim* [home] of all human beings." For Freud before Bachelard, this home/womb was also the site of male dreaming: "Whenever a man dreams of a place or a country and says to himself . . . 'I've been here before,' we may interpret the place as being his mother's genitals or her body."[34]

Bachelard places his study under the banner of "l'espace heureux" ["happy space"], which he renames "topophilie," thereby implying if never naming the possibility of another kind of relationship to (maternal) space that would be called "topophobie."[35] We find these two relationships at times overlapping, at times alternating, but virtually always inherently inseparable. This is to say that the record of male approaches to female space is fraught with ambivalence, with wide swings between affective poles, but rarely, if ever, with neutrality. Correlatively, the pattern that begins to emerge from a review of this record suggests that we should more specifically speak about the bounding, dividing, invading, sealing (and so on) of space than of space per se, for it is by means of such representational strategies that woman is spatialized and the resultant regions ambivalently confronted.

Witness the hysteria clinicians' play with this space in the guise of the discovery/exploration/conquest of female pathology. Medical reports of experimental techniques (among them manual stimulation and penetration of the genitals; tugging on pubic hair; the laying on of hands, leeches, cucumber and zucchini slices) sug-

---

[32] *The Russia House*, dir. Fred Schepisi, screenplay by Tom Stoppard, MGM, 1990.
[33] Gaston Bachelard, *La Poétique de l'espace* (Paris: Presses Universitaires de France, 1957), 26–27.
[34] Freud, "The 'Uncanny,'" *Standard Edition*, 245.
[35] Bachelard, *La Poétique de l'espace*, 17.

gest an approach to internal female topographies modeled on nineteenth-century imperialist doctrines: territorial exploration, invasion, and colonization. It is as if outer space, merely involuted, had become inner space, leaving unchanged the spirit of discovery and conquest that lingers still in twentieth-century media formulations of such a mission: "To boldly go where no man has gone before."[36]

Now certain reading experiences, according to reported accounts, sound a great deal like the doctors' voyages into female space. Here is Robert Darnton on reading the history of books: "In the brief span of two decades, the history of books had become a rich and varied field of study . . . so rich . . . that it now looks less like a field than a tropical rain forest. The explorer can hardly make his way across it. At every stop he becomes entangled in a luxuriant undergrowth of journal articles and disoriented by the crisscrossing of disciplines. . . . The history of books has become so crowded . . . that one can no longer see its general contours."[37] Darnton's reaction to the entangling textual underbrush—however rich, however luxuriant—is retreat. He moves quickly to separate himself from the distracting chaotic clasp of his lush tropical forest, posing boundaries and erecting classificatory lines: "To get some distance from interdisciplinarity run riot . . . it might be useful to propose a general model for analyzing [the subject]."[38]

Georges Poulet describes an initially similar textual encounter that ends otherwise. Here is Poulet's word on books:

> Lisez-moi, semblent-ils dire. Je résiste mal à leur demande. . . .
> D'aventure le sentiment qu'ils m'inspirent, je l'éprouve à propos . . . de
> vases et de statues. . . . N'est-ce pas parce qu'ils me donnent l'illusion
> qu'il y a quelque chose en eux que je pourrais percevoir en les regardant
> sous un autre angle? . . . Quel est ce dedans, cela m'intrigue et me force
> à tourner autour d'eux, comme pour trouver l'entrée d'une chambre
> secrète. Mais il n'y a pas d'entrée (sauf l'ouverture au sommet du vase, qui
> n'est d'ailleurs qu'un faux orifice). Le vase et la statue sont clos. Ils
> m'obligent à rester au dehors. . . . Prenez un livre, au contraire, vous le
> verrez s'offrir, s'ouvrir. . . . Le livre ne s'enferme pas dans ses propres
> contours; il ne s'y installe pas comme dans une forteresse. . . . Entre vous
> et lui les barrières tombent. Vous êtes en lui, il est en vous.

[36] The allusion, of course, is to the weekly voice-over introduction to the 1960s television series "Star Trek." I am told that the introduction to one of its contemporary sequels, "Star Trek: The Next Generation," has boldly altered the original mission and now proclaims, in gender-correct obedience to changing forms, "To boldly go where no *one* has gone before."

[37] Robert Darnton, "What Is the History of Books?" in *Reading in America: Literature and Social History*, ed. Cathy N. Davidson (Baltimore: Johns Hopkins University Press, 1989), 29.

[38] Ibid., 29.

Read me, they seem to say. I find it hard to resist their appeal. . . . This feeling they give me—I sometimes have it with . . . vases and statues. . . . Isn't it because they give me the illusion that there is something in them which, from a different angle, I might be able to see? . . . What this interior might be, that is what intrigues me and makes me circle around them, as though looking for the entrance to a secret chamber. But there is no such entrance (save for the mouth of the vase, which is not a true entrance since it gives access only to a little space to put flowers in). So the vase and the statue are closed. They oblige me to remain outside. . . . On the other hand, take a book, and you will find it offering, opening itself. . . . A book is not shut in by its contours, is not walled-up as in a fortress. . . . the barriers fall away between you and it. You are inside it, it is inside you . . .[39]

Poulet's rhetorical model presents no immediately apparent difference from Darnton's: a book is a space to be penetrated, a chamber to be entered, a barrier to be ruptured. The difference is not simply Poulet's greater (or at least more unreservedly expressed) pleasure, but a blurring of boundaries at just the point (of potential fusion, indistinction, merging) where Darnton draws the line(s). Darnton frets about losing sight of specific contours while Poulet celebrates such a loss of self-enclosed contours. Poulet's initial taking possession of textual space reveals itself to be finally as much a dispossession or abandonment of self, a merging or confusion of categories of self and other, inside and out ("you are inside it, it is inside you"). Something happens in the course of Poulet's description of reading that has the effect of replacing a model of incursion and border crossing by one of absorption and boundlessness. Poulet's initial tired entry into a book analogous to a woman's body unexpectedly proceeds to displace stereotypical alignments of male reading with bound setting or breaking, and female reading (especially as exemplified by the novel) with fusion and identity loss, by blurring distinctions between the two paradigms.

I want to emphasize, however, the more general persistence of a well-entrenched cultural model organized along bipolar lines of gender, genre, and mode of reading. Let us consider a contemporary genre constructed as antithetical to the novel. Serge Tisseron presents the comic strip as a genre preferred by boys because its form invites transgression, defies the law of logical narrative unfolding. The comic strip offers a freedom to skip from frame to frame, which is further elaborated by Tisseron as an inherent rootlessness of the genre, a homelessness specified as a repudiation of mother and woman: "Les héros de [bande dessinée] n'ont

[39] Georges Poulet, "Phénoménologie de la conscience critique," in *La Conscience critique* (Paris: Corti, 1971), 276–77; trans. as "Criticism and the Experience of Interiority," in *The Structuralist Controversy*, ed. Richard Macksey and Eugenio Donato (Baltimore: Johns Hopkins University Press, 1972), 56–57; trans. modified.

pratiquement jamais de parents ni de maison. . . . La maison, c'est la case, un
contenant qui ne doit rien à la mère ni à la féminité" ["Comic strip heroes practi-
cally never have parents or a house. . . . Their house is the frame, a container that
owes nothing to mother or to femininity"].[40] Here at last the novel confronts its
masculine counterpart: a genre whose formal structure of bounded frames suggests
a model of reading as separation, border making and breaking, disconnection. If
the novel encloses, shelters, absorbs its reader, the comic strip offers instead, in the
words of psychoanalyst Catherine Muller, "un univers en apesanteur, qui peut sa-
tisfaire un fantasme archaïque et masculin: celui d'un monde sans utérus" ["a
weightless universe that can satisfy an archaic and masculine phantasm: that of a
world without uterus"].[41]

The simultaneous containedness and capaciousness of the novel are emphasized by Jean Larnac, who (in 1923) defines it as "un moule élastique où l'on jette
tout ce que l'imagination, si dévergondée qu'elle soit, peut suggérer. Sans doute
[c'est] pourquoi il convient si bien aux femmes, ennemies de toute contrainte"
["an elastic mold in which one casts whatever the imagination, however shameless
it is, can suggest. Doubtless this is why it is so well suited to women, who are ene-
mies of all constraint"].[42] Larnac's remark about the novel strangely echoes Dr.
Charles Lasègue's mid-nineteenth-century definition of hysteria as the "corbeille
à papier de la médecine" ["wastepaper basket of medicine"].[43] These two intersecting comments suggest that the novel and hysteria are readily available containers,
receptacles for creative expansion.

It should be clear from the preceding quotations that there is a slippage, in conceptions of both female space and reading space, between representations of this
domain as physical or concrete, on the one hand, and abstract or metaphysical, on
the other. Monique Schneider's work on phantasms of femininity helps to explain
this shifting by discovering concrete woman's space as the fantasized locus of the
imagination. Schneider shows that witches, possessed women, and hysterics were
all seen as habitations or receptacles that could house any being, presence, or
force. Woman's inner space, by rights the child's abode, could as easily lodge spirits, demons, or the imagination:

> La dimension imaginaire . . . se trouve précisément localisée, assignée à
> résidence à l'intérieur de la matrice féminine: là est le foyer de tous les

---

[40] Serge Tisseron cited by Odile Cuaz, "La Lectrice et le cow-boy," *Le Monde*, 22 November 1991, 30.
[41] Catherine Muller cited by Cuaz, "La Lectrice."
[42] May, *Dilemme du roman*, 223.
[43] Quoted by Henri Cesbron in *Histoire critique de l'hystérie* (Paris: Asselin & Houzeau, 1909), 198.
See Chapter 2 for more on hysteria as a catchall diagnosis.

rêves et de toutes les divagations délirantes; le règne onirique est regardé
tout entier comme la concrétion de ces noires vapeurs exhalées par la
matrice.[44]

*The imaginary dimension . . . is precisely localized, made to reside inside the
female womb: that is the home of dreams and of all delirious wanderings; the onei-
ric realm is looked upon as the concretion of these dark vapors exhaled by the womb.*

Christopher Bollas, using terms perhaps not coincidentally reminiscent of
Schneider's thematics of possession, describes aesthetic experience as "a spell"
during which "time crystallizes into space." He goes on to derive the space of aesthetic experience ("the uncanny pleasure of being held" by a text, painting, so-
nata, etc.) from the infant's experience of maternal handling. This "first human
aesthetic," like all that will follow, is transformational, offering a form through
which the unintegrated self finds integration.[45]

In a conceptually related account of her own struggle with the creative process,
On Not Being Able to Paint, Joanna Field [Marion Milner] describes the psychic
barriers that render difficult adult reentry into that early "half-way house"[46] that
shelters childhood creativity: "a fear of losing all sense of separating boundaries;
particularly the boundaries between the tangible realities of the external world and
the imaginative realities of the inner world of feeling and idea; in fact a fear of
being mad."[47]

Both Bollas and Field are building upon D. W. Winnicott's work on transitional
space, the intermediate psychic area in which inner and outer reality can freely
merge for the infant originally fused with its mother—and later on for the artist,
aesthete, or religious believer. This transitional area molded by the mother provides the infant with a sheltered or safe zone that fosters a state of floundering and
unintegration—a state that facilitates a child's imagination sparked, an artist's inspiration, a reader's flash of insight.[48]

In their study of feminine identity in relation to constructs of pregnancy as
fusion and separation, saturation and emptiness, Fausta Ferraro and Adele

[44] Monique Schneider, *De l'exorcisme à la psychanalyse: Le féminin expurgé* (Paris: Retz, 1979), 125.
[45] Christopher Bollas, "The Aesthetic Moment and the Search for Transformation," *The Annual of
Psychoanalysis* 6 (1978): 385–86.
[46] Joanna Field [Marion Milner], *On Not Being Able to Paint,* foreword by Anna Freud (Los Angeles:
Jeremy P. Tarcher, 1957), 139.
[47] Ibid., 17.
[48] See D. W. Winnicott, "The Capacity to Be Alone," in *The Maturational Processes and the Facilitating Environment* (New York: International Universities Press, 1965), and "Transitional Objects," in
Playing and Reality (New York: Basic Books, 1971).

Nunziante-Cesaro suggest that woman's anatomically hollow space, insofar as it is space potentially open to creation, is metaphorically apt to evoke "la créativité psychique en termes génériques" ["psychic creativity in gendered terms"].[49] Jessica Benjamin articulates woman's inner space with intersubjective space, an avatar of transitional space, proposing a continuum "that includes the space between the I and the you, as well as the space within me." Through this articulation Benjamin points toward a de-essentialization of inner space while demonstrating its present cultural construction as female.[50] Feminists and other contemporary theorists thus reinhabit and revalorize a female-configured representation of aesthetic-creative space that was well rehearsed by nineteenth-century representations of hysteria.

In all such theorizings of aesthetic space, we find a recurrent network of themes: merging, loss of boundaries, disorientation, chaos, madness, creativity, and maternity. From here to hysteria is but a stumble, if we recall Diderot's oft-quoted words that, prey to hysterical delirium, "[la femme] revient sur le passé, qu'elle s'élance dans l'avenir, que tous les temps lui sont présents" ["{woman} relives the past, leaps into the future, and all time is present to her"], and the derivative nineteenth-century associations of hysterical delirium with "des exaltations singulières, bizarres, éloquentes, et même poétiques de l'imagination" ["singular, bizarre, eloquent, and even poetic exaltations of the imagination"].[51]

This shifting ground between aesthetic and hysterical space opens the way to some concluding speculations. Specifically, I want to suggest that hysteria as constructed by the nineteenth-century patriarchy is an ambivalent reconstruction of a lost nurturing space associated first with intrauterine fusion and later with a mother-child continuity that fosters creative play. I am not pleading a case for womb envy. Rather, I am arguing that this site of childhood merging, once repudiated, no longer seems quite safe. Regretted but rejected, familiar yet foreign, it is

[49] Fausta Ferraro and Adele Nunziante-Cesaro, *L'Espace creux et le corps saturé: La grossesse comme agir entre fusion et séparation*, trans. Simone Matarasso-Gervais (Paris: des femmes, 1990), 10. This is not a facile ode to maternal space. On the contrary, Ferraro and Nunziante-Cesaro signal the risk to women of corporeally retrieving originary (if phantasmatic) plenitude, for an anatomical filling of the inner hollow might exclude other creative modes of integration (such as knowledge, artistic creation, etc.) (96–97).

[50] See Jessica Benjamin, "A Desire of One's Own: Psychoanalytic Feminism and Intersubjective Space," in *Feminist Studies/Critical Studies*, ed. Teresa de Lauretis (Bloomington: Indiana University Press, 1986), 95. See, too, Benjamin's *The Bonds of Love: Psychoanalysis, Feminism, and the Problem of Domination* (New York: Pantheon, 1988), where she further explains the "inside" as the internal version of safe transitional space (128), and elaborates on the little boy's loss of that in-between space (due to repudiation of the mother) as cutting him off from the space within (163). Although Benjamin discusses inner space with a focus on proposing an alternative model for desire, her work is by implication helpful to thinking about aesthetics, creativity, and inner space.

[51] Denis Diderot, "Sur les femmes," in *Oeuvres complètes de Diderot*, ed. J. Assézat (Paris: Garnier Frères, 1875), 2:255. Brachet, *Traité de l'hystérie*, 285–86.

variously refashioned as female malady, devouring mother, muse. The altering is the token of repression.

The "desire of all reading women" with which I introduced these pages—that is, the yearning to be both poet and poem, author and novel, and to join with the aesthetic object—should then be understood as a desire whose gender specificity is constructed rather than essential, women's desire marking also the place of its repression by men. "Reading women" are placeholders, bookmarks, as it were, in the text of hysteria, bracketing a space that the medical men can no longer clearly read but do not quite dare erase.

PART TWO
EPISTOLARY NARRATIVES

Prologue

In the summer of 1846 Louise Colet and Gustave Flaubert met in the studio of the sculptor James Pradier, became lovers, and began a correspondence that treated of literary and other passions. At the time she was a prize-winning poet, novelist, and playwright eleven years his senior, a mother, and unhappily married; he was twenty-five and unknown. Their correspondence and very occasional trysts continued for roughly a year and a half; in March 1848 Flaubert, distressed by his lover's requests to meet, sent her a letter of rupture. The correspondence and liaison began again in July of 1851 when she sought him out upon his return from the Orient, and ended finally in the spring of 1854.

During the second phase of their correspondence and liaison Flaubert was writing *Madame Bovary* (which he began two months after their *retrouvailles*), and Louise Colet wrote (among other works) her verse narrative, *La Servante* (1853–54), one unit of a narrative poem cycle whose overarching title was *Poème de la femme*. (Seven narratives were originally planned, but only *La Paysanne* [1853], *La Servante*, and *La Religieuse* [1856] were executed.) *Madame Bovary* and *La Servante* are congruent texts not only by virtue of the overlapping chronology of their composition, but because each is about a woman who reads novels, reaches for the forbidden horizons they hold out, and falls into illness.

Of the almost daily exchange of letters during the almost five cumulative years of their two liaisons, five letters from Louise Colet are extant. The fate of the vanished letters is unknown. *

* Over the years, scholars have speculated on the disappearance of Colet's letters to Flaubert, some suggesting that they were destroyed—either by Colet's daughter, Henriette Bissieu, or by Flaubert's niece, Caroline Franklin-Grout. But in her forthcoming biography *Rage and Fire: A Life of Louise Colet, Pioneer Feminist, Literary Star, Flaubert's Muse* (New York: Simon and Schuster, 1994), Francine du Plessix Gray compellingly argues that Flaubert himself burned Colet's letters. Her evidence comes from an eyewitness account of an auto-da-fé by Guy de Maupassant, published in 1891 and reprinted in Georges-Emile Bertrand, *Les Jours de Flaubert* (Paris: Editions du Myrte, 1947), 198–200, and from Hermia Oliver's retelling of Maupassant's report in her book *Flaubert and an English Governess* (Oxford: Clarendon Press, 1980), 141–44. Maupassant tells of having been summoned to Croisset by Flaubert, in the year before his death, and of Flaubert's request for his company during a night of letter-burning. Toward morning, Maupassant observes, amid the letters perused and then tossed into the flames, a ribbon-wrapped packet containing a silk slipper, a lace handkerchief, and a faded rose. Flaubert speaks often and lovingly of such "relics," as he calls them—mementos given to him by Louise Colet—in his early letters to her.

4 THE PHYSIOLOGY OF STYLE

Sex, Text, and the Gender of Writing
Flaubert's Letters to Louise Colet

*Ils pouvaient peut-être connaître l'anatomie
d'une phrase, mais certes ils n'entendaient
goutte à la physiologie du style.*
GUSTAVE FLAUBERT TO LOUISE COLET,
30 SEPTEMBER 1853

● What reader of Flaubert's flood of letters to his new lover would not be tempted to name passion as their source? If, however, one at first approaches these epistles to Louise Colet as *love letters*, it soon becomes evident that the sense, balance, and even syntax of the compound term begins to shift as the pages turn. Are these letters written out of love, or are they meditations about a love of letters? Is the accent to be placed on love (desire, erotic passion, male and female sexual response) or on letters (epistles but also more generally belles lettres: writing, reading)?

Although the overt context of Flaubert's correspondence with Colet suggests that love is the message and letters the medium, the thematic and rhetorical thrust of his prose increasingly upsets the stability of such a formulation. As the correspondence progresses, even in its early period, but especially when it is renewed in 1851, after the first rupture, Flaubert's missives come to be dominated by matters literary: the writer's struggle with his own literary efforts, his corrections of Colet's manuscripts, his reactions to the book he is currently reading, his musings on language, style, and the tyranny of the blank page.

•   The ascendancy of letters does not, however, dictate the eclipse of love and sex. On the contrary, a discourse of sexual anatomy and physiology becomes the principal conduit through which Flaubert expounds on literary theory and practice. This discourse, whose control of clinical detail is in itself impressive, is further refined by its precise reproduction of conventions of sexual differentiation, which facilitate Flaubert's effort to chart a course toward literary perfection through the potential abysses of style. His reconstruction of a familiar dualistic code of sexual difference allows him to construct a similarly binary stylistic model. Good style, valorized as male, is described as hard, hairy, and muscular; it is alternately likened to testicles, bodily hair, and athletes' biceps. So we learn that "la vérité demande des mâles plus velus que M. de Lamartine" ["truth demands hairier males than Monsieur de Lamartine"], and that it is best to avoid "cette espèce d'échauffement, qu'on appelle l'inspiration, et où il entre souvent plus d'émotion nerveuse que de force musculaire" ["the heat of excitement called inspiration, often due more to nervous emotion than muscular force"], while the language of Montesquieu—which is not without merit, for Flaubert—contains "par-ci par-là des phrases qui sont tendues comme des biceps d'athlète" ["here and there sentences that are as taut as athletes' biceps"].[1] Poor style, on the other hand, is denigrated as female; it is soft and fatty. Whence this counsel to Louise Colet: "Tu as un côté de l'esprit . . . passionné et débordant quelquefois, auquel il faut mettre un corset et qu'il faut *durcir du dedans*" (2:79, 24 April 1852) ["There is a part of your mind . . . that is sometimes passionate and overflowing, which should be put in a corset and *hardened from within*"]. Bad style is overwhelmingly glandular; it often is breastlike. Unlike good style, which, like iron, is pumped through its master's corpus, it seeps through writing uncontrolled, like mother's milk or vaginal discharges: "Dans G[eorge] Sand, on sent les fleurs blanches; cela suinte, et l'idée coule entre les mots, comme entre des cuisses sans muscles" (2:177, 16 November 1852) ["G{eorge} Sand's writing reeks of vaginal discharges; it oozes and the idea drips between words, as if between thighs without muscles"]. But there is a remedy: "Il nous faut à tous *prendre du fer*" (2:509, 15 January 1854) ["We all need to *take iron*"]. Whereas bad style speaks shrilly and mimics other voices, good style is imperious and commands an audience, for it roars: "Je sens pourtant que je ne dois pas mourir sans avoir fait rugir quelque part un style comme je l'entends dans ma tête et qui pourra bien dominer la voix des perroquets et des cigales" (2:110, 19 June 1852) ["Yet I feel that I must not die without having forced style to roar as it does in my head, with enough strength to dominate the voices of parrots and cicadas"].

---

[1] These examples, as well as those that follow, are indicative of the pattern of the whole. Gustave Flaubert, *Correspondance*, ed. Jean Bruneau (Paris: Gallimard, 1973–91), 2:77, 24 April 1852; 2:252, 27 February 1853; 2:350, 6 June 1853. Unless otherwise noted, all references to Flaubert's *Correspondance* will be to this edition and will be provided in the text.

Pursuing the patterns apparent in this preliminary sketch, I read Flaubert's letters to Colet as a manual of style whose emblems are the clashing voices of the lion, the parrot, and the cicada, and whose rhetoric is modeled upon the course of his relationship with her and the conventions of sex, gender, and pathology prevalent in his era. To read style in terms of lived love and discursive convention admittedly implies a schematic separation of three elements that are in fact inextricably enmeshed; however, to embark on such a reading is to follow Flaubert's lead, and so provides my departure point.

As both writer and lover, Louise Colet is cast in the correspondence in the role of scapegoat for Flaubert, embodiment of a literary and an amorous style he disowns and which he expresses through myths of gender current in his milieu. This initial perspective yields, on the one hand, a miming of the tired script of woman's physiology inscribed as her social destiny and femininity pathologized as hysteria. On the other hand, it begins to reveal how Flaubert, in the very process of affirming the cultural text, unsettles its axioms by crossing back and forth over the very lines of sex, gender, and pathology that he reinscribes. This dislocation of cultural commonplaces relating to writing and the body will be my second concern; it will lead finally to a discussion of hysteria in Flaubert as that turning point at which the dichotomous constructions constitutive of the diagnosis, in the mid-nineteenth century (female/male, body/mind, fragmentation/cohesion) can no longer hold. Hysteria, erstwhile sexual marker, point of gender demarcation, becomes in these letters a point of indistinction, the place where gender (and other) distinctions fade into each other.

Although I attribute to Flaubert's literary intuition sporadic insights that transcend the ideological frame of his society, I do not want to claim that he was a lesser misogynist than his contemporaries, or that he had any semblance of a protofeminist consciousness. The following discussion will make clear that despite Flaubert's willed alienation from his society and his imaginative flights beyond it, he was a creature and a captive of the cultural unconscious of his time.

LES FLEURS BLANCHES DE L'ESPRIT

In the course of the self-lacerating stylistic pilgrimage that the writing of *Madame Bovary* constitutes for Flaubert, and which his letters record, he evolves a bipolar conceptual system that roughly corresponds to the stylistic methods and effects since canonized as realist and romantic. The positive axis of this Manichean model is defined by observation, mimesis, discipline, containment, and impersonality; the other is negatively defined by sentiment, lyricism, self-indulgence, effusion, and self-reference. The two paradigms of his analogical model are further identified as masculine and feminine. "Ce qui fait la force d'une oeuvre," explains Flaubert, "c'est la *vesée* [la virilité], comme on dit vulgairement, c'est à dire une longue énergie qui court d'un bout à l'autre et ne faiblit pas" (2:303, 13 April 1853)[2] ["What gives a work its force is virility; that is, a long-lasting energy that runs throughout and doesn't weaken"]. But the interests of the true and the mimetic are often foiled by the likes of Lamartine, Flaubert's stylistic nemesis and the quintessential model, in his correspondence, of an effeminate romanticism. In language that is always clinically graphic, but graphically inconsistent, Flaubert rejects Alphonse de Lamartine and his aesthetic followers as inadequate males or as castrati: "C'est un esprit eunuque, la couille lui manque, il n'a jamais pissé que de l'eau claire" (2:299, 6 April 1853) ["He is a spiritual eunuch, he has no balls, he never pissed anything but clear water"]; alternatively, he damns them as female, comparing their stylistic affectation to "des fleurs blanches de l'esprit" (2:310, 20 April 1853) ["vaginal discharges of the mind"].

Though this system of images is manifestly in place without the referential support of actual women and men (Lamartine functions as a sufficient but by no means necessary trigger), the images intensify in charge and in frequency when Flaubert taps Louise Colet's ink flow and body fluids as negative source for his system. When this happens, a logic that might be named *ad feminam* as well as *ad hominem* takes over his imagery: Flaubert, proponent of the "ligne droite géométrique" (2:40, 31 January 1852) ["straight geometric line"], plays straight man to Louise Colet's womanly meanders, striving repeatedly to contain lyricism's universal streaming by correcting Colet's bodily text and rewriting her verses. As poor style comes increasingly to be embodied, for Flaubert, by Louise Colet's femaleness, and pure style potentially by his own manhood, the literary quest becomes a more intimate kind of operation.

Flaubert, spiritual heir to the legendary Dutch boy, tries singlehandedly to stop the overflow of Colet's feminine literary sensibilities by recommending alterations of her female physiology. He finds her talent diluted by what he terms "le vague, la tendro-manie féminine" ["vagueness, woman's maniacal tenderness"], and advises accordingly: "Il ne faut pas, quand on est arrivé à ton degré, que le linge sente le lait. . . . Rentre, resserre, comprime les seins de ton coeur, qu'on y voie des muscles et non une glande" (2:304, 13 April 1853) ["Someone who has risen to your level must not allow her underwear to smell of milk. . . . Pull in, tighten, compress your heart's breasts, so that we see muscles there and not a gland"]. The extraordinary metaphoric violence of this request calls for comments I will temporarily defer. For the moment I want to follow Flaubert's more general metaphoric drift to point out that the milk metaphor quite ordinarily expresses woman's writing (and writing like a woman) in the *Correspondance*, and that milk in turn is easily and frequently replaced there by any one of a number of other body fluids that are usually

---

[2] As Jean Bruneau notes in his edition of Flaubert's *Correspondance*, *vesée* is a Norman term for *virilité* (2:1157).

but not necessarily endemic to women.[3] So at another point Flaubert counsels Colet: "Tu arriveras à la plénitude de ton talent en dépouillant ton sexe" (2:177, 16 November 1852) ["You will fulfill your talent by shedding your sex"]. But it is when Flaubert reads *La Servante*, Colet's verse narrative about a young peasant woman who (like Colet) loves books, loves a writer who abuses her, nourishes a secret desire to write (and, unlike Colet, fails), that the current of invectives reaches flood level. It spills out in a letter written to justify forty pages of criticism of *La Servante*: "Ne sens-tu pas que tout se dissout, maintenant, par le *relâchement*, par l'élément humide, par les larmes, par le bavardage, par le laitage. La littérature contemporaine est noyée dans les règles de femme" (2:508, 15 January 1854) ["Aren't you aware of how everything is being dissolved now, by *letting go*, by all that is damp, by tears, by chattering, by milk. Contemporary literature is drowning in menstrual flow"]. The declaration of literature's feminization rhetorically enacts its hystericization as well, according to nineteenth-century tenets. Through a kind of metonymic collapse of writer and text, woman and writing, the writing itself becomes that ill-wrought urn, that leaking vessel to which women, particularly hysterics, are more ordinarily compared. Woman's writing (and by extension, womanlike writing), by implication the hysteric's text, becomes the hysterical text. It is worth noting that Flaubert's construction of this overflowing body epitomized by the mortal threat of menstrual blood foreshadows a certain body of our contemporary theory relating feminine writing to surging body fluids. To recognize Flaubert as a precursory theoretician of *écriture féminine*, and the loved and loathed body of his Colet as one of its fearsome sources, is potentially to displace and revalorize the text of *écriture féminine*.[4] Correlatively, it is to unsettle all certainty about his own textual orientation.

[3] See, for instance, this commentary about *La Servante*: "Tu as fait de l'art un déversoir à passions, une espèce de pot de chambre où le trop-plein de je ne sais quoi a coulé. — Cela ne sent pas bon" (2:502, 9–10 January 1852) ["You made of art an outlet for the passions, a sort of chamber pot where the overflow of who knows what has dripped. It does not smell good"]. Flaubert follows his era's belief that *all* of woman's secretions, not only those obviously based in sexuality, are more considerable than those of their male counterparts. As Dr. Brachet put it:

> Tout le monde sait avec quelle facilité les larmes coulent chez la femme, combien la transpiration et la perspiration cutanée sont faciles et abondantes, combien la digestion est rapide, à cause de la formation plus prompte du suc gastrique et de la sécrétion plus prompte aussi de la bile; combien enfin les urines sécrétées semblent se presser de s'amasser dans la vessie pour être plus tôt évacuées.

> *Everyone knows how easily woman's tears flow, how ready and abundant are woman's transpiration and perspiration, how quick is her digestion because of her more rapid formation of gastric juice and her more rapid secretion of bile; finally, how urine, once secreted, seems in a hurry to collect in the bladder in order to be more quickly eliminated.*

J. L. Brachet, *Traité de l'hystérie* (Paris: Baillière, 1847), 67.

[4] My implication that *écriture féminine* is born of a male perspective on women's writing and women's bodies is deliberate and, though outside the purview of this discussion, merits further examination. As

For in passing one must recognize in the form of Flaubert's critique his own *re-lâchement*, his stream of reproach that knows no bounds. We might ask why *La Servante* among all of Louise Colet's works most powerfully unchannels Flaubert's ire. This text is arguably no more worthy of stylistic reproach than others of hers that he praises.[5] His stylistic censure is activated by other irritations, foremost among which is Colet's intimate relationship to her subject—a woman's aspirations, a woman's writing—a subject and a relationship that cannot be indifferent to him as he is writing his remarkably parallel *Madame Bovary*.

One might argue that Mariette of *La Servante* is an Emma Bovary better loved or at least more openly embraced by her creator. In fact Flaubert vehemently condemns Colet's lack of distance from her subject: "Tu as écrit tout cela avec une passion *personnelle* qui t'a troublé la vue" (2:502, 9–10 January 1854) ["You wrote all that with a *personal* passion that clouded your vision"]; he disapproves as well of her elevation of Mariette, who is for Flaubert "une femme supérieure" (2:482, 18 December 1853) ["a superior woman"]—which is to say, unlike Emma Bovary as Flaubert would have it most of the time, but very much like Louise Colet.[6] Is not then his reproach of Colet's insufficient distinction from her character a cover for the *doubling* of another difference: the double image of alterity that she and Ma-

---

for the menstrual metaphor, it should also perhaps be considered from a more literal standpoint. Flaubert's obsession with Louise Colet's menstrual periods is apparent from a reading of his letters, in which he refers to them by the code term "les Anglais." The obsession, explicitly related to his dread of paternity, is arguably not entirely absorbed, so to speak, by this fear. Consider, for example, his references to keeping as a "relic" a handkerchief soaked in Louise Colet's blood (1:273, 4–5 August 1846; 1:308, 23 August 1846). Whatever the explanation, the letters suggest that his rhythm of writing was interrupted or reinforced by the delays and arrivals of his lover's periods, hence the double reading of his statement that "la littérature contemporaine se noye dans les règles de femme" ["contemporary literature is drowning in menstrual flow"].

[5] Most noteworthy perhaps are some lines Colet wrote in commemoration of an early tryst in Mantes—lines Flaubert praised for containing "de vraies belles choses" ["some really fine things"]—although he protested that her description of him was too flattering (1:370–71, 30 September 1846):

> Comme un buffle indompté des déserts d'Amérique,
> Vigoureux et superbe en ta force athlétique,
> Bondissant sur mon sein tes noirs cheveux épars
> Sans jamais t'épuiser tu m'infusais la vie.   (1:370, n. 3)

> *Like an untamed buffalo from the American deserts,*
> *With the superb strength of your athletic prowess,*
> *Panting on my breast, and with your black hair flying*
> *Without ever tiring you filled me with life.*

[6] In fact Flaubert often writes to Colet to the effect that she is a superior woman, a woman better than the others, a woman like a man. On Flaubert's alternate embracing and repudiating of Emma, see Victor Brombert's classic but still timely commentary in *The Novels of Flaubert* (Princeton: Princeton University Press, 1966). For a view of Emma Bovary as a superior woman, see Mario Vargas Llosa's *The Perpetual Orgy: Flaubert and "Madame Bovary,"* trans. Helen Lane (New York: Farrar, Straus & Giroux, 1986).

riette jointly represent for him, which in turn reflects, in duplicate, his own difference from himself? For all the time Flaubert is marking off and distancing a certain writing style and a certain sensibility as distinctly feminine, even as he is determinedly grounding this gender-specific aesthetic sensibility in sexual difference, he is undermining the gender-sex connection by his own (intermittent) identification with a "feminine" style and sensibility.

DIKES, DAMS, AND AQUEDUCTS

Early in his correspondence with Louise Colet, Flaubert writes to her that when he is in love, this sentiment becomes for him "une inondation qui s'épanche tout à l'entour" (1:297, 12 August 1846) ["a flood that spreads everywhere around"]. In the same letter, the sentimental deluge spills over into aesthetics; Flaubert, reminiscing about his past, announces a writing project: "A quelque jour j'écrirai tout cela . . . cette poésie ruisselante et triste du coeur de l'adolescent, voilà une corde neuve que personne n'a touchée" (1:295–96, 12 August 1846) ["Some day I will write all that . . . the sad poetry streaming from an adolescent heart; there is a new and untouched subject"]. Although one might well argue that Flaubert had already poured forth torrents of such poetry in the juvenilia, he was to "write all that" again, now channeled—personified and transsexualized—in the daydreams and fantasies of the adolescent Emma.

In the interim decade Flaubert would, if nothing else, learn displacement and projection; he slowly became a veritable engineer of the psychic fluids, but ironically a victim as well of his own hydraulic construction. While working on *Madame Bovary*, he describes his creative self (in apparent negative contrast to Colet's verbal facility) as a clogged aqueduct: "Moi, je suis comme les vieux aqueducs. Il y a tant de détritus aux bords de ma pensée qu'elle circule lentement, et ne tombe que goutte à goutte du bout de ma plume" (2:469, 29 November 1853) ["I am like old aqueducts. There is so much debris on the edges of my thought that it circulates slowly, and can only fall by droplets from the tip of my pen"]. The work of channeling, plugging, damming, and diking that he brutally and unambivalently imposes upon Colet's brimming style is a more equivocal process where his own sensibilities are concerned: "Il est étrange," he remarks to Colet, "combien toutes mes rigoles se bouchent, comme toutes mes plaies se ferment et font digue vis-à-vis les flots intérieurs. Le pus retombe en dedans. Que personne n'en sente l'odeur, c'est tout ce que je demande" (1:437, early February 1847) ["It is strange how all my channels are becoming clogged, how all my wounds are closing and act as dikes for the inner floods. The pus flows back in. All I ask is that no one smell the odor"]. Flaubert's closing wish that no one smell the pus surely implies volition, even perhaps retention, yet the initial bewilderment before his own emotional damming suggests that this is an unwilled, externally imposed constraint. His ambivalence speaks in similar figures when he says of his heart "il a l'embouchure étroite et embarrassée, le liquide n'en sort pas aisément, il remonte le courant et tourbillonne" (1:421, 20 December 1846) ["its mouth is narrow and obstructed; the fluid cannot easily get out; it fights the current and whirls around"]. The heart blood's eddying resistance to containment—a resistance that Freud would later theorize as the "return of the repressed"—invites a reconsideration of any declared condemnation of overflowing sentiment.

Ink is the ideal cipher for an equivocation whose pairings of horror and desire, fear and pleasure are in other contexts only implied: its material foreignness to the body simultaneously displaces and permits symbolic continuity with the body fluids. Given Flaubert's image of his thought as a fluid that drips from his pen, we hardly need wait for the dying Emma Bovary to suffer from the bitter taste of ink or for a black liquid to stream from her corpse's mouth in order to understand ink as yet another figure in the very fluid symbolic economy of the body. Nowhere in fact is Flaubert's general ambivalence about flowing substances so explicitly articulated as in his mixed ode to the transubstantiated body fluid that ink represents for him: "L'encre est mon élément naturel. Beau liquide, du reste, que ce liquide sombre! et dangereux! Comme on s'y noie! comme il attire!" (2:395, 14 August 1853) ["Ink is my native element. It is a beautiful liquid besides, this dark—and dangerous— liquid! How one drowns in it! How it entices!"].

Flaubert's censured flow of Colet's womanly verse, but also the dammed-up streams of his own lyric youth, should then be carefully filtered for traces of the fatal attraction he much more freely attributes to ink. Flaubert's letters reinforce Peter Stallybrass and Allon White's belief that "disgust always bears the imprint of desire,"[7] but his expressed repugnance usually washes over desire's inscription. It is then helpful to find, as we plumb the torrents of disgust, occasional expressions of desire. They often cluster around her tears, which plague and fascinate and attract him: "Oh, si j'étais si sensuel que tu le crois, comme je les aimerais tes pleurs! Elles te rendent si belle quand elles coulent le long de tes joues pâles et vont mourir sur ta gorge chaude et blanche!" (1:331, 6 September 1846) ["Oh, if I were as sensual as you think me, how I would love your tears! They make you look so beautiful when they flow down your pale cheeks and go on to die on your warm white breast!"]. We can understand weeping as a sort of transitional fluidity, midway between the physiological and the moral: a nobler leaking, as it were, an incontinence of the soul. But Flaubert also voices to Louise Colet a vigorous nostalgia for what we might call his own contained "poetic phlegm":

[7] Peter Stallybrass and Allon White, *The Politics and Poetics of Transgression* (Ithaca: Cornell University Press, 1986), 191.

Vous êtes heureux, vous autres, les poètes, vous avez un déversoir dans
vos vers. Quand quelquechose vous gêne, vous crachez un sonnet et cela
soulage le coeur. Mais nous autres, pauvres diables de prosateurs, à qui
toute personnalité est interdite (et à moi surtout), songe donc à toutes les
amertumes qui nous retombent sur l'âme, à toutes les *glaires* morales qui
nous prennent à la gorge!

Il y a quelque chose de faux dans ma personne et dans ma vocation. Je
suis né lyrique, et je n'écris pas de vers.   (2:457, 25 October 1853)

*You are fortunate, you poets, you have an outlet in your verses. When something
troubles you, you spit out a sonnet and that eases the heart. But we poor devils who
write prose, to whom any personality is forbidden (especially to me), think of all the
bitterness that falls on our soul, of all the moral* phlegm *that catches in our throat!*

*There is something false in my person and in my vocation. I was born lyrical,
and I do not write verse.*

Flaubert's poets and prose writers, respectively spitters and swallowers of emotion, alternative versions of leaking women and dike-building men, are avatars of
his more celebrated pair of *bonshommes*: "Il y a en moi, littérairement parlant,
deux bonshommes distincts: un qui est épris de *gueulades*, de lyrisme, de grands
vols d'aigle, de toutes les sonorités de la phrase et des sommets de l'idée; un autre
qui fouille et creuse le vrai tant qu'il peut" (2:30, 16 January 1852) ["There are in
me, literarily speaking, two distinct fellows: one taken with hearing his own voice,
with lyricism, with great eagle flights, with sonorities of language and exalted
ideas; another who burrows into and digs up truth as much as he can"]. As the two
bonshommes, conceived as gender neutral, evolve, they undergo sexual differentiation. The lyrical *bonhomme*, repudiated, becomes a *bonne femme*, Flaubert's
repressed Other, and is externalized as the female principle, the eternal feminine:
the life flow he infuses into his creature Emma Bovary, whose rough draft is Louise
Colet.

Consider the metamorphoses of milk as representative of Flaubert's fluid creativity. Here first is what he writes to Louise Colet in his own name about their recent tryst: "J'avais dans l'âme des océans de crème" (2:102, 9 June 1852) ["I had
oceans of cream in my soul"]. Here now are his admonitions to Colet about her
style: "Il ne faut pas, quand on est arrivé à ton degré, que le linge sente le lait"
(2:304, 13 April 1853) ["Someone who has risen to your level must not allow her
underwear to smell of milk"] and "Ne sens-tu pas que tout se dissout, maintenant,
par . . . le laitage" (2:508, 15 January 1854) ["Aren't you aware of how everything
is being dissolved now by . . . milk"]. And here finally, this report of what Emma

86

•

Bovary feels after making love with Rodolphe for the first time: "Elle sentait son coeur, dont les battements recommençaient, et le sang circuler dans sa chair comme un fleuve de lait" ["She felt her heartbeat return, and the blood coursing through her flesh like a river of milk"].[8]

The inner oceans of cream are not only externalized and projected, in the course of their transformation into Emma's rivers of milk, but constricted and diluted. The pleasures of suffusion and fusion apparent in the initial lyric phrasing are doubled by a terror of drowning and dissolution often expressed elsewhere, in the letters to Colet, in terms of an ominous and irresistible drowning. He writes of style: "Je retrouvais toujours chez toi je ne sais quel ton noyé de sentiment qui atténuait tout, et altérait jusqu'à ton esprit" (1:446, 7 March 1847) ["I always found in you a certain tone drowned in sentiment that dimmed all the rest, and affected even your mind"]. He writes of love: "Ton coeur est une source intarissable, tu m'y fais boire à flots. Il m'inonde. Il me pénètre. Je m'y noie" (1:284, 8–9 August 1846) ["Your heart is an irrepressible source, you make me drink of it in torrents. It floods me. It penetrates me. I drown in it"].

Writing the crest of his ambivalent passion for Louise Colet, he is carried back to the ink-dark surge of the tides within. Flaubert transcribes the terrible lure of the siren's song from the echoing rush of his own inner seas.

FROM DISSOLUTION TO FRAGMENTATION: UNE ARABESQUE EN MARQUETERIE

Inundation is the most frequent but by no means sole phantasm of annihilation that haunts Flaubert's letters to Colet. Dissolution is closely related to fragmentation and disintegration, whose effects on the physical body and the writing corpus are registered with great regularity by Flaubert's devastated cries. At thirty-two, he laments: "Je vieillis, voilà les dents qui s'en vont, et les cheveux qui bientôt seront en allés. . . . Comme le néant nous envahit! A peine nés, la pourriture commence" (2:289, 31 March 1853) ["I am growing old, my teeth are going, and my hair will soon be gone. . . . How nothingness invades us! We are barely born when we begin to rot"]. "Comme mes cheveux tombent!" (2:448, 7 October 1853) ["How my hair is falling out!"] rages Flaubert later that year. His balding pate and rotting teeth—an ensemble he refers to as "ces décadences physiques" (2:426, 7

---

[8] Gustave Flaubert, *Madame Bovary*, ed. Jacques Suffel (Paris: Garnier Flammarion, 1979), 190; trans. Paul de Man (New York: Norton, 1965), 116. Note, too, an appearance of the same image used mockingly to describe his preparatory reading for the novel: "Voilà deux jours que je tâche d'entrer dans des *rêves de jeunes filles* et que je navigue pour cela dans les océans laiteux de la littérature à castels, troubadours à toques de velours à plumes blanches" (2:56, 3 March 1852) ["For two days I have been trying to enter the *dreams of young girls* and for that reason I have been sailing on the milky oceans of the literature of manor houses, and of troubadours wearing velvet caps with white plumes"].

September 1853) ["this physical decaying"]—punctuate his correspondence. Stylistic fragmentation, the literary analogue of anatomical decomposition, becomes an obsessive motif. Of his work on *Madame Bovary* he writes: "C'est une série de paragraphes tournés, arrêtés, et qui ne dévalent pas les uns sur les autres. Il va falloir les dévisser, lâcher les joints" (2:243, 29 January 1853) ["It is a series of set, crafted paragraphs that do not flow into each other. I will have to unscrew them, loosen the joints"]. He counsels Colet about her writing in similar terms: "Tu sais que les beaux fragments ne font rien. L'unité, l'unité, tout est là. L'ensemble, voilà ce qui manque à tous ceux d'aujourd'hui. . . . Mille beaux endroits, pas une oeuvre" (1:389, 14 October 1846)[9] ["You know that fine fragments are worth nothing. Unity, unity is all. The whole—that is what is missing in everyone's work today. . . . A thousand fine points, but not a work of art"].

It is important to establish that Flaubert's horror of decomposition is a steady background refrain in his letters; when he then accuses love in the name of Louise Colet of shattering his syntax, tearing his body and soul, we are hearing just one of many variations on a recurrent theme.[10] "C'est une chose étrange avec toi combien j'écris mal, je n'y mets pas de vanité littéraire" ["It is a curious thing that I write so badly to you; I don't bother with literary vanity"], he tells her in an unusual testimonial to love, continuing: "Mais c'est ainsi, tout se heurte dans mes lettres. C'est comme si je voulais dire trois mots à la fois" (1:367, 28 September 1846) ["But that is how it is; everything collides in my letters. It is as if I tried to say three words at once"]. He offers the following in analogous tribute to love's explosive power: "On ne se rencontre qu'en se heurtant et chacun, portant dans ses mains ses entrailles déchirées, accuse l'autre qui ramasse les siennes" (2:13, 23 October 1851) ["We only meet by colliding, and each one of us, carrying in his hands his torn guts, accuses the other who is picking up her own"]. In this world of dueling words and lovers, union brings disjunction, and life is a collision course with death. And as Emma Bovary was to find after the ball was over, wholes leave holes in their wake. "Son voyage à la Vaubyessard avait fait un trou dans sa vie" ["Her journey to Vaubyessard had made a gap in her life"], says the narrator of *Madame Bovary*,[11] echoing Flaubert, who in 1846 wrote to Louise Colet: "Tu as fait de mon existence une large brèche. Je m'étais entouré d'un mur stoïque; un de tes regards l'a emporté comme un boulet" (1:286, 9 August 1846) ["You have turned my existence into a

---

[9] See, too, his comments on the first *Education sentimentale*: "C'est ardent, mais ça pourrait être plus synthétique" (2:30, 16 January 1852) ["It is ardent, but it could be better synthesized"], and his criticism of Musset: "Personne n'a fait de plus beaux fragments que M[usset], mais rien que des fragments! pas une oeuvre!" (2:163, 25 September 1852) ["No one has produced finer fragments than M{usset}, but nothing *but* fragments! not a work of art!"].

[10] I want to resist the temptation to reduce Flaubert's fears of annihilation—even when at the hands of a woman—to psychoanalytic platitudes such as the "devouring woman" or the "vagina dentata."

[11] Flaubert, *Madame Bovary*, 89; trans. de Man, 40.

88 large breach. I had surrounded myself with a stoic wall; one of your glances demol-
• ished it like a cannonball"].

Here we have to imagine the "stoic wall" falling like hair, like teeth; the emotional "musculature," to use a preferred Flaubertian term, torn away so that no
barrier remains to separate inside and outside, to protect the self from the surging
waters within.[12] "Louise Colet" is a useful name in her lover's psychic vocabulary,
not only for love, but for whatever threatens to breach the dike of his existence—
which is perhaps to say, of his style.

For Flaubert perceives his own body, spirit, and text in a state of ongoing decomposition and dissolution—a state whose extreme form is vaporization—while
imagining Louise Colet as whole. Like a patchwork, he is "cousu de pièces et de
morceaux, plein de contradictions et d'absurdités" (1:426, January 1847) ["made
of stitched-together tatters and scraps, full of contradiction and absurdity"]. Occasionally Louise Colet can, like a good mother, reflect for him an (illusory) image
of his own wholeness:

> On m'a réveillé pour m'apporter ta lettre. . . . C'est venu comme un de
> ces bons baisers avec lesquels les mères réveillent leurs enfants, caresse
> matinale qui bénit toute la journée. . . . Entre les lignes, il me semble
> que je t'aperçois me sourire. Quand mes yeux s'arrêtent au bas des pages,
> je vois ton long regard tendre qui vient à moi. (1;353, 20 September 1846)

> *I was awakened to receive your letter. . . . It came to me like one of those delicious
> kisses with which mothers awaken their children, a morning caress that blesses the*

---

[12] Flaubert consistently uses the metaphor of muscles or musculature to mean disciplined style or writing, or contained sentiment. Thus, for example, he congratulates himself: "Style et muscles, tout est
souple encore" (2:206, 11 December 1852) ["Style and muscles, it is all still supple"], and he speaks ap-
provingly of sentences that are "tendues comme des biceps d'athlète" (2:350, 6 June 1853) ["taut like
athletes' biceps"]; on the other hand, he contrasts "force musculaire" to "émotion nerveuse" (2:252,
27 February 1853). Flaubert wears his musculature like an exoskeleton, the male equivalent of the
"corset" he advises Louise Colet to don to control the passionate overflow of her mind (see page 78,
supra).

Speaking of the fascist writing/imagination of soldiers in the Freikorps—but also more generally, of
male fantasies—Klaus Theweleit writes: "The person is split into an inner realm, concealing a 'numbly
glowing, fluid ocean' and other dangers; and a restraining external shell, the muscle armor, which contains the inner realm the way a cauldron contains boiling soup. The bubbling contents want to get out;
every one of the cited conjurations of war and civil war is toying with the possibility of that hot, locked-
up flood's erupting." Theweleit, *Male Fantasies*, trans. Stephen Conway (Minneapolis: University of
Minnesota Press, 1987), 1:242. The resonances between the metaphoric structures I find in Flaubert's
letters and those Theweleit finds in (soldier) males are overwhelming. His chapter "Floods, Bodies,
Histories" has been a great supportive presence for the writing of the present chapter, and has no doubt
influenced me in more ways than I am aware.

entire day. Between the lines, I think I see you smiling at me. When my eyes rest at
the end of the pages, I see your lingering tender gaze that comes to me.

Most of the time, however, his sense that she is "all of a piece" serves only to emphasize, by contrast, his own fragmentation—a fragmentation he sees daily reflected in the mirror. In the grips of a pre-Sartrean nausea, struck with the absurdity of grooming—that losing struggle against disarray, dirt, decay, and death—Flaubert finds only disintegration with the stubble in the mirror:

> Jamais . . . je ne me fais la barbe sans rire, tant ça me parait bête. . . . Tu
> ne le sentiras pas toi qui est d'un seul morceau, comme un bel hymne
> d'amour et de poésie. Moi je suis une arabesque en marqueterie, il y a des
> morceaux d'ivoire, d'or et de fer. Il y en a de carton peint. Il y en a de
> diamant. Il y en a de fer-blanc.   (1:308, 21–22 August 1846)

> *Never . . . do I shave without laughing, so stupid does it seem to me. . . . You*
> *could not understand this, you who are all of a piece, like a beautiful song of love,*
> *like poetry. But I am an arabesque of marquetry; there are pieces of ivory, of gold,*
> *and of iron. Some are of painted cardboard. Some are of diamond, some of tin.*

And yet there is an unmistakable nuance of pride, if not of gloating, in this comparison that only superficially privileges Louise Colet. To the integral harmony that his lover represents, Flaubert apposes himself as representing not total discordance or chaos, but rather a unity made of disparate parts: "une arabesque en marqueterie." Unity and fragmentation exist in tension in this intricate marquetry design, prefiguration of a cubist collage. The tension of a heterogeneous ensemble, a heteroclitic whole, made of bits and pieces—of tin as well as of diamond—implies a unity of art and not of nature. One begins to suspect that Flaubert's literary composition depends on the natural decomposition that obsesses him, and that he seeks even as he flees; for Flaubert before Wallace Stevens, death is clearly the mother of beauty.[13] In this context we can understand that curious insistence on separation and distance that Vincent Kaufmann has so aptly uncovered in Flaubert's letters to his lover, even during the period of their greatest intimacy. If it is true, as Kaufmann has argued, that the reason Flaubert wrote so

[13] See Wallace Stevens, "Sunday Morning," in *The Palm at the End of the Mind*, ed. Holly Stevens (New York: Vintage, 1972), 7:

> Death is the mother of beauty; hence from her,
> Alone, shall come fulfilment to our dreams,
> And our desires

much to Louise Colet was "pour trouer et traverser tout horizon d'attente" ["to pierce and to pass beyond the horizon of anticipation"], wasn't this so that he could then impose, at the site of the constantly renewed rupture, the artificial unity of writing?[14]

It is as if the very (en)closure of Colet's body presents a unity that must be disrupted in recognition of Flaubert's own fragmentation—and to furnish the artist's raw materials. So he must take apart her style, mutilate her body along with her woman's mind. Here we must recall the bound breasts; and we can take note, as well, of his persistent fetishization of Louise Colet—his sniffing of the purloined slippers he loves "autant que toi" (1:284, 8–9 August 1846) ["as much as you"], his handling of the locks of hair, the blood-soaked handkerchief—for fetishization is a form of disunification, a dismembering gesture. Fragment worship ("mes reliques" is the term Flaubert uses [1:308, 23 August 1846]) is a kind of compensation for a lost integrity, a loss that he repeatedly invokes: "Je n'ai eu que deux ou trois années où j'ai été entier (de dix-sept à dix-neuf ans environ)" (2:289, 31 March 1853) ["I was whole only for two or three years (when I was about seventeen to nineteen)"]. In other words, Flaubert as fetishist acts out the suffered loss by inflicting it in turn, while at the same time attempting to fill it synecdochically: by replacing the plenitude that his lover represented, with bits and pieces.

It is in the same light that we need to understand Flaubert's persistent impulse to turn Louise Colet into a hermaphrodite. In words that echo the stroke in which he suppressed the poetic flow with her breasts, he refashions her anatomy: "J'ai toujours essayé (mais il me semble que j'échoue) de faire de toi un hermaphrodite sublime. Je te veux homme jusqu'à la hauteur du ventre (en descendant). Tu m'encombres et me troubles et *t'abîmes* avec l'élément femelle" (2:548, 12 April 1854) ["I have always tried (but I believe I have failed) to make of you a sublime hermaphrodite. I want you to be a man down to your belly. You burden me and exasperate me and *ruin yourself* with the female element"]. This is a curious passage about which much could be said; what concerns me in particular is the brand of hermaphroditism Flaubert proposes, and the sex/gender relationship he implies. Initially, here as elsewhere, he appears to be anchoring gender in sex (understood for the moment as a biological given).[15] In other words, if he

[14] Vincent Kaufmann, *L'Equivoque épistolaire* (Paris: Minuit, 1991), 186. See, too, Martine Reid's excellent analysis of the distancing of the epistolary addressee, "Flaubert et Sand en correspondance," *Poétique* 85 (February 1991): 53–68.

[15] Of course, to posit sex as a biological (i.e., natural) given involves a major presumption, for, as scholars in various fields have shown in recent years, when we speak about sex we are always engaged with an ideological interpretation of sex; nature, as Roland Barthes put it some three decades ago, is always "parfaitement historique" (*Mythologies* [Paris, Seuil, 1957], 9). For more recent elaborations of the cultural construction of sex, see especially Suzanne J. Kessler and Wendy Mc-

removes her second(ary) sex characteristics, she will write in the masculine mode; biology, personality, and style therefore are tightly bound.[16] When we take a second look, however, his meaning shifts. If we read "upper" and "lower" halves of the body as they are conventionally coded, we get a (gendered) split between head and flesh, spirit and matter, which can be extended to the split pairing of gender and sex. (Gender is cultural; sex, natural.) What Flaubert then seems to be implying when he proposes this horizontal hermaphroditism is a gender/sex hybrid: what we call sex and gender do not have to correspond. In a similar vein he writes: "Je voudrais enfin qu'hermaphrodite nouveau tu me donnasses avec ton corps toutes les joies de la chair et avec ton esprit toutes celles de l'âme" (1:367, 28 September 1846) ["I would like, in a word, for you to give me, like a latter-day hermaphrodite, all the pleasures of the flesh with your body and all the pleasures of the soul with your mind"]. Later, still more bluntly: "Je voudrais que nous gardassions nos deux corps et n'être qu'un même esprit. Je ne veux de toi, comme femme, que la chair. Que tout le reste donc soit à moi, ou mieux, soit moi, de même pâte et la même pâte" (2:285, 27 March 1853) ["I would like us to keep our two bodies and be a single mind. I only want of you as a woman, your flesh. Let all the rest be mine, or better, be me, made of similar stuff and even the same stuff"]. Juxtaposed, these passages toy, however briefly, with the possibility of peeling gender off from sex, stripping sexual anatomy and physiology (which are again seen as given) of the very sex-role conventions to which he rhetorically adheres most of the time.

But there is madness in his method. We might more accurately speak of flaying than of peeling or stripping, for the separation Flaubert operates takes the shape of mutilation, dismemberment, vivisection. It becomes clear that Flaubert dreams of two sexes, one gender; two bodies, one mind: and the gender and mind, needless to say, are his. "J'avais cru dès le début que je trouverais en toi moins de personnalité féminine, une conception plus *universelle* de la vie" (1:366, 28 September 1846; my emphasis) ["From the beginning I believed I would find in you less of a feminine personality, a more *universal* conception of life"], he complains. Universality coincides contextually with masculinity; the masculine mind is gender neutral, and femininity is supplementary, an excrescence that should be removed.

Kenna, *Gender: An Ethnomethodological Approach* (Chicago: University of Chicago Press, 1978); Thomas Laqueur, *Making Sex: Body and Gender from the Greeks to Freud* (Cambridge: Harvard University Press, 1990); Emily Martin, *The Woman in the Body: A Cultural Analysis of Reproduction* (Boston: Beacon Press, 1987). For an excellent literary reflection on these problems, see Jessica Feldman's *Gender on the Divide: The Dandy in Modernist Literature* (Ithaca: Cornell University Press, 1993).

[16] An interesting slippage occurs here: neutered, she will be gender neutral, *which is to say that she will write like a man.*

That a rhetoric of aggression and separation, fragmentation and loss is used to describe the concept of hermaphroditism is quite remarkable. Most traditionally the reenactment of a primordial unity,[17] the *coincidentia oppositorum* or union of contraries, the hermaphrodite is here a figure of disjunction, Mircea Eliade's nineteenth-century "degradation of the [androgyne] symbol"—perhaps the only androgyne that the nineteenth century deserved.[18]

Very much a product of his time, Flaubert replicates, through the violence of his bodily revisions, the misogynistic discourse of the age. He distinguishes himself from this discourse, however, in that his version of it implicitly prefigures the complex and contradictory issues of the gender/sex debate that continues to divide and impassion us today. Having more or less essentialized women and women's writing in the body-bound ways I discuss, he nonetheless radically contradicts himself elsewhere, suggesting to Colet the arbitrariness of gender and of culturally imposed roles:

> La Nature, va, s'est trompée en faisant de toi une femme. Tu es *du côté des mâles.* Il faut te souvenir de cela toujours, quand quelque chose te heurte, et voir en toi si l'élément féminin ne l'emporte pas. . . . T'indignerais-tu si l'on disait du mal des Français, des Chrétiens, des Provençaux? Laisse donc là ton sexe comme ta patrie, ta religion, et ta province.   (2:421, 27 August 1853)

> *Nature made a mistake in making you a woman. You are* on the male side of the divide. *You must always remember that, when something offends you, and take care that the feminine element in you doesn't take over. . . . Would you be indignant if someone spoke ill of the French, of Christians, of people from Provence? So put aside your sex like your country, your religion, and your province.*

And in a reflection as noteworthy for its insight as for its blind spots, he recognizes (feminine) gender as a construct:

> La femme est un produit de l'homme. *Dieu a créé la femelle, et l'homme a fait la femme*; elle est le résultat de la civilisation, une oeuvre factice.

[17] See, however, Wendy Doniger O'Flaherty's perceptive comments in her fascinating study, *Women, Androgynes, and Other Mythical Beasts* (Chicago: University of Chicago Press, 1980), where she takes note of the ambiguous symbolic nature of androgyny: "Dangling before us the sweet promise of equality and balance, symbiosis and mutuality, the androgyne, under closer analyis, often furnishes better testimony to conflict and aggression, tension and disequilibrium" (334).

[18] Mircea Eliade, *Mephistopheles and the Androgyne*, trans. J. M. Cohen (New York: Sheed and Ward, 1965), 99.

Dans les pays où toute culture intellectuelle est nulle, elle n'existe pas (car c'est une oeuvre d'art, au sens humanitaire; est-ce pour cela que toutes les grandes idées générales se sont symbolisées au féminin?).

(2:284–85, 27 March 1853)

Woman is a product of man. God created the female, and man made woman; *she is the result of civilization, a work of imitation. In countries where intellectual culture is absent, she does not exist (for she is a work of art, in the humanitarian sense; is this why all the great general ideas are symbolized in the feminine?).*

The *femme/femelle* distinction anticipates contemporary notions of a gender/sex split, femininity then being presented as a constructed entity rather than a natural essence: an artifice designed by men for men.[19] One can certainly accuse Flaubert of farsightedness, of overlooking the equally contrived nature of masculinity (he, after all, is composed of "ces arabesques de marqueterie") and the necessarily imbricated processes of dual gender construction. Flaubert does not perceive that man creates himself indirectly, invents his own masculinity, when he constructs a feminine Other, when he fabricates the feminine *as* Other.[20]

However, it is precisely at the line of demarcation that Flaubert's vision begins to blur and simultaneously becomes visionary. Where distance separates from closeness, where woman is estranged from man and femininity is unmeshed from masculinity, all opposites also meet and coalesce. The specificity of femininity, albeit set up as difference—masculinity's constructed Other—turns out to be that it *includes* its Other. Having hyperbolically defined femininity in the essentializing, pathologizing terms that would come to be codified as hysteria, Flaubert then identifies with these terms, and, in the process of so doing, puts into question the reliability of the distinctions he draws.

THE VOYAGE IN

Much ink has been spilled, from Flaubert's day continuing through to our own, in an effort to diagnose (or dispute) his hysteria, and correlatively, to establish (or refute) his femininity. Let me emphatically state that this is exactly *not* my point, but that the reason such an effort seems to me wrongheaded *is.*

[19] Of course, the construct/essence dichotomy does not hold up when examined; constructs often perform the work of essentializing. See Diana Fuss, *Essentially Speaking* (New York: Routledge, 1989).
[20] One must illuminate the chiaroscuro truths of Flaubert's unilateral gender creation myth with Deborah Cameron's observation that "sex differentiation must be rigidly upheld by whatever means are available, for men can be men only if women are unambiguously women." Cameron, *Feminism and Linguistic Thought* (London: Macmillan, 1985), 155–56.

For well over a century, literary critics and their medical fellow travelers have combed the letters, diaries, and novels of Flaubert and his contemporaries in search of allusions to his physical symptoms, clinical treatments, medication, exposure to medical reports, sexual repression, sexual ambivalence. In the absence of medical evidence, they sought diagnostic clues or coverups. Was Flaubert a hysteric before the fact (that is, before medical science allowed men that diagnosis) or a mere epileptic? Did Flaubert have homosexual, bisexual, transsexual leanings that predisposed him to neurosis? Did he have feminine tendencies that might have made him a likely victim of hysteria, an inverted shadow of Emma Bovary? Was Flaubert Madame Bovary?

Roger Williams, taking his place in a long line of purveyors of such speculations, muses upon whether or not Flaubert could have been familiar with "the latest theories of neuroses or psychopathologies."[21] Anxious to trace Emma Bovary's nervous condition to a medical reality, he never pauses to consider that novelists and physicians are formed in a common cultural pool, and in turn mold similar cultural products; or, more radically yet, that novelists might have intuitions about cultural phenomena (including pathology) that precede or contradict medical "knowledge."[22]

The latter-day positivism that marks Williams's determined inquiry into pathological cause and effect, as it engages particularly with sexual identity, is ill-suited to Flaubertian writing and beside the point of his insights. The malady that Flaubert consistently refers to in his letters by such terms as "les nerfs," "la maladie de nerfs," "les affections nerveuses"—and that we can call hysteria (but the name matters very little)—could in fact be defined as the opposite of positivism. The property of Flaubertian nerves is transmigration and transition: they transgress boundaries, transpose categories and contexts, and, as we shall see, metamorphose the very metaphorical elements that give them form.

Despite Flaubert's vehement reprobation of all things wet and flowing, his nervous condition is frequently and unabashedly expressed by his own weeping:

> Mercredi dernier, j'ai été obligé de me lever pour aller chercher mon mouchoir de poche. Les larmes me coulaient sur la figure. Je m'étais attendri moi-même en écrivant, je jouissais délicieusement, et de

[21] Roger Williams, *The Horror of Life* (Chicago: University of Chicago Press, 1980), 167.
[22] Williams ponders, "While it is true that some of the revolutionary work which began to redefine the nature of hysteria . . . was published shortly *after* the publication of *Madame Bovary*, that does not necessarily prove that Flaubert was unaware of the theories" (167). He goes on to suggest that Flaubert might have had access to recent medical information through lectures given in Rouen or through his family because father and brother were physicians. It is the blithe assumption that literary malaise must necessarily derive somehow from medicine that I want to challenge. See Williams's bibliography for earlier sources of speculation about Flaubert's medical history.

l'émotion de mon idée, et de la phrase qui la rendait, et de la satisfaction
de l'avoir trouvée. — Du moins je crois qu'il y avait de tout cela dans cette
émotion, où les nerfs après tout avaient plus de place que le reste.

(2:76, 24 April 1852)

*Last Wednesday, I had to get up to go find my pocket handkerchief. Tears were
streaming down my face. I had moved myself to tears by writing; I took delicious
pleasure from the emotion of my idea, from the sentence that rendered it, and from
the satisfaction of having found it. At least I believe all of that was included in my
emotion, where my nerves after all took up more room than the rest.*

The dual allegiance of tears to body and soul makes them an ideal conduit for their
nervous tenor, which is always for Flaubert a form of transport between two poles:
"Je vivrai comme je vis, toujours souffrant des nerfs, *cette porte de transmission
entre l'âme et le corps* par laquelle j'ai voulu peut-être faire passer trop de choses"
(1:489, 11–12 December 1847; my emphasis) ["I will live as I live, always suffering
from my nerves, *this transmission portal between the soul and the body* through
which I have perhaps tried to transfer too many things"].

The ailment Flaubert abbreviates as his "nerves," figured here as a portal between the soul and the body, elsewhere plays a more transformational role. Still
charged with a mediating function within a traditional dualistic economy, the
nerves now more actively serve as a mechanism of conversion from the spirit to the
flesh: "Le chagrin, au lieu de me rester sur le crâne, a coulé dans mes membres et
les crispait en convulsions. C'était une *déviation.* . . . La *vocation* a été déplacée.
L'idée a passé dans la chair où elle reste stérile, et la chair périt" (2:127, 6 July 1852)
["My chagrin, rather than remaining on my skull, flowed into my limbs and
clenched them in convulsions. It was a *deviation.* . . . The *vocation* had been displaced. The idea passed into the flesh where it remains sterile, and the flesh per-
ishes"]. Such an account of his nervous attacks, also described as "des déclivités in-
volontaires d'idées, d'images" (2:218, 27 December 1852) ["involuntary declivities
of ideas, of images"], bears an uncanny resemblance to the mechanism Freud
would elaborate half a century later, and within the initial context of hysteria, as
conversion: simply put, the somatic expression of a repressed idea. Nonetheless,
such a coincidence of concept and expression should not necessarily be read as an
invitation to recuperate the Flaubertian "transmission portal" under the Freudian
banner of conversion hysteria. I would suggest instead that we subsume Flaubert's
antecedent version of conversion hysteria under the broader Flaubertian canopy
of transmission, which, as we shall see, includes myriad varieties of fusion, transfusion, transition, suspension of opposition within paired contraries.

This latter larger category would embrace a writing phenomenon we might call
literary transmigration:

Voilà une des rares journées de ma vie que j'ai passée dans l'Illusion, complètement, et depuis un bout jusqu'à l'autre. Tantôt, à six heures, au moment où j'écrivais le mot *attaque de nerfs*, j'étais si emporté, je gueulais si fort, et sentais si profondément ce que ma petite femme éprouvait, que j'ai eu peur moi-même d'en avoir une. . . . C'est une délicieuse chose que d'écrire! que de ne plus être *soi*, mais de circuler dans toute la création dont on parle. Aujourd'hui par exemple, homme et femme tout ensemble, amant et maîtresse à la fois, je me suis promené à cheval dans une forêt, par un après-midi d'automne, sous des feuilles jaunes, et j'étais les chevaux, les feuilles, le vent, les paroles qu'ils se disaient et le soleil rouge qui faisait s'entre-fermer leurs paupières noyées d'amour. (2:483–84, 23 December 1853)

This was one of the rare days of my life that I have spent in Illusion, completely, from start to finish. A little while ago, at six o'clock, as I wrote the word nervous attack, *I was so carried away, I shouted so loudly, and felt so profoundly what my dear woman was experiencing, that I feared that I might have one as well. . . . It is a delicious thing to write! to no longer be* oneself, *but to flow in all the creation about which one speaks. Today for example, man and woman together, lover and mistress at once, I rode a horse through a forest on a fall afternoon, under yellow leaves, and I was the horses, the leaves, the wind, the words they were speaking and the red sun that forced them to lower their eyelids flooded with love.*

That identification or indeed fusion of writer and text that Flaubert elsewhere censures in the name of Colet, he allows himself in the name of his *nerfs*. Once again nervous illness is a port of transit, a doorway between erstwhile separate domains, a well-traversed threshold. It fuses man and woman, lover and mistress, writer and character, writer-as-reader and text, anticipating Gérard Gasarian's contention that "l'hystérie est une maladie de lecture: elle survient au moment où le lecteur se méprend . . . [sur] son identité"[23] ["hysteria is a reading disorder: it comes about when the reader mistakes his or her identity"].

As the verb "circuler" suggests, Flaubert experiences the "literary disease" of mistaken identity as a *fluid* identity. This is a new but oddly familiar turn: it is in fact a return within the writer of his externalized Other. Now "homme et femme tout ensemble," self and Other, locus of a fused inside and outside, Flaubert can reappropriate female flow and feminine fluidity under the extraordinary rubric of his nerves. To qualify these processes still as "female" and "feminine" is, however,

[23] Gérard Gasarian, "La Figure du poète hystérique ou l'allégorie chez Baudelaire," *Poétique* 86 (April 1991): 177–78.

to continue to use a traditionally cleaved language and conceptual frame that his
nervous disorder invalidates. The culminating point of Flaubert's nervous malady,
the "attaque de nerfs" or nervous seizure, explodes the very notion of impermeable
contrasting categories: "Chaque attaque était comme une sort d'hémorragie de
l'innervation. C'était des pertes séminales de la faculté pittoresque du cerveau,
cent mille images sautant à la fois, en feux d'artifices. Il y avait un arrachement de
l'âme d'avec le corps" (2:377, 7 July 1853) ["Each attack was like a kind of hemor-
rhage of the nerve center. There were seminal discharges of the brain's imaging
faculties, a hundred thousand images exploding at once, in fireworks. The soul
and the body were torn apart"]. The generally female-related rush of blood (recall
the image of literature drowning in menstrual flow) more neutrally hemorrhages
here and is otherwise translated by semen (*pertes seminales*) instead of by the more
common Flaubertian metaphor of female discharges (*pertes blanches*). Female
and male lose their identity; the lyric lies down with the real. Body and soul, sex
and brain, inside and outside fuse in a shattering, erupting, streaming explosion of
solid-liquid indistinction.

It is at the moment of greatest fragmentation—when, convulsed, the body is in
pieces, out of control—that a reintegration of disparate realities is achieved. With
the ravages of illness comes the vision of healing, the image of wholeness. Flaubert holds up to his ailing nerves and flailing limbs the mirror of his writing, which
reflects psychic reunification and aesthetic harmony in place of corporeal
incoherence.

To constitute nerves and art as mirror images is of course a citation of that well-
worn nineteenth-century topos that compares, and often equates, madness and
genius. Flaubert, whose ear was ever sensitive to the banal ring of an *idée reçue*,
was only too aware of the risk of falling into that particular commonplace. He goes
to great (if sporadic) pains in his musings on nervosity to distinguish the nervous
from the artistic sensibility, despite frequent lapses that betray at least a vestigial belief in their identity. Here first is an attempt to differentiate art and nerves: "La Poésie n'est point une débilité de l'esprit, et ces susceptibilités nerveuses en sont une"
(2:127, 6 July 1852) ["Poetry is not a mental debility, and these nervous suscepti-
bilities are"]. Yet consider this ode to a sensibility that is indistinguishably nervous
and artistic:

> Certaines natures ne souffrent pas, les gens sans nerfs. Heureux sont-ils!
> Mais de combien de choses aussi ne sont-ils pas privés! Chose étrange,
> à mésure qu'on s'élève dans l'échelle des êtres, la faculté nerveuse
> augmente, c'est-à-dire la faculté de souffrir. Souffrir et penser seraient-ils
> donc même chose? Le génie, après tout, n'est peut-être qu'un raffinement
> de la douleur.   (2:443–44, 30 September 1853)

> There are natures that do not suffer—those of nerveless people. Lucky are they! But
> also, how many things are they deprived of! It is a curious thing how, as one rises on
> the scale of beings, the nervous faculty increases—that is, the faculty of suffering.
> Are suffering and thinking then the same thing? Genius, after all, is perhaps but a
> refinement of suffering.

Here Flaubert all but assimilates victims of nervous afflictions to the "happy few":
genius and illness overlap.

Some years later, in a pair of letters responding to some queries from Hippolyte
Taine as to the relative nature of nervous hallucination and artistic vision, Flaubert weighs resemblances and differences (3:562–63, 20? November 1866; 3:572–
73, 1 December 1866). I will not here enter into a detailed analysis of his comparative evaluation; I want only to single out a note of difference that will serve as a
conclusion. This particular comparison is significant within the context of my discussion because it links nervous hallucination and artistic vision in a configuration
of inversion—the very configuration responsible for the illusion of sameness created by a mirror image.[24] Flaubert cautions against confusing the two hallucina-
tory states: "Dans l'hallucination proprement dite, il y a toujours terreur, *on sent
que votre personnalité vous échappe,* on croit qu'on va mourir. Dans la vision poétique, au contraire, il y a joie. *C'est quelque chose qui entre en vous*" (3:562–63,
20? November 1866; my emphasis) ["With hallucination in the strict sense, there
is always terror, *you feel your personality escaping you,* you believe you are about to
die. With poetic vision, on the contrary, there is joy. *It is something that is entering
you*"]. The voyage out: a stream of nerves; the voyage in: a retrojected flow. Illness
turns out to be a facilitating condition for Flaubert, a means of resolving conflict
by forcibly reintegrating the ambivalently experienced elements that he has projected as the rejected feminine.[25] Flaubert sails into illness and drifts back to the
wave-washed shore of the very darkest continent of all.

[24] Here and throughout this chapter, my thinking has been inspired by Lacan's "mirror stage," although
I do not intend an application in any strict sense of Lacan's theory. (See Jacques Lacan, "Le Stade du
miroir comme formateur de la fonction du Je," in *Ecrits*, vol. 1 [Paris: Seuil, 1966].)
[25] One is reminded here of Freud's expression of the "flight into illness": the escape from conflict
achieved by symptom formation. See J. Laplanche and J.-B. Pontalis, *The Language of Psychoanalysis*, trans. Donald Nicholson-Smith (New York: Norton, 1973), 165.

5 REWRITING A WOMAN'S LIFE

Fluidity, Madness, and Voice in Louise Colet's *La Servante*

*[Le coeur des femmes] est un piano où l'homme artiste
égoïste se complaît à jouer des airs qui
le font briller, et toutes les touches parlent.*

GUSTAVE FLAUBERT TO LOUISE COLET, 24 APRIL 1852

*Et Gustave lui-même! oh! mon Dieu! mon Dieu! que je
plains et que j'aime les femmes! Quel drame je pourrais
écrire et j'écrirai sur leur destinée!*

LOUISE COLET, MEMENTO OF 22 MAY 1852

●   When we seek to reconstruct an epistolary dialogue, the enterprise is complicated infinitely if we find that one of the voices has been absorbed by the other: as the case of Colet and Flaubert suggests, we can recover only fragments. Reading Flaubert's letters to Colet, we occasionally distinguish phantom traces of her voice in his responses to her missing letters. Their spectrum of recoverability can be divided into three zones. In those cases where he cites her textually, we can reconstruct bits of her discourse. Consider, for example, specific passages of Colet's writings cited in Flaubert's letters: "Merci de tes vers sur Mantes, ils m'ont beaucoup plu, sois-en sûre. Il y en a de beaux, ceux-ci par exemple: 'Tout semblait rayonner du bonheur de nos âmes, . . .'" ["Thank you for your verses about Mantes; I can assure you that I liked them very much. There are some fine ones, these for example: 'Everything seemed to shine with the joy of our souls, . . .'"];[1] or similarly, "Je com-

---

[1] Gustave Flaubert, *Correspondance*, ed. Jean Bruneau (Paris: Gallimard, 1973–91), 1:347, 18 September 1846. Subsequent references to Flaubert's *Correspondance* will be to this edition and will be provided in the text.

mence à m'indigner de tes titres: *Poème de la femme; Ce qui est dans le coeur des femmes; Deux femmes célèbres; Deux mois d'émotion*" (2:310, 20 April 1853) ["I begin to be angered by your titles: *Poem of Woman; What Is in the Heart of Women; Two Famous Women; Two Months of Emotion*"].

In a second, hazier zone, Flaubert cites Colet indirectly and incompletely. We are tempted to engage in an imaginary reconstruction of Colet's discourse when we read: "Tu me dis que je t'ai envoyé des réflexions curieuses sur les femmes" (2:80, 24 April 1852) ["You tell me I sent you some curious reflections on women"], or "Tu dis, chère Louise, que mes lettres sont pour toi une toile de Pénélope" (2:462, 3 November 1853) ["You say, dear Louise, that my letters are like Penelope's cloth for you"]. However compelling it would be to decode such passages, any reconstruction of Colet's words involves considerable speculation on the reader's part. What aspects of Flaubert's thoughts on women struck Colet as so curious? When she compared his letters to Penelope's tapestry, was it because of the many rendezvous designated and canceled? Or because of his alternating exaltation and denigration of her love and of her texts? Or was she referring to another context that is lost to us?

Finally, in even less specific passages, Flaubert merely alludes to Colet's discourse, and any reconstructive attempt on the reader's part is pure guesswork: "Tu me demandes des explications à des choses qui s'expliquent d'elles-mêmes. Que veux-tu que je te dise de plus que je ne t'ai déjà dit et que tu ne sais déjà?" (1:420, 20 December 1846) ["You ask me to explain things that are self-explanatory. What more do you want me to say beyond what I have already told you and that you do not already know?"]. Unable to read Colet's prompting words, we cannot even appraise the validity of Flaubert's frequent summaries of her part of the dialogue: "Entre nous, je ne suis ni si haut ni si bas; tu me vulgarises ou me poétises trop" (1:348, 18 September 1846) ["Between us, I am neither so high nor so low; you vulgarize or poeticize me excessively"].

The very meager direct access we have to Colet's private words, in the form of various "Mementos" (her journal entries) and five letters to Flaubert published in the Bruneau edition of the *Correspondance*, pleads a compelling case for caution and skepticism in our reading of Flaubert's reading of Colet. Flaubert's confident basking in Colet's presumed tolerance for his frankness is often shown to be grossly misplaced, for Colet's own remarks suggest that she views her lover's candor as egotism in disguise. Witness, for instance, Flaubert's afterglow following a stream of abuse he has directed against Colet: "Oui, comme c'est bon d'avoir toi, car tu es la seule femme à qui un homme puisse écrire de telles choses" (2:304, 13 April 1853) ["Yes, how good it is to have you, for you are the only woman to whom a man can write such things"]. Consider then Colet's plaint in response, registered in a Memento some months later: "Que d'aspérités! comme il me blesse ou m'outrage naïvement!"[2] ["What harshness! How artlessly he wounds or insults me!"]. In her own voice Colet does not welcome censure with the alacrity ascribed to her in Flaubert's letter.

But such instances of double-stranded discourse are rare. Within Flaubert's letters to Colet, we hear only faint echoes of her epistolary voice; we read fragments of her texts revised by Flaubert's mastering text; we occasionally touch the rewoven tissue of her fears, her pleas, her love, her dreams. The very futility of the recovery mission confronts us with an intertextual structure of containment that prefigures the thematic core of Louise Colet's verse narrative *La Servante*, which I read as a surrogate for all her missing letters to Flaubert.[3] Colet's narrative introjects as subject a gendered structure of enclosure and subordination within which a woman's body and corpus are always preinscribed as male text.[4]

MARIETTE: THE BOOK

The protagonist of *La Servante*, a young Alsatian girl of humble birth, Mariette, one day finds a book in the garden of the château belonging to the marquise for whom she works. Mariette, whose *bovarysme* is unimpeded by the fact that the eponymous Emma was not yet fully formed when she herself was in the process of being created, is presented from the start as a victim of unfulfilled bibliophilic fantasies. When she then comes upon the little red book—red like an apple of knowledge set temptingly in her path—she is troubled, excited, overcome by a desire to which the narrator attributes her fall:

> Oh! pourquoi toucha-t-elle, agitée et ravie,
> A ce livre entr'ouvert sous l'ombrage oublié!

[2] Louise Colet, Memento, 4 December 1853, in Flaubert, *Correspondance*, 2:902. The largest and most readily available selection of Louise Colet's Mementos is published here; subsequent reference will be to this edition and will appear parenthetically in the text. Louise Colet began her Mementos in 1845, and continued writing them for the next ten years. She wrote these often intimate journal fragments on scraps of paper, envelopes, or whatever else was at hand. The original manuscripts are currently located in Avignon at the Fonds Colet, in the Médiathèque Ceccano (the municipal library).

[3] Although the Maupassant account I presented (see 76, *supra*) convinces me that Flaubert was responsible for the destruction of Colet's letters to him, I would speak of the loss of her letters in terms of the domination of her voice by his even if I were more skeptical about the identity of the culprit. Whatever historical accident suppressed her part of their correspondence and preserved his serves to reinforce the containing element of his letters.

[4] It is worth noting that this structure of female containment by a male text consistently reappears in Colet's writing. The female narrator's story in *Lui* is interrupted by the male protagonist's embedded narrative that appropriates roughly one-half of the text; in *La Paysanne*, when the heroine's lover returns from the war to find her buried, he exhumes her body, but the only part that has remained intact and identifiable is his own letter to her.

D'où viennent ces hasards qui perdent une vie?
Comment Dieu qui prévoit reste-t-il sans pitié?[5]

Oh! Why was she compelled to touch
This half-open book left in the shade of the trees!
What causes the misfortunes that doom a life?
How can God in his vision not take pity?

But the book that unbinds Mariette's desire is not just any book; it is the story of her life written before the fact:

Elle crut que ses yeux se couvraient d'un nuage,
Lorsqu'elle vit son nom sur la première page:
Mariette! (c'était le titre du récit),
Par Lionel de V. Elle s'arrête et lit.   (203)

She thought that her vision was clouded,
When she saw her name on the first page:
Mariette! *(it was the title of the book),*
By Lionel de V. She stops and reads.

Captivated by this literary mirror, Mariette stops and reads through to the end of her story, which entails loving a poet and dying in the prime of youth. When her more practical friend Théréson urges her to cast down the book, Mariette refuses:

"Je ne puis, je ne puis, je veux voir jusqu'au bout;
Cela me prend au coeur," répondait Mariette;
"Cette fille a mon nom et me ressemble en tout;
Elle aime ce que j'aime. . . ." Et ravie, inquiète,
Elle lisait toujours; à la fin du récit,
Sa figure était pâle et de pleurs inondée.   (203)

"I cannot, I cannot, I want to find out the end;
This touches my heart," answered Mariette;
"This girl has my name and resembles me in every way;
She loves what I love. . . ." And rapt, anxious,
She kept reading; at the end of the story
Her face was pale and flooded with tears.

---

[5] Louise Colet, *La Servante* (first edition, 1854), reprinted in *Femmes de lettres au XIXe siècle: Autour de Louise Colet*, ed. Roger Bellet (Lyon: Presses Universitaires de Lyon, 1982), 203. Subsequent references to *La Servante* will be to this edition and will be given parenthetically in the text.

I want to emphasize first the element of alienation that structures this scene of identification with the novel; Narcissus-like, Mariette is enthralled by the self seen as other in the novel ("cette autre Mariette") (203), which is to say, by the self seen by the other (Lionel de V., the author). The element of seduction inherent in this identification cannot be overlooked either: it courses through the passage in the repetition of the past participle *ravie*, calls attention to itself by invoking the Edenic model, and is displaced onto the embedded novel's hero, Léon:

> Mariette lui dit: "Ce qu'on lit semble vivre;
> On le sent, on y croit: ce Léon, son amant,
> Il existe, c'est sûr." Elle ferma le livre.   (203–4)

> *Mariette told him: "What one reads seems to live;*
> *One feels it, one believes in it: this Leon, her lover*
> *Exists, that is certain." She closed the book.*

The scene of reading weaves into a single shimmering design the three threads of seduction, identification, and alienation. Mariette's captivation by the novel suggests not only the seduction of fiction, but the fiction of seduction: the fabrication of identity, the identification of self as other that it brings into play.[6]

Reading is the veritable scene of seduction. Although Mariette will later become the mistress of Lionel de V. (who turns out rather fortuitously to be the marquise's brother), she is seduced initially (and primarily) by the novel. Lionel will seduce her only by virtue of a metonymic connection to his fictive namesake, Léon, and more generally, to his fiction, *Mariette*:

> Exaltée, affaiblie, à ce déclin du jour,
> Aspirant l'air en feu, s'oubliant elle-même,
> Ne se ressouvenant que du livre d'amour:
> "Oh! vous êtes Léon," dit-elle, "je vous aime!"   (217)

> *Exalted, weakened at this close of day,*
> *Breathing in the blazing air, forgetting herself,*
> *Remembering only the book of love:*
> *"Oh! you are Leon," she said, "I love you!"*

---

[6] These questions have been provocatively studied by Ross Chambers, who muses: "When we are seduced, are we not always seduced into conforming ourselves with an image: the simulacrum of one whom we believe can be loved?" *Story and Situation: Narrative Seduction and the Power of Fiction* (Minneapolis: University of Minnesota Press, 1984), 15.

104

•

So a plot template is established in the first five pages of *La Servante*, in the form of the embedded novel *Mariette*. The remaining forty-odd pages of the text are then devoted to testing the hegemony of this template: to what extent can Mariette's narrative (which for us as readers frames the template fiction, but which for Mariette is contained within it) be written otherwise? Is Mariette condemned to repeat *Mariette*, to read and reread her story *en abyme*? To what extent can a woman whose life appears before her as a man's completed novel go on to change the plot, rewrite the story?[7] To what extent can she escape her cultural emplottedness? Where are the alternative plot models, the myths, the languages that would allow a different novel to be written? If they do not exist, can they be invented?

These questions anticipate with uncanny accuracy those being posed by feminists today; most notably, they literalize, in the person of Mariette, would-be writer of books, the issues of feminine subjectivity, autonomy, and voice that Carolyn Heilbrun addresses metaphorically in *Writing a Woman's Life*.[8] What is literal, however, for Mariette is metaphorical for Louise Colet, who makes a great narrative effort, as we shall see, to distinguish her narrator's voice and its fate from Mariette's. So when we think about the revisability of specific containing plots in *La Servante*, we must consider how issues of plot containedness and autonomy are imbricated with broader cultural structures and restructurings at work in the narrative as well.

My reading of *La Servante* follows Colet's exploration of a woman's given position of enclosure within gendered conventions of plot, voice, language, and myth, her maneuvering within this space, and her efforts to chart a passage to an open space outside—a blank page, as it were. I do not claim that the text tells a clearly triumphant story of textual challenge and revision, but rather that it exposes with remarkable lucidity the powers of containment, and reveals with great pathos the difficulty of ever writing from an unmapped position outside gender constraints as long as we are situated by the language in which we write within traditional cultural plots.

[7] The description of the book is worth noting:

> Un petit livre rouge à riche reliure,
> Dont quatre griffes d'or marquaient les coins mignons.   (203)

> *A small red book, richly bound,*
> *With four gold stamps marking the delicate corners.*

This book is clearly an artifact, a cultural object, and the fact that Mariette appears always to be enclosed within it further suggests that she is contained within culture.
[8] Carolyn Heilbrun, *Writing a Woman's Life* (New York: Norton, 1984).

RECONSTRUCTING PLOT

Let us begin by flipping back to the opening pages of *La Servante* until we have arrived in the garden and have, with Mariette, spotted the forbidden fruit. Given the length of the episode, the fetishistic detailing of the book as physical object lying half-open—*entr'ouvert*, as if flashing its contents—and the narrative insistence on its seductive power, it is surprising to realize how very little we are in fact told about the plot of *Mariette*, despite its structural centrality within the plot of *La Servante*.

Although we hear a few background details about the Mariette of the embedded story (that she is a poor "daughter of the people," has a joyful if brief youth, and loves a man who is a poet), we know of only three actions that form the plot of *Mariette*: the heroine loves, is loved, and dies when she is twenty. Now, it is certainly not merely coincidental that these three actions correspond to the two essential narrative functions that define a woman's (resting) place in traditional fiction: devotion to a man, and death. Nancy K. Miller, among others, has long since noted that marriage and death are traditionally the only available ends for women in narrative;[9] Susan McClary has more recently shown, in her work on a wide range of Western musical genres, that narrative closure demands "the containment of whatever is semiotically or structurally marked as feminine"[10] and has further elaborated, in a reflection on Catherine Clément's work on opera, that "women are the inevitable victims of an art form that demands the submission or death of the woman for the sake of narrative closure."[11] And Clément, speaking of opera as "this spectacle thought up to adore, and also to kill, the feminine character,"[12] remarks on the diffusion in time and space of opera's recurrent plot of female loving and dying: "This perfect spectacle . . . repeats in this century the love stories of the last. It has overflowed the theater and the stage and produces operatic effects all over the place: in the movies, in musical comedy, in theater and in the texts of novels."[13]

I have paused to invoke these convergent observations from different disciplines in order to insist on the tradition within which Louise Colet is working, and which she before me is evoking in her framed narrative. *Mariette* is framed as a citation

[9] "Without marriage as telos there can be only death . . . or so it seems." Nancy K. Miller, *The Heroine's Text* (New York: Columbia University Press, 1980), 82. See, too, Carolyn Heilbrun's "What Was Penelope Unweaving?" in *Hamlet's Mother and Other Women* (New York: Columbia University Press, 1990), 103–11, for some related speculations on the dearth of narratives by which women can guide their lives.
[10] Susan McClary, *Feminine Endings: Music, Gender, and Sexuality* (Minneapolis: University of Minnesota Press, 1991), 15.
[11] Susan McClary, preface to Catherine Clément, *Opera or the Undoing of Woman*, trans. Betsy Wing (Minneapolis: University of Minnesota Press, 1988), xi.
[12] Clément, *Opera*, 6.
[13] Ibid., 12.

of the limited plot functions available to women within the dominant narrative tradition—limits which are emphasized by the minimalist plot summary—and as such, it is an urtext from which the framing text will depart and against which it will be played out. Through Mariette's reading and living of the novel she discovers, Colet anticipates Heilbrun's perception that "lives do not serve as models; only stories do that. . . . We can only retell and live by the stories we have read or heard."[14] In the gap she introduces between *Mariette* and Mariette's admittedly dismal but critically divergent life story in *La Servante,* and in a second breach she opens between Mariette's voice and the narrator's voice, Colet strategically demonstrates the difficulty of revising time-honored stories but, correlatively, the urgency for doing so.

Let us return to the point at which *La Servante* picks up the threads of *Mariette* in order to examine in greater detail the narrative strategies deployed to play them off against each other. What is *La Servante*'s answer to the feminine narrative functions put into circulation by the male author's novel? What becomes of love and marriage? And what of death? The heroine of *La Servante* ostensibly complies with the first expectation and foils the second; however, we shall see that in so doing, she complicates both.

After the fall comes still greater temptation. Novel reading leads to loftier horizons: Mariette's upwardly mobile dreams take her to Paris as the marquise's maid, once her mother's death has liberated her from provincial life. There she meets the marquise's ailing brother Lionel, author of *Mariette* and object of her infatuation, and nurses him back to health. In gratitude and temporary lust he bears her off with him, but his love rapidly gives way to domination and philandering, and Mariette's status as lover is redefined as servant.[15]

Lionel cruelly refuses Mariette's requests for education and mocks her desire to write, although he does not hesitate to take her on as amanuensis when he is too sick or drunk to transcribe his own thoughts. Mariette faithfully, doggedly, loves him nonetheless; she follows him, is abused by him, stoically suffers his beating, cheating, and drunken stupors. When finally he abandons her to run off with her childhood friend, Mariette attempts suicide but is rescued from a watery death in the Seine by her erstwhile disdained suitor, the honest but oafish miller, Julien. After a brief (but for Mariette, interminably boring) rest cure in the country in the midst of his thriving family, she returns to Paris and eventually purchases her in-

[14] Heilbrun, *Writing a Woman's Life,* 37.
[15] In fact all through this text Colet uses the category of servant as another name for woman, equating female heterosexual love with bondage. This does not mean that she tackles class issues in any real sense. Her recourse to a discourse of the lower classes and servitude remains essentially metaphorical, an example of what Elizabeth Spelman has deftly called "colonizing the language of suffering" in a lecture of the same name (University of Virginia, 5 November 1990).

dependence by dint of two years of hard domestic labor: she owns a *chambre de bonne* which is notably furnished with a bookshelf. A fatal encounter with Lionel leads, however, to a renewed liaison and continued misery until, victim of his own dissolute tendencies and of consumption, he expires—but not before quite literally seeing the light—"Lionel se redresse ébloui de clarté" (242) ["Lionel sat up dazzled by lucidity"]—and marrying Mariette on his deathbed. Then there is a lacuna in the text. After a corresponding blank on the page the next section begins. It is situated at the Salpêtrière Hospital in the midst of a city of madwomen, one of whom is Mariette. We are not told what precipitated her madness. The narrative ends with Mariette's clinging to a tree that she would climb, we are told, were it not for her straitjacket. She is muttering a chant that replays the provincial scene of the book's discovery.

There are several differences in the fate of the two Mariettes, the most obvious one being the iconoclastic survival of the frame story's Mariette at the end of the narrative. Despite the apparent similarity of her love plot to the model plot represented by the embedded story's Mariette, I would argue that the tone and the structuring of this plot call for a radically different reading.

The marriage scene that takes place on Lionel's deathbed in *La Servante* makes a mockery of marriage as institution and as plot; we see a union in form only, performed as an empty repetition of narrative conventions. Here is Lionel's dying flash of lucidity:

> "Oh! c'est donc toi l'amour que j'avais tant cherché?
> Oui, l'épouse, c'est toi! viens! je t'ai reconnue!"
> Et de ses doigts raidis au sien il met l'anneau
> Que mourante à sa main avait passé sa mère;
> Puis il l'enchaîne à lui d'une étreinte dernière,
> Comme pour l'emporter sur son coeur au tombeau!   (242)

> "Oh! *you* are the love I sought so long?
> Yes, *you* are the bride! come! I have recognized you!"
> And with his stiffened fingers he puts on hers the ring
> That his dying mother had placed in his hand;
> Then he draws her to him in a last embrace,
> As if to bear her off, clasped to him, to the grave!

The incipient rigor mortis suggested by the bridegroom's "stiffened fingers" emphasizes the equation of marriage and death that is evoked by Mariette's macabre nuptial embrace. In a sense, the marriage bed has always been a deathbed for Ma-

riette, for her union with Lionel has been represented in terms of suffering, abjection, and humiliation: in sum, as a death in life. But this is true only from the narrator's point of view; even after years of degradation, Mariette consistently and to
the end presents a face of love to Lionel: "Tant d'amour éclatait sur sa pâle figure"
(242) ["So much love shone on her pale face"]. When the narrator kills Lionel,
Mariette mourns him.

Marriage is not the only point at which Mariette and the narrator part ways.
There is a complex interplay between their two perspectives concerning the death
plot, and the embedded *Mariette* novel complicates matters further. Although the
narrator from the beginning has distinguished her perspective from Mariette's by
occasionally adopting the vocative in order to step back from her heroine and address nature conspiratorially about her, the first important conflict of perspectives
is prompted by Mariette's rapturous contemplation of the scene of her own death
in the novel. An ecstatic Mariette naively echoes an aesthetic tradition epitomized
by Edgar Allan Poe's assertion that "the death . . . of a beautiful woman is, un-
questionably, the most poetical topic in the world."[16] But a more cynical appraisal
of this tradition looms in the transition from Mariette's exaltation to the narrator's
irony:

> Elle s'arrête et lit:
> Oh! les belles amours! oh! l'histoire touchante!
> Que cette Mariette eut un heureux printemps!
> Pauvre, elle est adorée, elle rit, elle chante,
> Elle aime, elle est aimée, elle meurt à vingt ans!
> Elle meurt, et c'est là ce qu'on envie;
> La jeunesse s'éprend de ces rigueurs du sort.   (203)

> *She stops and reads:*
> *Oh! what sweet love! oh! what a touching story!*
> *What a happy spring this Mariette had!*
> *Poor, she is loved, she laughs, she sings,*
> *She loves, she is loved, she dies at twenty!*
> *She dies, and that is what is envied;*
> *Youth is infatuated with such hardships of fate.*

The narrative perspective changes in the last two lines cited; the switch is signaled
principally by the irony that abruptly makes its way into the text as the seductive-

---

[16] Edgar Allan Poe, "The Philosophy of Composition," in *Selected Writings of Edgar Allan Poe* (Harmondsworth: Penguin, 1967), 486. A clear example of the narrator's "asides" to nature in *La Servante*
begins: "Que lui disiez-vous donc, ô voix de la nature . . . ?" (201) ["What did you say to her, voices of
nature . . . ?"].

ness of dying young and in love gives way, through the repetition of "she dies," to
an intimation of the finality of death. The narrative distancing conveyed by the
impersonal pronoun *on* and by the aphoristic statement of the last line indicates
that our focus is no longer with Mariette reading *Mariette*, but with the narrator
watching Mariette as reader, appraising her responses, and judging them as indi-
cators of larger social patterns.

Colet frequently uses such a strategy whereby sympathy is elicited for Mariette
through a narrative identification with her point of view, which is withdrawn
whenever her character is too submissive, too complicitous with her ill-treatment.
This is one way of juggling irreconcilable subject positions: Colet wants to re-
count, from a feminine subject position, what it is like for a woman to live out the
plots written for her by men, but if she carries through to the traditional end point
without a twist, in order to show how well women have learned these plots, she
ends up replicating them.[17] This is why her narrator vacillates between identification with Mariette's suffering and repudiation of her weakness. To take up resi-
dence in either one of these positions would necessitate a choice between female-
associated submissiveness and male-associated critical distance: to write *as* a
woman or to write *for* a woman. Either stance reproduces patriarchal boundaries.[18] It is important that we recognize the systematic and strategic recurrence of
this kind of narrative maneuver, for the alternative is a naive and misogynistic mis-
reading that bypasses narratorial mediation in order to identify Colet thoroughly
and completely with her heroine.[19]

The death plot continues throughout the narrative to divide Mariette and the
narrator; it creates an internal struggle for control that no doubt reflects unresolved
narrative ambivalence. *La Servante* successfully resists Mariette's death, but not

[17] This writing experience would be an extreme version of the reading experience of split consciousness
that Judith Fetterley has dubbed *immasculation*, which consists of woman's being "co-opted into participating in an experience from which she is explicitly excluded; she is asked to identify with a selfhood
that defines itself in opposition to her; she is required to identify against herself." Fetterley, *The Resisting Reader* (Bloomington: Indiana University Press, 1978), xx, xii.

[18] The dilemma is current in contemporary feminist theory and has been formulated by Carol Thomas
Neely as "the dangers of being boxed in or locked out." Neely, "Feminist Modes of Shakespearean Criticism," *Women's Studies* 9 (1981): 5. See Toril Moi's suggestive discussion of Luce Irigaray's attempts to
escape specular constructions of femininity in Moi, *Sexual/Textual Politics* (London: Methuen, 1985),
137–39. See, too, Shoshana Felman's interrogation of Irigaray's positioning of herself as woman/the-
orist, echoed by Moi as by myself, in Felman, *La Folie et la chose littéraire* (Paris: Seuil, 1978), 140–
41. For a fascinating account of a similar attempt to combine conflicting subject positions, see Susan
McClary's analysis of Madonna's video, "Living to Tell," in *Feminine Endings*, 155–61.

[19] The unfortunate tendency to conflate female authors with their heroines, perhaps more pronounced
when a text is as polemical as *La Servante*, has no less misogynistic implications when practiced by a
woman than by a man. See Marie-Claude Schapira's "Peut-on encore lire *La Servante*," in Bellet,
Femmes de lettres. For some provocative comments on the assumption that women's fiction is necessarily autobiographical, see Christine Planté's article "Marceline Desbordes-Valmore: L'autobiographie
indéfinie," *Romantisme* 56 (1987): 47–58.

for lack of a death wish on her part. We see her on three separate occasions in the narrative leaning over parapets, lingering longingly at the edge of the river, as if teasing, defying the narrator; on the second of these occasions, she leaps, only to be saved from drowning by a narrator determined not to give in to this plot, even if she is tempted to play with it.

By the time Mariette has been plucked out of the Seine and married to a corpse, she has been essentially disengaged from the conventions of female plot. Denied death, widowed without having known marriage, she has bypassed narrative convention; she has outlived her plot. She is left in a literal no-man's land outside plot, outside language: it is the women's hospital called the Salpêtrière. There is a third alternative to female death and female submission: it is madness. But whereas death and marriage are closural states, bringing about narrative resolution, madness is a gaping space, a yawning question. The textual blank separating the double scene of Mariette's marriage to Lionel and his death from the Salpêtrière scenes corresponds to the lacuna that is madness. The text does not speak the cause of Mariette's folly; it simply moves into it.

Though female madness has been seen by some as woman's revolt against patriarchy, I do not want to champion Mariette's case, when I call it an *alternative* to death and marriage, as an overcoming of constraints or a celebration of the instinctual.[20] It seems particularly clear, in the present context, that madness is what is in excess of plot, or more specifically, that it is the price exacted for living outside plot. It is less a sign of successful revolt than a symptom of the ills incurred for venturing into a region beyond or between cultural codes. Such a region is reached in *La Servante* by means of a mythic journey into language.

REINVENTING LANGUAGE

What I have been calling the madness plot in *La Servante* is named for its end point; however, its evolution can be traced throughout the narrative inasmuch as it corresponds to a mythological voyage into language and then out again on the far side. The saga of Mariette is recounted in terms of a gendered passage from country to city, nature to culture, mother to father, concrete to abstract, unity to separation, imaginary to symbolic, voice to book. We see dramatized here—but also revised—a gendered myth of language acquisition that has changed little from the fiction of Colet's era to the theory of our own.[21] Given that Colet writes from the

[20] See Hélène Cixous and Catherine Clément, *La Jeune Née* (Paris: 10/18, 1975), for a debate on the hysteric as heroine/victim.

[21] In spite of the essential continuity, I will avoid the inevitably teleological approach that consists of fitting Colet's rendition of the myth within a contemporary theoretical framework. Although I cannot avoid looking back through my contemporary lens and will make comparisons to contemporary theory along the way, I want to give priority, inasmuch as is possible, to Colet's early version of the myth.

paradoxical position of a woman writing about a woman striving to write in an order in which woman and writing are incompatible categories, revision is inevitable; however, it should not be construed as deconstruction. As Colet shuttles her character between a presymbolic language represented as natural, material, fluid, embodied, and wordless, and a symbolic language represented as cultural, abstract, preinscribed, cerebral, and articulate, she reproduces conventional dualistic gender codes even as she valorizes them differently.[22]

Before turning to Mariette's wanderings in language, I want to make two qualifying points about Colet's occasional complicity with the patriarchal codes and conventions against which she is struggling. First, I want to argue that she is writing in large part as a witness, with the purpose of exposing rather than condoning such codes and conventions. This stance is most clear when she has her narrator explicitly distinguish her voice and perspective from Mariette's. If we take the discovery of the *Mariette* text as a model for this process, we might say, using Judith Fetterley's terms, that whereas Mariette is an assenting reader of this embedded text, the narrator positions herself as a resisting reader.[23] While this is the position she generally maintains throughout the narration, there are moments that appear to me (from my vantage point as a late twentieth-century reader) as lapses in her feminist reading, as a slackening of her resistance. This brings me to my second point, which is simply a reminder of the extent to which the voice of resistance adopted by a woman writing within male cultural, social, and literary conventions must systematically and painstakingly unbind itself from a tradition of assent. There is a good possibility that Colet was simply not a strong enough writer to emerge triumphant from a verbal battle with culture, for victory would have necessitated that she unlearn or unwrite the inflections of compliance contained within every utterance.

As Margaret Homans has pointed out, "although women writers past and present have made important and bold attempts to give voice to women's silenced story, we will perhaps never know the extent to which such revisionary myths (based on women's 'experience') have unintentionally reinscribed the pervasive androcen-

---

[22] It is interesting to note that the textual object of gender dichotomization for Flaubert is essentially conceived in terms of style, while for Colet it is more fundamentally voice. Although there is a certain amount of mixing (voice and style are at times presented as overlapping areas), the distinction strikes me as significant because it reflects the unquestioned assumption of voice for and by the male subject and its uncertainty for the female subject. On the prevalence of voice as metaphor in women's discourse and thinking, see Mary Field Belenky, Blythe McVicker Clinchy, Nancy Rule Goldberger, and Jill Mattuck Tarule, *Women's Ways of Knowing* (New York: Basic Books, 1986).

[23] In *The Resisting Reader*, Fetterley contends that the feminist critic must begin by becoming a resisting rather than an assenting reader, thereby beginning to exorcise the internalized male mind. She elaborates: "While women obviously cannot rewrite literary works so that they become ours by virtue of reflecting our reality, we can accurately name the reality they do reflect and so change literary criticism from a closed conversation to an active dialogue" (xxii–xxiii).

trism of our culture."[24] Inasmuch as my own discourse is, like Colet's, circumscribed by androcentric culture, but unlike Colet's, dually circumscribed because
I speak also from within a now institutionalized feminist subculture, my blind
spots are potentially doubled. Like Colet, I am in danger of unwittingly reinscrib-
ing androcentrism within my intentionally feminist reading. But also, because of
my own double inscription, I may unintentionally misread as points of resistance—as protofeminist attestations to the constraints of patriarchy—passages in
which Colet inadvertently relapses into androcentric conventions. These are risks
I can signal but not avoid. They usefully echo Colet's sense of finding her every
discursive venture recuperated by a preconstituted containing discourse.

Mariette's trajectory in language bears the shape of a revisionary family romance.
She moves out from an initial mother-identified state of preverbal communion
with nature to a liminal ground of literary aspirations that can begin to be realized
only upon the death of her mother. At that point, reborn in an aristocratic milieu
(but ironically as servant), she enters the realm of symbolic language under the illusory patronage of the lover who is author of her identity if not of her days. However, she can neither fully accede to the symbolic nor reenter the repudiated presymbolic domain, and caught between the two but belonging to neither, she falls
outside language into madness. I want to follow this four-stage itinerary in closer
detail, paying particular attention to its sharply dichotomous gendered spheres of
language.

For the child Mariette growing up in the provincial countryside, the world is
split into realities of mother and fantasies of otherness, the other world associated
with books, reading, education, and escape to Paris. The polarities are neatly represented in the first few lines, where we find Mariette and her childhood friend
Théréson posed in front of the village church, watching the coach setting off for
Paris. Mariette's aspirations are further defined, first in positive terms as bibliophi-
lia ("Mon voeu serait de vivre et de me renfermer / Dans cette salle au nord pleine
de livres rares" [201] ["My wish would be to live and to close myself off / In that
north room full of rare books"]), then in negative terms as the dismissal of her
suitor Julien on grounds of illiteracy ("Il ne sait pas lire" [207]).

With remarkable consistency, Mariette represents her mother as the obstacle
keeping her from the larger world of Paris and books. To Théréson's evocations of
Paris, she wistfully if dutifully responds: "A ma mère malade il faut songer avant"
(199) ["I must first think of my ailing mother"]; and to her employer's invitation to
serve in Paris, "Oh! moi, c'est ma plus chère envie / Mais ma mère est infirme, elle
mourrait sans moi" (204) ["Oh! as for me, that is my dearest wish / But my mother

---

[24] Margaret Homans, *Bearing the Word* (Chicago: University of Chicago Press, 1986), 14–15.

is ill, she would die without me"]. Momentarily deranged by the force of desire awakened in her by the discovery of Lionel's novel ("son coeur palpitait / Des désirs éveillés dans son âme de vierge; / Ce livre, ce voyage à Paris" [204] ["her heart palpitated / From the desires awakened in her virgin soul; / This book, this trip to Paris"]), Mariette reveals to her mother what is tantamount to an inverted death wish for her: "—'Ah! si vous guérissiez, je partirais comme elle'" (204) ["'Ah! if you were to get well, I would leave as she did'"]. Immediately repentant, torn between contrition and desire, pulled between mother and book, Mariette is for a time alternately nurse and reader:

> Elle ne quitta plus la malade affaiblie;
> Près d'elle elle faisait sa couture le jour
> Et relisait le soir, ardemment recueilli,
> Sans jamais se lasser son beau livre d'amour.   (205)

> *She no longer left the weakened patient;*
> *Beside her she did her sewing in the daytime*
> *And at night in ardent silence reread*
> *Her beautiful love story, never tiring of it.*

Soon afterward, however, her mother silently succumbs.[25] The mother's muffled moans and quiet death recede before the printed word when a letter fortuitously arrives summoning Mariette to serve the marquise in Paris. In a final apposition of motherworld and otherworld, girlish chastity and literary seduction, Mariette prepares for her departure by packing side by side the dress in which her mother robed her for her communion, and Lionel's novel: "Elle mit dans la malle, / Près du livre d'amour, la robe virginale" (207) ["She packed in her trunk / Next to the love story,

---

[25] Compare in the following citations the silence that surrounds the mother's death with Lionel's noisy passing:

> La mourante expira sans dire une parole.
> Une voisine entra. —"Silence! parlons bas!"
> Murmurait Mariette.   (206)

> *The dying woman expired without a word.*
> *A neighbor entered. "Silence! let us speak softly!"*
> *Murmured Mariette.*

> Et sa voix, où déjà le râle vient courir,
> Stridente, répétait: "Je ne veux pas mourir!"   (241)

> *And his voice, already traversed by the death rale,*
> *Repeated stridently: "I do not want to die!"*

the virginal dress"]. The apposition reveals itself more specifically as opposition when Mariette, book in hand and Paris bound, turns her back on her mother's house:

> Derrière elle éclata comme un bruit de sanglots:
> Elle crut que c'était sa pauvre mère morte
> Pleurant sur son départ et venant l'empêcher.   (207)

> *Behind her a sobbing sound burst forth,*
> *She thought it was her poor dead mother*
> *Crying over her departure and coming to stop her.*

As I follow Mariette's passage to a Paris represented by books, writing, artful language, and hypocrisy, I want particularly to emphasize the ways in which Colet apposes that sphere to the more dominant maternal voices of Mariette's early years; I want also to suggest that these two apposed spheres anticipate the domains that have more recently been theorized as *imaginary* and *symbolic* in Lacan's terms, and *semiotic* and *symbolic* in Kristeva's. I will be using the terms *presymbolic* and *symbolic* to avoid specifically aligning Colet's myth with Lacan or Kristeva so as not to inscribe it within a critical discourse that evolved more than a century later.[26]

Let us then consider closely Mariette's "mother tongue": the generally wordless, sometimes silent, but always transparent voice of nature. Mariette's childhood language is described as song ("Parler, c'est comme un air qu'on chante et qui console" [199]) ["Speaking is like singing a soothing melody"]. It is set against whispering breezes and singing birds and is itself compared to the babbling of finches (202). Mariette's wordless communion with the voices of nature is interrupted quite explicitly by her sighting of *Mariette*. The written word effectively silences nature's voice for her, as it will quite literally suppress the mother tongue, though Théréson stands by disapprovingly and insists: "J'aime mieux ma chanson" (203) ["I prefer my song"].

Now the parallels between Colet's story of a passage from a phase of preverbal communion to one of communication in language and the Lacanian and Kristevan narratives of a child's insertion into the symbolic order through a paternal interruption of the mother-child dyad and suppression of the maternal sphere attest

---

[26] Jane Gallop distinguishes Kristeva's *semiotic* from Lacan's *imaginary* as being a more positively valorized (more revolutionary, less closed) order. Jane Gallop, *The Daughter's Seduction: Feminism and Psychoanalysis* (Ithaca: Cornell University Press, 1982), 124.

to the consistency and longevity of cultural myth.[27] Colet's version, however, presents a few critical variants that dislocate the customary structural elements, serving to denaturalize a too-familiar story.

First, there is no father in *La Servante*, no figure of the Law to sever mother and daughter, no *nom du père* to inscribe the daughter as a separate being within language. Mariette, "little Mary" (by implication, "little mother"), bears no patronymic, and places herself under the sign of the mother in a rhetorical move that feminizes—maternalizes—the *pater* in the very act of naming him: "Marie est ma *patronne*," she declares (201; my emphasis). To anticipate charges of reading too literally, let me pass quickly to a more substantive matter for which the missing father is only a superficial sign. If Mariette's linguistic course runs parallel to contemporary theories of a passage from presymbolic plenitude to symbolic loss, it diverges from the theorized passage insofar as the move from presymbolic to symbolic for Mariette is gradual, nonviolent, and, most notably, initiated by the mother (that is, by nature as her surrogate). Prior to discovering the Book, but subsequent to acknowledging her yearning for books, Mariette, like so many other nineteenth-century heroines, sits before the open window communing with the world outside her confined sphere:

> Et les brises du soir qui venaient de la rive
> Avaient avec son coeur d'intimes entretiens.
> Que lui disiez-vous donc, ô voix de la nature,
> Longs échos alternés de la terre et de Dieu,
> Pour faire ainsi monter cette humble créature
> De sa calme ignorance à des rêves de feu?
> Elle ne connaissait encor que l'Evangile,
> Quelque récit naïf des conteurs allemands,
> Et la limpidité de son âme tranquille
> Ne s'était pas émue au trouble des romans.
> Pourtant vous l'attiriez et vous l'aviez saisie,
> Impétueux courant des coeurs faits pour aimer!
> Orages de l'amour et de la poésie,
> Elle vous pressentait sans pouvoir vous nommer!

[27] Freud's version of this myth equates the progress of civilization with a move from the material to the spiritual sphere, which he respectively qualifies as maternal and paternal. *Moses and Monotheism*, in *The Standard Edition of the Complete Works of Sigmund Freud*, trans. James Strachey, Anna Freud, Alix Strachey, and Alan Tyson, ed. James Strachey, 24 vols. (London: Hogarth, 1953–74), 23:112–15. For a good summary of the connections between culture and the mother's suppression, see Homans, *Bearing the Word*, 1–39.

Elle resta longtemps la tête rayonnante,
Comme voyant flotter son rêve au firmament,
Puis dans son petit lit s'endormit souriante,
Et les voix de son coeur lui parlaient en dormant.   (201–2)

> And the evening breezes that came from the shore
> Conversed intimately with her heart.
> What did you say to her, voices of nature,
> Echoing alternately from earth and from God,
> To make this humble creature rise up
> From her calm ignorance to burning dreams?
> She didn't yet know anything but the Gospel,
> And some German folk tales,
> And the limpidity of her tranquil soul
> Had not yet been stirred to excitement by novels.
> Yet you drew her and you seized her,
> Impetuous current of hearts made to love!
> Storms of love and of poetry,
> She sensed you without being able to name you!
> Her face radiant, she lingered,
> As if she saw her dream floating in the heavens,
> Then she fell asleep smiling in her small bed,
> And her heart's voices spoke to her as she slept.

I have quoted this passage in its entirety not only because it describes a prelapsarian (because prenovelistic) Mariette not yet fully inscribed in the symbolic order, still held in a symbiotic unity with a nature that converses wordlessly and intimately with her, but also because it implies that her aspirations to pass into the symbolic order emanate from within, and are generated by the maternally associated preverbal sphere. ("Que lui disiez-vous donc, ô voix de la nature / . . . Pour faire ainsi monter cette humble créature / De sa calme ignorance à des rêves de feu?") This is an effective rewriting of the myth, for it displaces the father's role as language giver, attributing this function instead to the mother's sphere, and signaling that the entry into the symbolic order is gradually prepared rather than precipitated by a rupture.[28]

---

[28] As Kaja Silverman more generally remarks, "[The mother] is traditionally first language teacher, commentator, and storyteller—the one who first organizes the world linguistically for the child, and first presents it to the Other. . . . The theoretical . . . equation of the maternal voice with 'pure sonorousness' must therefore be understood not as an extension of its intrinsic nature, or of its acoustic function, but as part of a larger cultural disavowal of the mother's role both as an agent of discourse and as a model for linguistic . . . identification." Silverman, *The Acoustic Mirror: The Female Voice in Psychoanalysis and Cinema* (Bloomington: Indiana University Press, 1988), 100.

Mariette's entry into the symbolic coincides with her cogito—her self-recognition in *Mariette*—and is therefore arguably signed by the book's author, "Lionel de V." But this surrogate *nom du père* becomes significant, becomes the sign of the new order into which she moves only because promptings from within the presymbolic order have already oriented her in this direction.

Mariette's sojourn in Paris, in writing, in the symbolic order is marked by disillusion, by alienation, by incompleteness, and by a sense of irretrievable loss. Whereas the voices of nature were transparent for her and rendered meaning immediate, meaning in Paris is mediated by an opaque language that cosmeticizes and distorts truth. Lionel's writing is the prime example of a pervasive disjunction of language and truth, appearance and reality. His poetry serves him well "pour farder en public un acte malséant" (217) ["to prettify an unseemly act to the public"]. His discourse is characterized by its duplicity, by a perpetual split between words and acts, language and sentiments: "Sa prose et ses vers juraient étrangement / Avec tous les instincts de son tempérament" (209) ["His prose and his verses clashed curiously / With all the instincts of his temperament"]. Lionel is a false mirror, a deforming echo:

> De tout ce qui séduit être l'écho sonore
> Et le semblant ému de tout ce qu'on adore
> Dire en accents profonds l'amour et la vertu
> Et les fouler aux pieds lorsque le chant s'est tu.   (218)

> *To be the sonorous echo of all that is seductive*
> *And the semblance of all that is tender and lovable*
> *To speak in reverent tones of love and virtue*
> *And to stomp on them when the song is over.*

The double face of language comes most clearly into view for Mariette when she understands that the lure of *Mariette* was false: she has entered into the promised language as object but not subject. Mariette might have yearned to be a poet and a poem, to paraphrase A. S. Byatt, but the lesson to be learned is that she can never author her own text.[29] She dares initially to dream of a partnership in letters, even after she has become resigned to submission in love:

> Elle rêvait déjà, doucement attendrie,
> Qu'après l'humble labeur, l'étude aurait son tour.   (217)

[29] In A. S. Byatt's novel *Possession* (New York: Random House, 1990), her character Ellen, the wife of a famous poet, writes of such adolescent ambitions in her journal (136). See epigraph to Chapter 3 (55, *supra*) for full citation.

> *Moved to sweet tears, she already dreamed*
> *That after her humble toil she would have a chance to study.*

But Lionel's response is negative:

> Mais à peine elle eut dit la première parole
> De ce secret espoir, qu'il s'écria, railleur:
> "Ça, la belle, ai-je l'air d'être un maître d'école?"   (218)

> *But scarcely had she spoken the first word*
> *Of her secret hope when he cried out mockingly,*
> *"Well, now, my dear, do I look like a schoolmaster?"*

Needless to say, Mariette will never be admitted to the subject position she seeks in language, although she does accede to a new position in language when she transcribes the words of a Lionel who is too drunk to handle a pen:

> "Pensez tout haut, et moi j'écrirai près de vous!
> Vous, l'esprit, moi, la main, cela me sera doux!"   (227)

> *"Think aloud, and I will write beside you!*
> *You, the mind, I, the hand—that will be sweet to me!"*

The role of amanuensis ironically realizes Mariette's desire to write, by literalizing it. The act that would serve to transcend her female destiny serves instead to materialize it.[30]

Mariette never completes the transition from presymbolic to symbolic, from matter to spirit, from concrete to abstract. Alienated within the order to which she aspired, she seeks traces of the maternally figured order she abandoned. She is in fact haunted by the sense of a lost plenitude whose absence phantasmatically intrudes upon her present:

> Mariette est en pleurs. Dans cette ville amère,
> Elle se sent frémir: elle croit voir sa mère,
> Comme si de sa tombe elle se relevait.   (219)

---

[30] Margaret Homans would perhaps read Mariette's role of scribe differently, for in *Bearing the Word* she suggests that a female author's representation of a female character as scribe constitutes a literalization of writing, and hence a recuperation of the maternal and the presymbolic (31–32). Despite my agreement with many of Homans's points, I cannot read Mariette's function as Lionel's amanuensis as other than an ironic degradation of her aspirations.

Mariette is in tears. In this harsh city,
She shudders; thinking she sees her mother,
As if she were rising from the grave.

Nostalgia repeatedly seizes upon the mother as the figure of disappeared unity:

Elle se souvenait de sa pure chimère
Qui riait sur les flots du grand Rhin écumant;
Aux bords du fleuve assise elle voyait sa mère,
Elle entendait Julien l'appeler tristement.
Ce n'est plus ton vieux Rhin, ce n'est plus ta jeunesse
Ce fleuve, ces palais se déroulant au loin;
Ces marbres, ces jardins que la lune caresse,
C'est Paris endormi qui ne te connaît point!   (224; my emphasis)

She remembered her pure chimera
That laughed on the streams of the great foaming Rhine;
She saw her mother sitting on the banks of the river,
She heard Julien sadly calling her.
This is no longer your Rhine, this is no longer your youth,
This river, these palaces looming in the distance,
These marble statues, these gardens caressed by the moon,
This is Paris asleep and a stranger to you!

Even nostalgia, however, seems to recognize an element of mythic reconstruction ("sa pure chimère") in the image of the flowing mother waters and the childhood communion with an embracing nature; even nostalgia hears reason enough to place rupture and loss within nature rather than after the Fall: "Oh! trompeuse est la voix de toute la nature" ["Oh! the voice of nature is deceitful"], says the narrator as a prelude to her Rhineland ode (224).

In fact mother, nature, plenitude, unity, satiety become increasingly problematic concepts for Mariette—and increasingly mythic constructs for the narrator. Images of fertility become sterility, flow turned to aridity, and mother's milk drying up appear frequently:

L'espérance, ici-bas, est la mère commune,
Et sa mammelle à tous offre un lait savoureux.
Mais aux lèvres du pauvre, il s'épuise ou s'altère.   (225)

Hope here on earth is our common mother
And her breast offers sweet milk to all
But on the lips of the poor, it dries up or turns.

When in desperation Mariette throws herself into the Seine in an attempt to recuperate a primordial union, the nurturing fluid is no longer there; the riverbed is
a tomb:

> Seine, que nos aïeux nommaient la nourricière,
> Ton lit n'est aujourd'hui qu'un immense ossuaire!   (232)

> *Seine, that our ancestors called the nurturer,*
> *Your bed today is but an immense ossuary!*

What this suicide manqué makes clear is the utter estrangement of the maternal
order Mariette reaches futilely to retrieve through death. The desired pseudo-
uterine fusion with the Seine (reinforced by the textual play with associations
between the river Seine and *sein*, "womb" or "breast") is recontained by a male
weave. Let us not forget that *Seine* is also that seine or net most literally represented
by Julien's fishermanly rescue:

> Le plongeur, détournant le sinistre courant,
> De sa robuste main la ramène au rivage.   (232)

> *The diver, fighting the sinister current,*
> *Brings her back to the shore with his robust hand.*

The robust hand that replaces "l'étreinte des flots" (232) ["the embracing waters"] is
another avatar of the protean seine, succeeding the maternal forms.[31] The containing seine/hand can also be read as a figure for the enclosing text, the patriarchal tissue that inevitably reappropriates female voice as if to confirm that even
maternity is a paternal concept.

　　Although Mariette's rescue from the water and her brief retreat into Julien's family are represented as a potential rebirth ("A sa sereine enfance elle espéra renaître"
[233] ["She hoped to be reborn to her calm childhood"]), return is not possible:
there can be no recuperation of a remembered childhood plenitude because that
plenitude, as we have seen, exists only as retrospective illusion. The desire that
provoked Mariette's initial departure has now become the ennui of a *déclassée*. Her
despair prefigures that of Emma Bovary, whose bitter existence would soon be so

---

[31] At a later point in the text, when Mariette is again leaning over the river, tempted by its flow, Lionel
reappears and provides her with "une invincible étreinte" (236) ["an invincible embrace"] that replaces
the once and threatened future "étreinte des flots."

unappetizingly served to her on a dinner plate: "Toute l'amertume de l'existence lui semblait servie sur son assiette, et, à la fumée du bouilli, il montait du fond de son âme comme d'autres bouffées d'affadissement" ["All the bitterness of life seemed served up on her plate, and with the smoke of the boiled beef there rose from her secret soul waves of nauseous disgust"].[32] Like Emma, Mariette is overcome by waves of existential disgust that mingle with the coarse odors of Julien's peasant table:

> Les viandes et le lard répandaient leurs vapeurs,
> Et le vin renversé tachait la nappe grise;
> Sur le reste des mets s'allongeait un vieux chat;
> Julien fumait sa pipe avec un air béat.
> La chambre regorgeait de ces odeurs mêlées
> Sans souci d'élégance, en famille exhalées;
> Le dégoût lui montait de la lèvre au cerveau.   (233)

> *The meats and the lard gave off their fumes,*
> *And spilled wine spotted the gray cloth;*
> *An old cat stretched out over the leftovers;*
> *Julien smoked his pipe beatifically.*
> *The room reeked of these mingled odors*
> *Let out in the simple intimacy of home;*
> *Disgust rose from her mouth to her brain.*

Reinsertion in the maternal order is no more tenable than was inscription in the paternal:

> Elle ne pouvait plus goûter leur quiétude,
> Son coeur s'était rouvert aux rêves enflammés,
> A la voix de l'amour, à celle de l'étude,
> A tous les horizons qui leur étaient fermés!   (233–34)

> *She could no longer swallow their calm*
> *Her heart had reopened to fiery dreams*
> *To the voice of love, to the voice of study,*
> *To all the horizons that were closed to them!*

[32] Gustave Flaubert, *Madame Bovary*, ed. Jacques Suffel (Paris: Garnier Flammarion, 1979), 99; trans. Paul de Man (New York: Norton, 1965), 47.

At the close of this scene of rescue, failed rehabilitation, and redeparture, the text has come full circle but resolved nothing. Although Colet clearly makes the point that the world inside the Lionel book is not equal to its cover and that Mariette cannot reclaim her birthright because she sacrificed it, she establishes as well that Julien's simple heart and beatific smile are not enough to make his confined life palatable. The lack of narrative clarity about what the right choice would be corresponds to the onset of Mariette's madness, which is rooted in the imperative for an absolute choice between two alternatives that might be designated, in J. P. Möbius's turn-of-the-century medical terms, as *civilization* or *milk*: "Proportionately as 'civilization' advances, fertility declines, the better the schools, the worse the confinements, less becomes the secretion of milk."[33] The daughter who would make her home fully in the symbolic must kill the mother. The daughter who would continue to reside in the maternal sphere finds all horizons closed.[34] Mariette is caught, then, between two spheres, unable to appropriate either her memories or her dreams, her voice or her pen.

After she leaves Julien's farm, we find her poised on a hill contemplating Paris. This pose is more accurately an equipoise, the emblem of her suspension between feminine and masculine, country and city, nature and culture, wordless communication and linguistic opacity. It is also a caricature of her upward mobility, her social climbing. Correlatively, it prefigures the madness scene at the end of the text, in which the heroine must be physically bound by a straitjacket to keep her from clambering into the trees.

In the final scene, we find Mariette wandering barefoot and disheveled among the trees in the courtyard of the Salpêtrière, hair loose and flowing, wearing a crown of straw, weeping flowerlike tears and songlike sobs. She has been saved from drowning, only to become Ophelia.

REWRITING OPHELIA

La Servante is framed by a five-page introduction, in the form of the *Mariette* text, and a five-page epilogue, which is written in the shadow of the Ophelia story. Both stories constitute sanctified cultural models against which the body of *La Servante* must define itself. In fact the story of Ophelia, who, like Lionel's heroine, loves a poet and dies young, amplifies but does not diverge from the archetypal patterns of *Mariette*.

---

[33] J. P. Möbius, "The Physiological Mental Weakness of Women," *Alienist and Neurologist* 22 (1901): 634.

[34] See Jean Wyatt's *Reconstructing Desire: The Role of the Unconscious in Women's Reading and Writing* (Chapel Hill: University of North Carolina Press, 1990) for an excellent analysis of the dichotomous choices awaiting the daughter who chooses not to travel the preassigned feminine path.

Colet spars with Ophelia as she does with *Mariette*, engaging with her plot but fracturing it, embracing but dislocating its central elements—its madness, song, silence, fluidity, fusion with nature, betrayed love, death—elements whose recasting would have been all the more unsettling to contemporary readers because of their familiarity with the Ophelia plot and character. *Hamlet* had been rediscovered in France in 1827, in a production in which a young Irish actress, Harriet Smithson, stole the show as Ophelia.[35] Smithson's long black veil, straw-strewn hair, and poetic delirium took Paris by storm; they were widely reproduced in prints and paintings, popular lithographs, and fashion design.[36] Trendsetters sported a "coiffure à la folle"—a black veil "with wisps of straw tastefully interwoven in the hair"[37]—which is faithfully reproduced in Mariette's mad scene:

> Jusqu'au sol ses cheveux, tels qu'un voile de deuil,
> Traînaient y ramassant des brins d'herbe et de mousse.   (245)

> *Her hair, hanging like a mourning veil,*
> *Swept the ground, gathering wisps of grass and moss.*

The Ophelia figure continued to haunt the French imagination well after the 1827 ground-breaking performance, notably during the period leading up to her 1853–54 reappearance in *La Servante*. George Sand represented her in *Indiana* in 1832; Musset and Hugo alluded to her in the 30s and 40s; Delacroix executed a series of paintings and lithographs representing Ophelia in the 1830s–50s. And in 1836–39 Louise Colet was part of a team of translators who collaborated with D. O'Sullivan and M. Jay on an annotated edition of *Chefs-d'oeuvre de Shakespeare*. *Hamlet* was one of the works studied.[38]

So when Colet becomes Ophelia's narrator, she brings with her not only a stock familiarity with the popularized Smithson interpretation, but also an editorial knowledge of the play and consequently an authority that lends to her plot revi-

[35] The Smithson performance was the most dramatic moment in a more gradual repatriation of the Ophelia character, who was infinitely more appropriate to the romantic spirit than to the measured enlightenment mind. See James M. Vest's *The French Face of Ophelia from Belleforest to Baudelaire* (Lanham, N.Y.: University Press of America, 1989) for the fascinating history of her vicissitudes.

[36] Smithson's Ophelia dominated theatrical, medical, pictorial, and literary iconography of the character for generations—arguably until well into the twentieth century. Elaine Showalter points out that Jean Simmons's Ophelia in the Laurence Olivier film of 1948 is still dominated by Smithson's interpretation of the role. Showalter, "Representing Ophelia: Women, Madness, and the Responsibilities of Feminist Criticism," in *Shakespeare and the Question of Theory*, ed. Patricia Parker and Geoffrey Hartman (London: Methuen, 1985), 83. See, too, Bram Dijkstra's account of Ophelia's nineteenth-century fortune, in *Idols of Perversity* (Oxford: Oxford University Press, 1986).

[37] Showalter, "Representing Ophelia," 83.

[38] Vest, *The French Face of Ophelia*, 148.

sions an element of both calculation and consequence. Her portrait of Mariette at the Salpêtrière, with her hair hanging long and unbound, is particularly obedient to Elizabethan conventions of representation, which coded disheveled hair as a sign of immodesty and sensuality often indicative of female dementia.[39] Her allusions to the gentleness of Mariette's madness—"Si doux et si placide est son égarement" (245) ["Her derangement is so placid and docile"]—also reflect the Shakespearean model, as does the Daphne-like fusing of woman and tree that we see in the affinity of Mariette's own limbs for tree limbs.[40]

The iconographically correct detail of Colet's Ophelia renders her plot modifications all the more conspicuous. Her most flagrant alterations—the transposition of the mad scene and the drowning scene and the transformation of lethal drowning into drowning manqué—give pause for thought. The interrupted suicide must be viewed as more than a response to a larger narrative tradition of women sacrificed to men's plots. It is also, more specifically, a reflection on an abiding association—generally inscribed in the discourse of hysteria and particularly imprinted upon Flaubert's thoughts about Colet's feminine style—of women with water and all things flowing.

Colet's invocation of Ophelia in response to Flaubert's denigration of her overflowing *style féminin* fights water with water. If Ophelia's drowning represents "the [masculine] necessity of drowning both words and feelings," as David Leverenz has argued, and further constitutes "a microcosm of the male world's banishment of the female, because 'woman' represents everything denied by reasonable men," then the homeopathic drowning of drowning that Colet writes into her Ophelia is a rescue operation: it combs not only the river for the heroine's body, but also her tears, for the feelings they contain, and her voice, for the drift of its words.[41] Mariette is an Ophelia who will not drown.

[39] See Maurice Charney and Hanna Charney, "The Language of Madwomen in Shakespeare and His Fellow Dramatists," *Signs* 3 (Winter 1977): 451–60. Note also the earlier portrait of Mariette, in the drowning scene, where her long hair is floating perilously toward the wheel of a mill (*La Servante*, 232).

[40] Woman as tree was a topos in nineteenth-century art and literature, a subset of the woman and nature theme. See Dijkstra, *Idols*, 93–101. Note also the similar allusion to the representation of Ophelia not only wearing but becoming the flowers that garland her, in Colet's description of Mariette's tears: "ses larmes sont les fleurs qui couronnent son front" (245).

[41] David Leverenz, "The Woman in *Hamlet*: An Interpersonal View," *Signs* 4 (Winter 1978): 303. Leverenz is referring specifically to Laertes' expression of grief at Ophelia's death:

> Too much of water hast thou, poor Ophelia,
> And therefore I forbid my tears; but yet
> It is our trick; nature her custom holds,
> Let shame say what it will: when these are gone,
> The woman will be out.

Shakespeare, *Hamlet*, ed. Edward Hubler (New York: Signet, 1963), 4.7.185–89.

That *La Servante* has at its core a woman's unsuccessful attempt to return to a feminine source is especially poignant in the light of Flaubert's reading of this text, in the *Correspondance*, as emblematic of a generalized cultural tendency toward effusiveness. The text of *La Servante*, in fact, moves like a thirsting Tantalus between wetness and dryness, flowing substances and desiccation. When Mariette turns her back on the maternal countryside for the city and the book, the omnipresent tears turn to ice. Although it is the kind of day "où tout semble pleurer" ["on which everything seems to weep"], as she departs, "la glace et le verglas couvraient le grand chemin" (207) ["ice and frost covered the highway"].[42] Mariette's Parisian debacle is repeatedly figured as lakes drying out or clear waters turning to mud. Here is the evocation of Lionel's debauchery:

> Tel on voit d'un beau lac quand l'eau vive est tarie
> Sur la vase monter les vapeurs des bas-fonds,
> Et sa rive autrefois verdoyante et fleurie
> Etale l'herbe sèche aux squelettes des joncs.   (212)

> *Just as one sees, when the source of a beautiful lake has dried up,*
> *The swamp vapors rising above the mud,*
> *And its formerly green and flowering bank*
> *Displaying dried grass and the skeletons of jonquils.*

Similarly, here is the image of Mariette's disillusionment:

> Mais voici qu'au matin, quand la paupière s'ouvre,
> Le beau fleuve limpide est un torrent fangeux.   (219)

> *But in the morning the eye opens to see*
> *That the beautiful clear river is a muddy torrent.*

And let us not forget that the life-giving, maternally-figured Seine becomes a bed of dry bones when Mariette plunges into its waters.

Bachelard calls water "le symbole profond, organique de la femme qui ne sait que *pleurer* ses peines et dont les yeux sont si facilement 'noyés de larmes'" ["the profound, organic symbol of woman who only can *weep* her suffering and whose eyes are so easily 'drowned with tears'"], and he refers to Laertes' grief before Ophelia's suicide as a sign of what is feminine in him, adding, "Il redevient homme—en redevenant 'sec'—quand les larmes ont tari" ["He becomes a man again—by 'drying out'—when his tears have dried up"]. Gaston Bachelard, *L'Eau et les rêves* (Paris: Corti, 1960), 113.

[42] Luce Irigaray has written some suggestive pages on the association of the feminine with the fluid, the masculine with the solid, and the privileging of the latter. Irigaray, *This Sex Which Is Not One*, trans. Catherine Porter with Carolyn Burke (Ithaca: Cornell University Press, 1985), 106–18.

So the drowning of drowning or the recuperation of the feminine never effectively happens in *La Servante*, and one might argue that Colet's narrative, like its
Shakespearean intertext, speaks ultimately to the "dissociation of sensibility" that
Leverenz locates in *Hamlet* as dichotomies of "role and self, reason and nature,
mind and body, manly and womanly, or the language of power and the language
of feeling."[43] It is in this dissociative state, this space of limbo between womanly
and manly codes that can never coincide, that Mariette's madness must be located.

The originality of Colet's representation of madness is that it is not defined, as is
usually the case, as that which speaks in woman's tongues, but rather as that which
lies in between feminine and masculine language. Feminine madness in Colet—
that reader's disease, dreamer's mobility, flowing sensibility, and inevitable silence,
forerunner of what would soon be popularized as hysteria—is a space of entrap-
ment, a snare that prevents free passage between feminine- and masculine-
identified states. By rooting Mariette's madness in the experience of reading (the
word *folle* significantly makes its first appearance in the text as Mariette finishes
Lionel's novel)[44] Colet both replicates and dislocates commonly accepted ideas
about the place of reading in the etiology of female hysteria. She attributes to the
novel a role in the evolution of Mariette's illness, but makes it clear that madness
occurs because the horizons opened by her reading are otherwise closed to her.
This amounts to an inversion of the establishment account, according to which
hysteria ensues when the horizons normatively closed to women are opened—
torn or rent—by novel reading.[45] Madness for Colet is that state or space of alienation that cannot be accommodated within either feminine or masculine spheres,
plots, or languages and that therefore results in the gaping openness, excess, and
muteness of the unencoded.

It is to achieve this sense of uncontainedness that Colet reorders Ophelia so that
her madness is no longer that which leads to another action (her suicide) and is
thereby subsumed or recontained by it. The madness of Colet's Mariette instead
stands alone outside enclosing structures, and resists closure. Colet's ironic strat-

[43] Leverenz, "The Woman in *Hamlet*," 308.
[44]
Elle [Mariette] ferma le livre,
Et le baisant le mit sur un beau mouchoir blanc.
"Es-tu folle?" dit l'autre [Théréson].   (204)

She closed the book,
And kissing it, placed it on a fine white handkerchief.
"Are you mad?" asked the other.
[45] This gap is later described by Baudelaire, another writer who understood hysteria well, as "un monde
où l'action n'est pas la soeur du rêve" ["a world in which action is not sister to dreaming"]. Baudelaire,
"Le Reniement de Saint Pierre," in *Oeuvres complètes*, ed. Claude Pichois (Paris: Gallimard, 1975–
76), 1:121–22.

egy in the last few pages of the text is to multiply discrete signs of enclosure (Mariette's straitjacket, Lionel's ring on her finger, the cell into which she is thrown in the last line of the text) that, in a more global sense, are completely powerless to contain or to structure the formless space of Mariette's madness.

Mariette at the Salpêtrière is twice removed from the maternal sphere of communication (she has twice repudiated it) and no longer inscribed in Lionel's text (when he dies, she is no longer within his frame). In her course from mother to father to limbo, she has moved from the plenitude of preverbal voice to the written word and then to incoherence. I want to insist that the fall outside language into the Salpêtrière is not a return to the source, to the silent communion of natural/maternal voice, but a plunge into a communicatory void.

Colet presents the Salpêtrière as a city of silence, a place where "tout bruit se tait" (242) ["all sound is silenced"]. Within the single page that introduces this scene, there are five references to the muted tongues and lives found there.[46] When sound is heard at all, it is babble or animal-like inarticulate noise. We hear the inmates "poussant des cris aigus comme le chat-huant" ["crying sharply like owls"] and "glapissant ou criant de bizarres paroles" (244) ["yelping or shouting strange words"]. The only other sound is song, as in the case of the idiots "chantant un refrain gai sur de plaintives notes" (244) ["singing a gay refrain in plaintive tones"] or, in the case of Mariette, whose own silence is broken by the metaphorical song of her sobs:

> Sa souffrance aujourd'hui, c'est sa beauté qui brille,
> Ses larmes sont les fleurs qui couronnent son front.
> Ses sanglots ignorés sont des chants magnifiques
> Que ceux de son amant n'égalèrent jamais.   (245)

> *Her beauty shines in her suffering today.*
> *Her tears are flowers that crown her brow.*
> *Her unheard sobs are magnificent songs*
> *That never were equaled by those of her lover.*

Here it is important to remember that music is traditionally associated with the irrational and with the feminine.[47] So when Mariette's weeping is exalted as song, I think we have to hear, beneath the trite romantic apotheosis of melancholy, the

[46] In addition to the citation given in the text, we read: "Drames froids et muets"; "Elles ne parlent pas"; "On n'entend pas leur plainte"; "A l'heure des repas, dans les longs réfectoires, / S'ouvrent, sans se parler, mille bouches sans dents" ["Cold mute dramas"; "They do not speak"; "Their plaint is not heard"; "At mealtime in the long refectories / A thousand toothless mouths open without speaking"] (242–43).

[47] See McClary, *Feminine Endings*; and Charney and Charney, "The Language of Madwomen."

128

•

echo of Ophelia's singing. Her echoing song serves not only as a textual acknowl-
edgment of Mariette's discursive breakdown (song being understood as the pure sonority of voice deprived of signifying content), but also as a reminder of the nexus,
embodied by her story, of women, madness, fluidity, and song.[48] The link between
fluidity and voice is especially pronounced in these verses, for the passage from
Mariette's suffering, shining beauty—which evokes tears without naming them—
to her tears, now named, then on to her sobs, and finally to her song, first phrases
female voice as inarticulate flow and then rephrases female fluidity as vocalization
and even, as "song," as incipient art. Colet's penultimate articulation—and ultimate revision—of this connection between voice and flow furnishes the grounds
for some concluding remarks. Her tendency to render creativity in metaphors of
voice (language and body) must be seen as a response to Flaubert's recourse, in his
own representations of creativity, to metaphors of flow.

RESTYLING VOICE: BETWEEN LANGUAGE AND BODY

When Julian Barnes translates the desired effect of Flaubert's fantasized "roaring
style," he replaces the French verb *dominer* with the English "to drown" rather
than with the more literal "to overpower" or "to dominate": "Still, I feel that I
mustn't die without making sure that the style I can hear inside my head comes
roaring out and drowns the cries of parrots and cicadas."[49] Barnes's translation
moves us from an apparent figuration of style as voice back to the underlying metaphoric pool from which Flaubert's discussions of creative power more commonly
derive. Whether fortuitous or cannily deliberate, his translation has the merit of
reminding us of the rhetorical alchemy by which Flaubert consistently turns female voice into fluid, in this way not only liquefying but liquidating it, as if to dissolve the Medusa he specifically embodied in Colet's voice when he wrote that it
had "un pouvoir . . . à faire dresser les pierres" (1:287, 11 August 1846) ["the
power to make stones rise"]. Colet reverses the metamorphosis when she trans-
forms flow into voice, albeit negativized voice. For although, as I have argued, the
voice we hear at the end of *La Servante* is wordless, Colet's narrator makes madness speak by framing its speechlessness.

   The transmutability of female vocality and fluidity speaks to an age-old mythic
construction serving to naturalize a cultural representation of women's voices as

---

[48] On the association of music with women, materiality, and sexuality, see McClary, *Feminine Endings*; Silverman, *Acoustic Mirror*; and Guy Rosolato, "La Voix: Entre corps et langage," *Revue française de psychanalyse* 37 (1974): 75–94.
[49] Julian Barnes, *Flaubert's Parrot* (New York: Knopf, 1985), 59. For the sake of comparison, here once
again is Flaubert's text: "Je sens que je ne dois pas mourir sans avoir fait rugir quelque part un style
comme je l'entends dans ma tête et qui pourra bien dominer la voix des perroquets et des cigales"
(2:110, 19 June 1852).

corporeal, continuous, irrepressible, perilous—and implicitly powerful. It is perhaps best embodied by the figure of the Sirens luring men to a watery death with
their song and most economically recapitulated by Bachelard's homonymic apposition of sea song and mother song: "Ce chant profond [de la mer] est la voix ma-
ternelle, la voix de notre mer"[50] ["This deep song {of the sea} is the maternal voice,
the voice of our sea {mother}"].

As Bachelard (following Flaubert) further stated, "Tout ce qui coule est de l'eau
. . . [et] toute eau est un lait"[51] ["everything that flows is water . . . {and} all water
is a milk"]. The identification of female voice with fluidity and, specifically, with
female body fluids, effectively contains this voice, and deprives it of its agency.
Following the model Kaja Silverman has developed in her work on female voice in
cinema, we can say that the process whereby female voice is embodied—interiorized or infused as body fluid potentially expressible through various organ holes—
is more accurately repressive, and that each of the holes or points from which a
woman's subjectivity is ostensibly to be expressed is in fact "the site at which that
subjectivity is introduced in her."[52] The embodiment of voice, although culturally
devalorized as feminine, is more generally one of the properties of human voice,
which, in Guy Rosolato's terms, is situated "between body and language."[53] The
feminization of embodied voice is then a gesture of projection (and rejection).

Our passage from Flaubert's representation of feminine voice as bodily effluvia
to be contained, to Colet's version of feminine voice as framed discourse, reverses
gender stereotypes: it moves us from the materiality of his model to the abstraction
of hers. For Flaubert's letters and Colet's reply in *La Servante* constitute a dialogue
about containment. He speaks in fluid metaphors of the need to channel a certain
lyric, romantic style and furthermore performs this channeling by his rhetoric of
female incorporation, while she responds by writing about the dispossession of female voice by male textuality, reinterpreting his containing discourse in narrative
terms. In this way Colet's text is a distorted reflection of Flaubert's, and the resultant glare works both to highlight and displace his enclosing discourse.[54]

I have emphasized here the narrative importance of Colet's poem (its internal
narrative structure and displacements and also the internarrative structure constituted by its discourse with Flaubert's letters). My reading flies in the face of a critical tradition that has consistently read Colet's verse narrative with the accent on
verse and has insistently followed Flaubert's standard in reading Colet's work with

[50] Bachelard, *L'Eau et les rêves*, 156.
[51] Ibid., 158.
[52] Silverman, *Acoustic Mirror*, 67.
[53] Rosolato, "La Voix." See, too, Silverman, *Acoustic Mirror*; and Roland Barthes, *Le Grain de la voix*
(Paris: Seuil, 1981).
[54] This is another version of the mimetic strategy Irigaray uses to displace male discourse. Irigaray,
Speculum of the Other Woman, trans. Gillian C. Gill (Ithaca: Cornell University Press, 1985).

her person as quintessentially romantic to the point of sentimental drivel, effusively lyrical to the point of bathos, and, most pointedly, hysterical.[55] Flaubert and the larger critical tradition here tacitly echo cultural associations of verse with the feminine, music, materiality, the body, and voice as pure sonority unmediated by meaning. Although Flaubert (who reportedly could neither write a line of verse nor carry a tune) paid nominal homage to the quality of Colet's verses, he simultaneously dismissed them as insignificant products of her body: "Je ne te sais nul gré de faire de beaux vers. Tu les ponds comme une poule les oeufs, sans en avoir conscience" (2:480, 18 December 1853)[56] ["I give you no credit for writing good verses. You lay them as a hen lays eggs, with no consciousness of what you are doing"].

My own claim is not that Colet deserves a place in the pantheon of aesthetic perfection; it is at once more modest and more complex. I want to be neither the apologist for her style nor the champion of her passions. I do, however, want to dissociate the two; and if I read *La Servante* as a text that could only have been written by a woman, it is because it displays a remarkable self-consciousness about women's position in patriarchal society, and not because it flows from Colet's lips in an oral/genital indistinction too often assigned by both her culture and ours to female discourse. Colet wrote her novel in verse or, in other words, imposed narrative form on her poetry. As such, she wrote a hybrid or even hermaphroditic text, according to gendered conventions of genre, once again manifesting a refusal to speak in a categorically feminine or masculine voice. It is this refusal to choose between two equally limiting alternatives that makes *La Servante* a protofeminist text in Nancy Miller's sense that feminist texts "protest against the available fiction of female becoming."[57]

The oppositional force of Colet's narrative can be gauged by Flaubert's scatological dismissal of it as "un déversoir à passions, une espèce de pot de chambre où le trop-plein de je ne sais quoi a coulé" ["an outlet for passions, a sort of chamber pot in which the overflow of who knows what has dripped"], and by his accompanying rejection of its anger: "Cela ne sent pas bon. Cela sent la haine" (2:502, 9–10 January 1854) ["That doesn't smell good. That reeks of hatred"]. Now, Flaubert's furious response to *La Servante* is prefaced by a leap to the defense of one of Colet's

---

[55] Julian Barnes, Jean Bruneau, and Marilyn Gaddis Rose are among the few commentators I have read who have written sympathetically of Colet. See Barnes, *Flaubert's Parrot*; Bruneau's preface to Flaubert's *Correspondance*; and Rose's introduction to her translation of Louise Colet, *Lui: A View of Him* (Athens: University of Georgia Press, 1986). And see Francine du Plessix Gray's forthcoming biography, *Rage and Fire: A Life of Louise Colet, Pioneer Feminist, Literary Star, Flaubert's Muse* (New York: Simon and Schuster, 1994), for a monumental revalorization of Colet's life and work.

[56] I owe the information about Flaubert's nonmusicality to Herbert Lottman, *Flaubert: A Biography* (Boston: Little, Brown, 1989), 66.

[57] Nancy K. Miller, *Subject to Change* (New York: Columbia University Press, 1988), 129.

former lovers, the poet Alfred de Musset, whom he loathes as both writer and man. Flaubert takes Musset (as do most subsequent readers) to be a thinly disguised referent for the Lionel/Léon character: "Pourquoi insulter Musset? que t'a-t-il fait?" (2:502, 9–10 January 1854) ["Why insult Musset? What has he done to you?"]. It is worth noting that variants on the name Léon are closely identified with Flaubert stand-ins in Colet's later romans à clef (*Une Histoire de soldat*: Léon, and *Lui*: Léonce). We also recall the lover Flaubert gave to Emma Bovary in the form of Léon. And we cannot suppress the leonine roar of disapproval with which Flaubert aspires to drown the voice of parrots and cicadas. Such echoes of the lion's part in the Flaubert-Colet dialogue suggest that Lionel's referential identity cannot be so unambiguously assigned.

My intent is not to substitute one biographical interpretation for another and certainly not to undertake at this concluding moment the biographical reading I have deliberately avoided through the body of my own text. I want rather to challenge the Lionel-Musset equation on the grounds that its referential specificity represents a much too facile reduction of a feminist text to a female vendetta. To read this text à la Flaubert as a purely personal expression is to infuse it within Colet's body as a sign of her leaking female physiology, and in this way to defuse its more general ideological force.[58]

It is the force of Colet's text as ideological commentary that prompts Flaubert's wrath, provokes the visceral outburst that he then projects as scatological critique of her style. His reaction to her anger is a revealing measure of the threat of a woman's voice that escapes containment, a woman's discourse that, unlike Mariette's, resists circumscription, and a woman's pen that dares to express the extent of its repression.[59] No wonder that he reinscribed Louise Colet, stripped of her autonomy, deprived of her pen, as Emma Bovary. But that is another story.

[58] Although in one of her Mementos Colet suggests that she will write about Musset (2:901–2, 1 July 1853), in another she reflects on Musset as a kind of Everyman, particularly comparing Flaubert to him: "Et tout en marchant je pensais que tous les hommes à des degrés près lui ressemblaient [à Musset], que G[ustave] en viendrait peut-être là un jour!" (2:896, 4 September 1852) ["And while walking, I thought that all men more or less resembled him {Musset}, that G{ustave} would perhaps be like that one day!"].
[59] On the link between the expression of anger and accession to power, see Heilbrun, *Writing a Woman's Life*, especially 14–25.

6 WRITING WITH A VENGEANCE

Writing *Madame Bovary,*
Unwriting Louise Colet

*Plus tard si je vis, si tu vieillis, j'écrirai peut-être
toute cette histoire qui n'en est même pas une.*
GUSTAVE FLAUBERT TO LOUISE COLET,
11 JUNE 1847

●   Recounting the definitive break, in 1854, between Colet and Flaubert, Herbert Lottman remarks that "we shall miss Louise Colet more than Gustave seemed to, for he was never again to express himself so expansively about his work-in-progress."[1] Echoing a tradition of dismissing the poet by recognizing her service as Flaubert's lover and principal correspondent during the *Bovary* years, Lottman nonetheless underestimates the uses of Louise Colet. For Flaubert's explicit commentary in the letters about his work-in-progress is less helpful to a reading of his novel than is the representation, throughout these letters, of their recipient as woman and writer. This is not to argue that Emma Bovary *was* Louise Colet, in a literary-realist or biographical sense, any more than she was Gustave Flaubert, but rather, that the writing of *Madame Bovary* corresponded to the process of constructing Louise Colet, and that the fictional and epistolary texts are dynamically interwoven.

We have followed earlier moments of this dynamic. The letters to Louise Colet

[1] Herbert Lottman, *Flaubert: A Biography* (Boston: Little, Brown, 1989), 126.

provide a log of a voyage of discovery not unlike a host of other nineteenth-century explorations of the self charted on the oceans and islands of the Other. Channel, port, vessel, *Muse*, Colet is used by Flaubert as metaphor, way point for the transport of his ideas, phantasms, desires, fears. We know when he asks her to stanch lyricism's milky flow that the "real woman" disappears; that *Louise Colet* is only a metaphor for conditions that transcend her; that at stake are his own ebbing and flowing resources. But the drama of Flaubert's journey toward his own heart of darkness does not dispel the questions raised by his literary imperialism. What of the appropriated waterways? What of the oceans crossed and channeled? What of Louise Colet?

Cast by the *Correspondance* in the role of Galatea to Flaubert's Pygmalion, Colet risks becoming her lover's creation. Flaubert had great designs for Louise Colet and did not hesitate to make them known: "Oh si je pouvais faire de toi ce que j'en rêve, quelle femme, quel être tu serais!"[2] ["Oh, if I could make you into the substance of my dreams, what a woman, what a being you would be!"]. We hear the frustrated ring of his creator's cry when he finds the form of the woman and the text unequal to the promise of the raw material. Her words are lost.

During the period Colet served as metaphor to Flaubert, however, she was herself writing, in *La Servante*, about the appropriation of women's lives and texts by men, and also about women's ways of reading, writing, and negotiating the reappropriation of their lives. I have shown that *La Servante* can be read as an open letter to Flaubert, a reclaiming and revalorization of subordinated voices. Colet does not celebrate woman's evasion of patriarchal containment; rather, she expresses and exposes such containment, evading a similar fate for herself by speaking its threat. We recall the sense of outrage conveyed by Flaubert's letters about this text. His fury, his desire for revenge through writing, aesthetically disciplined into writing with a vengeance, informs *Madame Bovary*, his own retelling of a woman's (failed) flight from social and ideological containment.[3]

There is a rhetorical foreboding of the contest of voices that would be constituted by Flaubert's letters, Colet's *La Servante*, and Flaubert's *Madame Bovary*, in his chosen image of a "roaring" style strong enough to overpower the voice of parrots and cicadas. The intention—attributed to the notably absent lion—to quell the other voices is strong testimony to their anticipated power. This power is activated in *La Servante*, in which Louise Colet, Flaubert's would-be parrot, speaks

---

[2] Gustave Flaubert, *Correspondance*, ed. Jean Bruneau (Paris: Gallimard, 1973–91), 2:467, 25 November 1853. All further references will be to this edition and will be given parenthetically in the text.
[3] Flaubert's term for this fury of revenge is "rage." "Je n'ai rien pour me soutenir qu'une espèce de rage permanente" (2:75, 24 April 1852) ["I have nothing to sustain me but a sort of permanent rage"], he writes to Colet, referring to his writing; and to Bouilhet, "J'ai rempoigné la *Bovary* avec rage" (2:573, 9 May 1855) ["I retackled my *Bovary* with rage"]. This last statement is made in a letter written two months after the definitive break with Colet.

instead in a different voice, a lyric voice, pronouncing a threat to the roar of domination. In response to the lion's projected roar, *La Servante* chronicles a feminine
subjectivity, realizing Flaubert's prophetic fears of the parrot's retort and the cicada's rebel song.

    Madame Bovary is Flaubert's answering roar of rage, his most bitter note of re-
venge, his longest letter in a correspondence already officially ended. Flaubert began work on the novel in September 1851, less than two months after his correspondence with Colet was renewed and less than two weeks after he surrendered
once again to her seductions. In January 1854 Flaubert responded in anger and at
great length to *La Servante*. In late April 1854 his letters ceased; in March of the
following year, when Colet learned he was in Paris and sought to see him, he wrote
her a letter of definitive rupture.[4] One year later, the manuscript was finished.
Even such a sketchy outline suggests that the works and lives of Colet and Flaubert
have intersecting chronologies whose ramifications for the novel need to be considered. Although her *Lui* (1859) achieved some notoriety as a novel of revenge, as
has her less remembered *Une Histoire de soldat* (1856), the motivating role of retaliation in the writing of *Madame Bovary* has been largely overlooked.[5]

    I will be reading *Madame Bovary* as a derivative of the letters to Louise Colet,
within the context of *La Servante* and Flaubert's reaction to it. But I will make the

---

[4] Much has been written about the rupture of Flaubert and Colet; there has been a great deal of speculation—but little more—as to the source of the break. The text of the final letter is as follows:

> Madame,
>   J'ai appris que vous vous étiez donné la peine de venir, hier, dans la soirée, trois fois, chez
> moi.
>   Je n'y étais pas. Et dans la crainte des avanies qu'une telle persistance de votre part, pourrait
> vous attirer de la mienne, le savoir-vivre m'engage à vous prévenir: *que je n'y serai* jamais.
>   J'ai l'honneur de vous saluer.
>
>   G. F.

(2:572, 6 March 1855)

> Madame,
>   *I understand that you troubled yourself to come to my house last night three times.*
>   *I was not there. And dreading the reprisals that such persistence on your part might elicit on*
> *mine, politeness obliges me to warn you: that* I will not be there *at any time.*
>   *With all due respect.*
>
>   G. F.

[5] No doubt the canonical status of *Madame Bovary*, its acceptance as high art, has to a certain extent
warded off analysis of its baser motives. For remarks on *Lui* and its source in revenge—against Flaubert
as well as, and even rather than, the ostensibly central figure of Albert/Musset—see Bruneau, in Flaubert, *Correspondance*, 2:1272; Marilyn Gaddis Rose in the foreword to her translation of Louise Colet's
Lui: A View of Him (Athens: University of Georgia Press, 1986), xv; Micheline Bood and Serge Grand,
L'Indomptable Louise Colet (Paris: Pierre Horay, 1986), 180.

Colet connection obliquely, turning first to Flaubert's more general uses of hysteria in constructing Emma Bovary and her daughter, Berthe, before making a case for his material reconstruction, in the body of Emma Bovary, of that particular stylistic figure of hysteria that he had named *Louise Colet*.[6] I will argue that the woman written is not only a reconstruction but also a restriction of the woman writer, who is recontained when she is cast in the mold of Emma Bovary, her feminine excesses indulged only to be finally condemned.

BERTHE/EMMA

In an early review of *Madame Bovary*, Baudelaire offered, in the guise of a rhetorical question, an elliptical interpretation that arguably still constitutes the most incisive and encompassing analysis of this novel. After pronouncing the adolescent Emma "le poète hystérique," Baudelaire goes on to extol hysteria:

> *L'hystérie! Pourquoi ce mystère physiologique ne ferait-il pas le fond et le tuf d'une oeuvre littéraire*, ce mystère que l'Académie de médecine n'a pas encore résolu, et qui, s'exprimant dans les femmes par la sensation d'une boule ascendante et asphyxiante (je ne parle que du symptôme principal), se traduit chez les hommes nerveux par toutes les impuissances et aussi par l'aptitude à tous les excès? (my emphasis)

> Hysteria! Why could this physiological mystery not serve as the foundation and bedrock of a literary work? *The Academy of Medicine has not as yet been able to explain the mysterious condition of hysteria. In women, it acts like a stifling ball*

[6] Benjamin Bart argues that "Louise Colet, in caricature, would be one of the principal models for Emma Bovary." Bart, *Flaubert* (Syracuse: Syracuse University Press, 1967), 156. My claim is not quite as mimetic, although there is tangible evidence of certain resemblances between Colet and Emma Bovary (the celebrated "amor nel cor" engraving on a gift from Colet to Flaubert that shows up in his novel as a maudlin gift from Emma to Rodolphe; an echo of Colet's bloodied handkerchief, which Flaubert possesses and writes to her about fondly and that turns up as another keepsake from Emma to Rodolphe; the fireworks in celebration of the Three Glorious Days, which Flaubert and Colet attended the night they met, reminding us of the fireworks of the Comices Agricoles in *Madame Bovary*; and so on). I read these details as coagulated points of a much more amorphous process linking Louise Colet and Emma Bovary (and Berthe); no one is a referent for the others, but rather they are all surrogates, substitutes for each other and personifications of forces, conditions, desires, and fears that I hope to articulate in these pages. For fuller details about these connections, see the following sources. On the "amor nel cor" engraving: Bood and Grand, *L'Indomptable Louise Colet*, 178; Gustave Flaubert, *Madame Bovary*, ed. Jacques Suffel (Paris: Garnier Flammarion, 1979), 218. On the bloodstained handkerchief: Flaubert to Colet, 1:273, 4–5 August 1846 and 1:308, 23 August 1846; *Madame Bovary*, 228. On the fireworks with a romantic overlay (fiercely satirized in the novel): Bart, *Flaubert*, 142; *Madame Bovary*, 181–83.

rising in the body (I mention only the main symptom), while in nervous men it can be the cause of many forms of impotence as well as of a limitless aptitude for excess.[7]

The interpretation Baudelaire suggests here intrigues me not only because I think he is right in identifying hysteria (as opposed to the more commonly cited adultery) as the bedrock of *Madame Bovary*, but because this tentative identification ("ne ferait-il pas") is couched in ambiguity. Itself open to interpretation, it is an invitation to reread more than just Flaubert's novel.

For the identification with *Madame Bovary* is never explicitly made: no particular text is named, the indefinite article is used ("*une* oeuvre littéraire"), and the verb appears in the conditional (thus hypothetical, even projective) mode. Baudelaire might just as well be suggesting hysteria as a more general literary source, even predicting its potential as a force of textual generation—a new muse. The richness of his comment lies precisely in its ambiguity; it says and means two things at once. I am insisting on this overdetermination because it serves to describe the course that my reading of *Madame Bovary* takes. What follows is an exploration of hysteria as it functions in this particular novel (as theme, as figure, and, ultimately, as narrative voice).[8] But more generally, if implicitly, it is an attempt to locate in *Madame Bovary* some keys to a subgenre that became promi-

---

[7] Charles Baudelaire, "*Madame Bovary* par Gustave Flaubert," in *Oeuvres complètes*, ed. Claude Pichois, 2 vols. (Paris: Gallimard, 1975–76), 2:83; trans. Paul de Man, in Flaubert, *Madame Bovary* (New York: Norton, 1965), 341, trans. modified. The article first appeared in *L'Artiste*, 18 October 1857 (six months after the bound edition of *Madame Bovary* was published and one year after the novel began to be issued in serial edition in *La Revue de Paris*).

[8] The notable omission here is (psycho)biography. The referential pathology of author or character is not the object of my focus, except to the extent that Flaubert or Emma converges with or diverges from representations of disease. The exact nature of both Emma's and Gustave's ailments (which are often conflated) has been much debated and often, I think, to little avail. For a summary and bibliography of such efforts, see Roger Williams, *The Horror of Life* (Chicago: University of Chicago Press, 1980); see my comments on Williams in Chapter 4. For the record, it is worth mentioning that Flaubert was a self-proclaimed hysteric at a time when this diagnosis was not yet officially available to men. (Although it is true, as I point out in my introduction and first chapter, that a few physicians had claimed hysteria for men as well as women by this time. However, this was not yet a received idea within the medical community, and certainly not within the lay community; it is therefore all the more striking that certain authors [among them Baudelaire and Flaubert] identified themselves or other males as hysterics, intuiting what medicine had not yet formulated at the time.) Flaubert borrowed from his own experience many of the details of Emma's visions, hallucinations, and convulsions. (See my citations in Chapter 4, and Williams, *Horror of Life*, chapter 3.) Flaubert's first recorded reference to his own hysteria is metaphorical; it coincides with the writing of *Madame Bovary*: he wrote to Louise Colet that his efforts to write the banalities of life were causing him to suffer "[des] hystéries d'ennui" (2:68, 8 April 1852). Although the term *hysteria* does not appear in Flaubert's novels, it occurs at least a dozen times in the *Correspondance* between 1852 and 1880. See Jan Goldstein's fascinating study, "The Uses of Male Hysteria: Medical and Literary Discourse in Nineteenth-century France," *Representations* 34 (Spring 1991): 134–66.

nent on the literary scene of the latter nineteenth century: the novel of hysteria. I
seek not only what the diagnosis can tell us about Emma Bovary, about Flaubert,   •
about the novel, but also what *Madame Bovary* has to say about hysteria, hysterics,
and their place in the nineteenth-century imaginary.

Madame Bovary stands roughly midway between two physicians' texts with which
it can profitably engage in intertextual dialogue: the entry "Hystérie" in the *Dictionnaire des sciences médicales* written by Louyer-Villermay in 1818, and the article by Charles Richet called "Les Démoniaques d'aujourd'hui," which appeared
in the *Revue des deux mondes* in 1880.[9] The former article (which appears to have
furnished many of the "clinical" details of Emma's ailment) occupies forty-six
dense pages in the *Dictionnaire*, the standard medical reference of the period;[10] it
presents the nosology, symptoms, causes, history, development, and recom-
mended treatment of the malady. The latter is the first in a series of three articles
written by Richet, who was, we recall, one of Charcot's disciples, in an attempt to
educate the public about hysteria, the Salpêtrière Hospital, and the Master's
teachings; rather curiously, one of the primary sources Richet's lesson on hysteria
draws upon is *Madame Bovary*.

   While Charcot's associate hails Flaubert as a precursor, citing literary evidence
in support of medical observation, Flaubert looks back to a medical source, which
in turn, I argue, is to a great extent culturally determined. The fluid relationship
among these three texts is, I think, emblematic of the larger pattern of reciprocal
influence marking narrative and medical discourses in the nineteenth century.
My comparison of these texts is shaped by the assumption that narrative and medical discourses are continuous, nonhierarchic, both enmeshed in a pervasive
ideology which, like Flaubert's ideal narrator, is invisible and omnipotent, everywhere and nowhere at once.

   When Charles Richet uses what he approves as the "descriptions exactes" (346)

[9] J.-B. Louyer-Villermay, "Hystérie," in *Dictionnaire des sciences médicales* (Paris: Panckoucke, 1818),
23:226–72; Charles Richet, "Les Démoniaques d'aujourd'hui," *Revue des deux mondes* 37 (15 January
1880): 340–72. Subsequent references to these articles will be given parenthetically in the text.
[10] The *Dictionnaire des sciences médicales* in fact figures explicitly in *Madame Bovary*. It is described as
constituting almost all of Charles Bovary's library: "Les tomes du *Dictionnaire des sciences médicales*,
non coupés, mais dont la brochure avait souffert dans toutes les ventes successives par où ils avaient
passé, garnissaient presque à eux seuls les six rayons d'une bibliothèque en bois de sapin" ["Volumes of
the 'Dictionary of Medical Science,' uncut, but the binding rather the worse for the successive sales
through which they had gone, occupied almost alone the six shelves of a pinewood bookcase"]. Flaubert, *Madame Bovary*, 66; trans. Paul de Man, 22–23. All subsequent citations will be taken from these
editions and will be noted in the text. If Charles was not in the habit of referring to the *Dictionnaire*,
Flaubert was. In a letter to Sainte-Beuve (3:277, 23–24 December 1862), he refers to the article on lep-
rosy as a source for a description in *Salammbô*. I am indebted to Lawrence Rothfield's "From Semiotic
to Discursive Intertextuality: The Case of *Madame Bovary*," *Novel* 19 (Fall 1985): 65, for bringing these
references to my attention.

138

•

of hysteria furnished by *Madame Bovary* to complete his professional description of the disease, he lets Flaubert's text speak for itself. Confident in his estimation that Emma is noteworthy among fictional hysterics as "[l'hystérique] la plus vraie" (348) ["the truest hysteric"], he lends to a page of running citations from *Madame Bovary* the voice of authority one might otherwise expect to emanate from excerpts of a clinical case study.[11]

While Richet apparently considers that Flaubert's anecdotal characterization of Emma's ailment needs no analysis, we might, in the interests of brevity and clarity, break down the passages he quotes into a simple list of symptoms denoted and connoted. Emma is then revealed to be capricious, histrionic, narcissistic, emotionally and financially extravagant, and prone to emotional swings, impulsive decisions, sexual fantasies, romantic whims, and acts of virile daring. She is given to fits of feverish chatter, periods of speechless lethargy, and, of course, bouts of reading. Her physical symptoms include paleness, palpitations of the heart, and sensations of suffocation.

If Richet dispenses with any attempt to impose nosological redefinition upon Flaubert's narrative, this is at least in part because such an enterprise would be redundant. In the first part of his article, prior to quoting from *Madame Bovary*, he enumerates the characteristics of hysteria. He might just as well have been summarizing Emma's case, for the two sets of symptoms are remarkably alike in content if not in style of presentation. The similarity invites some skepticism; it is not at all clear whether Flaubert in fact anticipated what would be accepted, some thirty years later, as the most medically accurate and up-to-date representation of hysteria, or whether the view of hysteria adopted by Charcot's group was based at least in part on literary and other popularly disseminated representations of it. There are clear indications, within Richet's exposition as well as externally, that by the time he was writing, the phenomenon he was describing was well known in spirit if not in name, and that a certain cluster of characteristics constituted the essence of a popular conception of "female nerves."[12] The complicity Richet maintains with his reader throughout the article implies their shared cultural preconceptions: "Je m'imagine que tout le monde connaît plus ou moins les bizarreries du caractère des femmes nerveuses" (342) ["I imagine that everyone is more or less familiar with the bizarre characteristics of nervous women"]; "Le caractère des

---

[11] The unexpected deference to a literary source in this doctor's article needs to be qualified by a reminder of his intended (literary) audience, which would doubtless have been better acquainted with novelistic heroines than with clinical patients. Nonetheless, the authority he is willing to give to Flaubert's fiction—especially at a time when doctors were generally suspicious of and hostile to literary representations of hysteria—cannot be dismissed.

[12] See G. Hahn, "Charcot et son influence sur l'opinion publique," *Revue des questions scientifiques* (July-August 1894): 230–61; Francisque Sarcey, *Le Mot et la chose* (Paris: Ollendorff, 1863), 280; Guy de Maupassant, "Une Femme," in *Chroniques* (Paris: 10/18, 1980), 2:111–15.

hystériques est fort étrange, comme chacun sait" (343) ["The character of hysterics is extremely strange, as everyone knows"]. His task here is less to introduce a new phenomenon than to clothe a familiar one in positivistic garb, to render it scientifically respectable: "Ce qu'on appelle les *nerfs* d'une jeune femme, c'est tout simplement de l'hystérie" (342) ["What is referred to as female *nerves* is simply hysteria"].

A notable exception to Richet's otherwise unmediated use of *Madame Bovary* provides a more revealing glimpse of the ideological underpinnings of the hysteria diagnosis. He concludes his lengthy series of quotations from the novel by qualifying Emma's case in passing as "hystérie légère" (349) ["mild hysteria"]. As he explains in a startling earlier passage, "cette hystérie légère n'est pas une maladie véritable" (346) ["this mild hysteria is not a true disease"]. For all Richet's insistence that Emma is "the truest of hysterics," he classifies her as a victim of merely mild hysteria—the kind that is not even "a true disease." The apparent inconsistency here can be cleared up if we read on. For mild hysteria is now redefined: "C'est une des variétés du caractère de la femme" ["It is one of the varieties of woman's nature"]. Richet elaborates:

> On peut même dire que les hystériques sont femmes plus que les autres femmes: elles ont des sentimens passagers et vifs, des imaginations mobiles et brillantes, et parmi tout cela l'impuissance de dominer par la raison et le jugement ces sentimens et ces imaginations.   (346)

> *One might even say that hysterics are more womanly than other women: their feelings are fleeting and intense, their imagination brilliant and mobile, and along with all that, they are incapable of dominating their feelings and imagination by reason and judgment.*

The "true disease" he refers to is not hysteria at all—in its mild or severe form—but femininity. Hysteria turns out to be just a way of labeling or highlighting the pathological feminine.

Richet here shows his mettle. He proves to be not only a strong reflector of nineteenth-century cultural stereotypes, but also (no doubt in spite of himself) an inordinately good reader of Flaubert; for his comments allow us to gloss Emma's nervous disorder as a euphemism for her femininity, and to relate her suffering to her female sexuality. I want to take this diagnosis one step further, suggesting that we think of her "female malady" as more precisely a case of *mothersickness*, which is my translation of "mal de mère," a term given as a synonym for hysteria by the *Dictionnaire des sciences médicales*. We should not leap to interpret this malady as the ennui of childbearing or childrearing. There is that, of course, in *Madame Bo-*

140 *vary*, but it is only a concretization of the more general, more fundamental afflic-
•   tion of having a womb.[13]

To sort through the implications this affliction has for *Madame Bovary*, I weave
back and forth between the novel and the dictionary. A reading of the *Dictionnaire*
yields, if not the verifiable source of Emma Bovary's hysterical traits, at the very
least a compendium of the era's understanding of such traits, and so an indirect
source. Emma is closely modeled upon an image of hysterics as described in this
article. Like them, she has "un tempérament nerveux, une sensibilité exquise . . .
une imagination brûlante . . . un coeur trop tendre ou facile à enflammer"
(*DSM*, 231) ["a nervous temperament, exquisite sensitivity . . . a burning imagination . . . an overly tender or easily inflamed heart"]. These characteristics, we
are told, reflect a tendency toward hysteria. Circumstantial factors that favor the
disease—factors that play a role in the etiology of Emma's illness—include "la lecture des romans" (235) ["the reading of novels"] and "une éducation molle" (231)
["a lax upbringing"]. One is reminded of Emma's convent upbringing:

> Vivant donc sans jamais sortir de la tiède atmosphère des classes . . . elle
> s'assoupit doucement à la langueur mystique qui s'exhale des parfums de
> l'autel, de la fraîcheur des bénitiers et du rayonnement des cierges. (70)

> *Living thus, without ever leaving the warm atmosphere of the class-rooms . . . she*
> *was softly lulled by the mystic languor exhaled in the perfumes of the altar, the*
> *freshness of the holy water, and the lights of the tapers.*   (25)

Other contributing factors are given as "les odeurs désagréables, fétides ou irri-
tantes" (231) ["unpleasant, fetid, or irritating odors"]; the phrase evokes that well-
known description, cited earlier, of Emma's mealtime despair:

> Mais c'était surtout aux heures des repas qu'elle n'en pouvait plus . . .
> toute l'amertume de l'existence lui semblait servie sur son assiette, et, à la
> fumée du bouilli, il montait du fond de son âme comme d'autres bouffées
> d'affadissement.   (99)

> *But it was above all the meal-times that were unbearable to her . . . all the*
> *bitterness of life seemed served up on her plate, and with the smoke of the boiled*
> *beef there rose from her secret soul waves of nauseous disgust.*   (47)

[13] On the nineteenth-century tendency to define the feminine as "an aptitude for maternity," see
Yvonne Knibiehler's provocative article "Le Discours médical sur la femme: Constantes et ruptures,"
Romantisme 13–14 (1976): 41.

Certain foods endowed with aphrodisiac properties, such as "les truffes, les cham-
pignons, . . . peut-être les fraises, les framboises" (232) ["truffles, mush-
rooms, . . . maybe strawberries, raspberries"] can also nurture hysteria. And what
about apricots? It is hard not to be reminded of Emma's spasms and the subsequent
illness provoked by Rodolphe's abandonment, but precipitated by the suffocating
aroma of a basket of apricots used to convey the letter of rupture. Monsieur Homais, as usual the voice of common wisdom, theorizes on the connection:

> Mais il se pourrait que les abricots eussent occasionné la syncope! Il y a
> des natures si impressionables à l'encontre de certaines odeurs! . . . Les
> prêtres . . . ont toujours mêlé des aromates à leurs cérémonies. C'est pour
> vous stupéfier l'entendement et provoquer des extases, chose d'ailleurs
> facile à obtenir chez les personnes du sexe, qui sont plus délicates que les
> autres.   (235)

> *It is quite possible that the apricots caused the syncope. Some natures are so*
> *sensitive to certain smells. . . . Priests . . . use aromatics in all their ceremonies.*
> *It is to stupefy the senses and to bring on ecstasies—a thing, moreover, very*
> *easy in persons of the weaker sex, who are more sensitive than we are.*   (150–51)

Moreover, Emma, with her fleshy lips, beautiful teeth, cascades of black hair, and
large dark eyes, matches the physical profile of women prone to hysteria, according to the *Dictionnaire*:

> On l'observe fréquemment . . . parmi celles qui ont . . . les yeux noirs
> et vifs, la bouche grande, les dents blanches et les lèvres d'un rouge
> incarnat, les cheveux abondans, le système pileux fourni et couleur de
> jais, et dont les caractères sexuels sont très-prononcés.   (234)

> *We frequently find it among women who have dark, lively eyes, a large mouth,*
> *white teeth and rose-red lips, a luxuriant head of hair, thick, jet-black body hair,*
> *and whose sexual characteristics are very pronounced.*

   Although there is a marked correlation between Emma's nervous traits and the
characteristics of hysteria as described by the *Dictionnaire*, two objections might
be raised at this point. In the first place, one wonders whether a merely thematic
correspondence would have constituted sufficient grounds for Baudelaire's accla-
mation of hysteria as "the foundation and bedrock of a literary work." And in the
second place, there is an important element of the *Dictionnaire* article that has no
manifest correlation with the presentation of Emma's case; I am referring to a fa-

miliar and pervasive emphasis in the article on the causal relationship between hysteria and the female reproductive system. From the beginning of the dictionary entry, hysteria is inextricably bound to female reproduction. "Il existe une maladie dont l'utérus est le siége" (228) ["There is a disease whose seat is the uterus"], we are told. The disease is classified within the genre "névroses de la génération" ["reproductive neuroses"] and the species "névroses génitales de la femme" (227) ["female genital neuroses"]; its synonyms, in addition to "mal de mère" ["mothersickness"], are given as "affection utérine, suffocation de matrice, étranglement de l'utérus . . . ascension de la matrice, névrose utérine" (226) ["uterine complaint, suffocation of the womb, strangling of the uterus . . . rising of the womb, uterine neurosis"].

But in the relatively rare event that a critic has discussed either Emma as mother, or her daughter Berthe, it has almost invariably been to remark on the absent mother or on the "diminutive role" played by the daughter.[14] (Let us not forget that Emma turns her head and faints when she learns that she has given birth to a daughter; the pattern is set.) Is it not paradoxical to insist on a correlation between a disease believed to be rooted in maternity and a novel about a woman who, though a mother, is arguably the least "maternal" of all mothers?

A revealing excerpt from Flaubert's correspondence can be used to counter both of these objections. In a letter to Louise Colet, Flaubert counsels her on what he considers the best way to incorporate observed reality into a literary work. Perhaps not coincidentally, Flaubert's advice is prompted by Colet's projected research visit to the Salpêtrière Hospital, where she intends to witness hysterics and various other madwomen firsthand in order to document the last scene of her verse narrative, *La Servante*. Here are Flaubert's instructions:

> Tu me dis que tu dois aller à la Salpêtrière pour [ta *Servante*]. Prends garde que cette visite *n'influe trop*. Ce n'est pas une bonne méthode que de voir ainsi tout de suite, pour écrire immédiatement après. On se préoccupe trop des détails, de la couleur, et pas assez de son esprit, car la couleur dans la nature a un *esprit*, une sorte de vapeur subtile qui se dégage d'elle, et c'est cela qui doit animer en *dessous* le style. Que de fois, préoccupé ainsi de ce que j'avais sous les yeux, ne me suis-je pas dépêché de l'intercaler de suite dans une oeuvre et de m'apercevoir enfin qu'il fallait l'ôter! La couleur, comme les aliments, doit être digérée et mêlée au sang des pensées. (2:372, July 1853)

---

[14] See, for example, Diana Festa-McCormick, "Emma Bovary's Masculinization: Conventions of Clothes and Morality of Conventions," in *Gender and Literary Voice*, ed. Janet Todd (New York: Holmes and Meier, 1980), 234.

*You tell me you must go to the Salpêtrière for [your] Servant]. Take care that this
visit does not influence you too much. It isn't methodologically sound to see all at
once, in order to write immediately afterward. One becomes too preoccupied with
details, with color, and not enough with its spirit, for color in nature has a spirit, a
kind of subtle vapor that is given off by it, and that is what should animate style
from beneath. How many times, preoccupied with what I had before my eyes, have
I not rushed to insert it immediately in a work only to realize later that it had to be
removed! Color, like food, must be digested and mixed with the blood of our
thoughts.*

This lesson intended to guide Colet toward the most effective integration of
madness within her text provides a crucial clue to Flaubert's integration of hysteria
within *Madame Bovary*, the writing of which he was struggling with daily at the
time of this letter. His caution that Colet not try to transcribe directly and in vivid
detail the madness she was to observe and would seek to convey is a reflection of his
own technique in *Madame Bovary*, where he is concerned not with the *letter* of
hysteria, but the *figure*: with what he calls here the *spirit*, "un *esprit*, une sorte de
vapeur subtile . . . qui doit animer en *dessous* le style." In counseling Colet to
avoid literal transcription, and *to let the spirit of madness animate her style from
beneath*, Flaubert uncannily rehearses the discovery Baudelaire would make,
when he read *Madame Bovary* four years later, that hysteria could function as the
foundation—"le fond et le tuf"—of a literary work.

If we superimpose Flaubert's letter and Baudelaire's review (to which Flaubert
not surprisingly responded: "Vous êtes entré dans les arcanes de l'oeuvre. . . .
Cela est compris et senti à fond"[15] ["You have entered the arcana of this work. . . .
You have a *profound* sense and understanding of it"]), we can reply to both potential objections at once. In *Madame Bovary* Flaubert does not in fact omit that aspect of hysteria considered during most of the nineteenth century to be its integral
component—namely, the female reproductive system. But he is less concerned
with its thematic representation ("[les] détails, . . . la couleur") than with its presence as a figure, a "subtle vapor" ("une sorte de vapeur subtile"): a fine haze per-
meating the atmosphere of his novel.[16] The *Dictionnaire* classification of this mal-

[15] Baudelaire, "*Madame Bovary*," 2:1120.
[16] My hypothesis that the writing of *Madame Bovary* involved Flaubert's transformation of hysteria
from letter to figure is supported by Claudine Gothot-Mersch's observations: "Les scénarios et les
brouillons, plus que la version définitive, mettent aussi en relief le côté hystérique du personnage. Certains textes nous montrent la jeune femme se livrant, dès Tostes, à des comédies qui trahissent un grave
déséquilibre. . . . [Des] hallucinations moins graves se rencontrent fréquemment dans les brouillons"
["The scenarios and rough drafts, more than the definitive version, accentuate the hysterical side of the
character. Some of the texts show us the young woman, from the early days in Tostes, indulging in
scenes that betray a severe imbalance. . . . Milder hallucinations show up frequently in the drafts"].

ady as a "generative neurosis" and a "female genital neurosis" finds its echo in *Madame Bovary*, for Emma's daughter is both metaphor and metonymy for her mother's womb, and thus integrally related to her hysteria.

Much as Emma's wedding cake with its cardboard stars and sugary dungeons synthesizes the novel's course while ironizing it, and much as the street organ with its miniature waltzers summarizes the Vaubyessard ball, Berthe recapitulates Emma: she is a reductive reprise, a negative miniature—her mother's parodic double.[17] Her very name contains within it the relentless pattern of Emma's destiny, for it shuttles between the ideal and the banal, invoking the one but evoking the other. "Berthe"—ostensibly chosen because "Emma se souvint qu'au château de la Vaubyessard elle avait entendu la marquise appeler Berthe une jeune femme" (124) ["Emma remembered that at the château of Vaubyessard she had heard the Marquise call a young lady Berthe"] (64)—is intended to signify elegance, pleasure, mobility, the well-born, and the viscount with whom she waltzed at the ball. But "Berthe" is phonetically attached to another memory—that of Les Bertaux, the farm where Emma was raised—and so with equal facility it signifies boredom, drudgery, stagnation, near-peasant origins, and a farmer father.[18]

The irony of the child's name is well matched by the circumstances of her birth. We might say that Emma has a double pregnancy, and two children, in the sense that she experiences everything twice, first in exalted and then in degraded form, and that Berthe is the child of the second pregnancy, the Other child. The first or imaginary pregnancy would have yielded a son: "Il serait fort et brun; elle l'appellerait Georges, et cette idée d'avoir pour enfant un mâle était comme la revanche en espoir de toutes ses impuissances passées" (122) ["He would be strong and dark; she would call him George; and this idea of having a male child was like an ex-

---

Claudine Gothot-Mersch, *La Genèse de Madame Bovary* (Paris: Corti, 1966), 194–95. Moreover, Flaubert's description in the *Correspondance* of his own initial contact with madwomen provides concrete details whose figurative equivalents are retained in *Madame Bovary*: "La première fois que j'ai vu des fous, c'était ici, à l'hospice général. . . . Dans les cellules, assises et attachées par le milieu du corps, nues jusqu'à la ceinture et tout échevelées, une douzaine de femmes hurlaient et se déchiraient la figure avec leurs ongles" ["The first contact I had with the insane was here, at the general hospital. . . . In the cells, seated and bound around the middle, naked to the waist and completely disheveled, a dozen women were screaming and tearing at their faces with their nails"] (letter to Louise Colet, 2:376, 7 July 1853). The traits figured by Emma Bovary—lasciviousness, self-destructiveness, incommunicativeness, constraint, marginality, alienation—are here concretely represented.

[17] It is worth noting that Charles sees Berthe as her mother's double: "Il voulait que Berthe fût bien élevée, qu'elle eût des talents, qu'elle apprît le piano. Ah! qu'elle serait jolie, plus tard, à quinze ans, quand, ressemblant à sa mère, elle porterait, comme elle, dans l'été, de grands chapeaux de paille! On les prendrait de loin pour les deux soeurs" (223) ["He wanted Berthe to be well-educated, to be accomplished, to learn to play the piano. Ah! how pretty she would be later on when she was fifteen, when, resembling her mother, she would, like her, wear large straw hats in the summer-time; from a distance they would be taken for two sisters"] (141).

[18] Moreover, this child named for nobility ends up as a déclassée; Homais will no longer allow his children to play with her once her financial ruin is assured.

pected revenge for all her impotence in the past"] (63).[19] This boy child, conceived in the afterglow of the Vaubyessard ball,[20] would have been the issue of the imaginary plot, the viscount plot—the positive pregnancy—while the baby girl, the child of the reality plot—the negative pregnancy—clearly belongs to Charles, the man who cannot even smoke the viscount's cigars.[21]

Certainly the daughter is named in memory of the Vaubyessard ball. But we need to recall that Emma's pleasures inevitably peak at the edge of abysses and that in this particular case, "son voyage à la Vaubyessard avait fait un trou dans sa vie, à la manière de ces grandes crevasses qu'un orage, en une seule nuit, creuse quelquefois dans les montagnes" (89) ["her journey to Vaubyessard had made a gap in her life, like the huge crevasses that a thunderstorm will sometimes carve in the mountains, in the course of a single night"] (40). Like the entire Vaubyessard episode it emblematizes, the name Berthe is hollow. Say it once, and you evoke a chateau filled with waltzing viscounts and marquises; say it again, and you hear its near homonym, *perte*—"loss, lack"—and you are back in the hole left by the trip to the Vaubyessard, a hole endlessly reopened by the child's torn stockings, her ripped blouses, and her vacuous reappearances in the novel (309, 361; de Man 209, 250).

What better name for the daughter who represents her mother's disillusionment, her lack of a son, than the very name of loss?[22] Berthe, as girl child, is the

[19] Dominick LaCapra summarizes the situation: "even her pregnancy was hysterical." *"Madame Bovary" on Trial* (Ithaca: Cornell University Press, 1982), 180.

[20] The ball takes place in October; we know that Emma is pregnant by the time she leaves Tostes in March. A revealing paragraph in the *Correspondance* lets us know that there was a vital link between the ball and the pregnancy in Flaubert's mind: "J'ai fini ce soir de barbouiller la première idée de mes rêves de jeune fille. J'en ai pour quinze jours encore à naviguer sur ces lacs bleus, après quoi j'irai au Bal, et passerai ensuite un hiver pluvieux, que je clorai par une grossesse" (2:63, 27 March 1852) ["This evening I finished scribbling the first idea from my girlish dreams. It will take me two weeks more to sail on blue lakes, after which I will go to the Ball, and then will spend a rainy winter that I will close with a pregnancy"].

[21] I am referring to the scene following Charles's discovery of what Emma presumes is the viscount's cigar case:

> Charles se mit à fumer. Il fumait en avançant les lèvres, crachant à toute minute, se reculant à chaque bouffée.
> "Tu vas te faire mal," dit-elle dédaigneusement.
> Il déposa son cigare, et courut avaler à la pompe un verre d'eau froide.   (89)

> *Charles began to smoke. He smoked with lips protruding, spitting every moment, drawing back at every puff.*
> "*You'll make yourself ill,*" *she said scornfully.*
> *He put down his cigar and ran to swallow a glass of cold water at the pump.*   (40)

[22] Naomi Schor suggests in her discussion of another nineteenth-century protagonist, Jeanne le Perthuis des Vauds of Maupassant's *Une Vie*, that "pushed to its logical extreme, one might say that all women are called Loss (Perte), since . . . loss is woman's lot." Schor, *Breaking the Chain: Women, Theory, and French Realist Fiction* (New York: Columbia University Press, 1985), 169.

boy's absence. She is at once reminder of the missing son and sign of what a son might find missing; as Dominick LaCapra suggests, she is "almost a literal figure of castration."[23] That is to say, she is also almost a literal figure of Emma's femininity, which Flaubert, in anticipation of Freud, represents as her recognition of a critical lack that could only be completely filled by a baby boy.[24] If Berthe/Emma prefigures Freud's model of femininity, she also recalls the similar and more overtly double-edged formula devised by Balzac's Vautrin: "La femme . . . est . . . la perte de l'homme"[25] ["Woman . . . is . . . man's loss"]. Woman is not only the incarnation of man's potential loss, but the feared instrument of this loss. Flaubert echoes Vautrin in a letter to Ernest Feydeau, in which he warns: "Mais prends garde d'abîmer ton intelligence dans le commerce des dames. Tu perdras ton génie au fond d'une matrice" (3:14, early February 1859) ["But take care not to damage your intelligence in commerce with ladies. You will lose your genius at the bottom of a womb"].

If we are to understand the ways in which Berthe as figure of her mother's anatomy embodies the spirit of her hysteria, we must at least begin to tease out a complex network of associations and differentiations concerning the womb, the phallus, castration, and hysteria. Let us recall the *Dictionnaire* explanation of why hysteria is necessarily the exclusive domain of women and, more specifically, why the female reproductive system should have an influence sufficiently powerful to induce the affliction, while the male reproductive system does not. Everything in this article suggests that it is the female rather than the male organs that generate hysteria because, on the one hand, they are located inside the body and are hidden, invisible, unknown, yet on the other hand, paradoxically, they are functionally more important, more complex—more powerful. Lest these factors seem etiologically irrelevant, let me supplement them with a direct quotation pertaining to the causality of female hysteria:

> Les organes de la génération ne peuvent être retranchés dans le sexe,
> tandis que l'appareil génital, tout extérieur chez l'homme, et chargé de
> fonctions plus limitées, semble former un système comme isolé, et qui
> peut être enlevé facilement. (229)

[23] LaCapra, *"Madame Bovary" on Trial*, 180.
[24] Sigmund Freud, "Femininity," in *The Standard Edition of the Complete Works of Sigmund Freud*, trans. James Strachey, Anna Freud, Alix Strachey, and Alan Tyson, ed. James Strachey, 24 vols. (London: Hogarth Press, 1953–74), 22:122–35. See, too, Schor's comment that "much before Freud, Flaubert well understood that in order for maternity to fully satisfy penis envy, the child must be male (which would condemn at least half of all women to inevitable neurosis)." *Breaking the Chain*, 22.
[25] Honoré de Balzac, *Splendeurs et misères des courtisanes*, in *La Comédie humaine*, ed. Pierre-Georges Castex, 12 vols. (Paris: Gallimard, 1976–81), 6:934.

The female reproductive organs cannot be cut off, while the male genital apparatus, entirely external and charged with more limited functions, seems to form an isolated system that can easily be removed.

This curious passage implies that hysteria belongs to women because they are anatomically more compact, less vulnerable than men. The explanation is clarified—and affirmed—a few sentences later:

> Remarquons enfin que si le rôle des organes génitaux féminins est beaucoup plus important, il commence et finit beaucoup plus tôt; en général, après quarante ans, la femme n'est plus apte à devenir mère; tandis que l'aptitude à procréer se prolonge chez l'homme presque indéfiniment, *comme si la nature avait voulu établir une compensation.*
>
> (229; my emphasis)

> *Finally, let us note that though the role of the female genital organs is much more significant, it begins and ends much earlier; in general, after age forty, woman can no longer have children, while the ability to procreate extends almost indefinitely in men,* as if nature had wanted to establish a compensation.

The second excerpt makes explicit what is only implied in the first: specifically, that the sexually exclusive definition of hysteria responds to an effort to compensate men for an apparent imbalance in the lot of the two sexes. Nature indemnifies men for the limited function of their genital organs by granting them extended fertility, and indemnifies them also for incurring the greater risk of loss, by assigning hysteria to women.

Hysteria, then, is an alternative form of castration visited upon women by men: "nature's compensation," or male revenge. Like the notion of female castration with which it is allied, it is already a fetish, a kind of compromise formation that strives to suspend and confuse polarities of masculine and feminine, presence and absence, outside and inside, supplementarity and lack.

We can turn once again to Berthe in order to elucidate Flaubert's use of hysteria as compromise. Because absence is this child's identifying feature, the few patterns that emerge from her otherwise inconsequential appearances in the novel become telling. Flaubert's representation of Berthe is distinguished by an incessant mobility whose extreme form—toward which my argument will develop—is fluidity. There is an emphasis on her comings and goings. What little we hear about her is dominated by accounts of her puppetlike entrances and exits. The comically repetitive quality of her peregrinations is evident in the following condensed sampling:

Emma fut prise . . . du besoin de voir sa petite fille . . . qui *avait été mise*
en nourrice. . . . Elle *retira* Berthe de nourrice (124–25, 139). Emma
. . . la *prit*. . . . Puis elle [la] *recoucha* (126). La servante *amena*
Berthe. . . . "*Emmenez*-la," dit [Emma] (151). "*Amenez*-la-moi!" dit sa
mère. . . . Elle la *remit* aux mains de la domestique (201). Elle *fit revenir*
à la maison sa petite fille, que son mari, durant sa maladie, *avait renvoyée*
chez la nourrice (241). "*Amenez*-moi la petite," dit-elle. . . . "Assez!
qu'on l'*emmène!*" s'écria Charles (337–38). On *avait conduit* Berthe
chez Mme Homais. . . . Charles, le lendemain, *fit revenir* la petite
(349, 359; my emphasis).

> *Emma was suddenly seized with the desire to see her little girl, who* had been put *to*
> *nurse.* . . . *She* took Berthe away *from the nurse (65, 76). She* took [her] up. . . .
> *Then she* put back *the little girl (66). The servant* brought Berthe. . . . "Take her
> away," *[Emma] said (85).* "Bring her to me," *said her mother.* . . . *She* gave her
> back *to the maid (124). Her little girl, whom her husband had* sent back *to the nurse*
> *during her illness,* returned home *(155).* "Bring *me the child," she said.* . . .
> *"Enough!* Take her away!" *cried Charles (232–33). They had* taken Berthe to
> Madame Homais's. . . . *The next day Charles had the child* brought back *(242,*
> *249).*

This constant shuttling motion is antithetical to Emma's ideal model of unrestricted movement, which she perceives as a typically male property: "Un homme,
au moins, est libre; il peut parcourir les passions et les pays, traverser les obstacles,
mordre aux bonheurs les plus lointains" (122) ["A man, at least, is free; he can explore all passions and all countries, overcome obstacles, taste of the most distant
pleasures"] (63). The question of where Emma herself is located on the continuum of movement is, however, a tricky one.

From the beginning, Emma is depicted as the essence of mobility; as Claudine
Gothot-Mersch remarks, she possesses "un dynamisme instinctif, qui contraste
avec le statisme de Charles"[26] ["an instinctive dynamism, in sharp contrast to
Charles's static nature"]. Her physical traits are carefully described to reinforce this
fundamental aspect of her being:

> Le grand air l'entourait, levant pêle-mêle les petits cheveux follets de sa
> nuque, ou secouant sur sa hanche les cordons de son tablier, qui se
> tortillaient comme des banderoles. . . . L'ombrelle, de soie gorge-de-
> pigeon, que traversait le soleil, éclairait de reflets mobiles la peau blanche
> de sa figure. (51)

[26] Gothot-Mersch, *La Genèse de Madame Bovary,* 102.

*The open air wrapped her round, playing with the soft down on the back of
her neck, or blew to and fro on her hips her apron-strings, that fluttered like
streamers. . . . The parasol, made of an iridescent silk that let the sunlight sift
through, colored the white skin of her face with shifting reflections.*   (12–13)

The static appearance of her everyday life is belied by "[sa] pensée vagabondant"
(56) ["her thoughts wandering"] (16), an offshoot of the voyage motif. Emma's escapes to Rouen, her unrealized departure with Rodolphe, her phantasmatic re-
treats to an idealized other world are recurrent manifestations of the general condition that Gothot-Mersch has named "la maladie de changer de place"[27] ["the
moving disease"].

Emma's malady, a perverse form of motion sickness, might otherwise be defined as a refusal to stay in (her) place. This was clearly the prevailing interpretation at the trial of *Madame Bovary*, when the novel was judged by Flaubert's contemporaries.[28] It is particularly revealing that the defense attorney, Sénard, basing
his case upon the same underlying assumptions about Emma as did the prosecu-
tion, argued that Flaubert intended his novel to be a cautionary tale about a
woman "qui *va chercher* le bonheur *ailleurs que chez elle*" ["who *goes looking* for
happiness *away from her own home*"]—a woman "qui a rêvé le bonheur *en dehors
de sa maison*" ["who dreamed of happiness *outside of her house*"].[29] Throughout
his pleading, Sénard continues to describe Emma's transgressions in spatial metaphors, metaphors that clearly imply that she has strayed from a woman's place.
"Conduite dans un couvent *hors de sa sphère*" (404) ["Taken to a convent *beyond
her sphere*"], she has had "une éducation *au-dessus de la condition dans laquelle
elle est née*" (392) ["an education *above the station into which she was born*"]; as a
result she is "*déviée*" (393) ["*deviant*"], unable to take care of "[les] devoirs de *sa position*" (392) ["the duties of *her position*"], unable to seek happiness "*dans sa maison*" (392; my emphasis) ["*in her home*"].

Twenty-two years later, and speaking from a medical position, Charles Richet
would echo Sénard's criticism of female upward mobility:

A Paris . . . et dans les grandes villes, où les jeunes filles des classes
inférieures et de la petite bourgeoisie reçoivent une éducation supérieure
à leur état social, l'hystérie est très fréquente.   (346)

[27] Ibid.

[28] As LaCapra has astutely argued, "A trial is a locus of social reading that brings out conventions of
interpretation in a key institution. *"Madame Bovary" on Trial*, 7.

[29] Réquisitoire, Plaidoirie et Jugement, in *Madame Bovary*, 414; my emphasis. Subsequent references
will appear in the text.

In Paris and in big cities, where young ladies of the lower classes and the petite bourgeoisie are educated beyond their social standing, hysteria is very frequent.

The doctor's etiological remarks, the lawyer's social commentary, and the novelist's literary portrait derive from a common source. Flaubert's vagabond, Sénard's social climber, Richet's overeducated hysteric are all latter-day versions of an ancient theory of hysteria preserved in the *Dictionnaire* term "ascension de la matrice" ["rising of the womb"] given as a synonym for hysteria. The nineteenth-century female wanderer embodies ancient Egyptian attributions of certain female behavioral disorders to a dislocated uterus that roves about the body, crowding other structures and impinging upon their functioning.[30] More specifically, she re-presents Plato's formulation of the womb as "an animal which longs to generate children" and which, if too long without child, may begin to stray and to work mischief in the body.[31]

If we are to contrast Emma with what Mario Vargas Llosa has called "those industrious procreating wombs, the women of Yonville,"[32] then I think we must do so in the parallel terms of that anguished barren animal, the roaming womb. Emma is the incarnation of the wandering womb, the ruling—but unruly—female organ that will not stay in place, that seeks to invade foreign, forbidden territory.

If we envision Emma's place on a spectrum of potential movement that stretches from unfettered male mobility to Berthe's rhythm of oscillation to female constraint or immobility, then Emma, as motion incarnate, appears to be ill-represented by her daughter and should perhaps be assigned instead to the male position. A closer look, however, compels us to rethink this position. If the paradigmatic womb is an animal straying about in the body, it is nevertheless a caged animal, and its wanderings are restricted.[33]

Although Emma is in many respects the essence of perpetual motion, she never effectively changes place; her movements are always constrained. The early, very animated description of her deliberately qualifies this animation: the flyaway wisps of hair, the apron strings twisting and billowing like streamers in the wind, the scintillating effect of the iridescent silk all bespeak a harnessed, tethered variety of motion, movement in place. Emma's musings as she awaits the birth of her child further specify the style of animation with which she is identified:

[30] My information comes from Ilza Veith, *Hysteria: The History of a Disease* (Chicago: University of Chicago Press, 1965).

[31] From Plato's *Timaeus*; quoted by Veith, *Hysteria*, 7–8. See my Introduction for greater historical detail.

[32] Mario Vargas Llosa, *The Perpetual Orgy: Flaubert and "Madame Bovary,"* trans. Helen Lane (New York: Farrar, Straus & Giroux, 1986), 24.

[33] Emma's confined motion typifies the situation of the nineteenth-century heroine, whose bound energy, as Schor has brilliantly shown, powers the nineteenth-century novel. See Schor, *Breaking the Chain*, especially "Unwriting *Lamiel*," 135–46.

Une femme est empêchée continuellement. Inerte et flexible à la fois,
elle a contre elle les mollesses de la chair avec les dépendances de la loi.
Sa volonté, comme le voile de son chapeau retenu par un cordon, palpite
à tous les vents; il y a toujours quelque désir qui entraîne, quelque
convenance qui retient. (122–23)

A woman is always hampered. Being inert as well as pliable, she has against her the
weakness of the flesh and the inequity of the law. Like the veil held to her hat by a
ribbon, her will flutters in every breeze; she is always drawn by some desire,
restrained by some rule of conduct. (63)

The image of an attached veil fluttering—palpitating—in the breeze repeats the
pattern of restrained motion but modifies it. Halfway between banality and pathology, the verb *palpiter* makes explicit the analogy between vacillating or oscillating motion and hysterical symptoms such as tremors, spasms, and convulsions.
Furthermore, the phrase "il y a toujours quelque désir qui *entraîne,* quelque
convenance qui *retient,*" which immediately follows and interprets the palpitating
veil simile, links the concept of palpitation to the back-and-forth pattern of motion
that will later be emblematized by Berthe's puppetlike existence.

Berthe, then, becomes a parody of Emma, of the wandering womb, and of
moving in place—a parody that gains in subtlety what it loses in certainty when it
is compared to an earlier version of the novel, which had Berthe in the throes of
convulsions shortly after Emma's death.[34] The identification of Emma with her
daughter suggests that she, like Berthe, belongs somewhere in the middle of the
range of movement, and that she represents a compromise formation, a figurative
correlative of the *Dictionnaire's* presentation of hysteria as nature's way of wounding women in recognition of—in retaliation for—their noncastratability. If un-
trammeled mobility is equated with masculinity and utter immobility with femininity, then Flaubert may well have created in Emma a degraded version of
the "hermaphrodite sublime" he tried so hard—and failed—to make of Louise
Colet.[35]

[34] Charles and Berthe are discussing death; Charles faints, "et, quand il revint à lui, elle avait des convulsions" ["and, when he opened his eyes, she was having convulsions"]. Flaubert, *Madame Bovary:*
Ebauches et fragments inédits, ed. Gabrielle Leleu (Paris: Conard, 1936), 1:574.
[35] "J'ai toujours essayé (mais il me semble que j'échoue) de faire de toi un hermaphrodite sublime" (letter to Louise Colet, 2:548, 12 April 1854) ["I have always tried (but I believe I have failed) to make you
into a sublime hermaphrodite"]. Flaubert's own identification with hysteria does not change his valorization of hysteria as degradation, for Louise Colet (and also for Emma Bovary and for women in general). Hysteria in women constitutes a mutilation, a loss; but when a male artist identifies with it, it becomes a supplement. As I contend in Chapter 4, hysteria allows Flaubert to be a (super)man with the
sensibilities and subjectivity of a woman.

EMMA/LOUISE

And so we appear to come full circle. Reading Emma's hysteria with contemporary medical texts establishes the fidelity of her case history to nineteenth-century conventions of pathology. What is not immediately obvious from this kind of reading—and what I want briefly to appraise before continuing—is the degree of refraction that occurs when Flaubert reproduces his era's image of hysteria. While it would be impossible to measure the angle of refraction—to do so would be tantamount to tracing the limits of Flaubertian irony—we must at least begin to evaluate its presence.

Two decades before Charcot realized the power of an *idée reçue* and became high priest of hysteria at the Salpêtrière, Flaubert read the medical dictionary and latched on to a rising cliché. I am using the *Dictionnaire* emblematically here; Flaubert could just as well have listened to people in the street. His awareness that medical and popular discourses of hysteria were fundamentally continuous is reflected by their interchangeability in *Madame Bovary*.[36] It doesn't really matter that the *Dictionnaire des sciences médicales* sits with uncut pages on the shelves of Charles Bovary's study, for its principal tenets (novels are a prime cause of hysteria in young girls, the fragrance of apricots is also pernicious, brunettes are highly excitable, and so on) emerge from the mouths of characters such as Monsieur Homais. The point is that the *Dictionnaire des sciences médicales*, whatever its authority as the voice of science, whatever its role as pillar of the medical institution, is essentially a dictionary of nineteenth-century medicine's received ideas. So it is not surprising that the entries related to hysteria in Flaubert's own *Dictionnaire des idées reçues* can be traced back to the medical dictionary:

> HYSTÉRIE. La confondre avec la nymphomanie.
> NERVEUX. Se dit chaque fois qu'on ne comprend rien à une maladie,
> cette explication satisfait l'auditeur.
> ROMANS. Pervertissent les masses.
> FILLES. Les jeunes filles: Eviter pour elles toute espèce de livre.
> BRUNES. Sont plus chaudes que les blondes (voy. BLONDES).

[36] For an opposing interpretation of *Madame Bovary* in terms of hysteria, see Rothfield's "From Semiotic to Discursive Intertextuality." His argument depends upon the underlying assumption—which runs exactly counter to my own—that "the system of medical presuppositions about hysteria did not exist as an encoded ideology based on a cliché . . . but as a part of a coherent discourse" (58). Neither can I entirely agree with Jan Goldstein's subtly argued claim for a literary subversion of the scientific discourse of hysteria, in "The Uses of Male Hysteria." Though literary insights into this discourse are often potentially subversive, they are usually recuperated by an underlying (and perhaps inevitable) ideological conservatism.

BLONDES.   Plus chaudes que les brunes (voy. BRUNES).

ROUSSES.   (Voy. BLONDES, BRUNES, BLANCHES et NÉGRESSES.)[37]

HYSTERIA.   *To be confused with nymphomania.*

NERVOUS.   *Said every time nothing is understood about an illness;*
            this explanation satisfies the hearer.

NOVELS.   *Pervert the masses.*

GIRLS.   *Young ladies: Avoid exposing them to any kind of books.*

BRUNETTES. *Are hotter than blondes (see BLONDES).*

BLONDES.   *Are hotter than brunettes (see BRUNETTES).*

REDHEADS.   *(See BLONDES, BRUNETTES, WHITE WOMEN, and*
            NEGRESSES.)

And so on. How does Flaubert's ironic reprise, in his own dictionary, of the conventions of hysteria presented in the medical dictionary, affect our reading of these conventions as they appear in *Madame Bovary*? I have no ready answer to that question; I can only point in what I think is the right direction by reiterating that *Madame Bovary* is bounded by medicine and its ironic double. I shall begin to elaborate on this framing by returning to Dr. Richet, who chronologically closes the series of texts with which I opened this discussion; his commentary, as we saw earlier, mediates between medicine and literature. Bringing to his appraisal of Emma Bovary the full authority of his medical knowledge, Richet passes judgment: "De toutes les hystériques dont les romanciers ont raconté l'histoire, la plus vivante, la plus vraie . . . c'est Mme Bovary" (348) ["Of all hysterics whose story has been told by novelists, the most lifelike, the truest . . . is Madame Bovary"]. Impervious to irony, Richet—the Homais of the Salpêtrière—evaluates Flaubert's hysteric and finds her to be a good copy.

If, somewhat arbitrarily, we assign to Richet the penultimate word in this conversation, it would be tempting to allow Flaubert the last laugh. But we should not too quickly or too gullibly decide that irony has the last word here. Any reading that addresses the question of Emma's hysteria must, like the novel, take its place between two dictionaries: the medical version and its literary subversion, taking care not to be blinded by Flaubert's irony in the second to his complicity with the first. In fact Flaubert's irony *covers* his complicity; it both includes and eclipses his collusion with the *doxa* he vociferously condemns as bourgeois discourse: *bêtise* and *idées reçues*.[38]

[37] Gustave Flaubert, *Le Dictionnaire des idées reçues*, in vol. 2 of *Oeuvres complètes*, ed. Jean Bruneau and Bernard Masson (Paris: Seuil, 1964), passim.

[38] Commentary on the workings of *bêtise* and *idées reçues* in Flaubert is infinite. My own thinking has been most influenced by Jonathan Culler's *Flaubert: The Uses of Uncertainty* (Ithaca: Cornell University Press, 1985); and LaCapra's *"Madame Bovary" on Trial*.

Flaubert's use of hysteria consistently exposes his discursive collusion with ideological constructs that he ostensibly rejects. In order to explore this problem I
move on to consider that particularly concentrated aspect of mobility—fluidity—
that links Emma Bovary intertextually to Louise Colet (the Colet we find in the
text of the *Correspondance*), and also binds her intratextually to Berthe. The contradictions and hypocrisies inherent in Flaubert's expression of double rage
(against Louise Colet and against bourgeois society) take me to a discussion of his
style as both recognition and denial of conflict: that is, as compromise and, finally,
as attempted resolution.

The identification of Louise Colet's style, in Flaubert's *Correspondance*, with
metaphors of her female flow—blood, tears, mucus, milk—is transcribed in his
imaging of Emma Bovary's temperament as it is embodied in her daughter,
Berthe. Once again, Berthe Bovary is a caricature of her mother, this time con-
densing Emma's lack of self-containment, her emotional overflow and fluctuating
dispositions. One might argue for the realism of the portrait of a child who sheds
an unceasing stream of tears, drools freely, vomits often, gets the colic, needs her
diaper changed, falls and bleeds (126, 148, 241; de Man 66, 82, 155). It is nonetheless arresting to find such a disproportionately large number of details devoted
to bodily leaks and drips in an otherwise vague portrait, particularly in view of the
fact that Berthe's portrait materializes the more abstract descriptions of Emma.
Berthe, presented as a system of perpetual drips, represents a condensation of
Emma, who is known to the bourgeoisie of Yonville for "ses airs évaporés" (157)
["her vaporish airs"] (89) and is similarly classified, in the words of her mother-in-
law, as "une évaporée" (220) ["a vaporish woman"] (my translation).[39] Given the
sources of these qualifications, which are commonplaces of the nineteenth-
century discourse of hysteria—"the vapors," in the parlance of the era—one
might be inclined to relegate them to the domain of ironic citation were it not
for the complicating factor that they find their place in a network of similar images characterizing Emma, her imagination, and her perceptions (and including
evaporation, vapor, haze, fog, clouds, mist) diffused throughout the narrative
discourse.[40]

---

[39] Her mother-in-law elsewhere continues in the same mode, blaming Emma's malaise on her leisure:
"Si elle était, comme tant d'autres, contrainte à gagner son pain, *elle n'aurait pas ces vapeurs-là*, qui lui
viennent d'un tas d'idées qu'elle se fourre dans la tête, et du désoeuvrement où elle vit" (157–58; my
emphasis) ["If she were obliged, like so many others, to earn her living, *she wouldn't have these vapors,
that come to her from a lot of ideas she stuffs into her head, and from the idleness in which she lives*"]
(90).

[40] I am not the first to speak of fog and haze in this novel. Tony Tanner writes some dazzling pages on
interior and exterior climate conditions in the novel, suggesting that Emma's fogginess may be explained by "her situation in a language dominated by a confusion of male ascriptions and descriptions
and prescriptions." Tanner, *Adultery in the Novel: Contract and Transgression* (Baltimore: Johns Hopkins University Press, 1979), 312. Tanner's comments on indistinction and the confusion of categories

So, for example, the malaise that overtakes Emma as Charles's wife is compared to that of a certain Guérin's daughter said to have had a fog in her head ("une manière de brouillard qu'elle avait dans la tête" [141; de Man 78]). At a later point in the narrative, when she takes communion while in the throes of brain fever after Rodolphe's abandonment, her entire being seems to vaporize: "Il lui sembla que son être . . . allait s'anéantir dans cet amour comme un encens allumé qui se dissipe en vapeur" (239) ["It seemed to her that her being, mounting toward God, would be annihilated in that love like a burning incense that melts into vapour"] (154).

We might then say that Berthe materializes Louise Colet's stylistic faults, while Emma etherealizes them. Or, to shift the terms of the analogy a bit, Berthe's liquidity is to Emma's vaporousness as the *woman* Louise Colet is to the *style* Louise Colet, with the first term on each side of the equation acting to embody, and the second, to abstract. We then have two extremes of a continuum that can be conveniently labeled "Berthe" and "Emma," with the proviso that this is a preliminary schematic representation of a textual rhetoric that we must eventually discuss as process rather than as static paradigm. For the character called Emma (who is, as we have seen, metonymically continuous with her daughter) herself includes both vapor and liquid: she coincides with an ongoing series of passages from a liquid to a vaporous state.

The outer and inner geographies of Emma's life are bathed in water. There is a predominance of liquid imagery in *Madame Bovary* used liberally as description and metaphor, the two modes often not clearly distinguishable.[41] Each of the three principal settings of the novel is water-based: Tostes, by its proximity to the sea; Yonville, by its site on the banks of the Rieule River; Rouen, by its position on the Seine. But the recurrent realist descriptions of these bodies of water flow imperceptibly into metaphorical geography, as when, for example, Emma and Rodolphe sit by the river before their projected elopement and "la tendresse des anciens jours leur revenait au coeur, abondante et silencieuse comme la rivière qui

---

are wonderfully provocative but seem to put Flaubert outside his writing as a nonparticipating observer and portraitist much of the time. Ross Chambers writes suggestively about environmental and discursive correlatives of Emma's malady (which he perceives as melancholy) and finds important connections between the fogs of her melancholy and modernity's truths found in cloudiness, confusion, and indistinction. Chambers, *Mélancolie et opposition: Les débuts du modernisme en France* (Paris: Corti, 1987). And Jean-Pierre Richard speaks of fluidity (primarily liquid rather than vaporous) within a nexus of processes (fusion, diffusion, dissolution, mutability) that are close to my own concerns. Richard, *Stendhal et Flaubert: Littérature et sensation* (Paris: Seuil, 1954).

[41] Rosemary Lloyd's brief but enlightening passage on water in *Madame Bovary* points out that the creation of (diegetic, emotional, or imaginative) space in this novel depends on a "constant oscillation between descriptive and metaphorical modes"; she uses the water motif as one illustration of such shifting. Lloyd, *"Madame Bovary"* (London: Unwin Hyman, 1990), 123–24; see also D. L. Demorest, *L'Expression figurée et symbolique dans l'oeuvre de Gustave Flaubert* (Geneva: Slatkine Reprints, 1967), 430–60.

coulait" (225) ["the tenderness of the old days came back to their hearts, full and silent as the flowing river"] (143). Similarly, but on a microcosmic level, there are the descriptions of Emma that evoke fluidity, if only in a passing detail, such as her hair flowing in "un mouvement ondé vers les tempes" (49) ["a wavy movement at the temples"] (11), or accumulated details that evoke mergings of the woman with her surroundings. Here is Emma in a warm winter moment when the frost begins to thaw: "L'écorce des arbres suintait dans la cour, la neige sur les couvertures des bâtiments se fondait. . . . [Son] ombrelle, de soie gorge-de-pigeon, que traversait le soleil, éclairait de reflets mobiles la peau blanche de sa figure. . . . On entendait les gouttes d'eau, une à une, tomber sur la moire tendue" (51) ["The bark of the trees in the yard was oozing, the snow melted on the roofs of the buildings. . . . {Her} parasol, made of an iridescent silk that let the sunlight sift through, colored the white skin of her face with shifting reflections. . . . Drops of water fell one by one on the taut silk"] (13). The metamorphic state signaled by the dripping bark, the melting snow, the drops of water falling onto the parasol is concentrated by the oscillating effect of the iridescent silk and the moiré, which often appears throughout the novel to intensify the protean effect of water images.

Emma's dreamscapes are of course no less waterlocked than the realist tableaux, only more exotically so. Riverbanks and sea breezes are joined by mountain lakes, grottoes, fountains, cascades, and gulfs, and by the appropriate accoutrements— swans, chalets, palm trees, gondolas, fishing nets, and guitars. The liquid images of her internal landscapes correspond to the fluidity with which the images succeed one another, and to the mobility of their display. Water imagery also appears alone, detached from diegetic moorings, to convey Emma's perceptive or affective states, as for instance the dark overpowering sea that translates her sense of impending doom when Rodolphe has rejected her plea for financial help: "Le sol, sous ses pieds, était plus mou qu'une onde, et les sillons lui parurent d'immenses vagues brunes, qui déferlaient" (333) ["The earth beneath her feet was more yielding than the sea, and the furrows seemed to her immense brown waves breaking into foam"] (228). Or again, there is the more positive image of a river of milk that suffuses Emma's consciousness after her lovemaking with Rodolphe: "Elle sentait . . . le sang circuler dans sa chair comme un fleuve de lait" (190) ["She felt . . . the blood coursing through her flesh like a river of milk"] (116).[42]

But if Emma's landscapes emerge from water, they drift into haze.[43] Her water-

---

[42] Although there is some truth to Demorest's observation that lakes, torrents, oceans, and waves represent in Emma's imagination "ce que l'amour a de terrible et de funeste" ["what is most terrible and catastrophic about love"], this is not categorically so because such images can and do bear positive tenors. Demorest, *L'Expression figurée*, 454.

[43] On the characteristic movement of expansion and diffusion in Flaubert, see Georges Poulet's classic studies "Flaubert," in *Etudes sur le temps humain* (Paris: Plon, 1949) and "Flaubert," in *Les Métamorphoses du cercle* (Paris: Flammarion, 1979).

based scenes, fantasies, dreams, and metaphors tend to dissipate, to be volatilized as fog, haze, or mist, to evaporate into the intangibility of disillusioned reverie. In many cases we can actually watch the transition process, the crossing from one state to another. One such passage moves us from fountains to their vaporous spray: "On entendait . . . le bruit des fontaines, dont la vapeur s'envolant rafraî-chissait des tas de fruits" (223) ["They heard . . . the noise of fountains, whose rising spray refreshed heaps of fruit"] (141). Another takes us from an illusory lake to the rising mists that both shroud and create it: "De la hauteur où ils étaient, toute la vallée paraissait un immense lac pâle, s'évaporant à l'air" (187) ["From the height on which they were the whole valley seemed an immense pale lake sending off its vapour into the air"] (114). Yet another excerpt puts before us what Emma views from an open window: "On voyait la rivière dans la prairie, où elle dessinait sur l'herbe des sinuosités vagabondes. La vapeur du soir passait entre les peupliers sans feuilles, estompant leurs contours d'une teinte violette, plus pâle et plus trans-parente qu'une gaze subtile arrêtée sur leurs branchages" (143) ["The river could be seen in the fields, meandering through the grass in sinuous curves. The evening vapors rose between the leafless poplars, touching their outline with a violet tint, paler and more transparent than a subtle gauze caught amidst their branches"] (78). Here the passage from river to vapor clearly signifies blurring, clouding, con-fusing, for the well-delineated curves of the river give way to the indistinct con-tours of the poplars.

The transition from water to vapor, however, is not written for us to read in every case; these are privileged insights, for much of the time we read the states sepa-rately. The haziness of Emma's perceptions, the vagaries of her dreams, the vague-ness of her desires are consistently figured in vaporous meteorological images—images that find their counterpart, and their reinforcement, in numerous associ-ated references to that shimmering, vacillating texture of moiré fabric, and in fre-quent recourse to the verb *miroiter*, "to shimmer, to glisten."[44] Verb, fabric, and meteorological metaphors share the element of change and changeability: fluctua-

---

[44] One example of the juxtaposition of these elements is the scene set before Emma one Thursday when she arrives at Rouen. She sees the city appear before her, "*noyée dans le brouillard.* . . . Ainsi vu d'en haut, le paysage tout entier avait l'air immobile comme une peinture; les navires à l'ancre se tas-saient dans un coin; *le fleuve arrondissait sa courbe* au pied des collines vertes. . . . On entendait le ronflement des fonderies avec *le carillon clair des églises qui se dressaient dans la brume.* . . . *Les toits, tout reluisants de pluie, miroitaient inégalement.* . . . Et son coeur s'en gonflait abondamment, comme si les cent vingt mille âmes qui palpitaient là eussent envoyé toutes à la fois *la vapeur des pas-sions qu'elle leur supposait*" (287; my emphasis) ["*drowned in the fog.* . . . Seen thus from above, the whole landscape seemed frozen, like a picture; the anchored ships were massed in one corner, *the river curved around* the foot of the green hills. . . . One heard the rumbling of the foundries, mingled with *the clear chimes of the churches, dimly outlined in the fog.* . . . *The roofs, shining from the rain, threw back unequal, glimmering reflections.* . . . Her heart swelled as though the hundred and twenty thou-sand souls palpitating there had all at once wafted to her *the passionate haze with which her imagination had endowed them*"] (190; trans. modified).

tion, oscillation, confusion, and indecision but also, more positively, exaltation, ethereality, possibility.

Emma is the center of consciousness that filters the haze of images before us (though as we will see, it exceeds her bounds, diffuses well beyond her). Contexts vary, but the language of vaporization is consistently conditioned by thin or expiring hopes, fantasy, illusion, disillusion, fading reveries, ennui. Here is Emma's incipient awareness of her stagnant life: "Comme les matelots en détresse, elle promenait sur la solitude de sa vie des yeux désespérés, cherchant au loin quelque voile blanche dans les brumes de l'horizon" (96) ["Like shipwrecked sailors, she turned despairing eyes upon the solitude of her life, seeking afar some white sail in the mists of the horizon"] (44). When she is saturated with her husband's dullness, "quelque chose de stupéfiant comme une vapeur d'opium l'engourdissait" (276) ["she felt a stupor overcoming her, as if from an opium haze"] (182; translation modified). At the opera in Rouen, absorbed in the performance of *Lucia di Lammermoor*, "il lui semblait entendre, à travers le brouillard, le son des cornemuses écossaises se répéter sur les bruyères" (248) ["she seemed to hear through the mist the sound of the Scotch bagpipes re-echoing over the moors"] (161). Returning to Yonville and Charles after a tryst with Léon, Emma looks back at Rouen: "A chaque tournant, on apercevait de plus en plus tous les éclairages de la ville qui faisaient une large vapeur lumineuse au-dessus des maisons confondues" (290–91) ["At every turn, they could see more and more of the city below, forming a luminous mist above the mass of houses"] (193).

Although the representation of Emma covers a spectrum that includes the liquid and the vaporous as its two extremes, and can therefore not be fixed in either position, the trajectory of her characterization consistently moves in the direction of dematerialization and volatilization. It moves counter to Flaubert's representation of Louise Colet, who, as we have observed, is constantly degraded by being rematerialized and reembodied. Emma's death is then all the more notable for its reversal of the customary process: dying, she is returned to liquid, to Berthe, and to Louise Colet.

The wetness we come to associate with Berthe and with Louise Colet anticipates Emma's death scene, which is dominated by a resurgence of liquidity: her tears, her vomiting, the beads of sweat, the regurgitated blood, the inky taste in her mouth, the black liquid that pours from her corpse's lips, the bodily dissolution (335–49; de Man 230–42). In graphic reminder of his recurrent complaint to Colet that everything was dissolving, Flaubert relocates femininity in a fluidity inseparable from dissolution and decay as Emma departs in a flood of inky vomit: "Un flot de liquides noir sortit, comme un vomissement, de sa bouche" (349) ["A rush of black liquid poured from her mouth, as if she were vomiting"] (242). More specifically, Flaubert's liquidation of Emma recirculates the elements that have

dominated his epistolary conversations with Louise Colet: ink, body fluids, feminine voice, creative flow, drowning. Emma takes her place after the Louise Colet
we know from the *Correspondance* and the Mariette we know from *La Servante* in
a series of women written into the restraining discourse of gender. But Emma also
takes her place as a woman who writes, again coming after Louise Colet and the
writer manqué Colet creates in the character of Mariette. Before Naomi Schor
had argued her compelling case for Emma as "the portrait of an artist, but the artist
as a young woman," one might easily have overlooked the representation of Emma
as writer.[45] Schor traces Emma's passage from the position of reader to the active
position of heroine, her desire to be not only a novel but a novelist, her acquisition, to this end, of the accoutrements of writing (blotter, penholder, envelopes,
writing case), and her desire for literary fame. In this framework her letters to Rodolphe suggest an incipient epistolary novel, and the suicide note is her last text.[46]
Although Schor's unveiling of Flaubert's portrait of Emma as author is too persuasive to be forgotten, the shrouding of her writer's persona in the text of the novel—
the fact that it *can* so easily be overlooked—is too significant to be dismissed.

I would displace Schor's emphasis on Emma's gender-related repression of her
own writing desire,[47] and stress instead the suppression/repression of Emma's writing on the part of Flaubert. Having followed the violence with which Flaubert cor-
rects Louise Colet's fluid-identified writing style, having then read *La Servante* as
the inscription of Colet's resistance to the drowning of her woman's voice, and having observed the fury with which Flaubert meets the finished manuscript (which
Colet publishes against his advice) we can better understand that Emma Bovary offered him an opportunity finally to make of Louise Colet "ce que j'en rêve" ["the
substance of my dreams"]: the chance to give form to his phantasms and to breathe
life into his wrath.

"*Ce poème est une mauvaise action*" (2:502, 9–10 January 1854) [*"This poem is
a bad action"*], Flaubert asserts upon reading *La Servante*, adding, "tu en as été
punie, car c'est une mauvaise oeuvre" ["you have been punished for it, for it is a
bad work"]. The invocation of talion law suggests not only judgment but warning.
Colet has been punished—but perhaps not enough. Dream and castigation, creation and correction: Emma Bovary is a better-chastised Louise Colet, a tenacious
disavowal of the power of her voice and a degradation of the authority of her ink.
Her voice definitively somatized as body fluids, reinfused in her body as vomit, she

---

[45] Schor, *Breaking the Chain*, 15.
[46] See, too, Nathaniel Wing's "Emma's Stories," in *The Limits of Narrative* (Cambridge: Cambridge
University Press, 1986), 41–77. Maria L. Assad has also spoken persuasively about Emma as writer,
and the inklike fluid as sign of a destroyed textuality. Assad, "Who Really Killed Emma Bovary?" (Paper
delivered at Eleventh Annual Nineteenth-Century French Studies Colloquium, Vanderbilt University, 17 October 1985).
[47] Schor, *Breaking the Chain*, 17.

160
•
is blotted out by a flood of regurgitated ink. Submerged in the return of her own re-pressed flow, she represents a critical reversal for Flaubert, who had seen *La Servante* as a prime example of contemporary writing drowning in the effusiveness of feminine style: "L'écriture contemporaine est noyée dans les règles de femme" (2:508, 15 January 1854) ["Contemporary writing is drowning in menstrual flow"]. Adjusting the balance, Flaubert drowns feminine voice in his writing.[48] Rewriting Colet's Ophelia, Mariette, who was saved at the last minute, rescued from the waters, Flaubert finishes the interrupted task. Emma is Ophelia re-drowned; the poison is a mere alibi of plot.

The liquidation of Emma Bovary might then be described as a purge. Indeed, Dr. Canivet, the celebrated medical expert called in from Neufchâtel, uses that very term after the emetic has done its work. "Diable! . . . cependant . . . elle est purgée" (339) ["The devil! yet she has been purged"] (233), he declares, perplexed that the sickness continues when the cause appears to have been removed. But only after death is Emma effectively purged—both *of* her liquidity and *from* the text. When the last black fluid has streamed from her cadaver's mouth (349), the text is once again set adrift in a cloud of vapors, and Emma all but evaporates:

> Les herbes aromatiques fumaient encore, et des tourbillons de vapeur bleuâtre se confondaient au bord de la croisée avec le brouillard qui entrait. . . .
> Des moires frissonnaient sur la robe de satin. . . . Emma disparaissait dessous; et il lui semblait [à Charles] que, s'épandant au dehors d'elle-même, elle se perdait confusément dans l'entourage des choses, dans le silence, dans la nuit, dans le vent qui passait, dans les senteurs humides qui montaient. (350–51)

> *The aromatic herbs were still smoking, and spirals of bluish vapour blended at the window with the entering fog. . . .*
> *The watered satin of her gown shimmered. . . . Emma was lost beneath it; and it seemed to him [to Charles] that, spreading beyond her own self, she blended confusedly with everything around her—the silence, the night, the passing wind, the damp odors rising from the ground.* (243)

By purging Emma, diffusing her body in a confusion of vapor, fog, and moiré, the text works to expurgate itself, cleansing itself of its stylistic leaks, of the residue of romanticism that trickles unpredictably forth from imperfectly buried springs. Having reproached literature for its embodied voice, Flaubert kills Emma to un-

[48] Is this the fantasized "roaring style" that would dominate—*drown*, in the happy translation by Julian Barnes—the other voices?

voice her body and disembody his own writing voice. This voice without body, without discernible identity, is set loose to wander, a fluid circulating force diffused in the narrative of *Madame Bovary*.

LOUISE/GUSTAVE

When we read the death of Emma Bovary, close to the end of the novel, we are reading the foregrounding of the beginning of the novel—a bit like what happens when we read the last book of Proust's *Recherche* and perceive the foundation for the novel's existence. As Marcel's evolution prepares the conditions for Proust's writing, the path toward Emma's demise is a working-through of Flaubert's style. One might say that the story of *Madame Bovary* recounts, in liquid and vaporous phases, the gestation of its style: it provides diegetic correlatives for the abstract problematics of writing.

Vaporization, a kind of dispersion of liquidity, is a figure of figuration: a dematerialization or abstraction of matter, a fading of boundaries, a blurring of identity. In other words, the generalized tendency toward evaporation in *Madame Bovary*, which is most strongly characterized by Emma but which pervades the novel's descriptive, thematic, and rhetorical networks, corresponds to the novel's stylistic tendencies, notably its unlocalizable narrative center and that fading of narrative, diegetic, and citational voices we call free indirect discourse.[49] It is therefore not surprising to find Flaubert's aesthetic ideal defined in terms similar to vaporization, in a letter to Louise Colet contemporaneous with the early period of writing *Madame Bovary*:

> Les oeuvres les plus belles sont celles où il y a le moins de matière. . . .
> Je crois que l'avenir de l'Art est dans ces voies. Je le vois, à mesure qu'il
> grandit, *s'éthérisant tant qu'il peut*, depuis les pylônes égyptiens
> jusqu'aux lancettes gothiques, et depuis les poèmes de vingt mille vers
> des Indiens jusqu'aux jets de Byron. La forme, en devenant habile,
> s'atténue. . . . Cet affranchissement de la matérialité se retrouve en tout.
> (2:31, 16 January 1852; my emphasis)

> *The finest works are the least material. . . . I believe that the future of Art lies in
> this direction. I see it as it matures,* striving to etherealize, *from the pylons of*

---

[49] Of the many excellent critical works devoted at least in part to an exploration of this crucial and complicated aspect of *Madame Bovary*, those I have found most helpful are LaCapra's *"Madame Bovary" on Trial* and Vaheed Ramazani's *The Free Indirect Mode: Flaubert and the Poetics of Irony* (Charlottesville: University Press of Virginia, 1988).

Egyptian temples to Gothic lancet arches, and from Indian poems of twenty
thousand lines to Byron's streaming verses. Form, as it advances, grows more
spare. . . . This liberation from materiality is to be found everywhere.

This praise of lightness, airiness, attenuation, dematerialization, and diffusion is once again reminiscent, by antithesis, of the liquid, cloying characterization assigned to Colet's style and of the reflection of this fluid style in the creation of Emma's daughter, Emma's environs, her appearance, the fluctuations of her fantasies and her desires. A flowing style, metonymically one with the ink that delivers it, may be assumed to have similar equivocal properties: beautiful and treacherous, it is both compelling and drowning. It is difficult to forget Flaubert's ambivalent ode to ink: "Comme on s'y noie! comme il attire!" (2:395, 14 August 1853) ["How one drowns in it! How it entices!"]. One understands the recourse to a "vaporization" of this style at once seductive and repulsive; it is a compromise that retains a certain essence while modifying its form. Dispersed, suspended in air, this style owns no source, no definition, no limitations. Everywhere and nowhere, it is spirit rather than matter: it is that madness that Flaubert advises Colet to observe at the Salpê-trière Hospital and then to diffuse in her writing as a subtle haze or "vapeur subtile."[50]

Practicing what he preaches to Louise Colet, Flaubert diffuses a fine madness into and throughout *Madame Bovary*, writes it as a subtle haze, vaporizes it as style. We have, then, a text about hysteria, but also, more crucially, a hystericized text: the vaporization of Emma Bovary's hysteria enacts the hystericization of Flaubert's novel. To speak of the vaporization of Emma's hysteria is to refer at the same time to the volatilization and diffusion of the pool of characteristics in which Flaubert both recognizes and abhors his own self, and that he identifies and punishes as Louise Colet; it is, by extension, to understand such diffusion as a conversion of inner ambivalence into the broad gestures and fine movements of style. To emphasize, however, the fundamental interchangeability of Louise Colet, Emma Bovary, the Flaubertian repressed Other, and feminine flow is to run the risk of masking the fact that what is being vaporized—but in that very process, harnessed—in their name is a social discourse whose exploitation, albeit volatilized, has unsettling ideological ramifications.

For once we have seen how the conceptual, metaphorical, and stylistic aura of *Madame Bovary* is permeated by the discourse of hysteria articulated at that time—and this, I think, is what Baudelaire perceived when he wrote, in more concrete terms, that hysteria was the very bedrock of the novel—and once we have seen *Madame Bovary* as a vengeful continuation of the letters to Louise Colet, the troubling but inevitable question of the authenticity of that other, conflicting proj-

---

[50] See my citation from this letter, 142, *supra*.

ect of revenge must be raised. I am referring to that long-term desire to strike out
against cliché, against *bêtise*, against the bourgeois spirit—a project epitomized
by, but not limited to, the plan for the *Dictionnaire des idées reçues*, designed to
humiliate its readers who would no longer dare speak "de peur de dire naturelle-
ment une des phrases qui s'y trouvent"[51] ["for fear of unthinkingly speaking one of
the sentences to be found there"]. The bitterness that emerges in this fantasy of in-
timidation, which is, in Jonathan Culler's words, "a desire for revenge and the
hope that the despair of language . . . might be visited on others," is otherwise expressed as a hatred of stupidity that gives rise to creative revenge: "Je sens contre la
bêtise de mon époque des flots de haine qui m'étouffent. Il me monte de la merde
à la bouche. . . . Mais je veux la garder, la figer, la durcir. J'en veux faire une pâte
dont je barbouillerais le XIXe siècle"[52] ["The stupidity of my age moves me to
waves of hatred that smother me. Shit rises in my mouth. . . . But I want to keep
it, to congeal it, to harden it. I want to turn it into a paste with which I will smear
the nineteenth century"].

But if *Madame Bovary* puts the current discourse of hysteria in the service of retaliation against Louise Colet, how can Flaubert claim in good faith to use writing
as a revenge against bourgeois discourse? When the personal settling of scores re-
sorts to the worn paths of social discourse, Flaubert is reduced to the level of *copiste*, intoner of received ideas. Retaliating against Louise Colet, Flaubert becomes society's accomplice or avenger rather than its vengeful antagonist.

One answer to this revenger's dilemma is irony: Flaubert can indulge in society's
clichés of hysteria and mock them too, if he takes a rhetorical stance that suggests
to the reader a knowing distance from a discourse that is inherent in, yet alien to,
the text. But irony is often an alibi for hypocrisy; like Charles Bovary, who gave
himself license to love Emma because he refrained from seeing her, Flaubert allows himself to subscribe to the *doxa* because he avoids acknowledging it as truth.
("Et, par une sorte d'hypocrisie naïve, il estima que cette défense de la voir était
pour lui comme un droit de l'aimer" [52] ["And he thought, with a kind of naïve
hypocrisy, that this interdict to see her gave him a sort of right to love her"] [13].)
His ironic repetition of a certain discourse implicitly affirms it, even while working to corrode it, because this discourse, mimed and undermined, is nonetheless
the signifying matter of the text. Flaubert's irony thus responds to a binary structure of thought within which incompatible perceptions sustain each other in un-
easy but unthreatened cohabitation—knowledge modifying belief, which in turn
reshapes knowledge. The functioning of such a structure depends on vacillation,
equivocation, and irresolution. Water, the essence of elusiveness and mutability,

---

[51] Flaubert, *Correspondance*, 2:209, 16 December 1852.
[52] Culler, *Flaubert: The Uses of Uncertainty*, 165–66; Flaubert, *Correspondance*, 2:600, 30 September
1855.

is its element; its visual emblem is moiré, the very tissue of undecidability, and its
psychic counterpart, the fetish.[53]

Caught between the Scylla and Charybdis of style—between crushing *bêtise*
and drowning sentiment—Flaubert chooses neither, and in refusing to choose,
risks both. This is another way of saying that irony is not easily contained or controlled, as some of Flaubert's most perceptive critics have shown in elegant detail,
in reference to *Madame Bovary*.[54] But I am also pointing out a similarity, thoroughly exploited by Flaubert, between such structures of ambivalence as irony
and the fetish, and the construction of hysteria. Like irony, like the fetish, hysteria
is a compromise formation. It is a means of retaining belief in a difference that
knowledge rejects.[55]

Signification abhors indistinction, and hysteria, entrenched in sex and gender
dichotomies, denies indistinction by buttressing a series of cultural and social differences. Yet the hysteric, even as she represents the epitome of femininity, is a figure of gender blurring and mixing. Hyperbolically feminine, she is a woman who
wants to be a man. Hysteria grounds difference, but also gives it the lie.[56] The cultural primacy of the nineteenth-century hysteric emblematizes a desperate concern with gender differentiation, which in turn responds to a compelling need to
channel the human condition: to mark off as separate the flow, change, disorder,
decay, and death that inhabit us all.[57] The hysteric is that model of pathology who
would ideally attract disease and dissolution and loss of control and, like a magnet,
cluster them cleanly within the circumscribed compass of female deviance, marginality, alterity. At the same time—as Flaubert's own identification with this
pathological model makes excruciatingly clear—she is a phantasmatic construction, an avowal of the generalized condition she is used to deny. Hysteria is struc-

[53] My understanding of the fetish, in the broad terms of a mode of perceiving reality, is indebted to Octave Mannoni's "Je sais bien, mais quand même . . . ," in *Clefs pour l'imaginaire ou l'autre scène*
(Paris: Seuil, 1969), 9–33.
[54] See Chambers, *Mélancolie et opposition*; Culler, *Flaubert: The Uses of Uncertainty*; LaCapra, "*Madame Bovary" on Trial*; Ramazani, *The Free Indirect Mode*; Wing, *The Limits of Narrative*.
[55] I am playing here with the traditional notion of the fetish—founded upon a belief in sameness despite knowledge of difference, upon the myth of castration, the (lost but replaced) maternal phallus,
and the denial of the "reality" of sexual difference—to suggest instead that the potential reality of sameness may be much more difficult to acknowledge than that of difference. (I am of course not referring
to anatomical differences but to a system of difference based upon them.)
[56] A contextually appropriate example is provided by a *boutade* attributed to Victor Cousin about
Louise Colet, whose hysteria was celebrated among the men of letters in her entourage: "Maxime mulier sum, sed virago" ["I am the epitome of womanhood, but a virago/but I act like a man"]. The pun is
reported by Bart in *Flaubert*, 143.
[57] My thinking here owes much to Dorothy Dinnerstein's *The Mermaid and the Minotaur: Sexual Arrangements and Human Malaise* (New York: Harper and Row, 1977), and to Sander L. Gilman's *Difference and Pathology: Stereotypes of Sexuality, Race, and Madness* (Ithaca: Cornell University Press,
1985).

tured like a fetish, and the hystericist—he who puts hysteria into discourse—
moves into the fetishist's position.[58]

Vaporization gives Flaubert a way out of the infinite equivocation of this binary
structure, an escape from the irony perilously close to hypocrisy, a release from the
endless oscillation of fetishistic perception. Vaporization works for Flaubert not
only as an element of plot, but as an aesthetic strategy. All the while that Flaubert
is feminizing mortality and loss, and concurrently identifying with a mutability
and flux inscribed in the name of woman, the narrative voice diffuses, disappears
in the fusing of disparate voices. The evaporation of the subject dissolves the dead-
lock of abdication and embrace. No compromise is necessary because there are no
longer antithetical positions: in fact there are no positions. As Roland Barthes remarks, *"On ne sait jamais [si Flaubert] est responsable de ce qu'il écrit* (s'il y a un
sujet *derrière* son langage)"[59] [*"One never knows {if Flaubert} is responsible for what
he writes* (if there is a subject *behind* his language"]. Flaubert saves himself from
drowning, and from colliding with *bêtise*, and—most significantly—from spin-
ning endlessly between the two, by suspending himself in that fine protective mist
that we variously call vaporization, hystericization, or the free indirection of style.

CODA: REFLECTIONS ON POISON
(OF ARSENIC, MERCURY, WATER, AND MIST)

Benjamin Bart reports that when Flaubert was doing the medical research for
Emma's death scene, he accidentally substituted the symptoms of mercury poisoning for those of arsenic, the appointed poison, having turned in error to the
wrong page in his medical source. Arsenic would not have induced an inky taste,
but mercury would have. Flaubert's mistake was all the more peculiar because he
himself was being treated with mercury at the time, for his syphilis.[60] In sum, an
uncanny slip of the page makes her poison his cure.

While I am wary about building an argument on anecdotal evidence, I can argue with confidence that the anecdote has metaphorical value, especially because
we find resonances of it in a letter Flaubert wrote not long afterward. Poison makes
another metaphorical appearance, here again linked with cure, when he writes in
1857 to Mademoiselle Leroyer de Chantepie describing how he cured himself of
his nervous condition: "Vous me demandez comment je me suis guéri des hallucinations nerveuses. . . . Je tâchais, par l'imagination, de me donner facticement
ces horribles souffrances. J'ai joué avec la démence et le fantastique comme Mith-

[58] Schor has quite rightly spoken of Flaubert's "typically fetishistic narrative voice." *Breaking the
Chain*, 136.
[59] Roland Barthes, *S/Z* (Paris: Seuil, 1970), 146.
[60] Bart, *Flaubert*, 307.

ridate avec les poisons" (2:716, 18 May 1857) ["You ask me how I cured myself of nervous hallucinations. . . . I tried, by imagining, to artificially induce horrible suffering in myself. I have played with dementia and fantasy as Mithridates played with poison"].

By way of reference to a king who in effect immunized himself by taking measured doses of poison, Flaubert introduces his own mithridatism. The second appearance of a cure by poison—that is, by attenuated doses of a fatal substance—supplemented by the timing of the letter (it was written one month after the publication of *Madame Bovary*) and by Flaubert's legendary undertaking of this novel as a cure for the romantic excesses of the juvenilia (notably, *La Tentation de Saint Antoine*)[61]—all this suggests that the writing of the novel was this cure. *Madame Bovary* was Flaubert's curative poison, the medium of his mithridatism: his inoculation with an attenuated form of a mortal substance.

He chose his poison: it was water. Playing with madness like Mithridates with poison, he volatilized the water, the emotional effusion, the rush of ink, the romantic flow. Poisoning himself gently, in measured doses, he turned liquid to vapor and cured his style; he vaporized hysteria and hystericized the text.

[61] Accounts to this effect are legion. See, for example, Bart, *Flaubert*, 243, and, of course, Flaubert's recurrent references to the self-disciplinary and self-punitive aspects of the writing of *Madame Bovary*, in the *Correspondance* of 1851–56.

PART THREE

LITERARY HISTORIES

7 THE LEAK IN CLOTILDE'S HEAD

Hysteria as Source of Zola's *Rougon-Macquart* Cycle

A nous de savoir quel anneau merveilleux confère . . .
une pareille puissance, au doigt de quel maître
il a été placé; quel jeu de pouvoir il permet ou suppose.
MICHEL FOUCAULT, *LA VOLONTÉ DE SAVOIR*

●   If we were to compile the various anatomical theories of textual origin
that implicitly constitute our literary tradition (and those that have been more explicitly promulgated in literature and criticism of the last decade), we could well
produce a companion piece to Freud's paper "On the Sexual Theories of Children."[1] In answer to the question "Where do babies come from?" Freud, as we
know, reports a series of juvenile hypotheses but stresses that those formed prior
to the knowledge of sexual difference are not gender specific. Responses to the
question "Where do stories come from?" however, apparently *are* predicated
upon sexual difference. Texts are either sired—and textual production is described by metaphors of penetration, insemination, and dissemination—or they
are given birth to, and their production is likened to gestation, labor, and deliv-

[1] Sigmund Freud, "On the Sexual Theories of Children," in *The Standard Edition of the Complete
Works of Sigmund Freud*, trans. James Strachey, Anna Freud, Alix Strachey, and Alan Tyson, ed.
James Strachey, 24 vols. (London: Hogarth Press, 1953–74), 9:209–26.

ery.[2] The female paradigm continues and intensifies, borrowing from the discourse of hysteria: texts may be woven from a woman's pubic hair, bled, lactated, or urinated into being (this last, Theodore Reik explains, because women "have a wider bladder").[3] Thus theories of textuality, while scarcely less phantasmatic than infantile sexual theories, are distinguished by their gender specificity.

Or so an overview would have it. But when we choose a text, read a given metaphor contextually, explore its thematic, structural, narratological implications, the metaphor in the text does not remain constant—that is, gender specific—for the problem of difference is, of course, no better resolved in the textual domain than within the confines of infantile sexual theory. My text is Zola's *Rougon-Macquart* epic, and my metaphor, following Zola, the female body.

Let me begin with a cautionary digression. Although I focus here on female figures of generation, I want first to locate these figures within the general narrative pattern. At roughly the same time that androgyny and hermaphroditism gained cultural currency, Zola was using sexual figures to represent fantasies of hermaphroditic authorship.[4] We might think of his narrative discourse as divided into two distinct categories—or more pertinently, two genres. This division is analogous to the dualism Flaubert was referring to when he remarked on the concatenation of realism and myth in *Nana*.[5] What Flaubert names *realism* is, of course, the dominant voice of Zola's narrative: in brief, it is a pseudoscientific mimetic discourse whose insistence on representation has been traced (notably by Aristotle in the *Poetics* and Freud in *Beyond the Pleasure Principle*) to children's attempts to master their environment through imitative play.[6] As D. A. Miller has argued in stronger terms, the practice of "classical" novelistic representation, which "assumes a fully

[2] For the best global analysis of paternal literary models and metaphors, see Sandra M. Gilbert and Susan Gubar, *The Madwoman in the Attic* (New Haven: Yale University Press, 1979). For a review of maternal literary models and metaphors, see Elaine Showalter's "Feminist Criticism in the Wilderness," in *The New Feminist Criticism*, ed. Elaine Showalter (New York: Pantheon, 1985), 243–70.

[3] See, for respective examples, Roland Barthes, *S/Z* (Paris: Seuil, 1970), 166; Susan Gubar, "'The Blank Page' and the Issues of Female Creativity," *Critical Inquiry* 8 (Winter 1981): 243–63; Hélène Cixous, "The Laugh of the Medusa," in *New French Feminisms*, ed. Elaine Marks and Isabelle de Courtivron (Amherst: University of Massachusetts Press, 1980), 245–64; Theodor Reik, quoted by Erica Freeman in her *Insights: Conversations with Theodor Reik* (Englewood Cliffs, N.J.: Prentice-Hall, 1971), 166.

[4] For some short but provocative pages on the fortune of the hermaphrodite in nineteenth-century French thought, see Michel Foucault's introduction to the English edition of the memoirs of Herculine Barbin, *Herculine Barbin: Being the Recently Discovered Memoirs of a Nineteenth-Century French Hermaphrodite*, trans. Richard McDougall, ed. Michel Foucault (New York: Pantheon, 1980), vii–xvii.

[5] "Nana tourne au mythe, sans cesser d'être réelle" ["Nana slides into myth, without ceasing to be real"]. Gustave Flaubert, *Correspondance*, 9 vols. (Paris: Conard, 1926–33), 8:388, 15 February 1880.

[6] Christopher Prendergast has used this evidence to suggest that a "profound psychic pattern [exists] between the principle of mimesis and . . . the desire for mastery." Prendergast, *Balzac: Fiction and Melodrama* (London: Edward Arnold, 1978), 181–82.

panoptic view of the world it places under surveillance," is a reinvention of nineteenth-century policing power.[7]

Furthermore, this fantasy of control staged by the techniques of realism is also explicitly articulated; both in the novels and in the theoretical texts, Zola's master voice speaks a language of conquest and mastery whose claims are plenipotentiary. "Tout dire pour tout connaître, pour tout guérir" ["To say all, to know all, to cure all"], proclaims Docteur Pascal, assimilating, by way of the verbs in his triple formula, Zola's three preferred master figures: the author, the scientist, and the doctor.[8] "Tous nos efforts aboutissent au besoin de nous rendre maîtres de la vérité" ["All our efforts lead to the need to become masters of the truth"], says Zola in *Le Roman expérimental*, speaking of the goal he ascribes to the naturalist novelists—a goal he alternatively describes as "la conquête lente de cet inconnu qui nous entoure"[9] ["the slow conquest of this unknown that surrounds us"].

I have thus far sketched a paradigm of discourse whose elements are realism, naturalism, observation, science, and mastery; following Zola, who almost systematically affixed the adjective *virile* to naturalist techniques, I will call this paradigm *male* and begin to consider its counterpart. The two discursive genres are suggestively juxtaposed in Zola's terms:

> Applaudir une rhétorique, s'enthousiasmer pour l'idéal, ce ne sont là que de belles émotions nerveuses; les femmes pleurent, quand elles entendent de la musique. Aujourd'hui, nous avons besoin de la virilité du vrai pour être glorieux.[10]

> *Applauding a turn of phrase, waxing enthusiastic for the ideal—such things are only fine nervous emotions; women cry when they listen to music. To be glorious today, we need the virility of truth.*

In other words, the virile model, "fait de logique et de clarté" ["made of logic and clarity"], is to be contrasted to its feminine counterpart, evoked as "un effarement sublime, toujours près de culbuter dans la démence"[11] ["a sublime bewilderment, always on the point of slipping into dementia"].

What Flaubert named *myth* in Zola corresponds to that paradigm alternatively labeled *inconnu, érotisme, lyrisme, poésie,* and *hystérie* by Zola; it describes an

[7] D. A. Miller, *The Novel and the Police* (Berkeley: University of California Press, 1988), 23.

[8] Emile Zola, *Le Docteur Pascal,* in *Les Rougon-Macquart,* ed. Armand Lanoux and Henri Mitterand, 5 vols. (Paris: Gallimard, 1960–67), 5:1022. Subsequent references to *Le Docteur Pascal* will be given parenthetically in the text.

[9] Emile Zola, *Le Roman expérimental* (Paris: Garnier Flammarion, 1971), 85, 86.

[10] Zola, "Lettre à la jeunesse," in *Le Roman expérimental,* 103.

[11] Zola, *Le Roman expérimental,* 93.

172
•

apparently subordinate discourse usually contained by its realist cover but that nonetheless constitutes a gap in this cover. Yet paradoxically, from the beginning (*Les Origines*, as the first novel is subtitled), this gap or crack, this embarrassing breach of textual integrity—this originary *fêlure*—is invested with a mythic priority. Inscribed on the body of the matriarch, Tante Dide, "notre mère à tous" ["the mother of us all"], the *fêlure* is linked not only to the propagation of the eponymous Rougon-Macquart dynasty, but also to the analogous textual generation. In Dide's immediate case, the *fêlure* generates "ces drames secrets, qui revenaient chaque mois" ["secret dramas that return every month"]: an inarticulate, uncontrolled discourse of desire that is displaced, as dumb show, to her hystericized body.[12] It is not by chance that Dide's secrets are staged monthly, as if to preserve a ritualized trace of the menstrual drama. For elsewhere in the cycle, as the *fêlure* is transmitted and transmuted, it is the source of secrets equally inseparable from secretions.

The hereditary secret resurges, in *La Joie de vivre*, in the form of Pauline's menstruation and again in the blood of Louise's childbirth. As Jean Borie remarks, "L'interdit du sang [chez Zola], l'horreur voluptueuse de le voir couler animent avec une belle urgence le jaillissement même de son écriture"[13] ["The blood taboo {in Zola}, the voluptuous horror inspired by its flow, animates and even compels the very surge of his writing"]. But there are other carriers available for the hereditary mystery. In *Nana*, as the courtesan lies dying, the flow of blood is transmogrified as "le bouillonnement de la purulence" ["the bubbling purulence"] and the "secret drama" that convulsed Dide's body, displaced to Nana's suppurating face, becomes her illegible epitaph.[14] A further transubstantiation, in *Pot-Bouille*, replaces blood with a juxtaposed stream of gossip and dirty dishwater, as the maids simultaneously flush their mistresses' secrets and their vegetable peels out the kitchen window into the courtyard below: "C'était l'égout de la maison, qui en charriait les hontes"[15] ["It was the sewer of the house; it carried all its shames"].

In the last novel of the cycle, *Le Docteur Pascal*, the *fêlure* makes its final, summary appearance. This novel, which I read as an allegory of Zola's hermaphroditic textuality, apposes his male and female paradigms of discourse, as personified by the doctor/scientist/author Pascal on the one hand, and his chimerical niece/ward/lover Clotilde on the other. When illustrating her uncle's treatises on botan-

---

[12] Zola, *La Fortune des Rougon*, in *Les Rougon-Macquart*, 1:136. Subsequent references to *La Fortune des Rougon* will appear in the text.

[13] Jean Borie, *Le Tyran timide* (Paris: Klincksieck, 1973), 127.

[14] Zola, *Nana*, in *Les Rougon-Macquart*, 2:1485; trans. George Holden (Harmondsworth: Penguin, 1972), 470. Subsequent references to *Nana* are to these editions and will be given parenthetically in the text.

[15] Zola, *Pot-Bouille*, in *Les Rougon-Macquart*, 3:107. Subsequent references to this novel will be given in the text.

ical heredity, Clotilde usually yields to the rigor of his realist aesthetic, applying herself with "une minutie, une exactitude de dessin et de couleur extraordinaire" ["an attention to detail, an extraordinary precision of design and color"]; however, she is at times given to wild, impressionistic renderings of the specimens: "C'était . . . parfois, chez elle, des sautes brusques, un besoin de s'échapper en fantaisies folles, au milieu de la plus précise des reproductions" (5:920) ["Sometimes she was overtaken by brusque mood shifts, by a need to escape into mad worlds of fantasy, in the midst of the most precise reproductions"]. Faced one day with Clotilde's most recent botanical fantasy, Pascal turns in exasperation to the housekeeper, who is mending clothes: "Pendant que vous y êtes, Martine, s'écria Pascal plaisamment, en prenant dans ses deux mains la tête révoltée de Clotilde, recousez-moi donc aussi cette caboche-là, qui a des fuites" (5:921) ["While you are at it, Martine," Pascal burst out jovially, taking between his two hands Clotilde's rebellious head, "would you also sew up this head, which is full of leaks"].

The leak in Clotilde's head—that is, her essential "gushiness"—is part of that insistent, if suppressed, female-associated paradigm of myth, fantasy, and extravagance, which, throughout the cycle, sporadically bursts, drips, flows, or spurts through its containing (realist) cover. Sexually loose, verbally incontinent, given to lyrical flow and to emotional overflow, women in Zola are repeatedly represented as "leaking vessels," to borrow a term from the seventeenth century.[16] Clotilde's leaking head, last avatar of the ancestral "cerveau fêlé" ["cracked brain"], is, then, the culmination of a series of Zola's creative excesses that are metaphorically incorporated by women. One easily imagines Zola, à la Flaubert, confessing his submerged projection: "Clotilde Rougon, c'est moi." In fact the cycle ends by displacing figurative authorship from Pascal to Clotilde. Although very early in the first novel, Pascal begins to show up on the sidelines of family dramas, listening hard and taking notes, he explains in the last novel that "ces dossiers ne sont pas destinés au public" (5:998) ["these files are not meant for the public"]. And when Pascal's documents are burned by his mother after his death, in an effort to launder the family secrets, only charred fragments remain. We then owe the *Rougon-Macquart* saga to Clotilde's retelling of the original story to which she was sole witness, before the auto-da-fé that destroyed all but the traces of its plot. *Les Rougon-Macquart* thus becomes Clotilde's story: a transgressive story, a violation of boundaries, a forbidden story "leaked" to the public.[17]

We might read the *Rougon-Macquart* cycle as a naturalist version of that para-

[16] See Patricia Meyer Spacks, *Gossip* (Chicago: University of Chicago Press, 1986), 39. For a comparison of this female aspect of Zola's metaphoric system to Balzac's more generally patriarchal system, see Janet Beizer, *Family Plots: Balzac's Narrative Generations* (New Haven: Yale University Press, 1986), 180–86.

[17] For an elaboration of Clotilde's role as author, see Janet Beizer, "Remembering and Repeating the *Rougon-Macquart*: Clotilde's Story," *L'Esprit Créateur* 25 (Winter 1985): 51–58.

174

•

ble of narrative presented by Diderot in *Les Bijoux indiscrets*. This would make the *Rougon-Macquart* a discourse displaced from *bouche* to *bijou*—from speech organ to sex organ—a discourse that persistently regenerates the text of its own sexual generation: a kind of anachronistic *écriture féminine*. The danger of such a reading is that it encourages some facile assumptions about Zola's (and Diderot's) texts. First, it suggests that these texts are celebratory evocations of female creativity. It then allows them to be too quickly and too unproblematically appropriated as evidence in the ongoing debate about what organ generates texts. In so doing, this reading overlooks important narratological factors. Specifically, it does not consider how female body metaphors are textually framed, and it bypasses the critical question of who is speaking.

Instead, we might retain the model of *Les Bijoux indiscrets* but displace our attention, as Michel Foucault does in his reading of this fable, away from the "bijoux parlants" toward that other jewel—the sultan's magic ring—whose stone, when rubbed, *"fait parler* les sexes qu'on rencontre" [*"gives voice* to any sex organs one encounters"]. Like the title of the thirteenth-century fabliau that originated the theme—*Du Chevalier qui fist les cons parler* [*Of the Knight who made cunts speak*]—Foucault helps us to recognize that the speaking subject is not the agent of discourse.[18] With a view toward exploring this imbricated structure of subject and object, toward tracing the discourse of the "jewels" to the master of the ring, I turn now to examine three representations of women's bodies in textual poses: first the erotic, in *Nana*; then the domestic, in *Pot-Bouille*; and finally, in more concentrated form and in the guise of a concluding statement, the obstetric, in *La Joie de vivre*.

UNCOVERING NANA

The Courtesan's New Clothes

Nearly three-quarters of the way through the novel that has been representing the life of the courtesan in all its nudity, Nana entertains a gathering of her paramours by expounding narrative theory.

---

[18] Michel Foucault, *La Volonté de savoir* (Paris: Gallimard, 1976), 104; my emphasis. For my information about Diderot's thirteenth-century predecessor, I am indebted to Aram Vartanian's helpful introduction to the critical edition of Denis Diderot, *Les Bijoux indiscrets*, ed. Aram Vartanian and Jean Macary, in *Oeuvres complètes* (Paris: Hermann, 1978), 3:3–18. For another use of *Les Bijoux indiscrets* as model for feminine discourse see Jane Gallop, "The Female Body," in *Thinking Through the Body* (New York: Columbia University Press, 1988), 72–77. In Gallop's appropriation of Diderot's parable, the female body confesses its secrets, although the confession is forced; in my own, the discourse belongs to a male agent and is projected onto the female body.

Nana causa avec les quatre hommes, en maîtresse de maison pleine de
charme. Elle avait lu dans la journée un roman qui faisait grand bruit,
l'histoire d'une fille; et elle se révoltait, elle disait que tout cela était faux,
témoignant d'ailleurs une répugnance indignée contre cette littérature
immonde, dont la prétention était de rendre la nature; comme si l'on
pouvait tout montrer! comme si un roman ne devait pas être écrit pour
passer une heure agréable!   (2:1369)

Nana chatted with the four men like a charming hostess. During the day she had
read a novel which was causing a sensation at the time. It was the story of a
prostitute, and Nana inveighed against it, declaring that it was all false, and
expressing an indignant revulsion against the sort of filthy literature which claimed
to represent nature—as if one could show all! as if a novel wasn't supposed to be
written as a pleasurable pastime!   (336–37; trans. modified)

The passage is remarkable not merely because courtesan turned literary critic
marks an unprecedented, and incongruous, switch from body language to literary
discourse, but because in order to dispute the claims of literary naturalism ("to represent nature"), Nana has recourse to a sexual metaphor: "as if one could show
all!" Narrative, says this metaphor, is an act of undressing, an exhibitionistic attempt to display what is euphemistically named (and thus, incidentally, veiled)
"all." We can hardly ignore the many scenes in which Nana, sex goddess and bed
partner of an empire, undresses before a mirror or strips for her lovers; nor can we
forget that she nightly displays herself to theater audiences as she stars in a performance of her own nudity.

Read literally, then, Nana's metaphoric denigration of realism is puzzling, but
no more so than the figurative condemnation. For Zola wrote "Le Roman expérimental," his treatise on narrative as scientific observation, even as he was preparing the outline for *Nana*. His position on realism is, of course, antithetical to the
one he ascribes to Nana. The realist procedure, he summarizes elsewhere, consists of rendering "la nature . . . dans son ensemble, sans exclusion aucune.
L'Oeuvre d'art . . . doit embrasser l'horizon entier"[19] ["nature . . . in its entirety,
without any exceptions whatsoever. The work of art . . . must take in the whole
horizon"]. To Zola's "One must tell everything," Nana impertinently replies,
"One cannot show all."

We have here a nexus of sexuality and textuality, body and narrative, showing
and telling, which is no less crucial for its paradoxical nature. For Nana's rebuttal

[19] Zola, Letter to Antony Valabrègue, in *Correspondance*, in *Oeuvres complètes*, ed. Maurice Le
Blond, 50 vols. (Paris: François Bernouard, 1928), 48:256, 18 August 1876.

of absolute revelation challenges the authority of the narrative plot that tells of the incessant disrobing of her body. And more critically, it threatens the very principle of Zola's narrative: if telling is showing and Nana, despite appearances, does not *show* everything, can narrative *tell* everything as Zola claims? The dissonance created by the clash of two voices (the authoritative narrative voice and the ostensibly less reliable voice of the protagonist) hints at the possibility that Nana, despite her presentation as a blind (and ultimately mute) force of desire, sees more and tells more about narrative than the official voice allows.

What follows is an inquiry into this agonistic game of show-and-tell as it is played out in the entire novel, where veils are alternately cast off and donned, curtains raised and lowered, barriers demolished and erected—and texts unraveled only to be rewoven. As Nana's commentary suggests, the dilemma we are exploring is at once sexual and textual. The thematic opposition of hide-and-seek, dress versus undress, cover versus discovery, is intimately related to narrative issues of representation and its limits. Zola here appropriates a nexus that, as Roland Barthes has noted, is etymologically inscribed within the very concept of textuality:

> *Texte* veut dire *Tissu*; mais alors que jusqu'ici on a toujours pris ce tissu pour un produit, un voile tout fait, derrière lequel se tient, plus ou moins caché, le sens (la vérité), nous accentuons maintenant, dans le tissu, l'idée générative que le texte se fait, se travaille à travers un entrelacs perpétuel; perdu dans ce tissu—cette texture—le sujet s'y défait, telle une araignée qui se dissoudrait elle-même dans les sécrétions constructives de sa toile.

> Text *means* Tissue; *but whereas hitherto we have always taken this tissue as a product, a ready-made veil, behind which lies, more or less hidden, meaning (truth), we are now emphasizing, in the tissue, the generative idea that the text is made, is worked out in a perpetual interweaving; lost in this tissue—this texture— the subject unmakes himself, like a spider dissolving in the constructive secretions of its web.*[20]

Barthes here proposes that we can conceive of texuality *either* as revelation *or* as process: mimesis or diegesis. I want to argue that a similar choice informs *Nana*. The show-and-tell metaphor (showing as telling and vice versa) is less than transparent and may well represent alternative rather than analogous modes of reading.

For while we might define *Nana* as a prolonged striptease, we must immediately

---

[20] Roland Barthes, *Le Plaisir du texte* (Paris: Seuil, 1973), 100–101; trans. Richard Miller as *The Pleasure of the Text* (New York: Hill and Wang, 1975), 64.

acknowledge that this is a compound term: a disjunctive. The novel unfolds in a
state of conflict and as such invites two disparate readings. It pretends to be a strip:
an unveiling, a disclosure, which is given as a social allegory, thus as a totalizing
revelation. But the transcendent allegory (the "message") is consistently eclipsed
by the story of desire (the would-be medium), much as the courtesan's unveiling is
more tease—promise and process—than disclosure and fait accompli, or strip.

Nana might be termed an exhibitionistic novel, because it displays, as plot mo-
tifs, questions of reading operative in all narrative. Staged thematically, dualities
of mimesis versus diegesis, closure and desire, metaphor versus metonymy call attention to themselves and invite a closer look.

We might begin by recollecting some specific intersections of showing and telling in the novel. When Nana makes her debut (simultaneously on stage and in the
novel), she is both a textual and sexual phenomenon—in that order. The daemonic attraction her body is soon to exert is preceded and equaled by the magnetic
effect of her printed name on the spectators, who are first her readers: "Dans la
clarté crue du gaz . . . de hautes affiches jaunes s'étalaient violemment, avec le
nom de Nana en grosses lettres noires. Des messieurs, comme accrochés au passage, les lisaient" (2:1097) ["In the crude gaslight, on the pale bare walls skimpily
decorated in the Empire style to form a peristyle like a cardboard temple, tall yellow posters were boldly displayed with Nana's name in thick black letters. Some
gentlemen were reading them, as if accosted on the way"] (20–21). "C'était une
caresse que ce nom. . . . Rien qu'à le prononcer ainsi, la foule s'égayait et deve-
nait bon enfant. Une fièvre de curiosité poussait le monde. . . . On voulait voir
Nana" (2:1100) ["The name was a caress in itself, a pet name which rolled easily
off every tongue. Merely by pronouncing it thus, the crowd worked itself into a
state of good-natured gaiety. A fever of curiosity urged it forward. . . . Everyone
wanted to see Nana"] (24).

Nana is, then, originally an effect of language, her name as much a force of
contagion as her body will become. But while her name is sexualized, her body becomes text, taking the place of the lines she does not deliver and the songs she cannot sing: "Dès ce second acte, tout lui fut permis: se tenir mal en scène, ne pas
chanter une note juste, manquer de mémoire. . . . Quand elle donnait son fa-
meux coup de hanche, l'orchestre s'allumait, une chaleur montait de galerie en
galerie jusqu'au cintre" (2:1113) ["From the second act onwards she was allowed to
get away with anything. She could hold herself awkwardly, sing every note out of
tune, and forget her lines—it didn't matter. . . . When she gave her special thrust
of the hip, the stalls lit up, and a glow of passion rose from gallery to gallery, until
it reached the gods"] (38).

We have here an initial displacement of the signifier from language to the
body—word made flesh. As the novel progresses, we in fact find the locus of mean-

178

•

ing repeatedly relayed from the word to the body. Thus, during Nana's liaison with Count Muffat, the lies she tells him are effaced by her physical presence: "Il comprit qu'elle mentait. Mais la sensation tiède de son bras, fortement appuyé sur le sien, le laissait sans force. Il n'avait plus ni colère ni rancune . . . son unique souci était de la garder là, maintenant qu'il la tenait" (2:1263) ["He could tell that she was lying, but the warm feel of her arm, as it leant heavily on his own, left him powerless. He felt neither anger nor rancour . . . his one thought was to keep her with him now that he had got hold of her"] (214). The true/false criterion of ordinary language yields to the sheer power of the physical signifier.

This shift of signifying fields is most dramatically rendered by Nana's final role as fairy queen in *Mélusine*: "trois poses plastiques d'une fée puissante et muette" (2:1471) ["three plastic poses of a fairy both potent and mute"] (454; trans. modified). Nana's swan song is silent: "Elle ne disait pas un mot, même les auteurs lui avaient coupé une réplique, parce que ça gênait; non, rien du tout, c'était plus grand, et elle vous retournait son public, rien qu'à se montrer" (2:1476) ["She didn't say a word; the authors had even cut the line or two they had given her, because they were superfluous. No, not a single word: it was more impressive that way, and she took the audience's breath away by simply showing herself"] (459).

Nana epitomizes what Naomi Schor has called, in reference to another of Zola's novels, "l'inquiétante étrangeté d'un corps saisi de sémiotique"[21] ["the uncanniness of a body stricken with semiotics"]. Nana's body becomes uncanny through a semiotic sleight of hand that would have us believe that we are reading body language rather than literary language. The text, replaced or repressed by the body it describes (and indeed creates), returns in the form of body language: the body as text or signifying corpus. This trompe-l'oeil effect reaches its peak when Nana's body serves as intertext for the journalist Fauchery. Seeking to satisfy his prurient curiosity about Countess Sabine's morality, Fauchery notices that she has a mole ("un signe") on her left cheek exactly like one Nana has. He reads this identifying mark as a sign of Sabine's potential depravity, deducing that her morality may be as similar to Nana's as her mole (2:1150, 1163). The signifier is quite obviously overdetermined, yet Fauchery's initial reading is confirmed in the course of the novel.

But it is not always this easy to affix a meaning to the semiotic charge invested in the body or—to shift the focus of Nana's metaphor a bit—to see what purportedly is being revealed. Philip Walker has remarked upon the intimate relationship in Zola's works between "sight and insight, vision and understanding."[22] As one might expect, given this rapport, when the visual field is obstructed, so, too, is the semiotic.

[21] Naomi Schor, "Sainte-Anne: Capitale du délire," *Cahiers naturalistes* 52 (1978): 106.
[22] Philip Walker, "The Mirror, the Window, and the Eye in Zola's Fiction," *Yale French Studies* 42 (1969): 52.

Thus Count Muffat's voyeuristic foray into the wings of the theater, past the
dressing rooms of the stars, corresponds to a desire (albeit repressed) to probe the
secrets of sexuality, to know the mysteries to which he has not been initiated. The
fact that the scene of seduction, however, is the theater, site of disguise, factory of
illusion, precludes the possibility of any real discovery. We watch Muffat, like a
child spying on his parents, peeking through curtain peepholes, squinting through
wall cracks, peering around half-opened doors, and averting his eyes from their
too-avid focus upon Nana's nominally veiled nakedness. Each aperture is as much
a barrier as an access to revelation, affording a glimpse that has neither time nor
space enough to crystallize as perception. Moreover, barriers removed yield new
barriers; layer upon layer, there seems always to be one more veil remaining.
Thus, when Muffat gains entry to Nana's dressing room and Nana appears nude,
her body is nonetheless veiled, first by a curtain and later by a qualifying statement
that covers both her nakedness and the prior description of it: "Elle ne s'était pas
couverte du tout, elle venait simplement de boutonner un petit corsage de percale,
qui lui cachait à demi la gorge" (2:1208) ["She had not covered herself at all, she
had simply buttoned on a little cambric bodice which half-hid her breasts"] (149;
trans. modified). One might argue that the essence of Nana's seductiveness lies in
this play of presence and absence; a presence that is never quite realized, an absence on the eternal verge of becoming present. What is erotic here, as Roland
Barthes has remarked more generally, is intermittence: "l'intermittence . . . de la
peau qui scintille entre deux pièces . . . entre deux bords; c'est ce scintillement
même qui séduit, ou encore: la mise en scène d'une apparition-disparition" ["the
intermittence of skin flashing between two articles of clothing . . . between two
edges. . . . It is this flash itself which seduces, or rather: the staging of an
appearance-as-disappearance"].[23]

In much the same way, what captivates in Nana is not what she unveils but the
veil itself, the challenge to a game of hide-and-seek. The veil takes the form of a
mask as Muffat, watching Nana put on her makeup, is "séduit par la perversion des
poudres et des fards" (2:1214) ["seduced by the perversion of powders and paints"]
(157; trans. modified). The perversion that seduces is quite literally a turnabout,
the imagined exchange of surface and depth; for the mask is an exaggerated surface
that holds out the (illusory) promise of a corresponding depth. Therefore, Muffat
accedes to nothing but his own desire; his attempts at sight and insight equally
thwarted, he leaves the theater breathing in "tout le sexe de la femme, qu'il ignorait encore" (2:1223) ["breathing in all the animal essence of woman, of which he
was still ignorant"] (166).

Thus far I have focused upon scenes in which the body as spectacle is incorporated within the larger context of the theatrical spectacle so that there is a *mise en*

[23] Barthes, *Le Plaisir du texte,* 19; *The Pleasure of the Text,* 10.

180 *abyme* of showing: a "show" within a show. The representational metaphor is not,
• however, always explicitly bounded by this mirroring effect, and it becomes useful
to consider some distinct but parallel attempts to unveil gender and genre—that is,
to locate the sources of sexual and textual disguise, or travesty.

We are at several points in the novel led through a series of successive screens—
behind the curtain, behind the backdrop, through the wings, behind closed
doors—to what Zola calls "l'autre côté du théâtre" (2:1215) ["the other side of the
theater"] (158). But the ostensibly "other" side yields much of the same: a prolongation of disguise and playacting that at one moment mixes a visiting "real-life"
prince with actors playing royal roles of mythology. The confusion is such that

> personne ne souriait de cet étrange mélange, de ce vrai prince, héritier
> d'un trône, qui buvait le champagne d'un cabotin, très à l'aise dans ce
> carnaval des dieux, dans cette mascarade de la royauté, au milieu d'un
> peuple d'habilleuses et de filles, de rouleurs de planches et de montreurs
> de femmes. (2:1210)

> *nobody dreamt of smiling at the strange contrast presented by this real prince, this*
> *heir to a throne, drinking a barn-stormer's champagne, and very much at ease in*
> *this carnival of the gods, in this masquerade of royalty, surrounded by dressers,*
> *whores, itinerant actors, and pimps.* (152; trans. modified)

In a world composed entirely of poseurs, one can hardly distinguish between theatrical roles and the roles of everyday life. Disguises turn out to be not so much illusions as illusions of illusion, masks that, to borrow Jean-Louis Baudry's definition, "feign dissimulation to dissimulate that [they] are nothing more than a
simulation."[24]

The representation/reality polarity is once again deconstructed when Nana, in
a radical departure from type-casting, stars as a duchess in *La Petite Duchesse*.
When the play folds (largely because of her inadequacy to the role), she shrugs it
off, resolved to play successfully an offstage version of the part: "Je vais lui en donner de la grande dame, à ton Paris!" (2:1346) ["I'll show Paris what a great lady is!"]
(310; trans. modified), she exclaims. And as all Paris watches, Nana's new persona
is launched—in markedly theatrical metaphors:

> Ce fut un lançage brusque et définitif, une montée dans la célébrité de la
> galanterie. . . . Et le prodige fut que cette grosse fille, si gauche à la
> scène, si drôle dès qu'elle voulait faire la femme honnête, jouait à la ville
> des rôles de charmeuse, sans un effort. (2:1346)

[24] Jean-Louis Baudry, cited by Severo Sarduy in "Writing/Transvestism," trans. Alfred MacAdam, *Review* (Fall 1973): 33.

It was a sudden and sure rise to stardom, a rapid climb to a gallant celebrity. . . .
And the remarkable thing was that this full-blown woman, who was so awkward on
the stage, so comical when she tried to play the respectable woman, was able to play
the enchantress in town without the slightest effort.   *(311; trans. modified)*

Nana's adopted role becomes the model, the referent, for the born-and-bred Parisian aristocracy: "Elle donnait le ton, de grandes dames l'imitaient" (2:1347) ["She set the tone; the great ladies imitated her"] (311; trans. modified). Reality is once more shown to be an extension of representation, a re-presentation of a representation. It is tempting to introduce here the concept of travesty in both its colloquial and literal acceptations: a mockery or deformation, and a dressing across or disguise. But the very essence of travesty is put into question because the concept of disguise implies the existence of a reality, a true identity behind the mask. All that can be discerned of the "essential duchess," however, is a cycle of masks: the flesh-and-blood duchesses are modeled on Nana's Paris rendition of her stage role, which in turn is an imitation, an interpretation of great ladies.

The fate of travesty is no different on the textual level. Travesty as literary genre presupposes a base test, an ordinary work that undergoes a subsequent deformation. The play in which Nana debuts, *La Blonde Vénus*, gives every appearance of travesty at first glance, for it is a burlesque representation of the amorous adventures of the pagan gods, a grotesque caricature of classical mythology. But the play is a more direct distortion of Jacques Offenbach's *La Belle Hélène*, itself a parody of the *Iliad* intrigue. And while the *Iliad* can be traced to Greek and then to Roman mythology, such a genealogy is popular or anonymous. So instead of an origin, we have a movement of infinite regress, an endless displacement of sources. The quest is further complicated by the fact that the scene of *La Blonde Vénus* is set on the terrain of *L'Assommoir*, the novel about Nana's mother and the story of Nana's own childhood. Michel Serres has suggested that Nana in her stage role of Venus, married to the blacksmith of the gods, "realizes" her mother's desired union with the Vulcan-like Goujet and thus plays out an intertextual incest.[25] Thus the return of *L'Assommoir* in *La Blonde Vénus* throws one more wrench in the search for textual origins, for it poses an alternative genealogy for the play, further disturbing the already complex pattern of linear descent from mythology.

We are reminded here of Barthes's remark that "le réalisme ne peut être dit 'copieur' mais plutôt 'pasticheur' (par une *mimesis* seconde, il copie ce qui est déjà copie) ["realism cannot be designated a 'copier' but rather a 'pasticheur,' {since} through secondary mimesis, it copies what is already a copy"].[26] The travesty of re-

---

[25] Michel Serres, *Feux et signaux de brume* (Paris: Grasset, 1975), 223.
[26] Roland Barthes, *S/Z* (Paris: Seuil, 1970), 61; trans. Richard Miller (New York: Hill and Wang, 1974), 55.

alism is no different; as layer upon layer of text is unpeeled, we can only situate the source in the vagueness of textuality.

As we move from genre to gender, sexual origins prove to be as elusive as textual origins. Transvestism, etymologically equivalent to travesty, plays an equally important role in the novel and is no less ambiguous a phenomenon. Nana's affair with Georges Hugon is precipitated by her dressing him up in her own clothing. In what Naomi Schor argues is "a rehearsal for the Sapphic love scenes with Satin,"[27] Nana disguises Georges as a girl and is then seduced by what is feminine in him: "Peu à peu, elle se sentait sans force. . . . Ce déguisement, cette chemise de femme et ce peignoir, la faisaient rire encore. C'était comme une amie qui la taquinait" (2:1239) ["Little by little, she felt her resistance melting. . . . This disguise, this woman's chemise and peignoir, renewed her giggles. He was like a girlfriend teasing her"] (185; trans. modified). This cannot be qualified as a transvestite love scene, however, because Georges's sexual identity is not firmly established. This boy dressed in woman's clothing in fact earlier appears looking like "[une] fille déguisée en garçon" (2:1152) ["a girl dressed up as a boy"] (84). One cannot properly speak of transvestism in a world where clothes make the man and the woman—where, that is, clothing defines rather than reflects sexual identity. The role of clothing as sexual determinant is personified by Madame Jules, the theater dresser whose name reflects her androgynous nature:

> Madame Jules n'avait plus d'âge, le visage parcheminé, avec ses traits immobiles des vieilles filles que personne n'a connues jeunes. Celle-là s'était desséchée dans l'air embrasé des loges, au milieu des cuisses et des gorges les plus célèbres de Paris. Elle portait une éternelle robe noire déteinte, et sur son corsage plat et sans sexe, une forêt d'épingles étaient piquées, à la place du coeur.
> (2:1208)

> *Madame Jules was a woman of indeterminate age, with the parchment skin and changeless features peculiar to old maids whom no one ever knew when they were young. She had shrivelled up in the torrid atmosphere of the dressing-rooms, among the most famous thighs and bosoms in all Paris. She invariably wore a faded black dress, and on her flat and sexless chest a forest of pins was stuck in where her heart should have been.*
> (149)

That the wardrobe mistress, purveyor of disguise, is characterized by her sexlessness serves to emphasize that costume creates sexual identity, which is as protean

---

[27] Naomi Schor, *Zola's Crowds* (Baltimore: Johns Hopkins University Press, 1978), 93.

as a change of clothing. As Virginia Woolf put it, "It is clothes that wear us and not we them."[28]

If sexuality, like textuality, has no determinate source, what are we to make of the many detailed descriptions of Nana's nudity? The problem can best be defined, I think, by a detour through the most explicit of a series of such passages: the celebrated scene in which Nana, with Muffat looking on, adoringly contemplates her body in the mirror. While her body and the various amorous poses she strikes are described with almost clinical precision, we (along with the count) do not see all. For in the midst of the anatomical detail, we find this screen: "Nana était toute velue, un duvet de rousse faisait de son corps un velours; tandis que . . . sa croupe et ses cuisses de cavale, . . . les renflements charnus creusés de plis profonds . . . *donnaient au sexe le voile troublant de leur ombre*" (2:1271; my emphasis) ["Nana's body was covered with fine hair, reddish down which turned her skin into velvet; while there was something of the Beast about her equine rump and flanks, about the fleshy curves and deep hollows of her body, *which veiled her sex in the suggestive mystery of their shadows*"] (223). I want to argue here (as in all the other passages in which nudity is declared, only to be denied by a covering statement) that the only thing veiling Nana's sex is text. If it is impossible to show what is behind the veil, it is because showing, in narrative, is always dependent on telling. And telling always interposes the veil of language between the reader and what it purports to reveal; or more accurately, it *replaces* revelation by the language that relates it.

Naomi Schor has pointed to the use of euphemism in the passage I have been discussing, particularly in reference to Nana's observation of "*d'autres parties de son corps*" (2:1270) ["other parts of her body"] (222). The euphemization of Nana's body, Schor proposes, represses not only her genitals but the absent phallus, and is thus a token of fetishism—that is, the denial of a phallic absence.[29] This interpretation becomes especially useful if we read it in the very broadest sense, understanding "phallus," in Lacan's terms, to mean "signifier."[30] We then have a paradigm—veil, text, euphemism, fetish, phallus, signifier—whose elements all refer to the simultaneous creation/repression of a signified. The veil is the signifier, the promise of a signified, of a plenitude of meaning, but it is also the obstacle that bars access to the signified. Euphemism is only the most obvious manifestation of the textual difference between telling and showing, the constantly renewed prom-

[28] This remark was brought to my attention by Sandra M. Gilbert, in "Costumes of the Mind: Transvestism as Metaphor in Modern Literature," *Critical Inquiry* 7 (Winter 1980): 391–417. See, too, Marjorie Garber's fascinating *Vested Interests: Cross-dressing and Cultural Anxiety* (New York: Routledge, 1992), which appeared too late to be integrated into this book.

[29] Schor, *Zola's Crowds*, 101–2.

[30] See especially Jacques Lacan, "La Signification du phallus," in *Ecrits*, 2 vols. (Paris: Seuil, 1966), 2:103–15.

ise to show what in truth never will—never can—be revealed. Like Penelope's tapestry, the text is that tissue constantly being unwoven and rewoven, alternately
promising and forestalling fulfillment.

Zola's theory of the *realist screen*, developed in the celebrated letter to Antony
Valabrègue, casts an interesting sidelight on the veil metaphor. While the metaphor works primarily as subtext in *Nana*, it is more directly confronted in Zola's remarks to Valabrègue. He writes the following:

> L'Ecran réaliste est un simple verre à vitre, très mince, très clair, et qui a
> la prétention d'être si parfaitement transparent que les images le traversent
> et se reproduisent ensuite dans toute leur réalité. . . . Il est certes difficile
> de caractériser un Ecran qui a pour qualité principale celle de n'être
> presque pas; je crois, cependant, le bien juger, en distant qu'une fine
> poussière grise trouble sa limpidité. Tout objet, en passant par ce milieu,
> y perd de son éclat, ou, plutôt, s'y noircit légèrement.[31]

> *The realist Screen is a mere windowpane, very thin, very clear, which pretends to be*
> *so perfectly transparent that images cross it and are then reproduced in all their*
> *reality. . . . It is, of course, difficult to characterize a Screen whose principal*
> *quality is that of almost not existing; I believe I can, however, evaluate it*
> *accurately by saying that a fine gray dust disturbs its limpidity. Any object that*
> *passes through this medium loses its vividness, or rather, is slightly darkened.*

This screen, medium that deposits a "fine gray dust" on the images it filters, is the
veil we have been discussing; it is none other than the printed text. Zola's description of the realist screen as that not-quite-transparent veil/tissue/text interposed
between the reader and the truth recalls (or, more accurately, foreshadows)
Barthes's suggestion that textuality be conceived of as "a generative idea . . . a perpetual interweaving" rather than as "a ready-made veil behind which lies . . .
meaning." Although Zola would ideally posit an image of transparency as the realist model, he admits the mediating presence, the determining presence, of the
text.[32]

It becomes evident that the theorization of realism as mimesis contains within it
an ambivalence similar to the thematized split in the novel between revelation and
veiling. Thus the discord thematically inscribed on and around Nana's body is in-

---

[31] Zola, Letter to Valabrègue, 255.

[32] Barthes, *Pleasure of the Text*, 64. While Zola here specifically addresses the referential aspect of the
realist illusion (that is, the belief in an identity of signified and referent), his remarks pertain also to the
semantic aspect (the belief in an identity of signifier and signified), which has been my primary focus.
My use of the terms *realist illusion*, *referential illusion*, and *semantic illusion* is based on Gérard Genette's definitions in "Proust et le langage indirect," in *Figures II* (Paris: Seuil, 1969), 248.

separable from a theoretical conflict that complicates and even polarizes our reading strategies. That is, do we read metaphorically, seeking meaning as revelation in closed, transparent totalizations? Or do we read metonymically, teased forward in time toward a meaning intermittently glimpsed but never postponed? These are the very questions naively formulated by Nana when she challenges narrative claims to "show all," insisting instead that a novel is written "pour passer une heure agréable."

Peter Brooks has proposed a dualistic model for narrative plot in which the metaphoric and metonymic processes are coextensive; while meaning in plot is dependent on the work of totalization and closure performed by metaphor, the very movement of plot relies upon the dynamism and deferral of metonymy.[33] Throughout Nana, however, the metaphoric and metonymic poles of reading are constantly placed in opposition. The double plot structure of the novel provides the most remarkable example of such a clash. Is the novel an allegory of the decline and fall of the Second Empire, the representation of "la pourriture d'en bas . . . se redressant et pourrissant les classes d'en haut"? ["the putrefaction from below, rising to putrefy the upper classes"?] Or is it rather "le poème du *cul*, et la moralité . . . le *cul* faisant tout tourner"? ["the poem of sex, whose moral is that sex is the motor of everything"?][34] Both statements were made by Zola, and both are borne out by the novel, but they represent very different readings. If Nana is about desire, if Nana herself is the figure of desire, then the novel tells of a profound disorder, a contagion of unfulfilled passion. If the novel is ultimately about the collapse of an empire, then the disorder is subordinated, bound by the allegory, and therefore recuperated within the order of plot. Similarly, the contagion is arrested as it yields to a higher level of signification, and passion is pacified, if not completely satisfied, by the conquest of a transcendent meaning.

We can turn to the microstructure of the novel for further illustrations of the conflict. How, for instance do we read the lingering bloodstain on the threshold of Nana's bedroom, remnant of Georges Hugon's attempted suicide? Is it a metaphor of Nana's guilt, a Lady Macbeth–like stigma that can never be removed? So Nana's maid reads it as she reiterates time after time: "Vous savez, madame, que ce n'est pas parti" (2:1447) ["You know, Madame, it hasn't gone"] (426). Or is it a metonymy, a contagious trace of shared guilt transmitted to all who cross the threshold? Such is Muffat's reading: "Muffat, que le trait de sang préoccupait . . . l'étudiait malgré lui, pour lire, dans son effacement de plus en plus rose, le nombre

[33] See especially Peter Brooks, "Freud's Masterplot: A Model for Narrative" and "Repetition, Repression, and Return: *Great Expectations* and the Study of Plot," in *Reading for the Plot: Design and Intention in Narrative* (New York: Knopf, 1984), 90–142. My thinking here and in the following pages is indebted to these studies of narrative plot and to D. A. Miller's *Narrative and Its Discontents* (Princeton: Princeton University Press, 1981).

[34] Zola, "Etude" for *Nana*, in *Nana* 2:1666, 1677.

d'hommes qui passaient" (2:1459) ["Muffat, whom the blood-stain preoccupied
. . . kept studying it in spite of himself, as if to discover from the degree to which it
had faded, how many men had passed that way"] (440).

The most interesting examples of dual readings involve Nana as one of the readers. For Nana consistently interprets metonymically, perceiving combinations and
contiguities rather than recuperative wholes. In one notable instance, the journalist Fauchery writes an article about Nana entitled "La Mouche d'or." The "official"
interpretation is clearly metaphoric:

> C'était à la fin de l'article que se trouvait la comparaison de la mouche,
> une mouche couleur de soleil, envolée de l'ordure, une mouche qui
> prenait la mort sur les charognes tolérées le long des chemins, et qui,
> bourdonnante, dansante, jetant un éclat de pierreries, empoisonnaient
> les hommes rien qu'à se poser sur eux, dans les palais où elle entrait par
> les fenêtres. (2:1270)

> *It was at the end of the article that the comparison with a fly occurred, a fly the
> colour of sunshine which had flown up out of the dung, a fly which had sucked
> death from the carrion left by the roadside and now, buzzing, dancing and
> glittering like a precious stone, was entering palaces through the windows and
> poisoning the men inside, simply by settling on them.* (221)

Nana's reading of the article, as revealed by the following dialogue, is quite
different:

> "A propos," demanda-t-elle, "as-tu lu l'article de Fauchery sur moi?"
> "Oui, 'La Mouche d'or,'" répondit Daguenet, "je ne t'en parlais pas,
> craignant de te faire de la peine."
> "De la peine, pourquoi? Il est très long, son article."
> Elle était flattée qu'on s'occupât de sa personne dans *Le Figaro*.
> (2:1267)

> *"By the way," she asked, "have you read Fauchery's article about me?"*
> *"'The Golden Fly?' Yes," replied Daguenet. "I didn't mention it because I was
> afraid of upsetting you."*
> *"Upsetting me—why? It's a very long article."*
> *She was flattered that the Figaro should concern itself about her person.* (218)

Nana reads the article as an extension of her person, as praise by force of accumulation. Later, at the racetrack, a horse named Nana takes the grand prix. In the

midst of crude jokes that make the horse Nana the metaphor of Nana's bestial nature, she herself is "heureuse de cette bête qui portait son nom" (2:1400) ["delighted by the animal bearing her name"] (372)—thrilled by this continuation of herself. Finally, when we return to Nana's bout of literary theorizing, we realize that the novel she is discussing, "a novel which was causing a sensation at the time . . . the story of a prostitute" (336), is the very book we hold in our hands. Nana has been reading *Nana*, the story of a prostitute and hence her own story, but also a story very much about narrative and how to read it, and so once again her own story. The heroine is eponymous not merely because the novel recounts her adventures, but because, as metanovel, it uses her adventure to explore its own dynamics. *Nana* also reads Nana—reads her as a dialogue between two theories of reading: metaphor versus metonymy, closure versus desire, revelation versus veiling.

Nana's body, "stricken with semiotics," textually afflicted, is the page upon which the narrative conflict is written. Her death in a sense effaces the conflict, for it renders the "page" illegible. Nana's body, ravaged by smallpox, is described, her face become "[une] bouillie informe, où l'on ne retrouvait plus les traits" (2:1485) ["{a} shapeless pulp, in which the features had ceased to be discernible"] (470). There is a nice irony in the fact that her lovers flee her decomposing body, fearing infection. For her death in fact marks the end of contagion. Dis-figured, she is cured of textuality. Desire is arrested by death as Venus makes way for Atropos: the atropical, the trope non-trope.

Metaphor appears to recuperate metonymy as Nana dies to be allegorically subsumed to the Empire's collapse. If as readers we nonetheless continue to feel that the desire plot is the "true" plot, I think this is so not only because it is the more perverse, but also the more subversive of the two available models. Nana, as the voice of desire, speaks to our desire as readers to keep reading, to escape the authority of a closure that is somewhat arbitrary. For the energy generated by Nana (by the desire plot) is not fully immobilized by the allegorical binding. The allegory is less a replacement than a displacement of desire, because the last words of the novel represent a remainder of textual energy and a renewed promise. The cry "A Berlin! à Berlin! à Berlin!"—like an echo of earlier cries for Nana—drifts up from the boulevard, swelling the curtains of her death chamber (2:1485). These curtains, a final manifestation of the veil interposed between the reader and the revelation, refer us once again to Nana's scoffing words: "as if one could show all!" Nana, the naive self-consciousness of the text, is here a wiser version of that other polymorphous pervert, the child in the tale "The Emperor's New Clothes." More conservative in her claims but more radical in her implications, Nana reminds all watchful eyes that she is ever clothed. Visionary in her denial of absolute vision, Nana reveals the veil and proclaims the truth of the text.

Pot-Bouille, or the Kitchen of Writing

La femme est le refoulé de l'homme.
La bonne est le refoulé de la patronne.
HÉLÈNE CIXOUS, *LA JEUNE NÉE*

Before telling of the courtesan's fall from glory into putrefaction, in *Nana,* Zola had narrated the rise of this "golden fly" from the dung heaps of Paris. In *L'Assommoir,* billed by its preface as "le premier roman sur le peuple . . . et qui ait l'odeur du peuple" ["the first novel about the people . . . that has the smell of the people"], he told of Nana's ascent from foul popular origins. Zola then went on, in *Pot-Bouille,* to map a course into new olfactory territory. *Pot-Bouille* would explore, according to the *Ebauche,* "la pourriture d'une maison bourgeoise" ["the rotting of a bourgeois establishment"].[35] While it is true that the proposed intent to portray bourgeois turpitude is realized in the course of the novel's revelations of the marriage markets, the adultery, bigamy, and passionless couplings—in short, the sexual and economic exploitation that lie behind a hypocritical facade of conventional morality and propriety—it is false to suppose that the score is evened here.

Though *Pot-Bouille* openly conveys Zola's point that bourgeois moral hypocrisy is equivalent to popular degradation, the novel also implies that it is the sins of the people that are visited upon the bourgeoisie. Because Zola cannot seem to narrate bourgeois infamy without having recourse to the people as its thematic and rhetorical source, his portraits in abjection cannot be unbound from class bias. Neither can they be separated from gender bias; for despite Zola's plotted blanket condemnation of the bourgeoisie in *Pot-Bouille,* the text of the masters' sins is written in the feminine: relayed from allusions to the unmentionable female maladies of their wives, it is then inscribed on the more expressive bodies of their maids.

The gynecological secrets contained within whispered conversations between men in the parlor are loudly and repeatedly exposed by the maids in the kitchen: "C'était l'égout de la maison, qui en charriait les hontes" (3:107) ["It was the sewer of the house; it carried all its shames"]. Rhetorically confluent with streams of dirty dishwater, rotting cooking wastes, and rank female secretions, the servantwomen's gossip serves as a narrative filtering system that works to purify the very pollution it is designed to convey. The text's recurrent return to the scene of the filthy inner courtyard, the contaminated kitchens, and the foul tongues and bodies of the maids as signifiers of bourgeois degradation effectively purges the bourgeoisie by deflecting the image of its impurity.

[35] Zola, *L'Assommoir,* in *Les Rougon-Macquart,* 2:373; Zola, *Pot-Bouille,* Dossier préparatoire, Bibliothèque Nationale, Département des manuscrits, Nouvelles acquisitions françaises 10321, folios 1–443, 382. *L'Assommoir, Nana,* and *Pot-Bouille* were written in 1877, 1880, and 1882, respectively.

We have heard a fair amount about *Pot-Bouille* as representation of bourgeois
hypocrisy but have barely begun to interrogate the ideological and semiological
hypocrisies of a representational process that rides upon the backs of the female
servants.[36] To open the question, I turn my attention in what follows to Zola's anatomical exposition of domestic sewage as abject source of his text. Correlatively,
I consider the punctual return of the kitchens, the sewers, and the maids, reex-
amining what has been called the novel's leitmotif in the more functional terms of
a ritual draining of bourgeois pollution—and, concomitantly, of the narrative discourse that relates it.[37]

The kitchen scenes that reappear regularly—almost rhythmically—in *Pot-Bouille*
are constructed at a metaphoric crossroads joining architecture, anatomy, and language. As we are periodically shuttled from the ornate second-empire facade and
public rooms of the apartment building to the four stories of kitchens arranged
over an inner pestilential courtyard—from salon to cesspool, as it were—we move
also from the silks and satins of bourgeois social attire into the malodorous, dripping inner cavity that is consistently assimilated to digestive, excretory, and sexual
space: "le boyau empesté," "le boyau noir," "le cloaque de la maison," "les murs
. . . ruissel[ant] d'humidité" (passim) ["the stinking bowel," "the black bowel,"
"the cesspool {cloaca} of the house," "the walls dripping with dampness"]. We slip
simultaneously to the dark underside of polite social discourse, the gossip or "dirt"
about the building's residents: "le linge sale de la domestique"; "les mots ignobles
. . . toute une débâcle d'égout, qui, chaque matin, se déversait là" (3:250, 269)
["the servants' dirty laundry"; "the foul language . . . the sewer overflow that
poured out there, every morning"].

As the kitchen interludes multiply, the connection between language and filth,
word flow and flushed wastes becomes increasingly emphatic. There is a progres-
sion from a metonymic association of words and pollution to a metaphoric equiv-
alence of the two. Statements such as "une volée de gros mots s'échappa de ce trou,
obscur et empesté comme un puisard" (3:106) ["a volley of dirty words burst from
this hole, dark and reeking like a cesspool"], or "des voix éclatèrent, le flot des ordures du matin montait, dégorgeait du boyau empesté" (3:250) ["voices broke out,
the morning sewage swept up, poured out of the stinking bowel"] give way to "un
flot boueux de gros mots monta de la cour des cuisines" (3:266) ["a muddy wave of

[36] The notable exception is Jean Borie's *Zola et les mythes* (Paris: Seuil, 1971), which does not retreat
before the question of Zola's complicity with the bourgeoisie. For a thorough discussion of Zola's representation of bourgeois hypocrisy, see Brian Nelson's *Zola and the Bourgeoisie* (London: Macmillan,
1983).
[37] In his preface to *Pot-Bouille*, André Fermigier writes, "Cette image du puits, du boyau, de l'égout, de
la cour sans air et sans lumière . . . est comme le leitmotiv du roman" ["This image of the cesspool, the
bowel, the sewer, the dark stifling courtyard . . . is like the leitmotif of the novel"]. Zola, *Pot-Bouille*,
ed. Henri Mitterand (Paris: Gallimard [Folio], 1982), 18.

foul talk rose from the kitchen courtyard"], "des gros mots dont les bonnes l'avaient éclaboussée" (3:272) ["filthy words that the maids had splattered on her"], or "la puanteur d'évier mal tenu, comme l'exhalaison même des ordures cachées des familles" (3:107) ["the stench of dirty drains, like the fumes of hidden family filth"]—the latter examples of language represented directly as dirt, contamination, and stench. Now, one might argue that this sewer synesthesia (the roar of the grease and the smell of the words) corresponds in an unsurprising way to the particular ignominy of gossip; however, glossing polluted waters as gossip does not account for the more perplexing fact that the constant stream of words thrown out the window as fetid kitchen slops or body wastes is marked as the very stuff of the novel.

Pot-Bouille is a patchwork of anecdotes, a collage of reported *faits divers*. The stories leaked from window to window and the words that splatter the courtyard are the constituent parts of the novel. In fact, as Henri Mitterand notes in the *Carnets d'enquêtes*, of all Zola's novels this one depended least on rigorous documentation; Zola relied instead on "oral documentation" that Mitterand elaborates as "quantité d'anecdotes ou de schémas d'anecdotes provenant des médisances des compères de Médan"[38] ["numerous anecdotes or anecdotal outlines whose source was the slander of the Médan cronies"]—in other words, the gossip of his cohorts. Despite an occasional reference to a mysterious retiring writer who quietly observes and then writes a novel so "dirty" that it lands him in prison (3:360)—the prototype of a naturalist author, planted in the text as a decoy—Pot-Bouille is represented as being generated by the pollution of leaking female bodies.

My insistence on the female identification of the often undifferentiated digestive/excretory/sexual effluvia originating in the kitchens of the novel is based on two different but mutually supportive kinds of evidence: on the one hand, affinities with an iconographic tradition of woman as leaking vessel and, on the other, the narrative centrality of a particular scene in the novel that crystallizes lexical and rhetorical traces diffused throughout.[39]

The tradition I refer to is perhaps best introduced by the story of Tuccia's sieve.[40] Tuccia, a priestess of Vesta accused of breaking her vows of chastity, cleared herself

[38] Emile Zola, *Carnets d'enquêtes*, ed. Henri Mitterand (Paris: Plon, 1986), 120.

[39] It is worth noting as well that a similar network of female bodies, filth, and sewage is found in Zola's "De la moralité dans la littérature," an article published a year earlier in his *Documents littéraires* (1881) and which he had written for *Le Messager de l'Europe*. Denouncing his hypocritical fellows who deny the raw veracity of novels like *Nana*, he writes: "Même lorsqu'une femme les éclabousse de son ordure, lorsqu'ils tombent une belle nuit dans un égout . . . ils gardent le silence. . . . si vous allez au-delà de la robe pour entrer dans la peau . . . vous les bousculez terriblement" ["Even when a woman splatters them with her filth, even when they fall one fine night into a sewer . . . they keep quiet. . . . if you go beyond the dress to penetrate the skin, you upset them horribly"]. Zola, "De la moralité dans la littérature," in *Oeuvres complètes, Documents littéraires*, ed. G. Sigaux (Paris: Fasquelle, 1927–28), 45:586.

[40] My comments about Tuccia owe much to Marina Warner's information in *Monuments and Maidens: The Allegory of the Female Form* (New York: Atheneum, 1985). Tuccia's story is recounted in the work of Pliny the Elder and Valerius Maximus.

of the charges by carrying a sieve full of water back from the river Tiber. This feat was a miracle because a sieve is an unsound vessel, like a woman's body, Marina Warner reminds us, "with its open orifices, dangerous emissions and distressing aptitude for change."[41] The chain of associations linking virtue, integrity, continence, virginity, and woman as vessel or container is evident and is emphasized by fertility, pregnancy, and maternity, which unseal the container and let its contents spill out.[42] Men's bodies are less often represented as vessels; and the many body fluids in fact common to men and women are nonetheless coded as female, as if the presence of a womb invoked the generic classification of container. So, for example, Abbot Odo of Cluny in the tenth century warns: "If men could only see what is beneath the flesh . . . they would be nauseated just to look at women, for all this feminine charm is nothing but phlegm, blood, humours, gall. Just imagine all that is hidden in nostrils, throat, and stomach. . . . We are all repelled to touch vomit and ordure even with our fingertips. How then can we ever want to embrace what is merely a sack of rottenness?"[43]

Although Tuccia herself is no longer a common figure in nineteenth-century iconography, the pattern of associations her story brings together continues to be pervasive. The nineteenth-century hysteric, represented as slave to her female secretions—but also, according to both medical and popular opinion, as prone to hypersecretion of gender-neutral body fluids—is an avatar of Tuccia and the ancient tradition she represents. We remember that the early nineteenth-century article "Hystérie" in the authoritative *Dictionnaire des sciences médicales* lists as harbingers of a hysterical attack "une effusion de larmes considérable . . . les clous, les furoncles, les abcès, les sueurs, les diarrhées, la salivation"[44] ["a heavy flow of tears . . . carbuncles, boils, abcesses, sweat, diarrhea, salivation"]. The hysteria doctors often stress that even normal women (that is, protohysterics) secrete tears, sweat, gastric juices, bile, and urine more quickly and in greater abundance than do men.[45] They are also prone to an analogous flow of chatter, gossip, exaggerations, and lies. So the physical and moral incontinence at the core of the Tuccia story are matched by a verbal incontinence also well known to the nineteenth century.

It is worth recalling the representation in a seventeenth-century emblem book, reported by Patricia Meyer Spacks, of "a leaking barrel as the type of the babbling as well as of the whorish woman."[46] Consider, too, the Renaissance topos that presents natural woman as "the gaping mouth, the open window, the body that 'transgresses

[41] Warner, *Monuments and Maidens*, 254.

[42] Ibid., 251.

[43] Cited by Warner, *Monuments and Maidens*, 251.

[44] J.-B. Louyer-Villermay, "Hystérie," in *Dictionnaire des sciences médicales*, vol. 23 (Paris: Panckoucke, 1818), 249.

[45] See, for example, J. L. Brachet, *Traité de l'hystérie* (Paris: Baillière, 1847), 67.

[46] Spacks, *Gossip*, 39.

its own limits' " in defiance of normative (i.e., tamed) "Woman" whose signs, as Peter Stallybrass has noted, were "the enclosed body, the closed mouth, the locked house."[47] The triple formula invoked by Stallybrass returns us to my earlier contention that the kitchen scenes of *Pot-Bouille* are dependent on a metaphorical superimposition of house, body, and language. I would like briefly to detail my own formulation and, simultaneously, to situate it in more specifically historical terms.

If in the nineteenth century women are still forbidden to leave domestic space, servants are more specifically confined, and the signs of their enclosure are more visible. Servants are increasingly relegated to kitchens, still unhygienic and poorly ventilated, which adjoin the toilets but are rigorously distanced from other rooms, and at the end of the day they retire to quarters materially separate from the masters' space—*chambres de bonnes* accessible only by way of back staircases from the kitchen.[48] These architectural modifications respond to an increasing repression on the part of the bourgeoisie of what Mikhail Bakhtin calls the grotesque body—the open, fluid body as process—which is consequently identified with the lower classes, who were, in the Goncourts' celebrated phrase, "plus rapprochés de la nature et de la sauvagerie"[49] ["closer to nature and to the primitive"].

We have, then, a multilayered mapping of class on the body and of the body on the house, which is further complicated by the conjugation of women and the people: the proletariat, as Susanna Barrows has shown, is consistently feminized (seen as uncontrollable, capricious, uncivilized, closer to nature and the body). Correlatively, proletarian women are represented as hyperfemale, hypernatural: matter compounded, as it were. So for example the Goncourts' journal relates an anecdote about a certain Dr. Camus who, called upon to vaccinate some upper-class young women and their chambermaids during a smallpox epidemic, observed that the skin of the high-society women felt like parchment, while the needle penetrated the flesh of the maids as if it were "une pomme qui jute. Oui, une pomme pleine de suc"[50] ["an apple dripping with juice. Yes, a succulent apple"].

[47] Peter Stallybrass, "Patriarchal Territories," in *Rewriting the Renaissance*, ed. Margaret Ferguson, Maureen Quilligan, and Nancy J. Vickers (Chicago: University of Chicago Press, 1986), 128, 127.

[48] See Monique Eleb-Vidal and Anne Debarre-Blanchard, *Architectures de la vie privée* (Brussels: Archives d'Architecture Moderne, 1989), 253–59.

[49] Edmond and Jules de Goncourt, *Préfaces et manifestes littéraires* (Paris: Charpentier, 1888), 55. Among Alain Corbin's always incisive passing comments on nineteenth-century intersections of politics and hygiene is the following astute analysis of the class distribution of odor: "La stratégie alors mise en oeuvre opérera clairement le partage entre le bourgeois désodorisé et le peuple infect" ["The strategy practiced clearly creates a split between a deodorized bourgeoisie and a putrid lower class"]. Corbin, *Le Miasme et la jonquille: L'odorat et l'imaginaire social, XVIII–XIXe siècles* (Paris: Flammarion, 1986), 64. On the grotesque body, see Mikhail Bakhtin, *Rabelais and His World*, trans. Hélène Iswolsky (Cambridge: MIT Press, 1968).

[50] Edmond and Jules de Goncourt, *Journal: Mémoires de la vie littéraire*, ed. Robert Ricatte, 3 vols. (Paris: Laffont, 1956), 2:721, 21 December 1876. For an excellent discussion of the metaphorical associations between women and the proletariat, see Susanna Barrows, *Distorting Mirrors: Visions of the Crowd in Late Nineteenth-Century France* (New Haven: Yale University Press, 1981).

The society women, whose parchmentlike skin evokes writing, surface, and the mind, are dry, desiccated, associated with the male principle, while the maids, linked to juiciness, food, and matter, incarnate fluid female depths.

When we then return to Zola's kitchens, the excremental, digestive, perspirational metaphors that often qualify the secreted gossip of the maids' quarters are more clearly legible as specifically female effluents, particularly once we read closely the scene of Adèle's childbirth. We look in on Adèle (who is pregnant with the unwanted child of one of the bourgeois masters) in the throes of discomfort one night in her room. Only gradually after various unfruitful trips to her chamberpot does she realize that the stomach pains she is having are not signs of intestinal trouble—"est-ce qu'elle allait avoir des coliques, maintenant?" (3:367)—["was she going to be colicky, now?"]—but of labor. As the scene develops, the birth process continues to be translated by an intestinal and excretory rhetoric that echoes the incessant descriptions of the kitchens and central courtyard:

> Des eaux ruisselèrent, ses bas furent trempés. . . . son derrière et son devant . . . n'étaient plus qu'un trou par lequel coulait sa vie; et l'enfant roula sur le lit, entre ses cuisses, au milieu d'une mare d'excréments et de glaires sanguinolentes.　　　　　　　　　　　　(3:369–70)

> *Her water broke, drenched her stockings. . . . all that was left of her bottom and her belly . . . was a hole through which her life ebbed away; and the child rolled out onto the bed from between her legs in a morass of excrement and bloody mucus.*

The umbilical cord and afterbirth, which are referred to repeatedly as "un boyau" ["a bowel"]—the preferred term throughout the novel for the pestilential courtyard—are deposited in Adèle's chamberpot. She then wraps the child in newspaper and leaves her in an alley—one more *fait divers* leaked from the depths of a dark polluted source. *Inter urinas et faeces* are born not only our lives but our words.

This is not the only time that writing is directly related to the horror of the maternal body. Earlier in the novel the concierge rages at the visible pregnancy of the only worker in the building, a boot stitcher who rents a *chambre de bonne*. His fury reaches phantasmatic proportions with the course of the pregnancy:

> "Ce ventre! ce ventre!"
> C'était ce ventre qui exaspérait M. Gourd. Un ventre de fille pas mariée. . . . Et son ventre avait grossi sans mesure, hors de toute proportion. . . .
> "Elle aurait dû prévenir, n'est-ce pas? on ne s'introduit pas chez les

gens, *avec une affaire pareille cachée sous la peau. . . . Et, regardez,*
regardez aujourd'hui! *elle ne tente rien pour le contenir, elle le lâche!"*

(3:254; my emphasis)

> *"That belly, that belly!"*
> It was that belly that exasperated Monsieur Gourd. The belly of an unmarried
> girl. . . . And her belly had swelled out of bounds, beyond all proportion. . . .
>   "She ought to have let us know, right? One doesn't room in a house with decent
> people with this kind of business hidden under the skin. . . . And look—just look
> at her today! She doesn't even try to hold it in, she lets it show!"

The hidden contents of this woman's body present the disturbing element: the
possibility of change, flux, overflow, the probability that inside and outside cannot
be maintained as separate categories. The openness of the boot stitcher's pregnant
body is emphasized by the fact that she is never named, only referred to as "la pi-
queuse de bottines," the repeated evocation of her occupation as maker of holes
translating her own permeable nature. And it is this woman's body, this unsound
container, that is here again linked to writing. The concierge's anger is directed
precisely at his perceived association of pregnant belly and writing: "Une maison
comme la nôtre affichée par un ventre pareil! car il l'affiche, monsieur . . . !"
(3:254) ["A house like ours labeled by such a belly! for it does label it, sir . . . !"].
Pot-Bouille, like the apartment building, is placed under the sign of the pregnant
belly, and writing, by implication, is a trace of the mother's body.[51]

We are led back to the maids' open mouths, bodies, and windows—the kitchen
of the novel, as it were—and to two unresolved questions originating there. Why
are the maids' material bodies designated as source of *Pot-Bouille*? And what is the
connection between the domestic generation of *Pot-Bouille* and the domestic
foundation of the novel's representation of the bourgeoisie? These are problems of
signification that can best be approached by considering *Pot-Bouille* as myth, in
Barthes's sense. When we look at the signifying structure of the novel, we can
easily recognize the maids in their kitchens as signifier of bourgeois moral turpitude. This sign is ambiguous, however, because the equation of domestic abjection and bourgeois turpitude would not be possible if maids and masters were
equal. The equation upon which the sign depends works only because there is, in
the imaginary of Second Empire France, a radical disjunction between the people

---

[51] In "De la moralité dans la littérature" as well, Zola indicates the female belly as source of naturalist
writing. Speaking of his critics, he comments: "Ils se fâcheront, en vous voyant avec les filles graves,
sérieux, un scalpel à la main, fouillant le ventre de ces jolies personnes, dont ils ne tiennent à connaître
que le satin" (45:586) ["They would become angry upon seeing you with honest girls, a scalpel in hand,
serious, burrowing around in the belly of these pretty creatures, for they only want to recognize the
satin"].

and the bourgeoisie. In other words, the initial sign assimilating the two classes also signifies something quite different: the reassuring survival of the class system. The duplicity of this myth—its particular version of the "jeu . . . de cache-cache" ["game . . . of hide-and-seek"] that Barthes poses as the essence of myth—lies in its flickering between the image of a shared popular/bourgeois filth and the implied distinction between two classes of dirt: the maids' "natural," material dirt on the one hand, and the metaphoric sullying of the bourgeoisie on the other.[52]

At roughly the time Zola was writing *Pot-Bouille*, Eugène Viollet-le-Duc wrote a strikingly lucid analysis of his century's architectural constructs of class, which present a usefully concrete analogue to the novelist's mythmaking. Distinguishing the aristocratic from the democratic state, he writes:

> Dans les châteaux comme dans les hôtels, la vie du puissant était à découvert; on ne trouvait ni étrange ni mauvais que les familiers, fussent-ils d'une classe inférieure eussent leurs entrées partout. C'était une existence en commun qui ne pouvait pas avoir d'inconvénients, parce qu'il n'y avait pas à craindre que les petits oubliassent jamais la distance sociale qui les séparait du maître.
>
> Il n'en est pas ainsi dans une société démocratique; c'est alors par une série de barrières matérielles que le maître peut se soustraire aux visées et empiètements des inférieurs.[53]

> *In chateaux as in mansions, the life of the powerful was open to view: it seemed neither strange nor undesirable that domestics, even of the lower classes, had access everywhere. Such a shared existence did not pose a problem because there was no fear that the lowly would ever forget the social distance that separated them from the master.*
>
> *This is not the case in a democratic society; in such a society the master must have recourse to a series of material barriers in order to remove himself from the designs and encroachments of his inferiors.*

Manifest physical segregation of the lower classes becomes increasingly necessary to the bourgeoisie after 1789, as rigid moral barriers are eroded. In a paradoxical sense, then, the imposing presence of material barriers speaks to the disappearance of more effective if less tangible social barriers. In much the same way, Zola's myth reinstates the barriers whose effacement he fears; the bar separating signifier from

---

[52] Roland Barthes, "Le Mythe, aujourd'hui," in *Mythologies* (Paris: Seuil, 1957), 203.
[53] Eugène Viollet-le-Duc, "17e entretien," in *Entretiens sur l'architecture* (Paris: Morel, 1863–72); cited by Eleb-Vidal and Debarre-Blanchard, *Architectures de la vie privée*, 258–59.

signified (domestics from masters) in the initial sign is the trace of this reimposed barrier.

As Viollet-le-Duc's commentary suggests, the sociopolitical changes attached to the democratization of France bring with them a semiological crisis, which I locate at the heart of Zola's novel.[54] How can difference be signified in an age when traditional founding distinctions no longer hold? As the title of the novel makes abundantly plain, we have in *Pot-Bouille* a melting pot: a very strong tendency toward coalescence, mixing, promiscuity, and flow—which is to say, the loss of clear distinctions. But we also have, in reaction, an insistent attempt to reestablish principles of differentiation. We have seen that this attempt is responsible for the mythological structure of the novel; I want to argue that it is also responsible for the periodic outbursts of the female abject, which, as we have seen, compose the novel's rhythmic structure and are designated as writing source.

The regular, repetitive emptying of material and verbal sewage suggests a ritual process, a ceremonial purging. For this reason I think a reading of these scenes needs to emphasize process rather than matter: the differentiation of impure from pure rather than the simple unloading of filth. If we understand dirt as the threat of heterogeneity, as "a category that has to do with boundaries," in Klaus Theweleit's words, or, similarly, borrowing Kristeva's formulation of the abject, as "ce qui perturbe une identité, un système, un ordre . . . l'entre-deux, l'ambigu, le mixte" ["whatever perturbs identity, system, order . . . the in-between, the ambiguous, the mixed"], then the hideousness of filth, slime, secretion, decay can be understood as a reminder of the fragility of the signifying process.[55] Dirt, or the instability of boundaries, mimes the perpetual risk run by a symbolic order based on discrimination and difference.[56] However, the ritualization of dirt as pollution or the unclean serves as a symbolic corrective to indistinction: a marking off of the impure that salvages the pure and, more crucially, guarantees the maintenance of difference. Just such a ritual purpose is served by the rhythmic return of domestic sewage in *Pot-Bouille*: pure and impure are sorted out in the kitchen of the novel, and a system of binary distinctions is traced in the blood and sweat of the maids. This demarcation, a kind of Ur-writing that emerges from the shadow of semiological

[54] The reflection of a signifying crisis by architecture and literature is doubtless not fortuitous. Philippe Hamon has written provocatively about the complicity between these two disciplines, their need to refer to one another, "comme si l'architecture renvoyait à la littérature, en une sorte de miroir . . . les questions fondamentales qui hantent cette dernière" ["as if architecture acted as a mirror for literature, reflecting the fundamental questions that haunt the latter"]. Hamon, *Expositions: Littérature et architecture au XIXe siècle* (Paris: Corti, 1989), 29.

[55] Klaus Theweleit, *Male Fantasies*, trans. Stephen Conway, 2 vols. (Minneapolis: University of Minnesota Press, 1987), 1:386; Julia Kristeva, *Pouvoirs de l'horreur* (Paris: Seuil, 1980), 12.

[56] Kristeva, *Pouvoirs*, 84.

crisis, underwrites Zola's text in much the same way that it supports his representation of the bourgeoisie.

If in both cases the signifying order is preserved by the maid, who performs a
kind of semiological laundering service, one is led to conclude that she functions
as a natural figure of difference. But in a rare moment of self-questioning, Zola's
text paints an auto-pastiche that undermines the very concept of nature, and perhaps of naturalism itself. Let me turn to this painting by way of conclusion.

Fairly early in the novel, Madame Josserand is hosting a tea party whose express
purpose is the marketing of her daughter Berthe. To this end, she displays, with
calculated nonchalance, this evidence of one of Berthe's many talents:

> Comme par hasard, une coupe de porcelaine se trouvait sur la table; au
> fond, encadrée dans la monture toute neuve de bronze verni, était peinte
> la Jeune Fille à la cruche cassée, en teintes lavées qui allaient du lilas clair
> au bleu tendre. Berthe souriait au milieu des éloges.   (3:55)

> *As if by chance, there was a porcelain cup on the table; on the bottom, in a rim of
> freshly varnished bronze, was the* Girl with the Broken Pitcher, *painted in washed-
> out hues varying from pale lilac to light blue. Berthe was smiling amidst the praise.*

Madame Josserand goes on to laud the realism of her daughter's style: "Pour le dessin, je le garantis! . . . Il n'y a pas un cheveu en plus ni en moins . . . Berthe a
copié ça ici, sur une gravure" (3:56) ["As for the drawing, I can guarantee it! . . .
There is not a hair too many or too few . . . Berthe copied it here, from an engraving"]. The mocking voice of Zola the naturalist is audible in this display of Berthe's
watered-down teacup art, copy of a copy of a copy, three times removed from any
observable model holding a broken vessel.

But if we shift our aesthetic orientation, looking at Berthe's venture from a symbolist rather than a realist viewpoint, it cannot be so readily dismissed. For the
painting Berthe has chosen to reproduce, Jean-Baptiste Greuze's *La Cruche cassée*
(the original of which the Louvre acquired in 1789) is a very apt symbolic self-
portrait of the thirdhand artist, particularly within the iconographic field of the
novel. Greuze's painting represents a nubile young woman with fresh face and
clouded eyes, a shattered earthenware pot slung over her right arm. With her
hands she clutches against her lower body a bunch of pink flowers wrapped in a
raised fold of her dress, and the spread of her fingers pressed to her pelvis against
the dress fabric replicates the jagged shape of the gash in her pot. This coy image of
lost virginity is emphasized by a thin stream of water flowing from a fountain directly behind the woman's left arm.

FIGURE 8. *Jean-Baptiste Greuze.*
La Cruche cassée.
(Paris, Louvre. © Photo R.M.N.)

Now, the citation of Greuze (and, indirectly, of the Tuccia legend) alludes to the unsound bodies of the maids and implicates Berthe as potential leaking vessel. Her reproduction of *La Cruche cassée*, replicated once more by her metonymic connection to the cups of tea she is serving to the guests, works as prophetic symbol. Later, after she is bartered in marriage and loses her chastity to a lover, the story of her adultery, first leaked by the maids "au milieu des épluchures et des eaux grasses" (3:269) ["amidst the vegetable peels and the kitchen slops"] and then spilled in her own tears (3:293), finally pours out in words: "Alors Berthe se confessa, d'abord en cherchant les mots, puis en lâchant tout" (3:320) ["Then Berthe confessed, first hestitating, then letting it all pour out"]. Berthe has become, in her mother's words, "[une] grande cruche" (3:344) ["{a} real crackpot"].

Zola's caricature of the artist as *copiste* is, of course, meant to be placed in contradistinction to a more kindred concept of the artist as naturalist, no doubt exemplified by the writer in *Pot-Bouille* who observes his neighbors and then writes an ugly but true novel—or better yet, by Zola himself. But to read *Pot-Bouille* as a rendering of nature is to make the same foolish claims for Zola as Madame Josserand does for Berthe. As Berthe painstakingly copies a reproduction of the Greuze painting, Zola paints his maids—so many *cruches cassées*—onto the bourgeoisie.

The aesthetic ambiguity of Berthe's art (failed realism or inadvertent symbolism?) reflects the ambiguities of Zola's naturalism and reveals his aesthetic ambivalence as well[57]—an ambivalence he would thematize a few years later in

[57] Might Zola's mockery of Greuze's sentimental painting contain an element of denied nostalgia? Twenty years earlier in a letter to Cézanne (16 January 1860) he admired the painting and expressed a longing to find the model—at the same time admitting that there probably was none, thereby echoing the realist/symbolist split:

> Dernièrement, j'ai découvert chez une de mes connaissances une vieille gravure enfumée. Je la trouvais délicieuse et je ne m'étonnai pas de mon admiration lorsque je la vis signée du nom de Greuze. C'est une jeune paysanne, grande et de rare beauté de formes: on dirait une déesse de l'Olympe, mais d'une expression si simple et si gracieuse que sa beauté se change presque en gentillesse. On ne sait trop ce que l'on doit le plus admirer, ou de sa figure mutine, ou de ses bras magnifiques; quand on les regarde, on se sent pris d'un sentiment de tendresse et d'admiration. . . D'ailleurs, Greuze a toujours été mon favori, et je suis resté longtemps devant cette eau-forte, me promettant d'aimer l'original, si un tel portrait, sans doute un rêve de l'auteur, peut en avoir un.   (Zola, *Pot-Bouille*, 3:1648, n. 1)

> *Recently, I discovered a smoky old engraving in the possession of an acquaintance. I found it delicious and was not surprised by my admiration when I saw that it was signed by Greuze. It is a young peasant girl, ample and unusually well shaped: one might say an Olympian goddess, but whose expression is so simple and so gracious that her beauty almost becomes gentleness. It is hard to know what is most admirable—her saucy face, or her magnificent arms; when looking at them, one is overcome by a feeling of tenderness and admiration. . . . Besides, Greuze has always been my favorite, and I lingered for a good while before this etching, promising myself to love the original, if such a portrait, probably a dream of its author, can have one.*

200 *L'Oeuvre.* There the artist Claude Lantier, who prides himself on painting only
• reality, struggles to rationalize—to naturalize—his representation of a female
nude on a boat in the middle of Paris:

> Claude s'entêtait, donnait des explications mauvaises et violentes, car il
> ne voulait pas avouer la vraie raison, une idée à lui, si peu claire, qu'il
> n'aurait pu la dire avec netteté, le tourment d'un symbolisme secret, ce
> vieux regain de romantisme qui lui faisait incarner dans cette nudité la
> chair même de Paris.[58]

> *Claude insisted, offered implausible and violent explanations, because he didn't
> want to admit the real reason, an idea he had that was too vague to be expressed
> clearly, a secret symbolism that tormented him, a holdover of romanticism that
> made him incarnate the very flesh of Paris in this nude body.*

Like Claude, Zola is prey to a "secret symbolism" that is responsible for his incarnation of the flesh of the bourgeoisie in the nudity of women, a nudity he struggles
to naturalize by referring it to the maids.[59]

To read Berthe's painted cup as a pastiche of *Pot-Bouille* is to reread Zola's naturalism, to destabilize the bracing role of female abjectness in his representation
of the bourgeoisie. Berthe's *Cruche cassée* suggests that Zola's painting of the
bourgeoisie should be attributed not to nature but to a coherent symbolist vision—
the symbolism of a vision that coheres to a certain ideology—and that his naturalism should be glossed as a symbolism naturalized by cultural codes.

THE BODY IN QUESTION

La Joie de vivre

Nana and *Pot-Bouille* turn on an omnipresent body that is endlessly deferred and
withdrawn. We have seen that Adèle's secret places (which are condensations of
domestic space) are constantly displaced as secretions, and that Nana's private
parts remain quintessentially *private*. When they are re-presented by Louise in the
childbirth scene of *La Joie de vivre*, they become quite simply *parts*: detachable,
observable objects. The scene of Louise's labor constitutes one of the rare instances, in Zola, where the female body is completely bared and its secret places

[58] Zola, *L'Oeuvre*, in *Les Rougon-Macquart*, 4:236.
[59] The citation from *L'Oeuvre* was brought to my attention by Peter Brooks's *Body Work: Objects of Desire in Modern Fiction* (Cambridge: Harvard University Press, 1993), 135. See his chapter 5 (123–61)
for a more extended commentary on Zola's treatment of the problem of representing the modern nude.

exposed. But nudity, like truth, turns out to be a *virtual* concept, dependent upon its antithesis, cover-up. When the last veil is lifted, when Louise is displayed, "découverte jusqu'à la gorge, le ventre à l'air, les jambes élargies" ["bared to the chest, belly up, legs spread"], both nudity and hidden truth have become conceptual impossibilities: "Cette nudité avait . . . disparu. . . . A la grande clarté brutale, le mystère troublant s'en était allé de la peau si délicate aux endroits secrets"[60] ["Her nudity had . . . disappeared. . . . In the harsh light, the troubling mystery had vanished from the delicate, secretive skin"].

Louise's body, fixed under "the harsh light" of Zola's naturalist scrutiny, resembles nothing so much as an entomological specimen splayed under a microscope, taken in charge by a superseding consciousness. The passage that focuses upon her body begins: "Louise n'était plus. Elle venait de s'abandonner comme une chose." ["Louise was no longer present. She had just given herself over, like a thing."] It ends: "Le médecin causait toujours" (3:1095–96) ["The doctor was still talking"]. The intervening description, bounded by these two statements, marks a passage from Louise's loss of consciousness to the narrative appropriation, via the doctor, of her immobilized body.[61]

Her lapse into unconsciousness allows the narrator's discourse to assume her body more completely and more perceptibly. When she faints, her absence provides an opening, creates the space for a narrative presence: "Elle restait là, sans même un frisson, étalant sa maternité ensanglantée et béante" (3:1096) ["She stayed that way, without even a shiver, exhibiting her bloody and gaping maternity"]. This *béance*, this organ gaping like a speechless mouth, constitutes a gap that the doctor/narrator can fill in with his own words. Here as elsewhere in Zola, female bodily discourse turns out to be a ventriloquist's discourse. Female speech is suppressed in order to be expressed as (inarticulate) body language, which is then translated—dubbed—by a male narrator. But the source of this projected voice can be traced through its phantasmatic imagery:

> A la grande clarté brutale, le mystère troublant s'en était allé de la peau si
> délicate aux endroits secrets, de la toison frisant en petites mèches
> blondes; et il ne restait que l'humanité douloureuse, l'enfantement dans
> le sang et dans l'ordure, faisant craquer le ventre des mères, élargissant
> jusqu'à l'horreur la fente rouge, pareille au coup de hache qui ouvre le
> tronc et laisse couler la vie des grands arbres.   (3:1096)

[60] Zola, *La Joie de vivre*, in *Les Rougon-Macquart*, 3:1096. Subsequent references to the novel will be given parenthetically in the text.
[61] We find essentially the same structure of mediation here as in the *Nana* scene, with the doctor's scrutiny now replacing the lover's. Both lover and doctor (and the distinction between the two is blurred by the doctor's name, *Cazenove*) perform a *mise en discours* of a mute (and therefore narratable) woman's form.

In the harsh light, the troubling mystery had vanished from the delicate secret skin, from the fleece curling all over in little blond tendrils; and only its suffering humanity was left, childbirth in blood and ordure, making mothers' bellies split, spreading the red crack to the point of horror, like an ax blow that splits open the trunk and lets the life of great trees ebb away.

When the mother's body is stripped and exposed to the harsh light of day, all it reveals in the presumed place of truth is a widening gash, a gaping, bleeding wound compared to a slash in an incongruously placed tree trunk. This wound, legacy of the "fêlure originaire," of the "première lésion," is, for Zola, not only the figure of female sexuality, but the central, driving image of his writing. It is a figure at once inspirational and daemonic.

In *Le Docteur Pascal*, in a passage whose language curiously echoes what I have just cited, Clotilde has this reproach for the doctor/author: "C'est une clarté terrible que ta science jette sur le monde, ton analyse descend dans toutes nos plaies humaines, pour en étaler l'horreur. Tu dis tout" ["Your science casts a terrible light on the world, your analysis enters all our human wounds, to expose their horror. You say all"]. And Pascal replies with his familiar refrain: "Tout dire, ah! oui, pour tout connaître et tout guérir" (5:992–93) ["To say all, oh yes! to know all and to cure all"]. His words take on a peculiar resonance when we recall that for Balzac, the writer's task was to "montrer la plaie"[62] ["to show the wound"]. Zola, whose doubts about literary identity are matched only by anxieties about sexual identity, would outdo his precursor: where Balzac set out to *show* the wound, Zola will *heal* it. The implications of such a therapeutic project are double: on the one hand, to stanch the flow of blood, or to heal female sexuality; on the other, to stanch the flow of words, or to cure the text.

It is precisely because his textuality is so dependent upon female sexuality that Zola is caught in a double bind, eager but ultimately unwilling to tell, know, and cure the wounded and wounding difference. This double bind is the fetishist's dilemma, perhaps best expressed by Octave Mannoni's now famous formula: "Je sais bien . . . mais quand même"[63] ["Of course I know {there is a difference} . . . but still"]. In Zola's reverse phrasing (in a statement that is once again an attempt to distinguish himself from Balzac), the mechanism of disavowal is remarkably similar: "Balzac dit qu'il veut peindre les hommes, les femmes et les choses. Moi, des hommes et des femmes, je ne fais qu'un, en admettant cependant les différences de nature."[64] ["Balzac says he wants to depict men, women, and things. As for me,

---

[62] Honoré de Balzac, letter to Hyppolyte Castille, in *Oeuvres complètes*, ed. Marcel Bouteron and Henri Longnon, 40 vols. (Paris: Conard, 1940), 40:642–52.

[63] Octave Mannoni, *Clefs pour l'imaginaire ou l'autre scène* (Paris: Seuil, 1969), 9–33.

[64] Zola, "Les Différences entre Balzac et moi," in *Les Rougon-Macquart*, 5:1737.

I consider men and women as one, while acknowledging, however, the differences of nature."] That is to say, "I do not acknowledge difference . . . but still."

Zola's stated ambivalence helps to explain why—with an inseparable mixture of horror and fascination—he plants a mutilated tree at the devastated site of Louise's genitals. For Zola, Louise is both castrated and not castrated. In this way, he covers or recuperates a loss with a gain that nonetheless marks off (and bears the mark of) privation: that privation upon which his writing depends.

What is of interest here is less the anatomical figure of loss than the figured loss of autonomy. When we recall that Louise loses, in rapid succession, bodily mastery, speech, and consciousness, thereby becoming representable, it begins to be evident that we need a definition of castration that incorporates a shift from the anatomical to the symbolic level. In her commentary on one of the classic Freudian examples of fetishism, the Chinese custom of binding a woman's foot and then being spellbound by it, Julia Kristeva usefully proposes that we understand castration as an exclusion indispensable to the constitution of a sociosymbolic order: "le dé-coupage d'une partie de l'ensemble pour que l'ensemble se constitue comme tel, comme une alliance homogène"[65] ["the cutting off of a part of the whole so that the whole can be constituted as such, as a homogeneous alliance"]. Just as the notion of revelation is dependent on secrecy, and nudity, on cover-up, the concept of coherence must be guaranteed by that of fragmentation, and the concept of identity by that of difference. But difference turns out to be a devalued same. Represented as less, woman is nonetheless introduced into the phallic order as its dregs. However, because she assumes the symbolic burden of the privation that is in fact imposed on all adherents to the social contract, her sign of lack is eventually valorized as a supplement: it is fetishized. Women are the refuse of society but also the guardians of its truths. Such a position, needless to say, hardly spells good news for women. Icons bear an uncanny resemblance to scapegoats.

Such a reading of the subtle transition from female castration to fetishization, from lack to plenitude, is especially useful to me at this point because it helps to return us from the particular clinical close-ups of Louise, Adèle, and Nana to Zola's more general use of anatomical metaphors of textuality. When the specific fetishistic images of the veil and the tree are elucidated as signifiers of both lack and secrets, they send us back to the founding metaphor—the recurring metaphor—of the *fêlure*, both gap and excess, lack become leak. Fetishism, as enacted by Zola, replicates the *fêlure*: the process of inscribing a crack, a fault, a lacuna within the text and then valorizing it as hidden signified, as signifying source.

It is worth emphasizing that woman can be blazoned as hidden signifier only when she has been introduced (as negative value) within the phallic order; that is, only once she has been fetishized. Therefore, when we associate the *fêlure* with fe-

[65] Julia Kristeva, *Des Chinoises* (Paris: des femmes, 1974), 91.

204 tishism, we have already implicitly dissociated Zola's text—at least in part—from
• its ostensibly female metaphorical source. Fetishism, or the process of making
woman appear to signify within a male symbolic order, depends upon a metaphorical shift from female to male anatomy. Or better still, it depends upon a *shifting
between* female and male anatomical figures, a dizzying vacillation that strives to
make difference an incessantly posed, eternally undecidable question.

8 HYSTERICIZING HISTORY

The Commune according to Du Camp

Les Convulsions de Paris

Si les Dieux sont partis, la Femme te reste.
FÉLICIEN ROPS TO EDMOND PICARD, 1878

● A certain strategy manipulated by rightist chroniclers seeking to disarm the political thrust of the Paris Commune consisted of pathologizing it.[1] Here is Zola: "C'était . . . une crise de nervosité maladive qui se déclarait, une épidémique fièvre" ["It was . . . the outbreak of a morbid nervous condition, a contagious fever"]. Now Jules Claretie: "L'état de Paris était encore plus pathologique que politique. La surexcitation cérébrale des derniers mois éclatait en un immense accès" ["The state of Paris was more pathological than political. The excessive cerebral agitation of the preceding months burst out in an immense fit"]. In a similar

[1] The Paris Commune was a revolutionary government formed by workers in Paris (and several other cities) in late March 1871, following a series of defeats suffered by the French army at the hands of the Prussians, the five-month siege of Paris by the Prussians, and an ensuing state of military, economic, and political chaos. Federal troops repressed the Commune two months later in a week-long massacre that left some twenty-five thousand mostly working-class insurgents dead. Notable as the first rise to power of a revolutionary proletariat, the Commune was generally censured by the bourgeoisie. In the intervening century, it has been appropriated as precursor by a number of leftist and extreme leftist movements.

205

but more explicit vein, Guy de Maupassant names the disease that figures so prominently in the rhetoric of anti-Communard literature: "La Commune n'est pas autre chose qu'une crise d'hystérie de Paris"[2] ["The Commune is nothing but Paris in the throes of a hysterical attack"].

The title of Maxime Du Camp's four-volume diatribe against the Commune, *Les Convulsions de Paris*, forecasts a work congruent with the rhetorical climate I have been referring to. The imagistic character of Du Camp's title immediately contradicts the claims of his introduction to tell only the facts in his historical narrative, which he represents as a documentary record of selected episodes of the Commune.[3] Indeed, the liminal figuration of political as pathological writes the metaphor large upon the body of the text, sustains it, suggesting that the hysterical body will be systematically inscribed, in the subsequent pages, upon the body politic. In other words, the figure in the title announces the extension of metaphor into allegory.

The *Princeton Encyclopedia of Poetry and Poetics* tells us that "we have allegory when the events of a narrative *obviously* and *continuously* refer to another simultaneous structure of events or ideas." Similarly, according to Northrop Frye, a narrative is allegory when an author indicates the relationship of images to ideas "explicitly," "continuously," and "systematically." Leonard Barkan speaks in like fashion, and more specifically addresses my own focus on the allegorical body: "An *extended* and *consistent* use of the human body image in a work is allegorical [when] it produces a *continuous* line of action *parallel* to the narrative itself."[4] But

[2] Emile Zola, *La Débâcle*, in *Les Rougon-Macquart*, ed. Armand Lanoux and Henri Mitterand, 5 vols. (Paris: Gallimard, 1960–67), 5:859. Jules Claretie, *Histoire de la révolution de 1870–71* (Paris: Aux bureaux du journal *L'Eclipse*, 1872), 636. I owe the citation from Claretie to Paul Lidsky's informative *Les Ecrivains contre la Commune* (Paris: Maspero, 1970), 54. Guy de Maupassant, "Une Femme," in *Chroniques*, 3 vols. (Paris: 10/18, 1980), 2:112. Maupassant satirizes in this article the inflationary use of the hysteria metaphor.

[3] Maxime Du Camp, journalist, art critic, novelist, editor, photographer, and inveterate voyager, is probably best known today as Flaubert's close friend and travel companion. Although some of his works were successful in his own time (*Les Convulsions de Paris* went through nine editions in twenty-five years), only his *Souvenirs littéraires*, a compendium of often vicious, specious, and extremely misogynistic literary gossip, remains in print today. In his youth he was an impassioned Romantic; in later life, he was a notorious conservative. This reputation barred him from delivering a funeral oration at Victor Hugo's gravesite, even though he was director of the Académie française at the time, for it was feared that a popular uprising might ensue. An often-linked strain of contempt for women and for the lower classes is a cross-generic trait of his writing.

[4] "Allegory," in *Princeton Encyclopedia of Poetry and Poetics*, ed. Alex Preminger (Princeton: Princeton University Press, 1974), 12; Northrop Frye, *The Anatomy of Criticism* (Princeton: Princeton University Press, 1973), 90; Leonard Barkan, *Nature's Work of Art: The Human Body as Image of the World* (New Haven: Yale University Press, 1975), 4–5, my emphasis. Angus Fletcher summarizes: "The traditional rhetoric set forth by Cicero, Quintilian, and the Renaissance rhetoricians asserts that allegory is a sequence of submetaphors which amount in aggregate to one single, continued, 'extended' metaphor." Fletcher, *Allegory: The Theory of a Symbolic Mode* (Ithaca: Cornell University Press, 1964), 70.

when we approach Du Camp's narrative expecting to find the title's projected body
casting a long convulsive shadow upon the disparate events of the Commune, we
are disappointed. The allegorical preconceptions set up by the title are frustrated
by the inconsistent structure of images that follows.

Les Convulsions de Paris is not unambiguously an allegory, if we understand
this figure to generate a consistently parallel structure of ideas, and if we define it
in terms of unity, continuity, and systematism. Neither, however, can it be dismissed as simply non-allegory. Although we find here no sustained discourse of
the hysterical body used to represent the Paris Commune, we do find that the
Commune is consistently conveyed by an extended body of discourse that may
best be named hysteria. What I am suggesting is that Du Camp's text shifts us from
an understanding of hysteria as a material body to the more fundamental notion of
the disease as a discourse, in the Foucauldian sense, that produces this body: man-
ufactures the diagnosis and the disease.

In the gap between title and text something changes; the work advances under
allegory's banner to reach us as unraveled fabric, presenting instead the scattered
elements of allegory. In the anticipated place of an integral image, we find a text,
Penelope-like, undoing itself even in the making, unmaking its representational
weave. Du Camp's perverse unmeshing of allegory—his fragmenting of the hysterical body—reveals more than a seamless allegory ever could, for it bares hysteria's constituent threads and exposes its textual functions.

There are two related but separate points to be emphasized here. First, the de-
allegorization of hysteria or disintegration of hysteria's allegorical body reorients
our attention to hysteria's generation, that is, to the separate strands of the discourse that produces it. Second, the ambivalence betrayed by first positing and
then undoing the hysterical body highlights the paradox of a figure both necessary
and intolerable to the text, a figure whose power the text endlessly works to incorporate yet vigilantly strives to dismember. What follows is an exploration of these
two avenues opened by *Les Convulsions de Paris*, which lead in turn to some reflections on the narrative structure and function of hysteria.

THE TATTERS OF ALLEGORY

Let us look first at the remnants of hysteria's allegorical body strewn through this
text. The title's convulsions, which initially establish the link between politics and
pathology, provide a recurrent—but nonetheless inconsistent—metaphor for the
upheavals that beset Paris during the Commune. We find that the condition
whose symptoms are the Commune's variously attributed convulsions, spasms,
and fits is subject to a plethora of diagnoses. Du Camp's Paris of 1871 is most frequently afflicted with epileptic seizures of a peculiar hybrid variety. "Un accès

208
•
d'envie furieuse et d'épilepsie sociale"⁵ ["A fit of furious envy and social epilepsy"]
is a typical explanation of events. But epilepsy is not a stable diagnosis here; Paris
suffers from a kaleidoscoping spectrum of available ills. There is hydrocephalus:
"La France a la tête trop grosse, et, comme les hydrocéphales, elle est sujette à des
accès de fureur maniaque. La Commune a été un de ces accès" (2:307) ["France
has a head too big for her, and, like hydrocephalics, she is subject to fits of maniacal furor. The Commune was one of those fits"]; kleptomania: "[les Communards]
en étaient . . . arrivés à un paroxysme qui les aveuglait et qui pourrait faire croire
qu'ils étaient atteints de cleptomanie aiguë" (4:145) ["{the Communards} were
struck by a paroxysm that blinded them and made it seem as if they were victims of
acute kleptomania"]; Saint Vitus's dance or chorea: "[Paris est] atteint de la danse
Saint-Guy politique" and "cette capitale [est] atteinte de chorée alcoolique et
meurtrière" (2:214, 3:125) ["{Paris is} afflicted with a political version of Saint Vitus's dance" and "this capital {is} afflicted with alcoholic and murderous chorea"];
ataxia: "la civilisation est ataxique; elle penche à gauche, elle va tomber" (4:326)
["civilization is ataxic; it is leaning to the left, it is about to fall"]; alcoholism: the
Commune empowers "le régime du *délirium tremens*" (1:85) ["the regime of *delirium tremens*"]; and, in extremis, death: "Le 25 mai, la Commune . . . s'agitait encore et ne vivait plus; mais les derniers spasmes de son agonie furent terribles"
(1:287–88) ["On the 25th of May, the Commune . . . was still stirring but was no
longer alive; yet the last spasms of its agony were terrible"].

Still unaccounted for are the numerous references to convulsions unyoked from
a controlling diagnosis: "ce paroxysme inconscient" (1:38) ["this unconscious paroxysm"], "un accès de folie furieuse" (2:213) ["a fit of furious madness"], "cet
accès de justice populaire" (4:208) ["this fit of popular justice"], "une des crises les
plus périlleuses" (4:7) ["one of the most dangerous seizures"], and so forth. The far-
flung diagnostic points designate a constellation less amorphous than one might
expect; the internal varieties of Du Camp's convulsion metaphor are entirely consistent with contemporary medical theories of hereditary degeneration. I am
thinking particularly of Jacques Joseph Moreau de Tour's "tree of nervosity,"
which shows hysteria, epilepsy, chorea, and convulsions to be offshoots of the
same branch, close cousins of prostitutes, criminals, utopians, and bad citizens,
who can follow their roots back to alcoholics and imbeciles.⁶

⁵ Maxime Du Camp, *Les Convulsions de Paris*, 4 vols. (Paris: Hachette, 1889), 1:vi. *Les Convulsions*
first appeared in 1878–79. Subsequent references to *Les Convulsions* will be to this edition and will be
given in the text.
⁶ Jacques Joseph Moreau de Tours, *La Psychologie morbide* (Paris: Victor Masson, 1859). Zola adapted
Moreau's tree as the model for the family tree of the *Rougon-Macquart*. (See figures 14 and 15.) In her
fascinating study of crowd theory in nineteenth-century France, Susanna Barrows mentions that crowd
theorists borrowed models for abnormal psychology from medicine. Predictably, then, crowds most
often act like women or alcoholics; and a network of familiar metaphors also compares crowd behavior

If convulsiveness is the symptom most obviously (if inaccurately) shared by Du
Camp's diagnoses of the Commune, it is closely shadowed by femininity. For
grammatical reasons, of course, the Commune is consistently referred to as *elle*
and, by extension, personified as a woman: "La Commune est bien malade; elle ne
tardera pas à mourir" (3:239) ["The Commune is quite ill; it/she will not be long in
dying"]. "La Commune oublie trop volontiers qu'elle est la fille—la fille mi-
neure—du Comité, et elle semble ne pas s'apercevoir qu'elle a plus que jamais besoin des conseils paternels" (4:97–98) ["The Commune too easily forgets that she
is the Committee's daughter—its underage daughter—and she seems not to notice
that now more than ever she needs paternal guidance"]. But grammatical gender
alone does not explain the feminine identification of this political body.

The Commune is feminized by association with a cluster of traits that connote
woman. We can best locate these womanly attributes by backtracking, abandoning
temporarily the figurative feminine to trace feminine presence in *Les Convulsions*. Women are not merely omnipresent but dominant in Du Camp's Commune. They are the driving force if not the ruling power of his narrative. Time
and again we see them, bloodthirsty maenads obedient to their animal instincts,
drunk with the taste of combat and eau-de-vie, speaking coarsely, dressing lewdly,
and undressing freely—sirens and sorceresses luring their menfolk into battle and
frequently plunging first into the fray. So prevalent is this configuration of traits
that almost any of Du Camp's descriptions of the *Communardes* is illustrative:

> Trois femelles animaient, enfiévraient les hommes, embrassaient les
> pointeurs et faisaient preuve d'une impudeur qui ne redoutait pas le grand
> jour. Jeunes, enivrées de bataille et d'eau-de-vie, elles apportaient un
> élément de débauche au milieu de la tuerie. (3:80)

> En sueur, les vêtements débraillés, la poitrine presque nue, [elles]
> passaient d'homme en homme et parfois criaient: A boire! (3:87)

> *Three bitches led on the men, kissed the gunners, and displayed an immodesty
> that did not try to hide itself. Young, drunk with battle and with eau-de-vie, they
> brought an element of debauchery into the bloodshed.*

> *Sweating, indecently covered, their breasts exposed, they went from man to man
> and sometimes called out for more drink.*

---

to that of savages, children, animals, the poor, and the insane. Barrows, *Distorting Mirrors: Visions of
the Crowd in Late Nineteenth-Century France* (New Haven: Yale University Press, 1981), 43. Du
Camp does not stray far from what we might call "crowd discourse."

210
•

These are not demure, compliant women, well fitted to a defined domestic space that would, in turn, confirm the ordered arrangement of family, class, and gender categories; on the contrary, they are destroyers of the social fabric: "Elles apprirent aux petits enfants à tout maudire, excepté la Commune" (2:61) ["They taught young children to curse everything—except the Commune"].[7]

These are women out of place—at a time when, as Susanna Barrow reminds us, even a single step could constitute transgression: "To conservatives in the late nineteenth-century any step, however tremulous, away from the foyer was denounced as a stampede toward anarchy."[8] These mobile women are viragos, as Du Camp succinctly puts it (2:62); women who would be men:

> Celles qui se donnèrent à la Commune—et elles furent nombreuses— n'eurent qu'une seule ambition—s'élever au-dessus de l'homme en exagérant ses vices. . . . Elles se déguisèrent en soldats . . . elles s'armèrent. . . . Elles se grisèrent au sang versé.   (2:60–61)[9]

> *The women who gave themselves to the Commune—and they were numerous— had a single ambition: to rise above man by surpassing him in evil. . . . They disguised themselves as soldiers . . . they took arms. . . . They got drunk on spilled blood.*

It begins to be clear that certain traits that would be valorized as virtues in men are called vices once women have displayed them. One representative portrait completes my point:

> Je m'imagine qu'elle était désespérée d'être femme, ou que tout au moins elle eût voulu être "la femme à barbe." . . . Dans la brutalité des opinions

---

[7] Michel Foucault suggests that one of the ways in which women were hystericized in the nineteenth century was to make their bodies coextensive with the social body, family space, and children's lives. Foucault, *La Volonté de savoir* (Paris: Gallimard, 1976), 137. And Barrows reminds us that French feminism took articulate form during the French revolution, so that any manifestation or hint of feminist (or even feminine) activity was associated with violent revolution and anarchy. *Distorting Mirrors*, 47–54.

[8] Barrows, *Distorting Mirrors*, 54. Or again, in the eloquent words of Louise Michel, who, condemned and deported for her revolutionary activity during the Commune, was one of the very women Du Camp ostensibly was describing: "Peut-être dans ce beau pays de France, la mode d'attribuer à un *cas pathologique* tout caractère de femme un peu viril est-il complètement établie" ["In this fine country of France, the trend of attributing any slightly virile characteristic a woman displays, to a *pathological case*, may well be completely established"]. Louise Michel, *Mémoires* (Paris: Maspero, 1976), 192.

[9] Also: "Les femmes faisaient effort pour s'élever à la hauteur des hommes; elles y réussirent; . . . dans plus d'un cas la victime aurait pu être sauvée si la femme n'était intervenue" (4:153) ["The women tried to rise to the height of the men; they succeeded; . . . in more than one case the victim could have been saved if a woman hadn't intervened"].

qu'elle émettait, dans la grossièreté de son langage, dans sa liberté
d'allures, pour ne pas dire plus, on sentait le regret d'être condamnée à
porter des jupes: elle ne détestait pas la violence masculine de certains
exercices, et si elle ne pratiquait ni la boxe ni la savate, elle aimait à
prendre un fleuret et à faire des armes.   (2:71)

*I imagine she was in despair at being a woman, or at the very least that she would
have liked to be "the bearded woman." . . . By the brutality of her opinions, the
coarseness of her language, the freedom of her movements—to say no more—one
sensed that she regretted being condemned to wear a skirt: she did not dislike the
masculine violence of certain activities, and though she practiced neither boxing
nor French boxing, she liked to take a foil and fence.*

Yet it is only because these ostensibly masculine women retain their essential female nature (which is to say that woman, like the people, is closer to the beast) that
they can so easily strip off the taming veneer of femininity, return to the creatural
state Du Camp attributes to one Marie Ménan, among others: "Elle avait je ne sais
quoi de sauvage qui rappelait l'effarement des oiseaux nocturnes subitement placés
au soleil. Elle fut cruelle sans effort, pour obéir à ses instincts" (3:81) ["She had a
certain wildness about her that was reminiscent of the agitation of nocturnal birds
suddenly put in sunlight. She was effortlessly cruel, in obedience to her instincts"].

The myth of the *pétroleuses* (which Du Camp perpetuates, all the while denying its veracity) is an inseparable current fed by this pool of atavistic female images.
A neologism coined in 1871 to designate the women of the Commune accused of
setting fire to Paris, *pétroleuse* was not always used in its strict (and quite possibly
specious) sense; its nimbus often explicitly included any woman associated with
the upheavals of 1871 and, by metaphoric association, implicitly surrounded the
more general category of woman when perceived as a threat to existing social and
symbolic structures.[10] So we find petroleum flowing like unstanched blood
through the tissue of Du Camp's narrative: "La furie allait toujours, n'écoutait rien
et entraînait les hommes. Un témoin m'a dit: 'Elle était tellement trempée de pétrole, que c'est un miracle qu'elle n'ait pas pris feu'" (3:84) ["The fury kept going,
listening to nothing and leading on the men. An eyewitness told me: 'She was dripping with oil; it's a miracle she didn't catch fire'"].

The *pétroleuses* are one of many nineteenth-century reincarnations of the ancient image of woman as "leaking vessel"—unsealed container unable to stop the

[10] For an excellent account of the women incendiaries, see Edith Thomas, *Les Pétroleuses* (Paris: Gallimard, 1963). Thomas uses the term to cover "toutes les femmes qui ont été mêlées au mouvement ré-
volutionnaire de 1871" ["all women who were involved in the revolutionary movement of 1871"] and
adds: "Ce n'est nullement péjoratif" (13) ["It is not at all pejorative"].

212

•

prodigious surge of sexual, reproductive, and other assorted body fluids and, by analogy, unable to monitor a loose tongue and a flow of lies or incoherent sounds: "Elles tiraient des coups de fusil au hasard, riant, criant, tutoyant tout le monde, ignobles à voir, plus ignobles à entendre" (3:80) ["They shot their guns randomly, laughing, shrieking, talking familiarly to everyone, vile to see, still more vile to hear"].[11]

The unchecked flow of petroleum issuing from the free circulation of *pétroleuses* through Du Camp's Paris is curiously at odds with his disparagement of those who believe in the "legend" of the women incendiaries. The accusation, he states, is "fausse. . . . Plus d'une erreur a été commise, et plus d'un malheur fut à déplorer" (2:286–87) ["false. . . . More than one error was committed, and more than one tragedy was mourned"]. Yet only a pen stroke away, he accommodates, nonetheless, the repudiated belief, declaring the legend "excusée sinon justifiée par le spectacle que l'on avait sous les yeux" (2:286) ["excused if not justified by the spectacle before our eyes"], adding that "si la Commune n'avait brûlé une moitié de Paris, on ne l'eût jamais crue capable d'en brûler l'autre moitié" (2:287) ["if the Commune had not burned half of Paris, one would never have believed it capable of burning the other half"]. It isn't true . . . but it could just as well be. This rhetorical slippage that preserves the belief it pretends to abandon describes the myth-mongering substructure of *Les Convulsions*, which everywhere inscribes as figure the beliefs it dismisses as fact.[12]

When Du Camp suggests that "on pourrait écrire un livre curieux: *Du rôle des femmes pendant la Commune*" (2:60) ["one could write a curious book: *On the role of women during the Commune*"], we should not be fooled by the contrary-to-fact construction of his proposal. Undaunted, he continues: "Le récit de leurs sottises devrait tenter le talent d'un moraliste ou d'un aliéniste. Elles avaient lancé bien autre chose que leur bonnet par-dessus les moulins; tout le costume y passa" (2:60) ["The narration of their foolishness should tempt the talent of a moralist or an alienist. They threw much more than propriety to the winds; all their clothes went that way"]. Du Camp has already written the "curious book" he is calling for; it is the one we hold before us, which implicitly records a discourse on the feminine in the Commune and, still more fundamentally, produces a discourse on the Commune *in the feminine. Les Convulsions de Paris* points out much more than the role of women in the Commune; it demonstrates (no doubt in spite of its author)

[11] See "The Sieve of Tuccia" in Marina Warner's *Monuments and Maidens: The Allegory of the Female Form* (New York: Atheneum, 1985) and Patricia Meyer Spacks's *Gossip* (Chicago: University of Chicago Press, 1986), 39.
[12] I am referring to the structure of fetishistic thought as elaborated by Octave Mannoni in "Je sais bien, mais quand même . . . ," in *Clefs pour l'imaginaire ou l'autre scène* (Paris: Seuil, 1969), 9–33.

La Femme émancipée, répandant la lumière sur le monde.

FIGURE 9. *Eugène Girard. "Emancipated Woman, spreading light over the world."* *(Caricature of a* pétroleuse.) *(Photo Bibliothèque Nationale, Paris.)*

how vital is the concept of woman to nineteenth-century narrative structures, even those that have ostensibly little to do with her.[13]

When we turn away from the explicit representation of women to look at the more general representation of the Commune, we find that the structuring categories do not change: the revolutionary events of 1871 are explained by the same recurrent cluster of characteristics that define femininity. Like women, the Commune is ruled by the primordial animal instincts, answers to the call of an atavistic wild: "La Commune . . . a simplement été la prédominance des instincts sur la loi" (4:23) ["The Commune . . . was quite simply the predominance of instinct over law"]. Once again we find the lower classes and women assimilated, reduced to the natural, the instinctual, the animal:

> On allait voir ce que peut faire un peuple sans mesure et sans instruction, lorsqu'il est livré à lui-même et qu'il se laisse dominer par ses propres instincts. L'intérêt de ceux qui avaient saisi la direction de ses destinées était de le surexciter, de l'amener à ce paroxysme inconscient où l'homme redevient la bête féroce naturelle.   (1:38)

> *We were about to see what an unruly and uneducated crowd is capable of, left to itself and surrendering to its own instincts. It was in the interest of those who had seized control of these lives to arouse the crowd, to goad it to that point of no return at which man once again becomes the natural savage beast.*

The web of themes spun around female sexuality (promiscuity, prostitution, debauchery, orgies, bacchanalia) returns in the vocabulary and images used to characterize the Commune, which is consistently referred to as "sabbat," "saturnales," "bacchanale," "débauche" ["witches' sabbath," "saturnalia," "bacchanalia," "debauchery"], compared to an orgy, and described as uninterrupted drunken revelry: "Pendant deux mois Paris fut en proie à l'ivresse furieuse" (1:38) ["For two months Paris was prey to a raging intoxication"].

The savage, the inflammatory, and the orgiastic are three rhetorical streams that feed Du Camp's Commune, epithetically called "cette débauche de sang, de pétrole et d'eau-de-vie" (3:255) ["that orgy of blood, oil, and eau-de-vie"], and they flow freely from a female-associated source ever brimming over its bounds. Transubstantiated as blood, oil, and wine, the female bodily secretions surge through this narrative, nourishing the network of images upon which it is constructed. A supplementary conversion turns oil into ink: "Ceux qui étaient . . . en état de

---

[13] This is, of course, the subject of Naomi Schor's persuasive *Breaking the Chain: Women, Theory, and French Realist Fiction* (New York: Columbia University Press, 1985).

FIGURE 10. *Georges Lacombe, Isis. This fin de siècle (ca. 1893–94) representation of Isis recalls the iconography of the* pétroleuse. *She is sculpted in polychrome wood; from her breasts spurts a blood-/flame-red milk that ambiguously nourishes/destroys the flowers and tree trunks over which it pours.* (Paris, Louvre. © Photo R.M.N.)

manier une plume ont écrit leur histoire, ils ont écrit le mémorial de la Commune. . . . Leur encrier aussi est plein d'huile de pétrole. . . . Leur prose éclaire autant que leur pétrole" (4:300, 305) ["Those who were capable of handling a pen wrote their history, they wrote a memorial to the Commune. . . . Their inkstand is also filled with oil. . . . Their prose is as inflammatory as their oil"]. By metonymic conversion, the oil-based ink of the Communards yields a ready flow of words, fictions, and lies: "Ce sont des bavardages sans fin. . . . Ils parlent, ils parlent, et lorsqu'on veut résumer leurs discours, on s'aperçoit qu'ils n'ont rien dit. . . . Les fables ou les calomnies dont ils se repaissent sont toute leur science" (4:27) ["This endless chatter. . . . they talk, talk, talk, and when one tries to summarize their words, it becomes apparent that they have said nothing. . . . The fables and the slander they feed on are their only resource"].

Related to the theme of gossip and fabrication, if not to the liquid medium that conveys it, is a ubiquitous motif of performance, spectacle, and disguise. The Paris Commune is pervasively described here by a theatrical paradigm that includes such terms as "spectacle, parade, cabaret, mascarade, cirque, bouffonnerie, baraque foraine, ménagerie, carnaval" ["spectacle, parade, cabaret, masquerade, circus, clowning, sideshow, zoo, carnival"], and its participants are regularly labeled "acteur, cabotin, fantoche, acrobate, paillasse, singe" ["actor, ham, puppet, acrobat, buffoon, ape"]. To begin, we can read here another version of the role-playing women we earlier found, and we might read both versions as an effort to derealize the Commune: if all Paris is a stage and the Communards are players, then once the curtain has come down the politics of revolt can be bracketed as a finished performance.

But Du Camp does not merely relegate the revolutionary elements to the apolitical domain of theatrical illusion. His tendency to evoke a particular end of the theatrical spectrum—circuses, fairs, masquerades—shifts the notion of representation to a more specific focus on popular culture, which, magnetlike, draws into its field some of the scattered points we have indicated: the orgy (feasting, drinking, dancing, singing, sexuality); the bestial (animal instincts, savagery); the anarchic. The emergent constellation—the carnivalesque—can be summarized as a world turned on its head, an inversion of hierarchies of gender, class, race, and of social, legal, and linguistic structures. It is an amplified rendition of the paradigmatic figure of woman dressed as soldier, leading man into battle.[14]

Du Camp's insistence on figures of reversal and on the systematic transgression of authority warrants closer attention. At times his evocation of power reversal or transgression is figurative. It is, for example, synecdochic when he speaks about

[14] Natalie Zemon Davis points out that "the female's position was [traditionally] used to symbolize not only hierarchical subordination but also violence and chaos." Davis, "Women on Top," in *Society and Culture in Early Modern France* (Stanford: Stanford University Press, 1975), 128.

the Communards' flagrant violations of spelling and grammar rules: "La Commune s'est toujours distinguée par un mépris hautain pour l'orthographe, la grammaire et la légalité" [1:45] ["The Commune has always distinguished itself by a
haughty disdain for spelling, grammar, and legality"]). And it is metaphoric when
he borrows a racist discourse to compare the Commune to "ces cours de rois nègres
dont les voyageurs nous ont conté l'histoire" (2:115) ["those courts of black kings
that travelers have told us about"]. More often, however, he explicitly reiterates his
lament of "the world upside down": "On vole tout simplement et avec désinvol-
ture. C'est le monde renversé" (4:137) ["They steal easily and offhandedly. The
world is turned upside down"]; "Pour ces gens, liberté signifie le pouvoir de tout
faire sans contrôle; égalité, participation à toutes les jouissances . . . fraternité,
utilisation de la communauté au profit de soi-même; c'est le renversement de la
proposition" (4:150) ["For these people, liberty means the power to do all with no
control; equality, participation in all pleasures . . . fraternity, use of the community for personal profit; the precept is turned on its head"]; "Le pivot du vieux
monde est faussé; la civilisation . . . penche à gauche, elle va tomber" (4:326)
["The pivot of the old world is warped; civilization is leaning toward the left; it is
going to fall"].

What shall we make of this discourse of carnival surging through Du Camp's
historical chronicle? We might start by invoking traditional anthropological perspectives, which suggest that ceremonies of reversal ultimately clarify and reinforce existing structures of order in a society.[15] Du Camp's rhetorical rites clearly
are staged to affirm existing bourgeois structures; his constant recourse to carnivalesque images of turnabout—to the arrogation of power by female, impoverished,
intoxicated, uneducated, libidinous elements of the populace—conveys anger
and disgust and is designed to arouse similar sentiments in the bourgeois hearts of
his readers. The Commune, then, can be presented as a momentary aberration,
an incursion of the lower into the higher spheres (the territory at stake being bodily,
social, cultural, linguistic, political, and economic), and its repression, a return to
the "natural" order of things. But the tissue of Les Convulsions is so thoroughly in-
filtrated by the carnivalesque as to be virtually inextricable from it. The force,
pulse, plot—in short, the narrative integrity of Du Camp's text—depend entirely
on the repeated expulsion of its carnivalesque Other, so that the symbolic center of
this text constantly recuperates its rejected margins.

Essential to my argument is Peter Stallybrass and Allon White's elaboration of
carnivalesque discourse as a displacement of carnival as social practice.[16] They

---

[15] Davis in "Women on Top" and "Reasons of Misrule" in Society and Culture argues that inversion
could undermine as well as reinforce existing power structures.
[16] Peter Stallybrass and Allon White, The Politics and Poetics of Transgression (Ithaca: Cornell University Press, 1986).

outline the gradual repression of the grotesque body of carnival by the emerging bourgeoisie, from the Renaissance onward, and a concomitant reconstruction of carnival as "all that which the proper bourgeois must strive *not to be* in order to preserve a stable and 'correct' sense of self."[17] But the very act of excluding the low, the vulgar, the disgusting simultaneously reproduces it, includes it, at the level of the imaginary. As Stallybrass and White aptly put it, "Disgust always bears the imprint of desire. These low domains, apparently expelled as 'Other,' return as the object of nostalgia, longing, and fascination."[18]

This theory of the symbolic return of the socially repressed begins to explain what is happening in *Les Convulsions de Paris* (which I take to be representative of the nineteenth-century collective imaginary), but I want to amend it on two counts. First, in Du Camp's text the carnivalesque answers to the name of woman; that is, woman is the primary symbol of the low, the disorderly, the insubordinate: the strongest, the most threatening construction of all that arouses disgust and desire.[19] Second, at stake in Du Camp's almost obsessive fascination with the carnivalesque (and most notably, with the carnivalesque spectacle) is not only the issue of how to represent the Commune, but the problem of how to represent the place from which one represents the Commune—or anything else. In other words, the emergence, within this account of the Commune, of a persistent lexical, thematic, and figurative emphasis on representation and the feminine is perhaps less significantly a function of Du Camp's perspective on the events of 1871 than it is a broader-based reflection of his anxiety about the shifting symbolic bases of representation. Let us consider this point.

THE FEMALE SYMBOLIC BODY

We have so far examined, in *Les Convulsions de Paris*, an extended background narrative, the dispersed discourse of hysteria used to convey historical events. Interrupting this narrative—piercing or punctuating it, to use Roland Barthes's concept of *punctum*, we have a series of points or snags. "*Punctum*, c'est aussi: piqûre, petit trou, petite tache, petite coupure" ["*Punctum* is also sting, little hole, spot, cut"], says Barthes. These are points at which the narrative weave is interrupted by

---

[17] Ibid., 178.

[18] Ibid., 191.

[19] In "Women on Top," Natalie Zemon Davis presents woman as the prime symbol of inversion. Her analysis of symbolic structures of early modern Europe remains essentially valid in the nineteenth century, with two additional impinging factors: the gradual rise of an activist feminism, with its accompanying threat for empowered men, and the gradual destruction, dramatically embodied by the French revolution, of earlier symbolic bases.

a detail that arrests our attention, diverts us from the Commune and the fragmented allegory that represents it.[20]

I want to close in on three of these details, three examples of what constitutes,
in my reading of *Les Convulsions*, the *punctum* of this text. Each focuses on a different mode of representation; they have little, if anything, to tell us about the
Commune, but together they provide crucial insights into Du Camp's representation of it.

Representing Photography. A discussion of the barricades constructed for the defense of Paris turns from fortification to photography: Du Camp relates that the
barricades played an aesthetic as well as a strategic role, for they became backdrops
for Communards eager to bequeath to posterity a soldier's costume and an elaborate military pose:

> Cette manie d'avoir son portrait sous travestissement militaire . . . arriva
> au paroxysme lorsque vint la Commune. . . . Les vitrines des marchands
> de gravures . . . disparaissaient sous les cartes photographiques
> représentant les membres de la Commune . . . revêtus d'uniformes d'une
> fantaisie parfois divertissante. . . . Comme d'infimes acteurs, ils aimaient
> à se revoir dans les oripeaux de leur rôle à succès.   (2:234–35)

> *This mania for having one's portrait in military disguise . . . reached its height with*
> *the advent of the Commune. . . . The display windows of print sellers . . .*
> *disappeared beneath photographs representing members of the Commune dressed*
> *in uniforms whose outlandishness was sometimes amusing. . . . Like minor actors,*
> *they liked to look back at themselves in the tinsel of their one hit role.*

Theatrical vocabulary abounds in Du Camp's descriptions of these "poses mena-
çantes" ["menacing poses"], these "attitudes peu naturelles" (2:234) ["unnatural attitudes"]; he represents the representational mode of these photographic sessions as
one of masquerade, role playing, dissembling, make-believe. But he paints the
product of these sessions differently:

> Ces photographies ne restaient pas toutes à Paris; beaucoup prenaient le
> chemin de Versailles, et servirent plus tard à faire reconnaître bien des

---

[20] Roland Barthes, *La Chambre claire* (Paris: Gallimard, 1980), 49. Barthes proposes what we might
consider to be a viewer-response approach to photography based on the analysis of two constitutive elements or themes: *studium*, which is a kind of broad cultural interest, and *punctum*, a much more piercing or poignant order of appeal. Barthes's terms (which I interpret liberally) are instrumental to my
reading of Du Camp, whose tableau of the Commune elicits a similar bilevel response from the reader.

malheureux qui se cachaient. . . . C'est de ce moment qu'on a installé à
la Préfecture de police un atelier photographique, qui permet de prendre
le signalement irrécusable des malfaiteurs.   (2:235)

> These photographs did not all remain in Paris; many took the road to Versailles,
> and later served to identify quite a few of the wretches who were in hiding. . . . At
> that point, police headquarters installed a photographic service that facilitated the
> positive identification of wrongdoers.

If the origin of these photographs was ludic, involving the free play of signifiers
and the unrestricted circulation of signs, the result—police identification—is rigorously controlling. From costumed poses improvised upon the sandbags to photography studio installed at police headquarters, the path these pictures take describes a parallel apposition of spectacular and referential conceptions of
representation. Du Camp's evident glee at the idea of these poseurs being caught
by their own game, held finally accountable to an unchanging identity beneath
the mask, translates his relief at the prospect that all may be right(ed) in the world
of signs; that signs, despite appearances, must ultimately be accountable to a fixed
referent. Masquerade is corrected as identification, theatricality superseded by referentiality; in the process, however, a gap has been introduced.

Representing Painting. Du Camp's vituperative denunciation of the Communards' toppling of the Vendôme column includes at its material and symbolic center a painting of a female nude, which he discusses in equally censorious tones.
The element of transition permitting the nonetheless startling shift from politics to
aesthetics is the artist and Commune activist Gustave Courbet, who purportedly
ordered the destruction of the Vendôme column and assuredly painted the nude
in question. A wrath that seems to know no bounds binds the creative and destruc-
tive acts in a puzzling causal relationship. "If he was vile enough to have painted
this, he must have torn down *that*," runs Du Camp's argument.[21]

While it appears that politics is being explained by aesthetics, something quite
different lies unarticulated within Du Camp's argument: one domain can explain

---

[21] The most succinct example of this logic underlying Du Camp's entire chapter on Courbet is the following. When Courbet was brought to trial for his role in the column destruction, he explained his action to the judge, according to Du Camp, in these terms: "J'étais honteux que l'on montrât cela comme
une oeuvre d'art" ["I was ashamed that it was displayed as a work of art"]. The president of the tribunal
responded: "Alors c'est un zèle artistique qui vous poussait?" ["So it was artistic zeal that moved you?"]
To Courbet's reply, "Tout simplement" ["Quite simply"], Du Camp in turn responds: "Ce 'tout simplement' est le pendant du portrait de femme dont j'ai parlé; on doit répondre l'un lorsque l'on a peint
l'autre" (2:211) ["This 'quite simply' is the extension of the portrait of a woman I spoke about; one has
to respond in that way when one has painted this"].

the other by way of a common symbolic structure. Du Camp's ravings take on a varnish of logic when we look at this structure. Here is his representation of Courbet's painting:

> Pour plaire à un musulman qui payait ses fantaisies au poids de l'or . . .
> Courbet . . . fit un portrait de femme difficile à décrire. Dans le cabinet
> de toilette du personnage étranger, on voyait un petit tableau caché sous
> un voile vert. Lorsque l'on écartait le voile, on demeurait stupéfait
> d'apercevoir une femme de grandeur naturelle, vue de face, émue et
> convulsée, remarquablement peinte, reproduite *con amore*, ainsi que
> disent les Italiens, et donnant le dernier mot du réalisme. Mais, par un
> inconcevable oubli, l'artisan qui avait copié son modèle d'après nature,
> avait négligé de representer les pieds, les jambes, les cuisses, le ventre, les
> hanches, la poitrine, les mains, les bras, les épaules, le cou et la tête.
> L'homme qui, pour quelques écus, peut dégrader son métier jusqu'à
> l'abjection, est capable de tout.   (2:189–90)

> *To please a Moslem who paid for his fantasies with their weight in gold, . . .*
> *Courbet . . . painted a portrait of a woman that is hard to describe. In the dressing*
> *room of this foreign personage, one could see a small picture hidden under a green*
> *veil. When the veil was drawn aside, one was awestruck by the sight of a life-size*
> *woman, seen from the front, agitated and convulsed, remarkably well painted,*
> *reproduced* con amore, *as the Italians say, and offering the last word in realism.*
> *But, by some inconceivable oversight, the artist who had copied his model from*
> *nature, had neglected to represent the feet, the legs, the thighs, the belly, the hips,*
> *the chest, the hands, the arms, the shoulders, the neck, and the head.*
> *A man who could degrade his craft to the point of abjection for a few coins is*
> *capable of anything.*

What constitutes for Du Camp the abject heart of this painting is I think not merely the female sex—which is all that remains on the canvas/page after he so coyly slashes the other body parts—but the positioning of female sexuality at the very core of symbolic systems, be they uncovered in aesthetic or political representations. For the painting he reveals here without naming it is Courbet's *L'Origine du monde*. As the title implies, the subject of this painting is a symbolic construction of sexuality and more specifically, as Linda Nochlin has remarked, a construction of the female genitalia as "the very source of artistic creation itself."[22]

We should not assume that the signifying structures of this painting remain con-

[22] Linda Nochlin, "Courbet's *L'Origine du monde*: The Origin without an Original," *October* 37 (Summer 1986): 77.

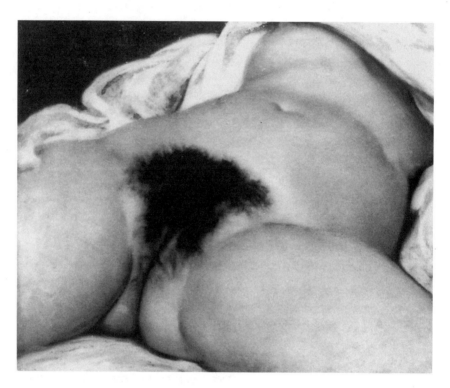

FIGURE 11. *Gustave Courbet,*
L'Origine du monde. *(Reproduced with
permission from Robert Fernier,* La Vie et
l'oeuvre de Gustave Courbet, *vol. 2.
Lausanne: Bibliothèque des Arts, 1979.)*

stant when it is embedded within Du Camp's narrative. I want to ask what world is being evoked in *L'Origine du monde* and why it is belatedly created, what brave new world this painting exemplifies within the narrative frame of *Les Convulsions de Paris*. We must reconstruct the Vendôme column before attempting an answer.

Constructed as a monument to the triumphs of Napoleon's Grande Armée, the Vendôme column was destroyed because it was a vestige of imperial legend. Whether we adopt Du Camp's rhetoric of the event as one more instance of a world turned on its head, Catulle Mendès's perception of it as an attack on "our victorious, superb fathers," Neil Hertz's psychoanalytic perspective of the toppled column as castration symbol, or Kristin Ross's Marxist reading of the demolition as "antihierarchical gesture," the association between column bashing and dismantling the reigning symbolic order—that of patriarchy—is evident.[23] The causal link between *L'Origine du monde* and the felling of the Vendôme column now becomes clearer. Rather like Victor Hugo's Claude Frollo, gesturing toward the printed book and then the cathedral, Maxime Du Camp brandishes Courbet's study of the female genitalia as he turns to the column's demolition, as if to say, "Ceci tuera cela" ["This will kill that"]. "Ceci" is not simply the painting we know from extratextual evidence to be *L'Origine du monde*; it is Du Camp's verbal representation of that painting, in which the body of the woman is not simply supine, decapitatated, and quadruply amputated, as Courbet had it, but also "émue et convulsée" ["agitated and convulsed"]. This description is completely supplementary to the body painted in *L'Origine*, which shows not a trace of a convulsion; but it supplies, through a curious chiasmus, the convulsed body announced by the title of *Les Convulsions de Paris* and withheld by its text.

I find in the apparent symbiosis of Du Camp's text and Courbet's painting authorization to superimpose their titles, whose structure is strikingly similar: a place (Paris, the world) and an event occurring there (an uncontrollable agitation, a beginning): together, fits and starts. Condensed, the titles describe a new order cutting through text and painting, cutting across political and aesthetic domains: a new Paris, a new creative principle, a fearsome new world whose symbolic center is mapped upon the core of the female symbolic body. Courbet, as maker and breaker of symbolic structures (though a more tempered view would present him as user and abuser of such structures), becomes the scapegoat upon whom Du Camp vents his rage, his fears, and his discomfort in the throes of symbol regeneration. He resists the shift with all his rhetorical might, displacing the convul-

---

[23] Du Camp, *Les Convulsions de Paris*, 4:137; Catulle Mendès, quoted by Kristin Ross in *The Emergence of Social Space: Rimbaud and the Paris Commune* (Minneapolis: University of Minnesota Press, 1988), 6; Neil Hertz, "Medusa's Head: Male Hysteria under Political Pressure," in *End of the Line: Essays on Psychoanalysis and the Sublime* (New York: Columbia University Press, 1985), 169–71; Ross, *The Emergence of Social Space*, 5.

sive female body to the margins of his text and dispersing its parts.[24] Dismembered, however, it reappears everywhere in his text as the phantom figure of the Commune.

Representing Voice. Incidental to Du Camp's account of the burning of the rue de Lille is an excursus on voice, language, and communication, and an implicit comparison of female and male empowerment in these areas. First we hear the women's response to the destruction:

> Dans la rue, c'était un indescriptible tumulte que dominait le cri des femmes, cri sans paroles, modulation suraiguë involontairement jetée par l'épouvante et qui vibrait au-dessus des rumeurs, comme un appel désespéré auquel nulle puissance surnaturelle ne répondait.   (2:94)

> *In the street there was an indescribable uproar dominated by women's screams, wordless screams, high-pitched involuntary cries prompted by terror, which vibrated over the din like a desperate appeal that no supernatural power answered.*

It is perfectly consistent with the dominant physical presence of women in this narration that the representation of female voice privileges its material aspect—in fact, thoroughly excludes the spiritual, the intellectual, and even the linguistic. Woman's voice is an involuntary, inarticulate vibration, a wordless cry: pure signifier hopelessly unmoored from any signifying potential.

This portrayal of woman's earthbound tones is all the more striking because it is immediately followed by an anecdote describing the discursive virtuosity of a man who talks with God:

> Le pasteur Rouville s'arrêta. . . . [Il était] fervent dans sa foi, éloquent, ayant une voix haute qui sait dominer le bruit, sachant par expérience qu'il n'est obscurité si profonde où l'on ne puisse faire pénétrer la lumière. . . . Seul, en présence du désastre qui le menaçait, il éleva son âme à Dieu.
>   (2:94–95)

> *Pastor Rouville stopped. . . . [He was] fervent in his faith, eloquent, with a loud voice that could dominate the noise, and he knew by experience that no darkness is so thick that light cannot be made to penetrate it. . . . Alone before the disaster that threatened him, he raised his soul to God.*

[24] Du Camp's description of Courbet's severed female torso repeats the amputating gesture, as he enumerates each of the absent parts (2:190).

After hearing Pastor Rouville's eloquent intervention, the attendant federal soldiers burst into tears and reach out to hug him; the incendiaries spare his house.
"He raised his soul to God," and God evidently answered, whereas woman's desperate cry echoes in a spiritual void.

Audible here is an echo of Baudelaire's reflections on the incongruous presence
of women in church: "Quelle conversation peuvent-elles tenir avec Dieu?"
["What can they possibly have to say to God?"], he asked.[25] Du Camp, like Baudelaire, echoes an age-old misogynistic discourse that presents femininity and
spirituality as mutually exclusive domains. Although the formless cries reverber-
ating in the rue de Lille are not those of women of the Commune, they are reminiscent of the babbling voices of Du Camp's *Communardes* and consistent with
the gendered rhetoric that represents the Commune, in *Les Convulsions de Paris*,
as material, sensual, and inarticulate.

Such digressions into photography, painting, and voice should be construed not as
intrusions of external material into the text but rather as extrusions from within, a
clumping or knotting of threads that otherwise weave the text. The *punctum* of
this text—well illustrated by the three details we have seen—is not only what
pierces or snags the narrative tissue, but also, more integrally, its very point.

The chilling ambiguity of the photography anecdote provides an introduction
to a crisis in representation woven into this text. Two polar readings of the photo-
graphed Communards posed upon the barricades permit no honest choice: both
are true. Disguise or identity, disguise *and* identity: mask and reference overlap.
Clear readings and stable meanings become impossible in a society that has lost its
symbolic bearings. As Lynn Hunt has persuasively argued, all political authority
requires a cultural frame within which to define itself, and every cultural frame
has a center where culture, society, and politics converge. If the cultural frame is
decentered—and this is what happened when the revolution desacralized the
king—a vacuum is created.[26] Hunt has shown how, in the decade following the
revolution, republican politics not only sought another representation of authority
(in the form of insignias, seals, statues), but also, more fundamentally, "came to
question the very act of representation itself."[27]

Du Camp's narrative confronts us with the aftermath of this symbolic decenter-
ing, its long-term indirect effects in all signifying domains. Constructed, like all
the artifacts of its time, upon a symbolic abyss, *Les Convulsions de Paris* obses-

[25] Charles Baudelaire, *Mon Coeur mis à nu*, in *Oeuvres complètes*, ed. Claude Pichois, 2 vols. (Paris:
Gallimard, 1975–76), 1:693.
[26] Lynn Hunt, *Politics, Culture, and Class in the French Revolution* (Berkeley: University of California
Press, 1984), 87–88.
[27] Ibid., 88.

sively works its unstable foundations into the texture of its narrative, everywhere questioning the possibility of representation but able to speak of little else.

In the face of the void, Du Camp posits, with considerable ambivalence, *L'Origine du monde*, verbally supplying the finishing touches to Courbet's work, exposing the painting with an energy and attention matched only by the terms of abuse he flings at it and its creator ("méprisable," "abjection," "dégrader" [2:189–90]). In place of the cultural framework swept away with the old regime, a cultural fiction that Jean-Marie Apostolidès has called "l'imaginaire du corps symbolique du roi"[28] ["the imaginary of the king's symbolic body"], Du Camp intuitively poses the imaginary of the new regime: the hystericized body of woman.[29] This body, matter unmastered in the throes of love, birth, illness, and death, is the energy source by which the text is run—and risks being overrun. Calling upon itself the wrath of its creator, this body, the stuff that allegories are made of, is instead fragmented, scattered to the far corners of the text, a torn and tearing thing. The demon with a forked tongue becomes a keening phantom.

Even in its integral allegorical form—a form that is always virtual in Du Camp's text—the powerful hystericized body is an empowering but not an empowered body.[30] For power, as Elaine Scarry has brilliantly shown, emerges from an interaction between physical and verbal acts in the course of which the body is transformed into the voice.[31] And as we have seen, it is precisely by the reverse transformation—by silencing the female voice and making the female body "speak" whatever is projected onto it—that Du Camp and others forge a monstrous female force that overpowers women.

[28] Jean-Marie Apostolidès, *Le Roi-machine: Spectacle et politique au temps de Louis XIV* (Paris: Minuit, 1981), 7.

[29] At stake here is not only the disease, but a much larger cultural framework or imaginary. See Michel Foucault's discussion of the hystericization of woman's body in *La Volonté de savoir*, 137; trans. Robert Hurley as *The History of Sexuality* (New York: Vintage, 1980), 104.

[30] Marina Warner, discussing an Amazon image of liberty that emerged in France in the first part of the nineteenth century, remarks: "By harnessing the figure of this outlaw . . . the Liberty image brings her under control. . . . every society will define its own 'wild' differently and then try to annex it." Warner, *Monuments and Maidens*, 292. Jacqueline Carroy suggests an intriguing causal relation between the trauma of the Commune and mounting Charcotian (spectacular) hysteria, suggesting that the latter was necessary to explain and defuse the former. Carroy, "Une Femme, des récits et des foules," *Revue internationale de psychopathologie* 41 (1991): 323–32. I find these analyses convincing but also want to argue for a more positive narrative need for the figure of the hysteric: inspiration as well as scapegoat, she offers patriarchal discourse a way out. But, as I explain in the body of my text, I do not think this is good news for women.

[31] Elaine Scarry, *The Body in Pain: The Making and Unmaking of the World* (Oxford: Oxford University Press, 1985), see especially 45–59. Speaking about torture, Scarry observes that "even where the torturers do not permanently eliminate the voice through mutilation or murder, they mime the work of pain by temporarily breaking off the voice, making it their own, making it speak their words, making it cry out when they want it to cry, be silent when they want its silence, turning it on and off" (54).

VENUS IN DRAG, OR REDRESSING THE DISCOURSE OF HYSTERIA

Rachilde's *Monsieur Vénus*

J'avais quelques raisons d'originalité, de commodité
aussi, en allant trouver le préfet de police du moment
pour lui demander, le plus simplement du monde,
la permission de m'habiller en homme. . . . Il ne me
restait qu'à vivre en mauvais garçon et je laissai
derrière moi la robe de la petite oie blanche,
de la demoiselle qui demandait au Jésuite,
son précepteur, le miracle de la . . . transfiguration!
Le métier de femme de lettres . . . ressemble un peu à
celui des actrices toujours obligées à la représentation.

RACHILDE, *POURQUOI JE NE SUIS PAS FÉMINISTE*

● In his 1889 preface to the second edition of *Monsieur Vénus*, Maurice Barrès describes the novel as "le spectacle d'une rare perversité" ["the spectacle of unusual perversity"].[1] In 1986, Bram Dijkstra calls *Monsieur Vénus* "a role-reversal novel . . . an early example of the unthreatening reversal games [characteristic of] . . . the past century."[2] In the time separating Barrès and Dijkstra,

---

[1] Rachilde, *Monsieur Vénus* (Paris: Flammarion, 1977), 5; trans. Madeleine Boyd (New York: Covici, Friede, 1929), 19. Subsequent references to *Monsieur Vénus* will be given parenthetically in the text and will be to these editions. Boyd's translation is generally faithful to Rachilde's text and tone, but tends toward prudishness when Rachilde's prose becomes purplish. In such cases I have modified the translation (and have so indicated) to correspond more closely to the original French. There is a recent translation of *Monsieur Vénus* by Liz Heron (London: Dedalus, 1992) which I have not yet seen as this book goes to press.

[2] Bram Dijkstra, *Idols of Perversity* (Oxford: Oxford University Press, 1986), 337. Dijkstra's reduction of *Monsieur Vénus* to a game of sexual inversion represents a traditional treatment of the novel. Several feminist readings of the novel have astutely shown that the theme of sexual inversion is not a mere game, but implicates (and works to deconstruct) broader categories and symbolic structures. See Micheline Besnard-Coursodon, "Monsieur Vénus, Madame Adonis: Sexe et discours," *Littérature* 54

228

•

Monsieur Vénus loses its shock value: the rare spectacle becomes only another round in an innocuous series of games. This is not terribly surprising; one might expect that a century's difference would bring in tow a reading difference. More remarkable than the change is the continuity: both appraisals of Rachilde's novel emphasize a turnabout. Charged with "perverting" or "reversing" convention, the novel is locked in a structure whose binarity we know to be dependent on unitary dominance. I want to argue that *Monsieur Vénus* embodies much less a reversal than a dispersal of convention—a more radical challenge than can be accommodated by the inversion figure.

First a concession: anyone familiar with the plot—or even attentive to the oxymoronic title—of this novel might initially be tempted to read binary logic as its natural order and inversion as its prime mover. *Monsieur Vénus* tells of a young aristocratic woman, an amateur artist named Raoule de Vénérande, who meets Jacques Silvert (*dit* Jaja), a young male *fleuriste*, or flower-maker, and is ravished by his beauty. She sets him up as her mistress in an elegantly appointed apartment and outfits him in lavish, flowing fabrics. The text is punctuated by a series of trysts featuring cross-dressing, sadomasochistic scenes in which Raoule plays aggressor to Jacques's victim, and by violent sexual rivalries that circulate among Raoule, Jacques, and a supporting cast: her soldier suitor and his prostitute sister. The four are pitted against each other in kaleidoscoping patterns of homo- and heterosexual desire, which climax in the sacrifice of Jacques to Raoule's jealousy following his attempted infidelity with the soldier. Raoule's final trysts are with death—or, more accurately, with its effigy. We find her, dressed now as a woman, now as a man, in a sumptuous bedchamber, clasping a wax cast of Jacques's body.

This plot summary is indicative of a masculine/feminine turnabout that affects clothing, profession, temperament, gender pronouns and inflections, social, financial, and sexual positions—not to mention power. My reluctance to privilege inversion as the master trope of this novel has nothing to do with denying its operation; it has everything to do with recognizing the contexts within which it operates both extra- and intratextually—contexts that complicate and destabilize. This means considering, on the one hand, how figures of reversal in the text are related to contemporary reading conventions and, on the other, how they function within the tissue of Rachilde's writing. We have initial access to both domains—and a means of mediating between them—in the form of the preface I referred to earlier, written by Maurice Barrès five years after the novel's original publication.

(May 1984): 121–27; Melanie Hawthorne, "The Social Construction of Sexuality in Three Novels by Rachilde," *Michigan Romance Studies* 9 (1987): 49–59; Véronique Hubert-Matthews, "Androgynie et représentation chez quatre auteurs du dix-neuvième siècle: Balzac, Gautier, Sand, Rachilde" (Ph.D. diss., University of Virginia, 1993); Dorothy Kelly, *Fictional Genders: Role and Representation in Nineteenth-Century French Narrative* (Lincoln: University of Nebraska Press, 1989): 143–55.

Much like an author's own preface, this one is an instrument of the text: it serves **229** to direct our reading. But if, like any threshold, it leads inside, it also opens onto the outside. It is a mirror held up to the book, but a mirror that is always two-sided and that also reflects the reading public: its beliefs, its desires, its fears, its patterns of reception. I am suggesting that we read the preface to *Monsieur Vénus*—much as Dominick LaCapra reads the trial of *Madame Bovary*—as "an index of conventions or norms of reading in the larger public."[3] As Barrès takes on the role of defense attorney for the novel (which was never literally brought to trial but was banned shortly after its 1884 publication in Belgium), his argument, anticipating its audience, is necessarily saturated with fin de siècle conventions of interpretation. The preface reads the novel, but it reads double. At the same time, the novel reads the preface. *Monsieur Vénus* may, in fact, best (and only apparently anachronistically) be understood as a deconstructive reading of its own preface, for it responds to and unsettles the ideologically grounded conventions of interpretation reproduced by this preface.

THE PREFACE: CROSSING THE THRESHOLD

In what follows I situate myself on the unsteady prefatorial threshold between *Monsieur Vénus* and its nineteenth-century public, crossing over and back in both directions. My stance mimes the opening scene of the novel, which places Raoule de Vénérande in a similarly problematic threshold position: "La clef étant sur la porte, elle entra; mais sur le seuil, une odeur de pommes cuisant la prit à la gorge et l'arrêta net" (23) ["The key was in the door, she entered, but the smell of apples cooking filled her throat and stopped her short upon the threshold"] (33). Raoule enters, but is stopped short. She is on the doorsill—and so not yet inside—but enveloped by the odor that surrounds her. Even as this sentence draws our attention to the threshold—the dividing line—it blurs the distinction between outside and inside. The evident problematizing of spatial borders is compounded by an interrogation of other boundaries: most notably, gender difference, class distinction, and textual limits. Expecting that the flower-maker Marie Silvert will be a woman, Raoule asks Jacques, "Est-ce que je me trompe, monsieur?" ["Am I mistaken, Monsieur?], to which he replies, "Pour le moment, Marie Silvert, c'est moi" (24) ["For the time being, I am Marie Silvert"] (34). As she stands at the threshold, Raoule suggests crossing the barrier segregating the aristocracy from the people. And finally as the reader, with Raoule, enters the text, the liminal status of the opening lines is obscured by a sign of extratextual intrusion into the text. This quite material sign (*Marie Silvert, fleuriste, dessinateur* [23] [*Marie Silvert, flower-*

---

[3] Dominick LaCapra, *"Madame Bovary" on Trial* (Ithaca: Cornell University Press, 1982), 16.

maker, designer] [33]), rendered in the text by italics, is the inaugural instance of a practice that will gradually become pervasive. The italics signal a discourse that is both inside and outside the text: a discourse whose mere presence speaks its assimilation yet whose typographic difference marks a foreign provenance. I will come back to this.

Barrès in his preface admits no such zone of shadow, no such threshold site of fusion and confusion. He quite simply offers a privileged means of access to Rachilde. I do not mean to use the woman here in place of her work, although one could say that it is precisely such a metonymic slide, albeit reversed, that regulates Barrès's approach to a novel that is for him irrevocably—and salaciously—conflated with the woman who wrote it. "Rachilde n'a guère fait que se raconter soimême," says Barrès; "Son livre n'est qu'un prolongement de sa vie" (14, 17) ["Rachilde has done nothing but tell her own story"; "Her book is the prolongation of her life"] (22, 24). His introduction to the novel quickly becomes the exhibition of a child-woman whose rather equivocal wares he is trying to sell. He promises that the reading of *Monsieur Vénus* will climax in "[une] émotion violente" (5) whose force builds from the following traits ascribed to its author: her youth, her innocence, her ignorance, her perversity, her hysteria.

Barrès creates a woman-text whose appeal is based on the superimposition of three phantasmatic faces of woman: the hysteric, the whore, and the polymorphously perverted nymphet. Rachilde, "cette fiévreuse" (13) ["that feverish young woman"] (21), writes a novel that Barrès more specifically attributes to "une des plus singulières déformations de l'amour qu'ait pu produire la maladie du siècle dans l'âme d'une jeune femme" (14) ["one of the most extraordinary deformities of love which the *maladie du siècle* has produced in the soul of a young woman"] (22). He otherwise identifies her novel as a psychological symptom (20; 27). But it is the image of Rachilde as seductive girlchild that is most alluring to Barrès. This Gallic Humbert Humbert reflects at length and with evident relish on "les jeunes filles [qui] . . . sont gouvernées uniquement par l'instinct, étant de petits animaux sournois, égoïstes et ardents" (14) ["young girls {who} are governed only by their instincts, being small animals, tricky, selfish, and passionate"] (22). He savors every reference to Rachilde's excessive ignorance (the epistemological reinforced by the sexual), and he takes particular delight in identifying innocence as paradoxical source of her rather more knowing novel, marveling at "ce vice savant éclatant dans le rêve d'une vierge" (6) ["the refinements of vice, bursting from the dreams of a virgin"] (20).

Barrès's persistent emphasis on Rachilde's paired ignorance and innocence finally calls attention to itself, letting us suppose that knowledge's vacuum is more precisely an evacuation of knowledge: process rather than essence. The calculated production of what we might call an "ignorance effect"—a salable image of sensual and intellectual deprivation—merits further scrutiny, less in tribute to Barrès's insistence than in recognition of the marketing strategies in which it is grounded.[4]

In his effort to promote *Monsieur Vénus*, to explain why the novel is a masterpiece,[5] Barrès repeatedly invokes Rachilde's tender age and sex: "Ce qui est tout à fait délicat dans la perversité de ce livre, c'est qu'il a été écrit par une jeune fille de vingt ans. Le merveilleux chef-d'oeuvre!" (5–6) ["The nicety of the perverseness of this book lies in the fact that it was written by a young girl of twenty. A marvellous masterpiece!"] (19–20). The repeated references to her puerility, chastity, and wholesome upbringing signify sexual purity, which is in turn the signifier of ignorance: Rachilde has "des yeux qui ignorent tout" and "l'ignorance d'une vierge" (6, 16) ["eyes which ignore everything" and "the ignorance of a virgin"] (20, 24). The degree to which sexual inexperience (itself already a specious assumption) is generalized as ignorance *tout court* is surprising; more curious is the conclusion that Rachilde's (presumed) innocence disqualifies her intellectual capacity to write *Monsieur Vénus*. "Certes," the prefacer assures us, "la petite fille qui rédigeait ce merveilleux *Monsieur Vénus* n'avait pas toute cette esthétique dans la tête. . . . Simplement elle avait de mauvais instincts" (13) ["Of course the little girl who wrote this marvellous *Monsieur Vénus* did not have such aesthetics . . . in her head. . . . She simply had bad instincts"] (21). He elaborates: "Rachilde, à vingt ans, pour écrire un livre qui fait rêver un peu tout le monde, n'a guère réfléchi; elle a écrit tout au trot de sa plume, suivant son instinct" (14) ["At twenty Rachilde wrote a book which amazed everybody, and wrote it with scarcely any reflection; she wrote easily, following her instincts"] (22).

The logical extension of Barrès's argument is that *Monsieur Vénus*, a novel born of the coupling of innocence and ignorance, should have spontaneously aborted; innocence and its incestuous bedfellow, ignorance, should breed only the blank page. But—by intervention of the new godhead, pathology—the marriage of feminine innocence and ignorance engenders (by immaculate conception) vicious knowledge.

The lesson Barrès teaches is that *Monsieur Vénus*, a novel that draws from his pen such adjectives as "abominable, canaille, impur" (5–20, passim) ["daring, vulgar, impure"] (19–27, passim), is written not with the head but with the (female) instincts. In order to write her knowing novel, Rachilde had no need to know (to understand or to have experienced) what she wrote; she simply gave free rein to her nerves, unleashed her instincts and feelings: "Pour les écrivains de cet

---

[4] See Eve Sedgwick's illuminating comments on the reification of innocence (as exemplified by Diderot's *La Religieuse*) in "Privilege of Unknowing," *Genders* 1 (Spring 1988): 102–24.

[5] In an 1888 letter to Rachilde, reproduced in the Flammarion edition of *Monsieur Vénus*, Maurice Barrès expresses his desire to write "vingt belles pages où j'expliquerais comment et en quoi ce livre là est un chef d'oeuvre" (9) ["twenty beautiful pages, explaining how and why it is a masterpiece"] (17).

ordre, le roman n'est qu'un moyen de manifester des sentiments que l'ordinaire de la vie les oblige à refréner" (17) ["To such writers, the novel is only a means of expressing that emotion which the humdrum of life obliges one to repress, or at least to conceal"] (24–25). Barrès is invoking a kind of "blood knowledge" of vice, a "natural viciousness" carried by the female of the species.

We need not waste time pondering the inconsistencies evident in this portrait of the young woman artist as cretin. The contradictions inherent in Barrès's presentation of *Monsieur Vénus* as virginal fantasy on the one hand and, on the other, sordid "autobiographie de la plus étrange des jeunes femmes" (20) ["autobiography of the most peculiar of young women"] (27–28) cannot be rationally resolved; they can only be understood as inscriptions of the more global nineteenth-century discourse about sex that Michel Foucault calls "sexuality."[6] Barrès's comments on Rachilde (on the novel as woman) constitute a virtual mapping of the power/knowledge apparatus Foucault calls the "hystericization of the female body": a three-pronged strategy by which woman's body is equated with sexuality, appropriated by pathology, and identified with the social body (which I take to mean language, among other things). Barrès's perceptions about *Monsieur Vénus* have little to do with the novel and much to do with the grid he imposes upon it, a grid already in place that organizes his reading. As Leo Bersani has observed in reference to another phantasmatic context (the representation of AIDS), "The messages most likely to reach their destination are messages already there."[7]

Barrès's reading strategy, by analogy to what Foucault calls a "power/knowledge strategy," can be described as the hystericization of the textual body: the preface reads the text by applying to it a grid whose essential components are, as we have seen, hypersexuality, pathology, and bourgeois family values. We might suppose that the preface was intended to trigger a parallel reading strategy in its public. But the very production of this preface is evidence that such a strategy was already in place and did not need to be deliberately activated. In a sense, then, this threshold text is self-effacing. As it would mark off the contours of the text, it shades into indistinction, blurring the border—becoming the blurred border—between reader and text. As it would guide the reader to the text, it cannot help but reveal that the reader is already in the text and the text preinscribed in the reader.

The conflation of a text's writing and its reception, the collapsing of limits between inner and outer textual space, the implosion of the extratextual into the text: these are the occult forces of Barres's preface that Rachilde takes on as her subject. *Monsieur Vénus* is about the male colonization of female textuality and of woman *as* textuality: it is a novel that parodies its own reception, writes the intrusive reader into its text. This internalization of a predicted response—Rachilde's quite literal inspiration—is nowhere clearer than in her liberal use of italics.

[6] Michel Foucault, *La Volonté de savoir* (Paris: Gallimard, 1976), 137.
[7] Leo Bersani, "Is the Rectum a Grave?" *October* 43 (Winter 1987): 210.

TYPING DIFFERENCE: THE USE OF ITALICS

The italicizing of words and phrases—a practice that appears on the first page and then with gathering force as the novel advances—typographically formalizes the foreignness of a discourse whose source is given as external to the text.[8] Surging forth in the midst of a text dominated by roman type, italic characters introduce not only a different discourse, but also the very idea of differentiation, the splitting off that creates difference.[9] Within the italicized discourse, and dominating it, is a subdiscourse on gender, itself the paradigmatic marker of difference: roughly half the italicized forms represent gender pronouns, gender-inflected nouns, adjectives, verbs, and gender-specific terms (such as *Mlle, neveu, maîtresse*).

The gendering of italics presents a *mise en abyme* of the production of difference: a demarcation of demarcation whose overemphasis undermines the possibility of ever telling what the difference is. When Jacques is designated by the italicized pronoun *il* or Raoule by the noun *femme* (70, 71), the italics call into question the linguistic code or convention that assigns gender. But when, alternatively, Jacques is referred to by an italicized feminine pronoun (*elle, la* [92]) or when Raoule's discourse is marked by italicized masculine inflections ("'Je suis *jaloux*,' rugit-elle" [99] ["'I am a *jealous fellow*,' she roared"] [100; trans. modified]), the italics become part of a multilayered cross-dressing more difficult to interpret. What is being challenged in the latter examples is not so much convention as the text's interrogation of convention. The italicization of forms that might otherwise appear to be offered as inverted revisions of linguistic conventions suggests the rejection of a simple reversal mechanism. What is at stake is less any particular sign or signs than the process of referentiality, especially as based on a sexually determinable notion of difference. In the italicized moment at which the *il* of Jacques is recoded as *elle*, there is a flicker of uncertainty, a shadow cast on the apparently transparent connection linking gender with people and language. The demarcation of the text's re-markings of gender alienates the narrative voice, destabilizes its authority, suggesting a fundamental indistinguishability of self and other, inside and outside, originality and citation, sincerity and irony.

Such an interrogation of differentiation pervades the use of italics in *Monsieur Vénus*, even when gender is not specifically at issue. We can divide Rachilde's use of italics into categories ranging from most to least distanced or differentiated from the narrative voice, although we find that the text ultimately reveals these divisions to be illusory. I turn first to the most conventional, most encoded form of italics,

---

[8] Italics appear, on the average, about every third page in the Flammarion edition; in the central section of the novel they occur more frequently (approximately every page, often with multiple appearances on a page).

[9] Claude Duchet's excellent study of Flaubert's use of italics has enriched my understanding of Rachilde. See Duchet, "Signifiance et insignifiance: Le discours italique dans *Madame Bovary*," in *La Production du sens chez Flaubert*, ed. Claudine Gothot-Mersch (Paris: 10/18, 1975), 365.

which quite clearly separates "foreign" discursive elements from the narrative discourse proper, as when, for example, Rachilde offers the book title *Les exploits de
la Brinvilliers* (75), the sign *Marie Silvert, fleuriste, dessinateur* (23), or the Angli-
cism *high-life* (110). In each of these cases the italics label as Other a citation from
an easily identifiable code. Additional examples, however, range along a gradient
according to which the origin of the italicized words or citation loses specificity
and, eventually, distance from the text.

The next most differentiated category of italics in *Monsieur Vénus* explicitly attributes its origin to a specific code: "Tante Elisabeth n'était pas sans savoir que *son
neveu*, comme elle appelait souvent Raoule . . ." (42); "Marie . . . était bien per-
suadée maintenant que cette folle . . . leur reviendrait plus sage, plus protectrice,
plus *cossue* enfin, selon son expression faubourienne" (61); "Ayant une idée fort
vague de *la haute*, selon l'expression si souvent répétée de sa soeur . . ." (112); "On
s'imaginait . . . l'individu *complet* dont parlent les récits fabuleux des brahmanes"
(171) ["Aunt Elizabeth did not know that *her nephew*, as she often called
Raoule . . ." (50); "Marie . . . was firmly convinced now that the crazy woman
. . . would come back . . . calmer and more generous, more *in the money*, as she
crudely expressed it" (66); "Since he had a very vague idea of the life of the *upper
crust*, as his sister often called them" (112); "They seemed to be that *complete* individual spoken of in the fabulous tales of Brahmins"] (166).[10] In one of two intermediate cases, the source of the italicized discourse is explicitly attributed but is
anonymous ("cette virilité d'une heure qu'on appelle *la fatuité*" [102] ["that
ephemeral virility called *vanity*"] [103]), while in the other, conversely, the source
is particularized but only indirectly ("Il [Raittolbe] se contenta donc de révéler à
Raoule la situation exacte . . . [et] avoua que, pour *calmer* l'humeur dangereuse
de Mlle Silvert, il avait cru nécessaire de céder à *sa fantaisie*. . . . Il terminait en
déplorant l'*accès de vivacité* dont Jacques avait été victime" [138] ["He contented
himself by revealing to Raoule the exact location . . . he acknowledged that, in order to *mollify* Mademoiselle Silvert's dangerous temper, he had thought it necessary to yield to her *fancy* for him. . . . He ended by regretting the *anger* of which
Jacques had been the victim"] [136]). In this latter example, the use of indirect discourse lets us identify the implied source of the italics.

At the vaguest, least differentiated end of the spectrum, the discursive source is
neither specified nor, except for the italics, is it even labeled as Other. When, for
instance, we read "on l'avait fait *si fille* dans les endroits les plus secrets de son être,
que la folie du vice prenait les proportions du tétanos!" (220) ["they had made him
such a whore in the depths of his being, that the madness of vice took the proportions of tetanus!"] (211; trans. modified), or when we are told that "Raittolbe, bien

---

[10] I have added italics where missing in Boyd's translation and will continue to do so in subsequent citations. I have modified the translations from Boyd's pages 66 and 112.

qu'il eût été jusque-là un honnête homme, *avait le siècle"* (97) ["Although he had always been a gentleman till then, Raittolbe *had caught the century"*] (98; trans. modified), there is no mark of reference; we must ourselves supply a subject and verb of attribution, however vague: an implicit "comme on dit" that labels the italicized elements as citation and refers them to the anonymous pool of social discourse. This least differentiated use of italics, marked only typographically, works as much to assimilate the italicized portions of the text to the narrative discourse as to alienate them from it. A link on a discursive chain stretching from the extratextual to the text itself, nonspecific italics are as akin to nonitalicized forms of citation as they are to other, more deictic uses of italics.

When we read that Raittolbe *"avait le siècle,"* we intuitively refer the italicized words to a collective voice, not only because no specified voice can be heard, but because in the expression "avoir le siècle" ["to catch the century"] we recognize Rachilde's variant of "la maladie du siècle" ["the disease of our times"], a euphemism for hysteria, and the fin de siècle's cliché self-diagnosis (a cliché repeatedly reproduced by Barrès in his preface). Rachilde's reissued form of the euphemism ironizes it. Stylistically fractured and typographically reset, her variant points out the exaggerated linkage of history and disease by pathologizing the era.

But irony is not produced here by italics alone. Italics serve merely to heighten the distancing effect that is otherwise present everywhere in the novel. This particular case, in which italics are used to emphasize the ironic repetition of an *idée reçue*, slides almost imperceptibly into a tissue of similarly ironized, though unitalicized, commonplaces about hysteria, sexuality, masculinity, femininity, and art. As we see the text integrate its italicized Other (offering no designation of discursive source) and, conversely, as we hear the narrative voice speak in Other (not always italicized) tongues, it becomes apparent that the entire novel is a caricatural citation of fin de siècle stereotypes. In other words—words I paraphrase from some comments Ross Chambers has made about *Madame Bovary*—if this text is indistinguishable from its social matrix, a competent reader must put the entire novel in quotes and engage in a sentence-by-sentence ironic reading.[11]

But Rachilde is not Flaubert. Why then attribute to her the awareness of a Flaubert rather than that of a Bouvard or a Pécuchet? What if her relentless repetition of the social discourse of her time is not a sign of resistance but of compliance? Why assume Rachilde is society's gadfly rather than its scribe? These are extremely sticky questions that I cannot definitively resolve, partly because I think it likely

---

[11] "Dans la mesure où . . . le texte ne se distingue pas de sa matière sociale, le lecteur devra être capable de 'mettre des guillemets' au *roman entier*, et de maintenir phrase par phrase une lecture ironique." Ross Chambers, *Mélancolie et opposition: Les débuts du modernisme en France* (Paris: Corti, 1987), 192. Chambers goes on to suggest that such a reading ("une lecture simplement ironique") is insufficient.

that they do not have either/or answers. Without ruling out complicity, however, I want to make a provisional argument for contestation: for a series of formal strategies that when brought to bear upon citation create an ironic field that ultimately turns repetition into difference. Operating singly or, more often, in combination, these strategies include but extend beyond italicization, embracing other attributed forms of quotation (direct and indirect) as well as the stylistic alteration, exaggeration, reversal, and sheer accumulation of cliché locutions or topoi.

As we explore the citational structure of *Monsieur Vénus*, the functioning of the strategic mechanisms that both shape and re-form it begins to emerge. In addition, the discourse cited—the social discourse—more specifically reveals its identity as the discourse of hystericization, and we hear in Rachilde's citations from it strong echoes of the preface by Maurice Barrès that would be written five years later. For purely organizational purposes, my discussion of this discourse is divided into the following categories: gender (gender/power roles and gender reversal); science (clinical hysteria and heredity); and the semiotic body. These rubrics correspond to somewhat arbitrary divisions of an essentially continuous discourse; in fact, the categories overlap at many points.

THE DISCOURSE OF GENDER

Threaded through the novel are a series of gender-related topoi only too familiar to readers of nineteenth-century novels. The *fleuriste*-turned-courtesan Jacques Silvert is a citation of an *idée reçue* that equates the occupation of flower-making with loose morals and prostitution.[12] Jacques's rides through the Bois with Raoule de Vénérande also repeat a convention, *l'heure du Bois*, whose formulae are also closely adhered to: Jacques, the beautiful lower-class consort, discreetly hidden in the back of the carriage so as to see without being seen, is given an introduction to society by Raoule, who points out the principal players on that stage and recounts what goes on behind the scenes. Even his indolent, submissive pose is a citation: "Il resta couché au fond de la voiture, tout près d'elle, la tête abandonnée sur son épaule, répétant de ces bêtises adorables qui rendaient sa beauté plus provocante encore" (109–10) ["He stayed close to her in the carriage, lying down with his head upon her shoulder, repeating sweet nothings which rendered his beauty still more provocative"] (109; trans. modified). Jacques's fearful intuition, in the face of the

---

[12] See, for example, the discussions in Emile Zola's *L'Assommoir* about the inappropriateness of the occupation for a young girl, at the point at which the area of Nana's apprenticeship is being decided. (Zola, *L'Assommoir*, in *Les Rougon-Macquart*, ed. Armand Lanoux and Henri Mitterand, 5 vols. [Paris: Gallimard, 1960–67], 2:681–82.) Nana does become a flower-maker, and the sequel to her story, recounted in the remaining pages of *L'Assommoir* and then in *Nana*, supports her family's prediction and her century's received wisdom.

moneyed, well-born travelers of the Bois, that he will one day be abandoned when
his rich, aristocratic lover takes a spouse from among her own, is also a citation
from a familiar gender code that dichotomizes mistress and wife: "—Ah! disait-il
souvent, se serrant contre elle avec effroi, tu te marieras, un jour, et tu me quit-
teras!" (110) ["'Ah!' he used to say, cuddling up to her, frightened, 'some day you'll
marry and you'll leave me!'"] (110).

In the preceding examples, it is of far greater importance that we recognize, in
Rachilde's discourse, citations from a dominant gender code than that we insist
upon the fact that in her versions of the code, the conventional gender positions
are reversed. Gender inversion in these and many other cases is a strategic technique used to emphasize, by defamiliarizing, the conventions that are inverted—
conventions that might otherwise pass as natural.

Even such a preliminary review of inverted citation in *Monsieur Vénus* should
suggest that reversal is not, as has been claimed, the dominant figure in this novel;
only one among a number of ironizing strategies, it is, like the others I consider,
subordinate to the regime of repetition. Precisely, if paradoxically, because reversal is in the service of repetition (it serves, alongside its companion strategies, to assure a dizzying proliferation of repetitions), it gains a subversive power rather than
remaining a mere dependent (thus conservative) form of social discourse.

Reversal plays a double role in this novel, for it is not only a formal strategy bearing upon citation but itself a citation as well, one more cliché mobilized from the
fin de siècle reserve. Mario Praz has long since demonstrated that reversal—more
precisely, gender reversal—is a literary commonplace that pervades the nineteenth century, returning in ever-changing garb.[13] In passing, we should invoke
the feminized romantic hero, the androgyne, the femme fatale; more specifically
(but not exhaustively) we might mention René, Mademoiselle de Maupin, Séra-
phîta/Séraphîtüs, Mathilde de la Mole, Emma Bovary, Foedora, La Zambinella.

So when Rachilde puts Jacques into a woman's nightgown (73) or gives him
rounded thighs that "effaçait leur sexe" (55) ["make his sex uncertain"] (61), when
she equips Raoule with "une panoplie d'armes de tous genres et de tous pays" (36)
["weapons of all kinds and of all countries"] (45) and repeatedly dresses her in male
garb, the commanding mode is citation and not reversal. In other words, we must
think of gender reversal primarily as a unit, as a compound convention cited by
Rachilde. Admittedly the distinction between Rachilde's use of gender reversal,
on the one hand, in complicity with convention and, on the other, as a defamiliarizing strategy is not always clear-cut. When, for example, Raoule imperiously
cries to Jacques, "Suis-je le maître, oui ou non" (103) ["Am I master, yes or no?"]
(104) or when she warns him, "Tu dois t'apercevoir . . . que, de nous deux, le plus

[13] Mario Praz, *The Romantic Agony*, trans. Angus Davidson (1933; reprint, Oxford: Oxford University Press, 1970).

homme c'est toujours moi" (99) ["You must feel . . . that I am the better man of
the two!"] (100), the effect of the gender/power inversion cliché is ambiguous.
"Master" and "man" could here be understood as nominal power shifters, as metaphors shifting power from man to woman without, however, changing the phal-
locentric power base. Or they could be understood as subversions of gender conventions, if we emphasize the fact that a conventional identification of power with
(masculine) gender is being cited *in a different voice*; by regendering the citing
voice, the convention by which mastery and masculinity are conceptualized together is denaturalized. We cannot choose.

We might imagine *Monsieur Vénus* organized along two principal axes: the axis
of citation and the axis of formal strategies. The point at which the two axes intersect is reversal. At this site of convergence, reversal folds over upon itself (that is,
upon gender reversal), doubles, becomes something akin to a double negative. Although in theory we would expect gender reversal reversed to yield a positive
value—a confirmation of convention—in effect, this doubling is an alert: it unsettles and confuses the reader, highlighting and destabilizing the cited discourse
of gender. Examples abound; the following are particularly clear.

Raoule, in full male attire and acting the role of a man seducing his virgin bride,
is making love to Jacques. At the height of passion, however, she bares her breasts
("pour mieux sentir les battements de coeur de Jacques" [198] ["to feel the beating
of Jacques' heart better"] [192]) and destroys the fiction, reverses the citation of
gender reversal: " 'Raoule,' s'écria Jacques, la face convulsée . . . 'Raoule, tu n'es
donc pas un homme? tu ne peux donc pas être un homme?' . . . Et le sanglot des
illusions détruites, pour toujours mortes, monta de ses flancs à sa gorge" (198)
[" 'Raoule, aren't you a man? Can't you be a man?' And the sob of lost illusion, for-
ever dead, came from the innermost part of his being"] (192). This is a case of
double-cross-dressing: Jacques is betrayed when Raoule in drag returns to a female
identity, and the reader's expectations are tricked when Raoule's undressing re-
dresses the gender reversal cliché. Language, moreover, changes gender in this
novel as easily as Raoule and Jacques change clothes. In the quotation " 'Je suis *jaloux!*' rugit-elle affolée" (99), the female speaker (Raoule) adopts a masculine-
inflected adjective, only to revert to a female identity, exposed (like Raoule's
breasts) in the feminine pronoun and the following feminine-inflected adjective.[14]
The accumulation of such grammatical hermaphrodites is disconcerting; Raoule's
suitor Raittolbe might be speaking for the reader when he pleads: "Tâchons de

[14] Examples of fluid sexual identity abound. When, for instance, Jacques is compared to the Venus
Callipygous—his body feminized—his virility (phallicity) is immediately emphasized (55; 61). And in
another incident, Jacques enters Raittolbe's apartment dressed in drag; later Raoule enters dressed in
drag; finally both leave together in regular attire, to the great confusion of the valet de chambre (217;
208).

nous entendre! . . . Adoptons *il* ou *elle*, afin que je ne perde pas le peu de bon sens   **239**
qui me reste" (91) ["Let us come to an understanding! . . . Let's stick to either *he* or
she so that I won't lose the few shreds of common sense I have left"] (92–93).[15]

Rachilde's appropriation of gender conventions continues, the irony building as
commonplaces of gender slide into stereotypes of hysteria, passing by way of
clichés about femininity. Chided by Raittolbe for rearranging a planned meeting,
Raoule cites all the commonplace explanations before he has the opportunity to
propose any one of them: "'Rien ne doit vous étonner, puisque je suis femme,' ré-
pondit Raoule riant d'un rire nerveux. 'Je fais tout le contraire de ce que j'ai
promis. Quoi de plus naturel?' " (81) ["'As I am a woman nothing ought to astonish
you,' Raoule answered, laughing nervously. 'I do the opposite of what I promised.
What can be more natural than that?'"] (83). Implicit in this overdetermined response is a string of clichés about femininity: woman does not conform to reason,
woman is unpredictable, woman is mobile and capricious, woman is natural,
woman is prisoner of her nerves. It is the stockpiling of citation, the overdetermination, that is here responsible for the ironic texture.

Raoule's presence in the novel, the coherence (such as it is) of her character, is
due to the expansion and development of this citational network. Everywhere we
hear repeated the litany of cliché characteristics (animal-like, sneaky, ardent, perverse, instinctual, nervous, pathological) that structured Barrès's discourse on
women. Raoule, dubbed "la nerveuse" (33), is aroused by Jacques's beauty: "Mlle
de Vénérande recula jusqu'au lit; ses mains nerveuses se crispèrent dans les draps;
elle grondait comme grondent les panthères" (55) ["Mademoiselle de Vénérande
went back to the bed; her nervous hands clutched the sheets; she was roaring, as
panthers roar"] (61). Hysteria rears its lustful head, and Barrès's ardent beast is
roused once more. Or again: "Raoule se leva; un tremblement nerveux la secouait
tout entière" (29) ["Raoule arose, a nervous tremor shook her all over"] (39).
Jacques is once again the *agent provocateur*. When Raoule lingers in his small,
poorly ventilated apartment, her nervous condition is aggravated: "Ses nerfs se sur-
excitaient dans l'atmosphère empuantie de la mansarde" (31) ["Her nerves were
over-excited by the suffocating atmosphere of the garret"] (40). This passage
should be read in the context of nineteenth-century treatises on hysteria, which
typically warn of just such pernicious effects of fetid odors and noxious air. We
may therefore take Raoule's nervous response to close air as our introduction to a
series of citations that let us hear the clinical along with the popular discourse of
hysteria.

[15] On the generally accepted idea that truth and sexual identity are intimately bound, see Michel Foucault's lapidary introduction to the English translation of Herculine Barbin's *Herculine Barbin: Being
the Recently Discovered Memoirs of a Nineteenth-Century French Hermaphrodite*, trans. Richard
McDougall, ed. Michel Foucault (New York: Pantheon, 1980): vii–xvii.

THE DISCOURSE OF SCIENCE

There are intermittent echoes in *Monsieur Vénus* of the most recent clinical cant about the disease. Although I want to reiterate, in passing, that it is impossible to isolate scientific from popular discourses, given their common ideological bed-rock, I can nonetheless indicate unmistakable citations of the teachings of Char-cot and his group at the Salpêtrière. Raoule in her coupé abandons herself to a state of nervous exhilaration: "la tête en arrière, le corsage gonflé, les bras crispés, avec de temps à autre un soupir de lassitude" (34) ["her head thrown back, her breasts heaving, her arms clasped. From time to time she gave a sigh of fatigue"] (43). This pose reproduces an *arc de cercle* or the spasmodic muscle contracture known as opisthotonos: the bowed-back body position Charcot made famous when he standardized the hysterical attack, organizing it into four largely invariable phases that he then subdivided into attitudes and movements. The *arc de cercle* was located in the second major phase, known as "la période de grands mouve-ments ou de clownisme." The opisthotonus associated with hysteria bears a marked resemblance to the attitude of a body in the throes of passion. As Bram Dijkstra has recently pointed out, this convulsive woman (whom he designates by the unfortunate epithet "The Nymph with the Broken Back") becomes a fin de siè-cle topos of painting.[16]

Rachilde cites the Salpêtrière once again in a rather long-winded paraphrase of "retrospective medicine," the practice, widely indulged in by the Charcot circle, of reinterpreting history and art of the past (usually representations of daemonic possessions) according to current medical tenets: that is, recuperating the spiritual in the name of the scientific— specifically, in the name of the hysteric.[17] Rachilde borrows the discourse of retrospective medicine and uses it periphrastically to an-nounce her heroine's capricious decision to marry that plebeian object of her de-sire, Jacques Silvert: "Raoule, folle comme les possédées du Moyen Age qui avaient le démon en elles et n'agissaient plus de leur propre autorité" (176) ["Raoule, as mad as those people of the middle ages who were possessed of devils and were no longer reponsible for their actions"] (170). To the ears of any *initié* of the period, "folle comme les possédées du Moyen Age" immediately translates as "hysterical." The extension of the more quotidian epithet into an unwieldy peri-

---

[16] Dijkstra, *Idols*, 101.

[17] Jan Goldstein has brilliantly shown the anti-clerical political underpinnings of this teleological ven-ture. Goldstein, *Console and Classify: The French Psychiatric Profession in the Nineteenth Century* (Cambridge: Cambridge University Press, 1987), 371. As Goldstein points out, although "retrospective medicine" (so dubbed by Emile Littré in 1869) was a new label, the practice was not entirely new, hav-ing been used in passing in support of the monomania diagnosis earlier in the century; however, only among the Charcot group did retrospective medicine become "an intensively cultivated genre" (Gold-stein, 370, n. 159).

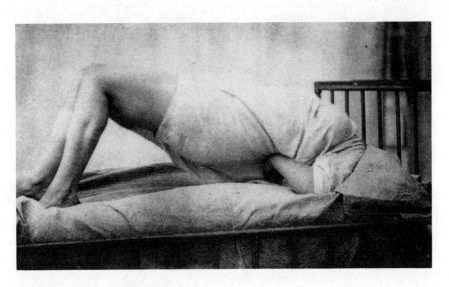

FIGURE 12. *"Arc de cercle."*
(Published in D. M. Bourneville and P. Régnard,
Iconographie photographique de la Salpêtrière 3, 1879–80;
photo B.I.M., Université René Descartes, Paris.)

phrasis flaunts its citational nature; the phrase appears to be borrowed, out of place, drawn from another (more specialized) discursive register.

This other register—the medical discourse of hysteria—makes one explicit, directly quoted foray into *Monsieur Vénus*. Near the beginning of the novel, Rachilde, like any qualified clinical practitioner of the era, supplies the etiology of Raoule's malady:

> Un jour, Raoule, courant les mansardes de l'hôtel, découvrit un livre; elle lut, au hasard. Ses yeux rencontrèrent une gravure, ils se baissèrent, mais elle emporta le livre . . . Vers ce temps, une révolution s'opéra dans la jeune fille. Sa physionomie s'altéra, sa parole devint brève, ses prunelles dardèrent la fièvre, elle pleura et elle rit tout à la fois. [Sa tante], inquiète, craignant une maladie sérieuse, appela les médecins.   (39–40)

> *One day, Raoule, rummaging in the garrets of the mansion, discovered a book which she read by chance. She saw an engraving, and turned away, but she took the book with her. . . . About that time there was a change in Raoule. Her expression altered, her words became brief, her eyes became feverish, she laughed and cried at the same time. [Her aunt] grew uneasy and, fearing a serious illness, called the doctors.*   (48)

Like Emma before her, Raoule catches novelsickness. The *cause morale* as well as the symptoms of her hysteria follow the textbook pattern, conforming to the spirit of Tissot's much-paraphrased warning that novel reading in adolescent girls would invariably lead to hysteria several years later.[18] The doctor's prognosis and recommendation for treatment also comply with decades of professional and folk wisdom, which finds hysterics, nymphomaniacs, and whores closely related. Although the Charcot circle officially denied the commonplace association between hysteria and lust, their preachings often implicitly corroborated the age-old comparison.[19] Raoule's doctor, however, says aloud and in caricatural terms what his real-world Salpêtrière confreres for the most part dared only whisper:

> Un cas spécial. . . . Quelques années encore, et cette jolie créature que vous chérissez trop, à mon avis, aura, sans les aimer jamais, connu autant

---

[18] For an elaboration of the novel's role in hysteria, see Chapter 3.

[19] Sigmund Freud, writing of his time spent studying at the Salpêtrière, reports Charcot's sotto voce comment on the etiology of hysteria: "It is always the genital thing . . . always . . . always . . . always." This statement is, of course, a flagrant contradiction of his official position on the matter. Freud, "On the History of the Psycho-Analytic Movement," in *The Standard Edition of the Complete Works of Sigmund Freud*, trans. James Strachey, Anna Freud, Alix Strachey, and Alan Tyson, ed. James Strachey, 24 vols. (London: Hogarth, 1953–74), 14:1–66, 14.

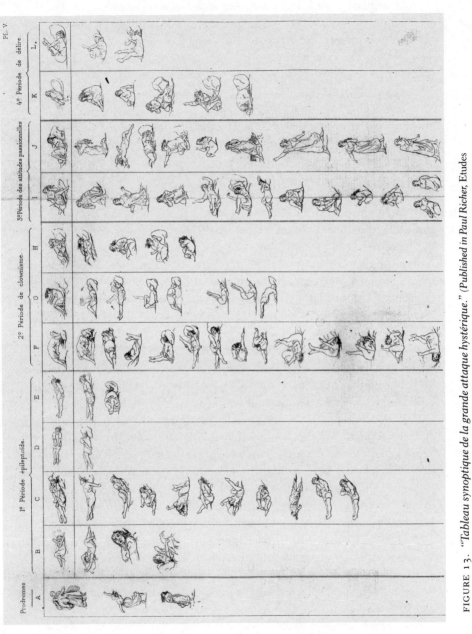

FIGURE 13. *"Tableau synoptique de la grande attaque hystérique."* (*Published in Paul Richer, Etudes cliniques sur la grande hystérie ou hystéro-épilepsie, 1881; photo B.I.M., Université René Descartes, Paris.*)

d'hommes qu'il y a de grains au rosaire de sa tante. Pas de milieu! Ou
nonne, ou monstre! Le sein de Dieu ou celui de la volupté! Il vaudrait
peut-être mieux l'enfermer dans un couvent, puisque nous enfermons les
hystériques à la Salpêtrière!   (40–41)

> *A very special case. A few years more, and that pretty creature whom you love too*
> *much, I think, will, without ever loving them, have known as many men as there*
> *are beads on her aunt's rosary. No happy medium! Either a nun or a monster! God's*
> *bosom or passions! It would, perhaps, be better to put her in a convent, since we*
> *put hysterical women in the Salpêtrière!*   (49)

There is a double postulation at work here: while he is equating hysteria and female eroticism, the doctor is also comparing hysteria to nunhood. If, as he suggests, religious life is a sublimated but parallel form of female eccentricity, then
the opposition of hysteric and nun yields to a convergence. While the doctor pre-
scribes the convent and chastity, Tante Elisabeth's confessor, representing the
other side of the nineteenth-century debate, suggests the "true" (and truly atavistic) remedy: "Mariez-la!" (40) ["Marry her."] (49). The two sides of the debate are
clearly invoked here. On the one hand, hysteria is causally related to lubricity;
therefore, prostitutes are more and nuns less inclined to the ailment than are other
women: chastity is a prophylactic or cure. On the other hand, hysteria is causally
related to sexual continence; therefore, nuns are more and prostitutes less inclined
to the malady than are other women: sex is the best medicine. The juxtaposition of
these conflicting theories is mutually corrosive.

Hystericizing discourse is most explicitly demystified, however, in a sentence of
ambiguous origin. We find Raoule's soldier suitor, Raittolbe, frustrated by her at-
tentions to the young *fleuriste*, "jurant qu'il ne reviendrait jamais chez cette hystérique, *car, selon ses idées, on ne pouvait qu'être hystérique dès qu'on ne suivait pas*
la loi commune" (65) ["swearing to himself that he would never come back to that
hysterical woman. *In his opinion anyone who did not follow ordinary rules must be*
hysterical"] (70; my emphasis). Though the form this phrase takes is that of indirect
discourse, the speaker is the narrator's puppet; the concept that hysteria is defined
by individuality, thus by marginality, demonstrates a lucidity, a self-consciousness
that we know to be beyond Raittolbe (he is not a strong enough vessel for this
thought). A gaping disproportion yawns between the expressed idea that hysteria
may have as much to do with diagnosis as with symptoms and Raittolbe's capacity
to have (much less express) such an idea; this space is inhabited by narrative consciousness alone.

Rachilde's novel records not only stereotypical hysteria, but also its inscription
within the larger discourse of pathological genealogy. The presentation of Ra-

childe's hysteric follows the same protocol as any clinical "présentation des malades" of the period, which begins to describe the patient by reconstructing a degenerative genealogy, a pathological heredity to which his or her condition can be ascribed. It is not unusual to find, in the section called *Observations* that appears in most treatises, accounts such as the following:

> Mère hystérique sans attaques; père maladif, attaqué de gastralgie depuis vingt-cinq ans. Un frère bien portant, un autre frère gastralgique, une soeur hystérique avec attaques.[20]

> —*Père*, . . . sobre, sujet à des céphalalgies; il est en convalescence d'une pleurésie. [Son *père* aurait eu une paralysie. —Aucun autre accident nerveux dans la famille.] *Mère* . . . bien portante; étant jeune, elle a eu des *migraines*. . . . [*Père*, . . . il faisait des excès de boisson. —*Mère*, bonne santé.][21]

> Son père . . . est alcoolique. Sa mère, morte tuberculeuse, a eu des *attaques d'hystérie*. Enfin, l'on trouve dans sa famille une grand'mère maternelle encore hystérique, bien qu'elle ait atteint l'âge de 82 ans, et *deux tantes* maternelles toutes deux atteintes d'*hystérie*. Voilà des antécédents d'une importance capitale, quatre hystériques et un alcoolique dans la même famille![22]

> *Mother is hysterical without attacks; father is sickly, has suffered from gastralgia for the past twenty-five years. There is a healthy brother, another gastralgic brother, a hysterical sister with attacks.*

> —*Father*, . . . *sober, prone to cephalalgia; convalescing from pleurisy. [His* father *probably was paralyzed.* —*No other nervous disorder in the family.]* Mother . . . *healthy* . . . *had* migraines *when young.* . . . *[*Father . . . *excessive drinking—* Mother, *good health.]*

> *His father* . . . *is an alcoholic. His mother, dead from tuberculosis, had* hysterical attacks. *Finally, his family reveals a maternal grandmother who was also* hysterical, *although she lived to eighty-two, and* two maternal aunts *who were* hysterical *as well. Such antecedents are of capital importance, four hysterics and an alcoholic in the same family!*

[20] P. Briquet, *Traité clinique et thérapeutique de l'hystérie* (Paris: Baillière, 1859), 56.
[21] Désiré-Magloire Bourneville and P. Regnard, *Iconographie photographique de la Salpêtrière* (Paris: Progrès Médical, 1878), 124. The brackets appear in Bourneville and Regnard's text.
[22] Jean-Martin Charcot, *L'Hystérie*, ed. E. Trillat (Toulouse: Privat, 1971), 178.

As Charcot astutely noted (and fervently believed), "La fatalité antique [est] aujourd'hui remplacée par la fatalité héréditaire"[23] ["The fatality of antiquity is replaced today by the fatality of heredity"]. Heredity becomes destiny in the late
nineteenth century, and the branches of the *arbre généalogique* twist and turn, for
the family tree doubles as a tree of degeneration.

Jacques Joseph Moreau de Tours's "tree of nervosity," whose branches graphically represent hysteria, epilepsy, prostitution, alcoholism, and criminality as
closely related phenomena, is one of the best mappings the fin de siècle has left us
of its phantasms. Evil has clearly metamorphosed as pathology in Moreau's schematic rendering of the generational transmission of vice. Moreau's tree can be
supplemented by two other essential artifacts: Bénédicte Auguste Morel's myth of
degeneration and Jules Déjerine's genealogical tables. Morel postulates the inher-
itance, over the course of four generations, of a carefully predicted, evolving series
of abnormalities originating in the founding generation's exposure to intoxicating
agents (alcohol, poor diet, crowded living conditions, etc.). Déjerine's seventy
"tableaux généalogiques" trace the congenital sources of different forms of marginality ("hérédité du meurtre," "hérédité de la folie," "hérédité de la débauche"
["inherited murder/madness/debauchery"]—to name a small sampling).[24] All of
these myths were, of course, taken up and elaborated by Zola, who personified
every leaf on the tree of degeneration in his five-generation *Rougon-Macquart*
cycle.

Rachilde repeats her lessons well, and she has them indirectly repeated by
Raoule, who, child of the times, shields her madness behind the following "expli-
cation lucide": "Son père avait été un de ces débauchés épuisés que les oeuvres du
marquis de Sade font rougir, mais pour une autre raison que celle de la pudeur. Sa
mère . . . avait eu les plus naturels et les plus fougueux appétits" (39) ["Her father
had been one of those worn-out debauchés who blush at the work of the Marquis
de Sade, but not from prudery. Her mother . . . had had the most natural and violent of appetites"] (47–48).[25] Jacques, too, can do nothing but play out the fate
dealt him by his heredity: "Jacques était le fils d'un ivrogne et d'une catin. Son
honneur ne savait que pleurer" (58) ["He was the son of a drunkard and of a whore.
His honor could only weep"] (64; trans. modified). Like Raoule, he is aware that

---

[23] Ibid., lesson entitled "Hystérie et dégénérescence chez l'homme," 143.
[24] Jacques Joseph Moreau de Tours, *La Psychologie morbide* (Paris: Victor Masson, 1859); Bénédicte
Auguste Morel, *Traité des dégénérescences* (Paris: Baillière, 1857); Jules Déjerine, *L'Hérédité dans les
maladies du système nerveux* (Paris: Asselin & Houzeau, 1886). There is a good general account of the
work of Moreau, Morel, and others in George Frederick Drinka's *The Birth of Neurosis* (New York: Simon and Schuster, 1984).
[25] It is worth emphasizing that the sins of her parents are offered by the child Raoule to her teachers in
explanation of her own vices; Rachilde's text thereby reflects (ironically or not) how thoroughly theories
of heredity were meshed into the social fabric.

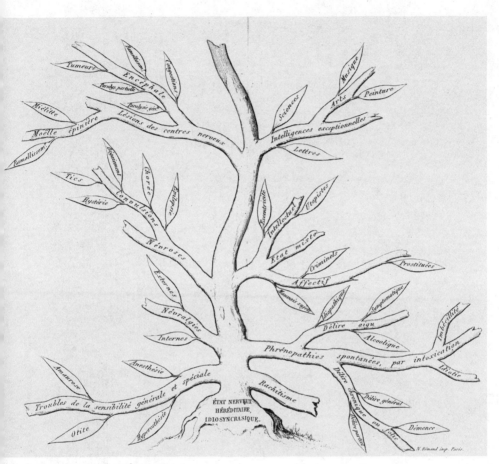

FIGURE 14. *Tree of nervosity.*
*(Published in J. J. Moreau de Tours, La Psychologie
morbide dans ses rapports avec la philosophie de
l'histoire, 1859; photo B.I.M., Université René
Descartes, Paris.)*

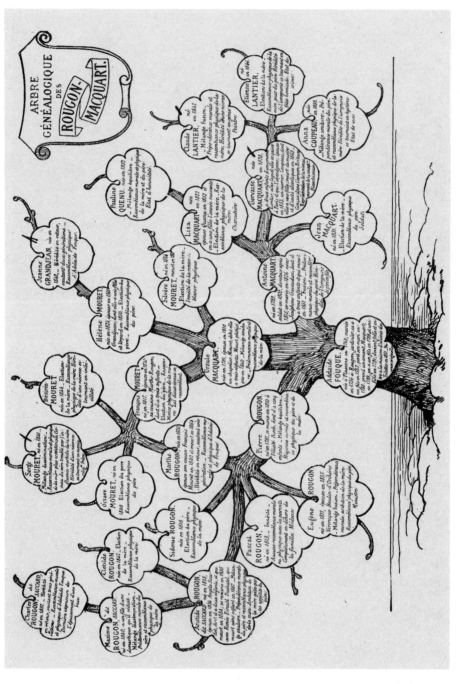

FIGURE 15. *Family tree of the Rougon-Macquart dynasty.* (*From Emile Zola,* Une Page d'amour
[*Paris: Charpentier, 1878*]; *photo Pauline Page.*)

his fate is indelibly inscribed in his blood, and he accepts as inevitable the consan-
guinity of vice, which he holds wholly responsible for his leaving Raoule's embrace to offer himself to her suitor: "Ensuite, rien n'était de sa faute! . . . La prostitution, c'est une maladie! Tous l'avaient eue dans sa famille: sa mère, sa soeur;
est-ce qu'il pouvait lutter contre son propre sang?" (220) ["And it was not his fault!
. . . Prostitution is a disease! They all had had it in his family: his mother, his sister; could he struggle against his own blood?"] (211). Using Raoule and Jacques as
mouthpiece, Rachilde is quoting the substance, if not the letter, of two lines from
the *Oresteia* (*Les Erinnyes*, 2. 5)—a citation that Charcot facetiously placed in the
mouths of two of his more pitiable hysterics, "deux malheureuses créatures . . .
des dégénérés, des déséquilibrés, des faibles intellectuellement et moralement"
["two sad creatures . . . degenerates, unbalanced creatures, intellectually and
morally feeble"]:

> Qu'avons-nous fait, ô Zeus, pour cette destinée?
> Nos pères ont failli: mais nous qu'avons-nous fait?[26]

> *What have we done, oh Zeus, to deserve this fate?*
> *Our fathers failed: but what have we done?*

The citation, twice removed from its source when it appears in *Monsieur Vénus*, is
further distanced by Rachilde's couching it in indirect and free indirect discourse;
not attributable to any specific voice, it appears and reappears in her text as the
voice of repetition: cliché, *idée reçue*, *bêtise*.

We have so far considered, through Rachilde's mimicry of them, only those topoi (gender and power, the clinic and heredity) through which hysteria's discourse
wields its marginalizing, disempowering effect. Rachilde's manipulation of a final
(and only artificially separate) topos, which I call the semiotic body, traces the process whereby the disabling of the hystericized body paradoxically becomes an enabling force for the discourse that produces it.

THE DISCOURSE OF THE SEMIOTIC BODY

A reversal mechanism is once again in operation here, for the body at stake in this
text is not, as is conventionally the case, female; it is the sometimes transvestite but
nonetheless decidedly male body of Raoule's mistress, Jacques. Clearly, the focus
of hystericizing discourse is partitioned in this novel. Raoule receives the label of
hysteric, along with the nervosity, the capriciousness, the lubricity that fall under

[26]Charcot, "Hystérie et dégénérescence chez l'homme" in *L'Hystérie*, 142.

it (although one might argue that the hysteria effect, whose contagion we well know, spreads to Jacques as well over the course of the novel). Jacques's share is less notably hysteria (in the clinical sense) than hystericization, or the aura created by hysteria's discourse: the reduction of the person to the body and of the body to its sexuality, the pathologizing of this sexuality, and its conversion into a semiotic force.

At this point the medical and linguistic meanings of *semiotics* overlap: that branch of medicine whose purpose is to interpret bodily signs or symptoms is harnessed by a sociolinguistic system that finds larger cultural meanings in such symptoms. Jacques's body traverses a semiotic spectrum in this novel, alternately becoming a poem, a text, a painting, a sculpture: in short, a semiotic object to be read, deciphered, interpreted, viewed, written, painted, and molded. Before we turn to specific examples of this aesthetic apotheosis, it may be useful to recall briefly both the broad tradition within which women in the nineteenth century are identified with texts and other objets d'art and the narrower, hyperbolic version of this tradition, which turns hysterics into mystics or poets and their bodies into inscriptions of their oeuvre.

When Balzac's Duchesse de Langeais dies, a victim of her passion, her grieving lover Montriveau is advised by a friend to think of her as no more than a book read in childhood, and Montriveau concurs: "Oui, . . . car ce n'est plus qu'un poème" ["Yes, . . . for all she is now is a poem"]. In Prosper Mérimée's *La Vénus d'Ille*, a bronze but otherwise uncannily lifelike Venus is given to the narrator as an exercise in reading: he must not only interpret the words engraved on her pedestal and the inscription on her arm, but also give meaning to the marks on her body and decipher the character traits imprinted on her face ("dédain, ironie, cruauté *se lisaient* sur ce visage" ["disdain, irony, cruelty could *be read* all over this face"]). And in Zola's *L'Oeuvre*, Christine Lantier, the model for her husband's masterpiece, is sacrificed for her own painted image; woman is replaced by man's representation of her.[27]

These excerpts from a century's archives begin to reconstruct a certain aesthetic economy in which female bodies are stifled into textuality, smudged into painting, or, in the catchall phrase used by Sandra M. Gilbert and Susan Gubar, "killed into art."[28] The particular reliance of realist fiction on the binding of female energy has been elegantly analyzed by Naomi Schor, who suggests that the feminocentrism of

---

[27] Honoré de Balzac, *La Duchesse de Langeais*, in *La Comédie humaine*, ed. Pierre-Georges Castex, 12 vols. (Paris: Gallimard, 1976–81), 5:1037; Prosper Mérimée, *La Vénus d'Ille*, in *Carmen et autres nouvelles*, 2 vols. (Paris: Livre de Poche, 1983), 2:89; Zola, *L'Oeuvre*, in *Les Rougon-Macquart*, vol. 4.
[28] Sandra M. Gilbert and Susan Gubar, *The Madwoman in the Attic* (New Haven: Yale University Press, 1979), 17.

the nineteenth-century novel can be attributed to this necessary relationship between representation and woman.[29]

If the hysteric is—as doctors and novelists alike consistently represent her—a hyperbolic woman, "femme plus que les autres femmes,"[30] then we can extend Schor's argument to cover the disproportionate place of hysteria in the late nineteenth-century novel: that is, to explain this novel's dependence on the hysteric's incapacitation. We have already explored the fin de siècle (clinical and fictional) text's appropriation of the hysteric's mute or inarticulate body, which is then pressed into service as a vehicle for any meaning the colonizing text seeks to express. Jules Claretie's *Les Amours d'un interne* provides the most concise, most literal illustration of this process. Let us briefly recall the scene in which the hysteric Mathilde lies unconscious at the Salpêtrière, surrounded by young interns who are observing their teacher while he traces letters on her bare skin with his fingernail. The doctor's touch leaves a raised, weltlike inscription on the woman's flesh, like a mystic's stigmata, and this text, impressed like a brand on her body, remains legible for hours, earning her the title "papier à lettres vivant"[31] ["living writing paper"]. This appellation bears witness to an instant of textual lucidity, for it is an implicit admission—revealing the underside of the woman-as-art topos—that Mathilde is not, after all, herself a text but only the blank page upon which the male doctor can write any message he chooses. Her body is being used as "a medium of communication between men," phrasing I borrow from Anthony Wilden's discussion of crimes of violence perpetrated by men on women's bodies. Rather than speaking, Mathilde (again, in Wilden's terms, via Lacan) is "being spoken."[32]

Rachilde's sustained citation of this topos throughout her novel is charged with a certain shock value; the reversal of convention, whereby a *male* body is appropriated as textual surface by a *female* creative force, defamiliarizes the conventional power relationship and thus puts it into question. The semiotic conversion of Jacques's body originally takes poetic form. The poetry must, however, be replaced within the context of its writing in order for the cliché to emerge fully. The situation is as follows. Raoule's spurned suitor Raittolbe takes advantage of her absence to accost Jacques. The interview ends badly: Raittolbe—ostensibly provoked by Jacques and Raoule's perverse relationship—brutally beats Jacques. But there is

---

[29] Naomi Schor, *Breaking the Chain: Women, Theory, and French Realist Fiction* (New York: Columbia University Press, 1985), 144.

[30] Charles Richet, "Les Démoniaques d'aujourd'hui," *Revue des deux mondes* 37 (15 January 1880): 346.

[31] Jules Claretie, *Les Amours d'un interne* (Paris: Dentu, 1881), 312.

[32] Anthony Wilden, "In the Penal Colony: The Body as the Discourse of the Other," *Semiotica* 54 (1985): 40, 77.

a strong suggestion that the attack is prompted more by the soldier's repressed desire for Jacques than by a desire for revenge.[33] Following this incident, fearful of Raoule's anger, Raittolbe sends her a letter in which he attempts to justify the beating as the outcome of a quarrel. Jacques, on the other hand, takes no steps to communicate his version of the story to Raoule:

> Jacques n'ignorait pas l'adresse de Raoule, mais la pensée de se plaindre ne lui vint pas. . . . Jacques, dont le corps était un poème, savait que ce poème serait toujours lu avec plus d'attention que la lettre d'un vulgaire écrivain comme lui. (139)

> *Jacques knew Raoule's address, but he never thought of complaining. . . . Jacques, whose body was a poem, knew that his poem would always be read more attentively than any letter from such a vulgar writer as he.* (136–37)

His body stands in for the epistle he doesn't send; his body *is* the message. Let us remember that the textualization of Jacques's body, however breathtaking this body may be in itself, is Raittolbe's doing. Jacques's flesh is legible only once it is marked, "zébrée de haut en bas de longues cicatrices bleuâtres" (142) ["streaked from top to bottom with long, bluish scars"] (140; trans. modified).[34] He is Raittolbe's text, and once Raoule has deciphered the inscription, she finds the message unambiguous: "Raoule, à genoux, comptait les traces brutales. . . . 'Assez,' rugit Raoule . . . 'cet homme t'a vu! Cela me suffit, je devine le reste. . . . Il faut que j'efface chaque cicatrice sous mes lèvres ou je te reverrai toujours nu devant lui'" (143–44) ["Raoule, on her knees, was counting the brutal marks. . . . 'That's enough,' roared Raoule . . . 'that man saw you! That's enough for me! I can guess the rest. . . . I must rub out every scar with my lips, or I shall always see you naked

---

[33] "[Raittolbe] s'empara du bras de Jacques. Celui-ci eut un rapide mouvement de recul et sa manche flottante s'écartant, Raittolbe sentit la chair nacrée sous ses doigts. . . . Raittolbe . . . sauta sur la maudite créature dont la robe de velours lui semblait à présent les ténèbres d'un abîme. . . . 'Ah! tu sauras ce que c'est qu'un vrai mâle, canaille!' . . . hurlait Raittolbe, saisi par une colère aveugle dont il ne s'expliquait peut-être pas bien la violence" (133–34) ["{Raittolbe} seized Jacques's arm. The latter shrank back and as his billowing sleeve left his arm bare, Raittolbe felt the mother-of-pearl skin beneath his fingers. . . . Raittolbe . . . jumped upon the damnable creature whose velvet gown appeared to him now like the darkness of an abyss. . . . 'Now you know what a real man is like, scoundrel!' Raittolbe howled, seized by a blind anger whose violence he could not understand"] (131–32; trans. modified).

[34] Earlier in the novel, Raoule is moved to invoke poetry when she first catches sight of Jacques's nude body: "Poème effrayant de la nudité humaine, t'ai-je donc enfin compris; moi qui tremble pour la première fois en essayant de te lire avec des yeux blasés" (55) ["The terrible poetry of human nudity, I understand it at last. I who tremble for the first time in trying to read it with blasé eyes"] (61). It is significant that the poem, at this preliminary point, is more generally one of human nudity and that Raoule is still struggling to read the message, which becomes legible only once Raittolbe marks the exquisite writing surface.

before him'" (140–42). As Raoule's lips give way to tooth and nail, the work of era-
sure is accomplished by violent superscription, by the layering of scar over scar,
trace upon bloody trace. Jacques becomes a palimpsest. In and of himself neither
poet nor poem, artist or painting, he is instead a periodically reinscribed tablet or
canvas passed back and forth in an ongoing conversation between Raoule and
Raittolbe.[35] "Jacques," says Raoule, rather astutely, "n'est plus qu'une plaie, c'est
notre oeuvre" (156) ["Jacques is only a wound; he is our work of art"] (153; trans.
modified).

Armed with these words and our knowledge that Raoule is an artist who paints
nudes, we might speculate, albeit fancifully, that Jacques is one of them—perhaps
even the one she has hanging in her bedroom: "une académie masculine n'ayant
aucune espèce d'ombre le long des hanches" (37) ["a male nude, with no shading
along the thighs"] (46; trans. modified). We leave the realm of speculation, however, at the end of the novel, for Raoule's aesthetic metaphor is explicitly realized
when she has Jacques quite literally "killed into art." Finished off in a duel and reproduced as a wax mannequin, "statue de cire," Jacques is no longer mere oeuvre
but chef-d'oeuvre: "Ce mannequin, *chef-d'oeuvre* d'anatomie, a été fabriqué par
un Allemand" (228) ["This wax figure, an *anatomical masterpiece*, was fabricated
by a German"] (217; my emphasis throughout; trans. modified).

So the novel ends—not, however, without previously having alluded to
Raoule's part in a collaboration with the German artist-cum-technician responsible for Jacques's waxen image:

> Le soir de ce jour funèbre, [Raoule] se penchait sur le lit . . . et, armée
> d'une pince en vermeil, d'un marteau recouvert de velours et d'un ciseau
> en argent massif, se livrait à un travail très minutieux . . . Par instants,
> elle essuyait ses doigts effilés avec un mouchoir de dentelle. (224–25)
>
> *On the evening of that mournful day, [Raoule] bent over the bed . . . and, armed*
> *with silver pincers, a velvet-covered hammer and a silver scalpel, engaged in a*
> *very delicate task. . . . Occasionally she dried her tapering fingers with a lace*
> *handkerchief.* (215)

The allusion is clarified when Jacques's effigy is described:

[35] Although Jacques dabbles in painting, his artistic pretensions are dismissed. Raoule evaluates one of
his paintings: "un paysage sans air, où rageusement cinq ou six moutons ankylosés paissaient du vert
tendre, avec un tel respect des lois de la perspective, que, par voie d'emprunt, deux d'entre eux parais-
saient posséder cinq pattes" (30) ["a heavy landscape, where five or six stiff sheep were grazing on a field
of pale green, with so little regard for the laws of perspective that, between them, two appeared to have
five legs"] (39). Another character, the artist Martin Durand, offers an appraisal that is more direct but
no more positive: "il n'a pas une ombre de talent" (163) ["he has not got the slightest trace of talent"]
(158).

un mannequin de cire revêtu d'un épiderme de caoutchouc transparent. Les cheveux roux, les cils blonds, le duvet d'or de la poitrine sont naturels; les dents qui ornent la bouche, les ongles des mains et des pieds ont été arrachés à un cadavre. (227)

> *a wax figure covered with transparent rubber. The red hair, the fair eyelashes, the gold hair of the chest are natural; the teeth which are in the mouth, and the nails on the hands and feet have been torn from a corpse.* (216)

Putting aside for the moment the grotesquely spectacular nature of this representation, I want to consider it more specifically as a spectacle of cliché: Rachilde's final, paroxysmic performance of a dizzying array of citations from the fin de siècle *doxa*. For while we recognize that Jacques's death and aesthetic reincarnation cite a myriad of nineteenth-century heroines "killed into art," the reproduction of his body is not cast of any single element: it is a collage of citations as well as of material parts.

THE SPECTACLE OF CLICHÉ

Jacques's immortalization in the form of a wax statue is a very specific quotation; its source is the *atelier de moulage* together with the *musée des moulages* at the Charcot Salpêtrière. There, in the mid 1870s, Charcot inaugurated the practice of casting in wax the convulsed or otherwise distorted bodies of his patients. This technique—one among many that would gradually aestheticize pathology—served no particular medical purpose (Charcot, after all, relied upon living demonstrations for his lectures and his own experimentation); it served essentially to create museum pieces, to preserve pathology as an art form.[36]

Jacques's wax double is a rather special copy of the Salpêtrière castings, however, for it comes equipped with "un ressort, disposé à l'intérieur des flancs, [qui] correspond à la bouche et l'anime" (228) ["a spring hidden inside the thighs {that} connects with the mouth and gives it life"] (217; trans. modified). Because the preceding sentence tells us that Raoule (in alternating male and female attire) visits the statue at night, embracing it, kissing it upon the lips, we can assume that there is a reference here to necrophilia, whose fortune in the late nineteenth century hardly needs to be elaborated.

[36] For an account of the specific practice of sculpting or casting at the Salpêtrière, see Georges Didi-Huberman, *Invention de l'hystérie: Charcot et l'iconographie photographique de la Salpêtrière* (Paris: Macula, 1982), 33–34 and 122–24; and Jules Claretie's novelized recounting of the same in *Les Amours d'un interne*, 112, 222. Didi-Huberman's entire book is a brilliant account of and reflection on the transformation of hysteria into spectacle at the Salpêtrière.

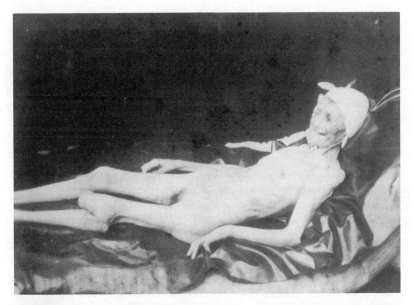

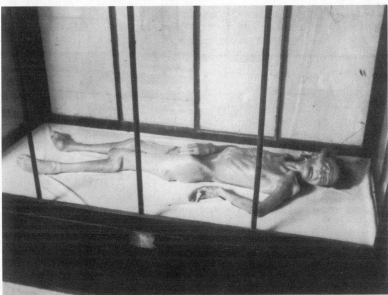

FIGURE 16. *Top: Photograph of a patient
from one of Charcot's clinical dossiers.
Bottom: Wax cast of same patient.*
(Reproduced with permission of Bibliothèque
Charcot, La Salpêtrière, Paris)

•

Following this decadent tableau, the novel's bland last sentence seems anticli-
mactic: "Ce mannequin . . . a été fabriqué par un Allemand" (228) ["This wax figure . . . was fabricated by a German"] (217; trans. modified). The conclusion appears at best disappointing and at worst irrelevant. When we recall, however, that
the ghoulish "masterpiece of anatomy" is in fact a collaborative effort, and when
we then look more closely at the collaborators, what emerges is the conjugation of
two clichés. The cooperation of Raoule and the German presents us with a phantasmatic fin de siècle alliance of superwoman and superpower: a sex and a nation
each grown too knowledgeable, too strong, too competitive, too threatening. We
recall that the Commune fueled the already highly inflammable nineteenth-
century imagination with the incendiary image of the *pétroleuse*. The literal (if
perhaps mythic) image of women reputed to have set fire to much of Paris during
the Commune rapidly spread to include any and all women involved in the revolutionary movement of 1871, and eventually included as well any women perceived as being out of their place, out of (male) control, in competition with men,
and often, symptomatically, in trousers.[37] This image of a female menace, of
women as destroyers—literal cutthroat competitors of men—was further inflated
over the course of the next two decades by the passage of the Camille Sée Law of
1880, which provided for state-funded secondary education for women, and the
passage in 1884 of more liberal divorce laws, which allowed women to initiate divorce proceedings. Already beginning to take shape in the 1880s was the mythic
specter the 1890s would call the *femme nouvelle*, the overeducated, overambitious
woman who inverted gender roles and dislocated bourgeois values.[38]

The equally threatening stereotype of the German can also be traced back to the
same period, for the Commune was, of course, roughly contemporaneous with
the Siege of Paris and the French defeat in the Franco-Prussian war. This humili-
ating defeat was generally interpreted as proof that France had declined militarily
in the nineteenth century because she had allowed Germany to outstrip her scientifically and industrially. Germany emerged from this period perceived not only
as the enemy but also as a threatening supertechnological force.[39]

By condensation, the *pétroleuses* and the besiegers of Paris become the joint
forces that "unmanned" France. The two phantasmatic Others that converge his-
torically and mythically in 1871 continue to haunt the French imagination in tan-
dem a decade later, their respective roles virtually unchanged: the German fabricates the mannequin—that is, supplies the necessary technical knowledge and

[37] For an extended analysis of the role of the *pétroleuses* in the nineteenth-century imaginary, see
Chapter 8.
[38] See Claire Goldberg Moses, *French Feminism in the Nineteenth Century* (Albany: State University of
New York Press, 1984).
[39] See Goldstein, *Console and Classify*, 348.

skill—while Raoule, the trouser-wearing, corpse-mutilating maenad, is responsi- **257**
ble for the grisly detail work.[40] The lifelike mannequin they create, a combined
marvel of technology and art, demands a closer look. Our glance, however, need
not be excessively penetrating in order to reveal that the "chef-d'oeuvre d'anatomie," image of anatomical perfection, is in fact a body in pieces. For we know that
the vision of ideal wholeness is constructed by supplementing the wax image with
myriad fragments of the body it represents. The plucked hairs, the teeth and nails
torn from Jacques's corpse complete the representation, but in so doing, they de-
compose it. Even as they produce an effect of hyperrealism, these body remnants
deconstruct the very concept of mimetic realism by destroying the integrity of the
referent, flaunting by their mere presence the fragmentary, defective status of the
real.

Rachilde insists, in other words, that the statue can be no more than its separate
parts—no greater and no more coherent than the bits and pieces of the social discourse that produces it (among which is the fiction of its creation by Raoule and
the German). Neither body snippets nor discursive fragments can be recuperated
in the name of mimetic realism because the realist aesthetic is merely another citation writ large on this body and contradicted by its finer features. Among these,
the fine hairs Raoule plucks from Jacques's cadaver are of particular (if unexpected)
relevance to the fate of realism's clichés. Now, if we very schematically posit the
defining characteristics of traditional realism as totalization and the detail (the first
accomplished by means of the second) and if we also accept that the process
whereby the realist detail is totalized or idealized is often fetishistic in nature (an
absent referential plenitude is artificially replaced), then we might read a good deal
between the hairs reaffixed to the wax body.[41] We might recall being shown Raoule
armed with silver tweezers ("*armée* d'une pince en vermeil" [224; my emphasis])
engaged in a very detailed task ("un travail très minutieux" [225]). We might then
be tempted to describe this labor of plucking and later reattaching hairs as fetishistic in the extreme.

Except for two qualifying factors. First, the fetish (etymologically related to the
factitious) is by definition an artificial (though not necessarily inorganic) supplement to the real, whereas here we have the real supplementing art. Second, the fetish, as figured in traditional anatomical terms, is a phallic substitute whose effect,
in more abstract terms, is one of essentialization, centralization, fixation, and

---

[40] The rising German and declining French birthrate in the years after 1870 was cause for great anxiety
in France, as was German industrial expansion, often cited as an explanation for the French defeat in
1870. See Debora L. Silverman's chapter four in *Art Nouveau in Fin-de-siècle France: Politics, Psychology, and Style* (Berkeley: University of California Press, 1989) for an informative account of the menace posed to the bourgeois family by the *femme nouvelle*.
[41] For a fascinating analysis of interconnections between realism and the detail, see Naomi Schor's
Reading in Detail (New York: Methuen, 1987), which informs my reading of *Monsieur Vénus*.

unity. But in Rachilde's version, where what is at stake is replacing "les cheveux roux, les cils blonds, le duvet d'or de la poitrine" (227) ["the red hair, the fair eyelashes, the gold hair of the chest"] (216), there is, quite to the contrary, a sense of randomness, dispersal, displacement, and plurality: a scatter effect peculiarly emphasized from the beginning of the novel when Raoule first takes note of Jacques's hirsuteness: "Il en avait partout" (55) ["He had curls everywhere"] (61). There is, in the emphatic and sustained attention paid to every form and site of male hair, an apparent defetishizing of the phallus and a reinvestment in a more general erotics of the body—a reinvestment similar in its erotic detailing to a fetish but that I hesitate to call fetishistic precisely because it is general, mobile, and diffuse.

A challenge to my argument for defetishizing this body arises, however, in the form of that curious detail of the statue that I mentioned previously: "un ressort, disposé à l'intérieur des flancs" (228). How are we to read this "spring" between the legs of the statue? Is it a metaphor whose purpose is to insist that the mannequin is anatomically correct? Or is it a sign that the mannequin has been anatomically corrected—hence a prosthesis—in other words, a fetish? To complicate matters, I should add that an explicit displacement from hair to phallus takes place much earlier in this novel when, immediately following the observation on the omnipresence of Jacques's curls ("il en avait partout"), we are told "il se serait trompé, par exemple, en jurant que cela seul témoignait de sa virilité" (55) ["he would have been mistaken, it is true, if he had sworn that they were the only proof of his virility"] (61). This initial displacement sets a precedent that reopens the possibility—though not the certainty—of fetishism: that is, of a phallic recuperation of all the dispersed tufts, strands, and lashes. Perhaps they are only displaced.

But does it really matter whether the odd emphasis in *Monsieur Vénus* on hair and hair transplants constitutes a fetish or not? Or is the issue unnecessary and undecidable—a matter of splitting hairs, as it were—a distraction from the larger issues of representation and cliché? Only apparently. The premise underlying my exploration of this area thus far, which I would like to address more explicitly now, is that the statue, "masterpiece of anatomy," should also be read as the anatomy of representation according to Rachilde. At stake in our reading of the mannequin's anatomy is our interpretation of the representational aesthetic informing *Monsieur Vénus* and, therefore, the way we read this text.

If we opt for a nonfetishistic representation of the statue, as I tend to, we read body and text as decentered and detotalized, a collage of corporeal remnants or citational fragments. The text, in this case, presents no cohering vision or overarching meaning: it simply repeats, sometimes to breaking point, the tired images of its day. Jacques, who in life is a repository of cliché, a representation of fin de siècle stereotypes, becomes in death (which is to say, in art) a copy of a copy, a representation of himself as representation: the self-referential body of cliché—or, in short, Rachilde's parrot. (After all, says the narrator of *Un Coeur simple*, "Tous les perroquets s'appellent Jacquot" ["All parrots are called Jacquot"].[42] The statue, in other words, is a simulacrum: an avatar of the mannequins called *simulacra*[43] that in Caesar's time held victims to be burned in honor of the gods. It is no mere copy, but a representation based on absence, mimetic void, referential sacrifice. If we view the statue as simulacrum, we are, of course, substituting, for the deconstructed realist aesthetic, a once iconoclastic perspective long since recuperated as modernist aesthetic.

If, on the other hand, we choose to read a fetishized version of *Monsieur Vénus*, the novel becomes a story of perversion, a story about pathology, or, as Barrès sees it, a perverted, pathological narrative. In short, the citations are read for their semantic content rather than their cliché emptiness; irony is unread; ideology is transparent. Bodily fragments and discursive shards are idealized, in this case, reinstated in an interpretive whole, and recuperated by a mimetic vision.

The problem these two alternatives pose for me is that all the while I adopt the first, I cannot dismiss the second, largely because it is inscribed as a possibility in the very uncertainty of Rachilde's text. On the microcosmic level, Rachilde produces consummate ambiguity by presenting a defetishized image of the mannequin's body along with the possibility of refetishizing it—and ambiguity is, of course, the very stuff of fetishist dreams. On the macrocosmic level, I find overwhelming irony in the novel's cliché structure and read Rachilde as iconoclastic, a breaker (or at least a batterer) of the verbal icons of her culture. At the same time, I recognize ironic repetition as repetition nonetheless and find ironic mimicry and compliant performance not always distinguishable. And I have before me, irrevocably present in the republished edition of the novel, the preface by Maurice Barrès, evidence that *Monsieur Vénus* can also be read as a maker, or at least an affirmer, of the same icons I see dented or cracked. Furthermore, we cannot avoid reading text and preface together, not only in the antagonistic sense I suggested previously (the novel as deconstructive reading of its preface), but also as complicitous: Rachilde, after all, accepted Barrès's offer to introduce her novel, and we can only assume she read his text and approved it before publication. The book, in other words, is a package, and it is wrapped to sell—to cater, paradoxically, to the reigning ideology against which I have argued Rachilde's irony is directed.

The two original alternatives, once examined, suggest a plethora of interpretations. Let me briefly evoke a sampling. (1) Rachilde is using ironic repetition to de-

[42] "[Le perroquet] était placé auprès de la porte, et plusieurs s'étonnaient qu'il ne répondait pas au nom de Jacquot, puisque tous les perroquets s'appellent Jacquot" ["{The parrot} was put next to the door, and several people were surprised that he didn't answer to the name of Jacquot because all parrots are called Jacquot"]. Gustave Flaubert, *Un Coeur simple*, from *Trois Contes*, in *Oeuvres complètes*, ed. Jean Bruneau and Bernard Masson, 2 vols. (Paris: Seuil, 1964), 2:174.
[43] I owe this information to Didi-Huberman, *Invention de l'hystérie*, 267.

260
•

construct the ideology I have called hystericization. Her text (and her irony) are appropriated by Barrès; the irony changes sides. (2) Again, assume Rachilde is using repetition ironically; consider now, however, that the addition of the preface only accentuates Rachilde's irony by illustrating its target. (3) Assume instead that Rachilde is a compliant performer of the passwords and bywords of her time; she gratefully accepts Barrès's sincere offer to champion her novel. (4) As in the previous case, assume that Rachilde is a compliant consumer of the *doxa* but consider now that Barrès's gratefully received preface ironizes the novel he appears to be championing. (5) Continuing to posit Rachilde's compliance, let us consider the possibility that the confrontation of Rachilde's nonironic novel and Barrès's nonironic preface results nonetheless in a textual irony. (6) The reader chooses any of the above interpretations and consequently falls victim to a textual irony.

If we decide to refuse irony, we risk becoming irony's dupe. But if we make any specific irony our choice, we refuse the mobile irony that inhabits the text and risk the same fate. How, then, do we settle this dilemma? I don't think we do; I don't think we can. I persist in my ironic reading of *Monsieur Vénus*, all the while admitting that the irony of irony is its inclusion of naive repetition. Speaking for irony, I find myself in the somewhat bewildering position of speaking as a fetishist: "Je sais bien . . . mais quand même"[44] ["I know . . . but all the same"]. If it is true, as Nathaniel Wing has suggested, that irony "serves as an alibi for a fetish,"[45] then we might conceive of the ironist as the fetishist's apprentice, reaching out for all readers, ensnaring them in a tangle of ambiguity, uncertainty, and indecision from which there is no escape. Irony quite possibly makes fetishists of us all.

---

[44] This is Octave Mannoni's formulation of the structure of the fetish and, more generally, of fetishistic thinking. Briefly elaborated: the fetishist knows that an old cherished belief is false but nonetheless . . . (continues to believe it). The *nonetheless* is not articulated: it *is* the fetish. Mannoni, "Je sais bien, mais quand même . . . ," in *Clefs pour l'imaginaire ou l'autre scène* (Paris: Seuil, 1969), 9–33. The existence of a perplexing pamphlet by Rachilde, *Pourqoui je ne suis pas féministe* (Paris: Editions de France, 1928), only fortifies the irony of *Monsieur Vénus*. Despite the title and the blatantly misogynistic pronouncements sprinkled throughout this text, the politics of its author defy definition. The narrative voice, prone to contradiction, evasiveness, ambiguity, and paradox, may or may not be ironic at any given moment. Chameleonlike, Rachilde's narrator can never be located behind the rapid succession of rhetorical disguises she—like the actress/woman of letters of this chapter's epigraph—takes on. In her excellent intellectual biography (in progress) of Rachilde, "Rachilde's Paroxysms of Chastity," Melanie Hawthorne helps to reinterpret as writing strategies some of the paradoxes of both Rachilde's politics and her style.

[45] Nathaniel Wing, *The Limits of Narrative* (Cambridge: Cambridge University Press, 1986), 77.

POSTCRIPT

Speculations on Dracula, Frankenstein, and Rachilde's Monster

Rachilde's narrative and mine come to a halt before the exhibit of Jacques's wax effigy. Last in a series of textually posed bodies, his is given more precisely in repose, an ironic citation of the archetypically female semiotic body but also a shadow of his former self. For if earlier in *Monsieur Vénus*, Jacques's living body was compared to an epistolary poem of desire passed between two other characters—a poem explicitly offered in lieu of a letter[1]—it is now simply a dead letter. Adorned with the tooth-and-nail detailing we recognize as Raoule's signet, sheathed in rubber, and consigned to a walled-in chamber, Jacques's body is signed, sealed, and withdrawn from circulation. Cast in wax—a seal on the letter of flesh—the statue

---

[1] "Jacques n'ignorait pas l'adresse de Raoule, mais la pensée de se plaindre ne lui vint pas. . . . Jacques, dont le corps était un poème, savait que ce poème serait toujours lu avec plus d'attention que la lettre d'un vulgaire écrivain comme lui" ["Jacques knew Raoule's address, but he never thought of complaining. . . . Jacques, whose body was a poem, knew that his poem would always be read more attentively than any letter from such a vulgar writer as he"]. Rachilde, *Monsieur Vénus* (Paris: Flammarion, 1977), 139; trans. Madeleine Boyd (New York: Covici, Friede, 1929), 136–37. Subsequent references will be to these editions and will be given parenthetically in the text.

lies in apposition to the "living writing paper" of Mathilde's dermographic body with which I opened this book, and provides the space for a postscript.

Finished with assorted appliqué bits torn from Jacques's corpse, the partly molded, partly patchworked statue invites an equivocal message. For Raoule is the modern Frankenstein, and Jacques is her monster. Unlike Mary Shelley's creature, who was the product of fragments scavenged from disparate graves and charnel houses, Rachilde's creation, reconstituted from his own cadaver, is ostensibly a self-made man. But the allusion to reflexivity and, by extension, to the autonomous, self-enclosed modern individual—what constitutes the modernity of this Frankensteinian model—does not dispel its monstrousness: that quality belonging to any creature, object, activity, or thought that cannot be classified, that combines categories, and crosses conceptual borders. The lifelike mannequin mixes the synthetic and the organic, technology and art, death and life, says that no boundary can assure their distinction. And its organic appliqués, tantamount to exposed sutures on the rubber surface, suggest that the whole could become unstitched, fall into constituent pieces. These monstrous parts, as I suggested earlier, are analogous to the citational composition of *Monsieur Vénus*. They are the bits and pieces of stereotype: the Other's discourse that is worked into the text and whose demarcating italics, like so many dissolved sutures, have been mostly lost or absorbed.

It is perhaps inevitable that the influence of a text that everywhere evokes the problematic of liminality should infiltrate my own text, where I now find, in the form of the monstrous, the insistent return of the grotesque—a term I applied earlier to the statue but bracketed for the sake of pursuing another line of thought. *Monster* is a preferred term in *Monsieur Vénus*. It appears (sometimes in the adjectival form *monstrueux/se*) twelve times in the novel and refers to Jacques, to the passion that joins him with Raoule, and to Raoule—in descending order of frequency.[2] Curiously, all the designations of monstrosity figure *before* Jacques's apotheosis. The apparent displacement of the "monster" label does not merely indicate that the monstrosity of his final hybrid form goes without saying. More significantly, it suggests that what is most monstrous in this novel—its inexorable fluidity, its disregard for boundaries, its dissolution of distinctions—exceeds its final representation by the statue. The monstrous, given its associations with mobility, can only be represented—fixed as allegory—in the form of the statue and, therefore, attenuated or arrested there.

From the first page of the novel, where Rachilde situates Raoule on an apartment threshold—a line partitioning space but in context also separating genders, social classes, reader and writer, literary text and social text, original and citation—she begins also to undermine the work of differentiation that a threshold os-

---

[2] I have not included in my count numerous allusions to monsters or monstrosity that do not use the term, such as *démon*, *maudite créature*, *grotesque*, and so on.

tensibly performs. The subversiveness of *Monsieur Vénus* is embodied by the protean forms of Jacques and Raoule and by the mobility of desire they everywhere
put into play—a mutability and mobility whose eroding of sexual, gender, and
class distinctions inevitably sweeps away the foundations of binary thinking and of
meaning as we know it. With Jacques's death, wax reincarnation, and immobili-
zation in a rubber sheath within a walled chamber, there is at least a gesture toward
recontaining transgressive forces. Dressed ("revêtu" [227]) only in transparent rubber, his virility cast in relief, Jacques as statue defies sexual indeterminacy.[3] But if
the transgressive elements of this novel are not diffused throughout the final tableau as they are in the rest of the novel, neither are they dispelled: rather, they are
concentrated in the life-and-death indistinction of a dead man reincarnated as a
rubber doll, an inanimate object artificially animated ("un ressort . . . l'anime"
[228]) so that death and life are no longer separate provinces.

Fine, says my reader. We are growing used to geographical flux. Shifting
boundaries are a sign of our times. We can redraw the lines. But has hysteria been
wiped off the map? And I must in response ask the reader's indulgence, ask for a
moment's patience so that I can move even further afield in order to return to my
point. As the good doctor Van Helsing, hero of another book of the undead, reminds us, "In this, the quickest way home is the longest way, so your proverb say."[4]
I quote Van Helsing advisedly, not only because his words are apt and his spatial
metaphor fitting, nor only because he makes his point in an appropriately hybrid
fusing of Dutch and English, nor only because my citation of his citation reproduces that blurring of sources I have been speaking about. I turn to Van Helsing
also because he is a hunter of monsters—more precisely, a vampire slayer—and
because he leads the group that stalks and traps the monster I have not yet discussed
but who has been lurking behind much of what I have said. This monster is of
course Dracula. He finds his way into hysteria's narrative by an indirect textual
path that crosses different eras and different media, and he enters by way of "The
New Blood Culture," a *New York Times* commentary by Frank Rich prompted by
the late 1992 release of Francis Ford Coppola's *Bram Stoker's "Dracula."*[5]

As Rich reads it, Coppola's film is about AIDS and, more specifically, about the

---

[3] In the original 1884 edition, however, the sentence that I am glossing here from the 1889 edition was
extended, so that it read: "Un ressort disposé à l'intérieur des flancs, correspond à la bouche et l'anime,
en même temps qu'il fait s'écarter les cuisses." Rachilde, *Monsieur Vénus: Roman matérialiste* (Brussels:
Auguste Brancart, 1884), 228. ["A spring hidden inside the thighs corresponds to the mouth and animates it, and simultaneously opens the thighs"] (my translation). The first edition clearly retained, to
the end, the sexual ambiguity of the rest of the novel—an ambiguity reduced, whether for aesthetic or
moral reasons, in the fourth (1889) edition. I am grateful to Véronique Hubert-Matthews for alerting
me to the 1884 variant.
[4] Bram Stoker, *Dracula* (New York: Doubleday, 1927), 292. Further references will be given in the text.
[5] Frank Rich, "The New Blood Culture," *New York Times*, 6 December 1992, "Styles of the Times"
section. Further references will be given in the text. *Bram Stoker's "Dracula,"* dir. Francis Ford Coppola, Columbia Pictures, 1992.

subliminal fantasies that surround the disease. He offers as evidence the raging presence of blood in this movie on the various levels of plot, dialogue, and cinematography. He describes Coppola's *Dracula* as "an orgy of bloodsucking, bloodletting and blood poisoning" (1), refers to the portrayed exchange of blood with "lubricious vampire victims" as "unsafe sex," and remarks that even babies are prey to the mysterious illness labeled by one bewildered doctor a "'disease of the blood unknown to all medical theory.'" As if in illustration of the unknown invader, the camera, Rich continues, at one point pauses for "an extended microscopic view of what appears to be rampaging blood cells" (11). And as if in confirmation of Dracula's observation that "'blood is too precious a thing in these times,'" the screen is often tinted "capillary red," so that the viewer's perspective is suffused with blood (11). The camera captures the predator as well in shrouds of mist and fog—vapors that are alternative fluid forms.

This, Rich says, is a film for our times, a film that plays to the fears of "further AIDS invasions of the national bloodstream" (1). Pinpointing the superb timeliness of *Dracula* to political events coincident with its mid-November 1992 nationwide opening, Rich notes that the distraction of the recent presidential election was no longer present, that the ensuing easing of the previously dominant economic fear left room for other demons, and that the much-publicized possible lifting of the ban on homosexuals in the military unleashed phobias about contamination through casual contact—phobias fed by increasing public awareness that AIDS is not confined to homosexuals, hemophiliacs, and drug users.

I find Rich's argument that Coppola's *Dracula* taps into the terror of our times insightful and utterly convincing. I also, however, find Rich's very focused historicism blinding to the larger historical context. For the full title of Coppola's film, as Rich mentions, is *Bram Stoker's "Dracula."* The naming of the author of the 1897 novel in the movie title alludes to an intended fidelity of Coppola to Stoker, film to novel, postmodernism to Victorianism, and to the echoing of one fin de siècle's phobias by those of another. When Rich calls Coppola's movie "this unfaithfully anachronistic retelling of [Stoker's horror tale]" (11), one wonders if he read the book, which includes every verbal reference to blood that the film does (and more), which hypostatizes blood as milk and semen, and which everywhere vaporizes vampires to mist and fog, the better to help them penetrate houses, rooms, and bodies, the better to let them infuse their poisonous fluids into unsuspecting bloodstreams. Like Jonathan Harker, who looks for the monster in the mirror and finds only his own image, Rich finds in Coppola's *Dracula* an anachronism that is the reflection of his own chronological bias.

Nowhere is the chronological error as clear as when Rich glosses "the new blood culture" as "the bizarre pop byproduct of a national obsession with all bodily fluids" (1). Any of us who has witnessed nineteenth-century phantasms about bod-

ily fluids accumulate in hysteria's corpus will have difficulty perceiving our contemporary blood culture as new. All of the eroticized terror of fusion, infusion,
and transfusion that Rich associates with "the new blood culture" ostensibly provoked by the AIDS virus already pervades Stoker's 1897 novel.

To better situate Stoker's *Dracula* on its own historical turf, I could speak here of
the engulfing fluids of hysteria and syphilis, those particular pathologies that gave
nineteenth-century desire its lethal force, but I prefer to do so only in passing, for I
want to deliteralize the fluid component of all these diseases—without, of course,
denying their reality or their specificity. The very dissimilarity of AIDS and hysteria—the fundamental fact that one is fatal, one is not—is especially important,
for it suggests that the overlapping discourses through which each is perceived contain common phantasmatic undercurrents.

We have already seen how the threat of overflowing body fluids associated with
hysteria dematerializes into the more abstract—but no less terrifying—menace of
undifferentiation that touches the physical and social body alike (although part of
the point is that such distinctions cannot be maintained). I want now briefly to suggest that Stoker's monster materializes and dematerializes similar threats, and that
we must therefore rehistoricize (that is, bihistoricize) and dematerialize the discourse of fluidity in Coppola's film. Only then can we evaluate the continuity between the new blood culture, vampirism, the leaking of hysterical bodies, and,
more abstractly, the dissolution of discursive boundaries that is at work in *Monsieur Vénus*.

The reiterated cry of Stoker's madman Renfield ("The blood is the life! The
blood is the life!" [142]) serves as a superfluous reminder that the color of Stoker's
prose is as unambiguous as the tint of Coppola's screen. Blood is not only spilled or
sucked or transfused everywhere in this novel; it is evoked metaphorically when it
is not explicitly flowing. It also symbolically replaces semen and milk. The three
fluids are graphically superimposed when, in an image conflating fellatio and
nursing, we see Mina Harker's face pushed down to suck from a spurting wound on
Dracula's chest: "His right hand gripped her by the back of the neck, forcing her
face down. . . . The attitude of the two had a terrible resemblance to a child forcing a kitten's nose into a saucer of milk to compel it to drink" (282). As Christopher
Craft has suggested, the confluence of fluids and the anatomically shifting images
of this tableau most vividly represent the subversion of gender boundaries that is
everywhere threatened in this novel.[6]

But gender is not the only dualism undone in this novel, and bodily fluids are
only the symbolic carrier of a generalized dissolution of boundaries most literally
represented by the location of Dracula's castle "just on the borders of three states"

---

[6] See Christopher Craft, " 'Kiss Me with Those Red Lips': Gender and Inversion in Bram Stoker's *Dracula*," *Representations* 8 (Fall 1984): 125–26.

yet unmarked on all maps and in all guides (2). The boundaries crossed and duly noted by Jonathan Harker on his voyage east will, of course, be recrossed in both directions by Dracula and by Van Helsing's band of vampire fighters; the traversal of geographic borders will be most sensationally echoed by vampirization and blood transfusions. But as Stephen Arata has argued, penetrations of the body in Stoker's tale, analogous to invasions of the body politic, articulate Victorian fears of reverse colonization, and the dread mixing of blood corresponds to a horror of miscegenation.[7] (Dracula describes the blood that flows in his veins as "the whirlpool of European races" [29].) The polyglot dictionary to which Jonathan Harker must have recourse (6) in order to make his way through the linguistic babel of his Transylvanian passage is emblematic of the general polymorphism of this novel, which is a composite of letters, diaries, transcribed phonograph diaries, telegrams, newpaper articles, and travelogue. Slithering through this monstrous assemblage of genres—"just as a lizard moves along a wall"—is the novel's eponymous anti-hero, hybrid without a species: "What manner of man is this, or what manner of creature is it in the semblance of man?" (35). Dracula, in Craft's well-chosen phrasing, is "a border being who abrogates demarcations, makes . . . distinctions impossible. He is *nosferatu*, neither dead nor alive but somehow both, mobile frequenter of the grave and boudoir, easeful communicant of exclusive realms."[8]

In Dracula's sexually ambiguous mouth ("white sharp teeth, behind the full lips of the blood-dripping mouth" [282]), Craft puts some unanswerable questions that speak graphically to the monstrous polymorphism of desire here represented: "Are we male or are we female? Do we have penetrators or orifices? . . . And what about our bodily fluids, the red and the white? What are the relations between blood and semen, milk and blood?"[9] Dracula feeds on nubile young women, but homoerotic desire is represented nonetheless by a narrative that both represses a thirst for young men (as when Jonathan Harker cuts himself shaving and is saved from the fangs of the beast—in the nick of time, as it were—by his crucifix) and displaces it (by the banding together of men in the hunt for Dracula).

The mobile sexuality figured by Stoker's dripping vampire mouth leads in two different but mutually significant directions: it announces Coppola's similarly fluid vision of monstrosity, and it repeats the image of another—differently monstrous—mouth (the wax statue's) in which coded dualities are dissolved in a bloodless dry irony. Distinctions between masculine and feminine, organic and synthetic, death and life are undermined in Jacques's reconstructed mouth, a wax orifice implanted with real teeth and animated by a decidedly phallic spring worked presumably by Raoule's (ambiguously) feminine hand. Fused here, too,

[7] Stephen D. Arata, "The Occidental Tourist: *Dracula* and the Anxiety of Reverse Colonization," *Victorian Studies* 33 (Summer 1990): 621–45.
[8] Craft, "'Kiss Me with Those Red Lips,'" 117.
[9] Ibid., 109.

are categories of sex and text; for if the sensationalizing description of the statue **267**
most immediately evokes a lewd rubber doll, not far behind comes the realization
that this is also a ventriloquist's dummy, and that the spring that works the mouth
is a narrative device. Once again sex talks, but its words are manipulated. Evocations of wax statues, cadaverous erotica, cross-dressing, bodies killed into art—so
many citations from a decadent lexicon—are dead letters, reminders that necrophilia and logophilia are inextricably crossed and fused.

The figurative fluidity everywhere operative in *Monsieur Vénus* usefully ab-
stracts the more literally represented fluidity of many of the hysteria texts I have
discussed. Rachilde's novel in fact speaks more significantly, though implicitly,
about hysteria through its constant invocation and abrogation of binary categories
than it does through explicit citations from hysteria's discourse. By deliteralizing
this discourse and miming the cultural work hysteria is charged with, *Monsieur
Vénus* acts as a bridge between the hysteria texts and the monster narratives, to
which I will return by way of rearticulating hysteria's strongest undercurrents.

My words on Coppola necessarily incorporate words on Stoker as well. For Coppola's *Bram Stoker's "Dracula,"* from the awkwardly deliberate title on, is a study in
citation.[10] The film everywhere cites the fluidity that pervades the novel, and simultaneously fluidifies citation, blurs its distinguishing traces. Coppola's script reproduces, and his camera reinvents, not only the literal fluidity of Stoker's novel
(the blood, the symbolic sexual transfusions, the tears, the mists), but also Stoker's
emphasis on traveling, on crossing borders, on changing forms and kaleidoscoping
histories. The camera lingers insistently on Jonathan Harker as he crosses over the
threshold of Dracula's castle. Lucy, freshly recruited to the ranks of the undead,
"walks beyond the grace of God, a wanderer in the outer darkness." Dracula's
fifteenth-century princess is reincarnated as Victorian maiden. Thickly billowing
fog unwraps Dracula's gallant young prince persona, who slips suddenly into the
devil's shape, which evanesces and leaves in its place a swarming horde of rats. A
storm rages across the screen with the synesthetic howl of wolves. Lucy's severed
head fades into a roast on a platter. Eyes gleam red like bloodied mouths and pierce
the darkness like fangs, and bleeding fang marks metamorphose into glinting orbs.
Intermittently the film toys with the possibility of stopping the flow of blood, of
time, of shapes, of sense. Dracula reaches out to wipe away Mina's tears and turns
them into a fistful of diamonds. He begs for release from his intermediate state in
the finality of death: "Give me peace."

Coppola's movie plays alternately with exceeding its own boundaries and recontaining the excess. The opening scenes precede the title (in flagrant defiance of the
monumental image of this title inscribed in bronze) and reach back beyond Bram
Stoker's story to folkloric accounts of Vlad the Impaler. And the closing scene is

[10] In fact, when the title appears on the screen, the citation begins. The film begins a few minutes earlier, preceding Stoker's narrative with folkloric background.

followed—after the movie has to all intents and purposes ended, the soundtrack has faded out, and the credits have been shown—by the swelling tones of Annie Lennox singing "Love Song for a Vampire." Soundtrack and movie are renewed for several minutes. There is a kind of overflow effect on either end, as if the movie could not be contained by its pretended frame. Midway through, Dracula and Mina meet in London and see at the cinematograph what appears to be a replay, in early moving pictures style, of the first few (Vlad the Impaler) scenes of the film— as if to recapture the runaway material within firm boundaries. But Coppola's camera has already filmed several immediately preceding frames of London streets in the same early moving pictures style of the film within the film, as if in mockery of the borders that turn out to be dysfunctional quotation marks.

The citational foundation of *Bram Stoker's "Dracula"* might otherwise be translated as double vision. As such, it is emblematized by a young prince Dracula in Victorian dandy form, sporting a pair of modish blue-tinted glasses perched rakishly on his nose. Peering through and over his glasses at the fifteenth-century princess Elisabeta reincarnated as Mina, he tells her: "I have crossed oceans of time to find you." Telescoping four hundred years in his mobile perspective, he two-times Mina with Elisabeta as Coppola does the phantoms of this fin de siècle with those of the last, crossing time with space, juxtaposing two epochs, and two incarnations.

Double-crossing these crossovers, Coppola echoes with the rhetoric of his camera the overarching shift between metaphors of double talk (citation) and metaphors of seeing double that is implicit in his dual perspective. The interchangeability of mouth and eye, speech and sight, message and vision, language and camera is metaphorically or metonymically invoked in this film by special effects that turn fang punctures into wolves' eyes, monster eyes into wine goblets, or the eye of a peacock feather into the mouth of a tunnel. These transformations belie the insistent authority of ocular images in this film. Coppola gives us eyes—monstrous roving eyes—everywhere superimposed on the screen, often for the space of a barely perceptible moment, and ranging in form from the literal to such metonymies as binoculars or glasses, to visual puns (the "eye" of a storm) that slide vision once again into language. In the process, Coppola, true to his name—*coppo*, Italian for "eye socket"—but again mixing media, leaves his signature in visual translation. Faithful namesake of the itinerant optician/magician of E. T. A. Hoffmann's "The Sandman," cited by Freud as a master of the uncanny, our Coppola, too, is an oculist, purveyor of "fine eyes, beautiful eyes."[11] Signing his text, crying

---

[11] Cited by Sigmund Freud in "The 'Uncanny.'" I quote here and in note 12 from the 1925 translation by Alix Strachey in Benjamin Nelson, ed., *On Creativity and the Unconscious* (New York: Harper and Row, 1958), 134, which I prefer to the later *Standard Edition* translation (Freud, "The 'Uncanny,'" in *The Standard Edition* [London: Hogarth Press, 1953–74], 17:229).

his wares, this hawker of vision bleeds eyes into mouths that gloss what we see as what we have the words to speak and, conversely, what we can say as what we have the eyes to read.

Borrowing Coppola's lens, I have made hysteria disappear, only to make it reappear in a monster's mouth. I wanted—in words I borrow from Freud, who in turn borrowed Hoffmann's image,—to "look through the fell Coppola's glasses."[12] Through them I saw a monstrously altered but radically continuous discourse. Turning back now to look once more through Frank Rich's eyes, I see an image of a blood culture that behaves differently than the one that Coppola represents. Rich's "new blood culture" tends to recontain both its terrible fluidity and its unceasing monstrosity. When he neatly situates the Draculean hyperconsciousness of fluidity within our own historical moment and more specifically identifies it with AIDS, foreclosing its nineteenth-century context, he reproduces the containing gesture of the vampire hunters or the hysteria doctors: he draws a containing circle as if to enclose what by definition must, as Coppola shows, spill over all bounds.

As Coppola makes us see, the new blood culture is the old blood culture. In defiance of its citational frame, Coppola's Bram Stoker's "Dracula" bleeds Stoker into Coppola, novel into film, gynophobia into homophobia, hysteria into AIDS, and one fin de siècle into another. Dracula, like hysteria, is about bodily fluids that defy the sanctuary of our human frames and seep through the hermetically separated safe houses of gender. It is about blood, and tears, and sex. And it is about the "watery clasp" of words that must flow into and become whatever they would grip and control.[13] Coppola's Dracula is most markedly fluid in its intertextual play, in its watery embrace of a nineteenth-century source that speaks the uncontainability of desire, of death, of time, and of the texts we write for them.

[12] Freud, "The 'Uncanny,'" in On Creativity, 137; Standard Edition, 17:230.
[13] The citation is from Robert Graves, "The Cool Web," in New Collected Poems (New York: Doubleday, 1977), 27. Graves writes of "throwing off language and its watery clasp."

BIBLIOGRAPHY

Ackroyd, Peter. *Dressing Up, Transvestism and Drag: The History of an Obsession.* New York: Simon and Schuster, 1979.

Agulhon, Maurice. *Marianne au combat.* Paris: Flammarion, 1979.

Allen, James Smith. *In the Public Eye: A History of Reading in Modern France, 1800–1940.* Princeton: Princeton University Press, 1991.

Apostolidès, Jean-Marie. *Le Roi-machine: Spectacle et politique au temps de Louis XIV.* Paris: Minuit, 1981.

Aragon, Louis, and André Breton. "Le Cinquantenaire de l'hystérie." *La Révolution surréaliste* 4 (15 March 1928): 20–22.

Arata, Stephen D. "The Occidental Tourist: *Dracula* and the Anxiety of Reverse Colonization." *Victorian Studies* 33 (Summer 1990): 621–45.

Ardener, Shirley, ed. *Women and Space: Ground Rules and Social Maps.* London: Croom Helm, 1981.

Armstrong, Nancy. *Desire and Domestic Fiction.* Oxford: Oxford University Press, 1987.

272
•
Assad, Maria L. "Who Really Killed Emma Bovary?" Paper delivered at the eleventh annual Nineteenth-Century French Studies Colloquium, Vanderbilt University, 17 October 1985.

Bachelard, Gaston. *L'Eau et les rêves.* Paris: Corti, 1960.

——. *La Poétique de l'espace.* Paris: Quadrige/P. U. F., 1957.

Bakhtin, Mikhail. *Rabelais and His World.* Translated by Hélène Iswolsky. Cambridge: M.I.T. Press, 1968.

Balzac, Honoré de. *La Comédie humaine.* Edited by Pierre-Georges Castex. 12 vols. Paris: Gallimard, 1976–81.

——. *Oeuvres complètes.* Edited by Marcel Bouteron and Henri Longnon. 40 vols. Paris: Conard, 1940.

Barbin, Herculine. *Herculine Barbin: Being the Recently Discovered Memoirs of a Nineteenth-Century French Hermaphrodite.* Translated by Richard McDougall and edited by Michel Foucault. New York: Pantheon, 1980.

Barkan, Leonard. *Nature's Work of Art: The Human Body as Image of the World.* New Haven: Yale University Press, 1975.

Barnes, Julian. *Flaubert's Parrot.* New York: Knopf, 1985.

Barrows, Susanna. *Distorting Mirrors: Visions of the Crowd in Late Nineteenth-Century France.* New Haven: Yale University Press, 1981.

Bart, Benjamin. *Flaubert.* Syracuse: Syracuse University Press, 1967.

——. "Male Hysteria in *Salammbô.*" *Nineteenth-Century French Studies* 12 (Spring 1984): 3–21.

Barthes, Roland. *La Chambre claire.* Paris: Gallimard, 1980.

——. *Le Grain de la voix.* Paris: Seuil, 1981.

——. *Mythologies.* Paris: Seuil, 1957.

——. *Le Plaisir du texte.* Paris: Seuil, 1973. Translated by Richard Miller as *The Pleasure of the Text.* New York: Hill and Wang, 1975.

——. *S/Z.* Paris: Seuil, 1970. Translated by Richard Miller. New York: Hill and Wang, 1974.

Baudelaire, Charles. *Oeuvres complètes.* Edited by Claude Pichois. 2 vols. Paris: Gallimard, 1975–76.

Baym, Nina. *Novels, Readers, and Reviewers: Responses to Fiction in Antebellum America.* Ithaca: Cornell University Press, 1984.

Beizer, Janet. *Family Plots: Balzac's Narrative Generations.* New Haven: Yale University Press, 1986.

——. "Remembering and Repeating the *Rougon-Macquart*: Clotilde's Story." *L'Esprit Créateur* 25 (Winter 1985): 51–58.

Belenky, Mary Field, Blythe McVicker Clinchy, Nancy Rule Goldberger, and Jill Mattuck Tarule. *Women's Ways of Knowing.* New York: Basic Books, 1986.

Bellet, Roger, ed. *Femmes de lettres au XIXe siècle: Autour de Louise Colet.* Lyon: Presses Universitaires de Lyon, 1982.

Benjamin, Jessica. *The Bonds of Love: Psychoanalysis, Feminism, and the Problem of Domination*. New York: Pantheon, 1988.

———. "A Desire of One's Own: Psychoanalytic Feminism and Intersubjective Space." In *Feminist Studies/Critical Studies*. Edited by Teresa de Lauretis. Bloomington: Indiana University Press, 1986.

Bercherie, Paul. *Genèse des concepts freudiens*. Paris: Navarin, 1983.

Bernhardt, Sarah. *Ma Double Vie*. 2 vols. Paris: des femmes, 1980.

Bernheimer, Charles. *Figures of Ill Repute: Representing Prostitution in Nineteenth-Century France*. Cambridge: Harvard University Press, 1989.

Bernutz, G. "Hystérie." In *Dictionnaire de médecine et de chirurgie pratique*. Edited by Jaccoud. Vol. 18. Paris: Baillière, 1874.

Bersani, Leo. "Flaubert and Emma Bovary: The Hazards of Literary Fusion." *Novel* 8 (Fall 1974): 16–28.

———. "Is the Rectum a Grave?" *October* 43 (Winter 1987): 197–222.

Bertrand, Georges-Emile. *Les Jours de Flaubert*. Paris: Editions du Myrte, 1947.

Besnard-Coursodon, Micheline. "Monsieur Vénus, Madame Adonis: Sexe et discours." *Littérature* 54 (May 1984): 121–27.

Bollas, Christopher. "The Aesthetic Moment and the Search for Transformation." *The Annual of Psychoanalysis* 6 (1978): 385–94.

———. "The Transformational Object." *International Journal of Psychoanalysis* 69 (1979): 97–107.

Bood, Micheline, and Serge Grand. *L'Indomptable Louise Colet*. Paris: Pierre Horay, 1986.

Borie, Jean. *Le Tyran timide*. Paris: Klincksieck, 1973.

———. *Zola et les mythes*. Paris: Seuil, 1971.

Bouillet, Louis. *Lettres à Louise Colet*. Edited by Marie-Claire Bancquart. Paris: Presses Universitaires de France, 1973.

Bourneville, Désiré-Magloire, and P. Regnard. *Iconographie photographique de la Salpêtrière*. Paris: Progrès Médical, 1878.

Brachet, J. L. *Traité de l'hystérie*. Paris: Baillière, 1847.

Bram Stoker's "Dracula." Directed by Francis Ford Coppola. Columbia Pictures, 1992.

Briquet, P. *Traité clinique et thérapeutique de l'hystérie*. Paris: Baillière, 1859.

Brombert, Victor. *The Novels of Flaubert*. Princeton: Princeton University Press, 1966.

Brooks, Peter. *Body Work: Objects of Desire in Modern Narrative*. Cambridge: Harvard University Press, 1993.

———. *Reading for the Plot: Design and Intention in Narrative*. New York: Knopf, 1984.

———. "Storied Bodies, or Nana at Last Unveil'd." *Critical Inquiry* 16 (Autumn 1989): 1–32.

274
•

Bruttin, Jean-Marie. *Différentes Théories sur l'hystérie dans la première moitié du XIXe siècle*. Zurich: Juris Druck, 1969.

Byatt, A. S. *Possession*. New York: Random House, 1990.

Cameron, Deborah. *Feminism and Linguistic Thought*. London: Macmillan, 1985.

Cappellanus, Andreas. *The Art of Courtly Love*. Edited by Frederick W. Locke. Translated by John Jay Parry. New York: Frederick Ungar, 1957.

Carroy, Jacqueline. "Dédoublements: L'énigmatique récit d'un docteur inconnu." *Nouvelle Revue de psychanalyse* 42 (Fall 1990): 151–71.

——. "Une Femme, des récits et des foules." *Revue internationale de psychopathologie* 41 (1991): 323–32.

Carroy-Thirard, Jacqueline. "Figures de femmes hystériques dans la psychiatrie française au 19e siècle." *Psychanalyse à l'université* 4 (March 1979): 313–24.

——. "Hystérie, théâtre, littérature au XIXe siècle." *Psychanalyse à l'université* 7 (March 1982): 299–317.

——. "Possession, extase, hystérie au 19e siècle." *Psychanalyse à l'université* 5 (June 1980): 499–515.

Cesbron, Henri. *Histoire critique de l'hystérie*. Paris: Asselin & Houzeau, 1909.

Chambers, Ross. *Mélancolie et opposition: Les débuts du modernisme en France*. Paris: Corti, 1987.

——. *Story and Situation: Narrative Seduction and the Power of Fiction*. Minneapolis: University of Minnesota Press, 1984.

Charcot, Jean-Martin. *L'Hystérie*. Edited by E. Trillat. Toulouse: Privat, 1971.

——. *Leçons sur l'hystérie virile*. Edited by Michèle Ouerd. Paris: Le Sycomore, 1984.

Charney, Maurice, and Hanna Charney. "The Language of Madwomen in Shakespeare and His Fellow Dramatists." *Signs* 3 (Winter 1977): 451–60.

Chesler, Phyllis. *Women and Madness*. New York: Doubleday, 1972.

Cixous, Hélène. "The Laugh of the Medusa." In *New French Feminisms*. Edited by Elaine Marks and Isabelle de Courtivron. Amherst: University of Massachusetts Press, 1980.

Cixous, Hélène, and Catherine Clément. *La Jeune Née*. Paris: 10/18, 1975.

Claretie, Jules. *Les Amours d'un interne*. Paris: Dentu, 1881.

——. *Histoire de la révolution de 1870–71*. Paris: Aux bureaux du journal *L'Eclipse*, 1872.

Clébert, Jean-Paul. *Louise Colet*. Paris: Presses de la Renaissance, 1986.

Clément, Catherine. *Opera or the Undoing of Woman*. Translated by Betsy Wing. Minneapolis: University of Minnesota Press, 1988.

Colet, Louise. *Une Histoire de soldat*. Paris: Alexandre Cadot, 1856.

——. *Lui, roman contemporain*. Paris: Librairie Nouvelle et A. Bourdelle, 1860.

——. *Lui: A View of Him*. Translated by Marilyn Gaddis Rose. Athens: University of Georgia Press, 1986.

——. *Memoranda*. Reprinted in *Correspondance* by Gustave Flaubert. Edited by Jean Bruneau. 3 vols. Paris: Gallimard, 1973–91.

——. *La Paysanne*. Paris: Perrotin, 1853.

——. *La Religieuse*. Paris: Perrotin, 1856.

——. *La Servante*. Paris: Perrotin, 1854. Reprinted in *Femmes de lettres au XIXe siècle: Autour de Louise Colet*. Edited by Roger Bellet. Lyon: Presses Universitaires de Lyon, 1982.

Corbin, Alain. *Le Miasme et la jonquille: L'odorat et l'imaginaire social, XVIII–XIXe siècles*. Paris: Flammarion, 1986.

Craft, Christopher. "'Kiss Me with Those Red Lips': Gender and Inversion in Bram Stoker's *Dracula*." *Representations* 8 (Fall 1984): 107–133.

Cuaz, Odile. "La Lectrice et le cow-boy." *Le Monde*, 22 November 1991, 30.

Culler, Jonathan. *Flaubert: The Uses of Uncertainty*. Ithaca: Cornell University Press, 1985.

Czyba, Lucette. *Mythes et idéologie de la femme dans les romans de Flaubert*. Lyon: Presses Universitaires de Lyon, 1983.

Danahy, Michael. *The Feminization of the Novel*. Gainesville: University of Florida Press, 1991.

Darnton, Robert. "What Is the History of Books?" In *Reading in America: Literature and Social History*. Edited by Cathy N. Davidson. Baltimore: Johns Hopkins University Press, 1989.

Daudet, Alphonse. "A la Salpêtrière." *Chronique médicale* 1 (January 1898): 15–18.

Dauphiné, Claude. *Rachilde*. Paris: Mercure de France, 1991.

Davis, Natalie Zemon. *Society and Culture in Early Modern France*. Stanford: Stanford University Press, 1975.

Déjerine, Jules. *L'Hérédité dans les maladies du système nerveux*. Paris: Asselin & Houzeau, 1886.

Delboeuf, J. "Une Visite à la Salpêtrière." *Revue de Belgique* 54 (15 October 1886, 15 November 1886): 121–47, 258–75.

Delpit, Albert. *Le Mariage d'Odette*. Paris: Plon, 1880.

Demorest, D. L. *L'Expression figurée et symbolique dans l'oeuvre de Gustave Flaubert*. Geneva: Slatkine Reprints, 1967.

Diderot, Denis. *Les Bijoux indiscrets*. Edited by Aram Vartanian and Jean Macary. In vol. 3 of *Oeuvres complètes*. Paris: Hermann, 1978.

276 ———. "Sur les femmes." In vol. 2 of *Oeuvres complètes de Diderot*. Edited by J.
•   Assézat. Paris: Garnier Frères, 1875.

Didi-Huberman, Georges. *Invention de l'hystérie: Charcot et l'iconographie pho-tographique de la Salpêtrière*. Paris: Macula, 1982.

———. "Une Notion de 'corps-cliché' au XIXe siècle." *Parachute* 35 (1984): 8–14.

Dijkstra, Bram. *Idols of Perversity*. Oxford: Oxford University Press, 1986.

Dinnerstein, Dorothy. *The Mermaid and the Minotaur: Sexual Arrangements and Human Malaise*. New York: Harper and Row, 1977.

Donne, John. Elegie XIX, "To His Mistris Going to Bed." In *Poetry and Prose*. Edited by Frank J. Warnke. New York: Random House, Modern Library, 1967.

Drinka, George Frederick. *The Birth of Neurosis*. New York: Simon and Schuster, 1984.

Du Camp, Maxime. *Les Convulsions de Paris*. 4 vols. Paris: Hachette, 1889.

Duchet, Claude. "Signifiance et insignifiance: Le discours italique dans *Madame Bovary*." In *La Production du sens chez Flaubert*. Edited by Claudine Gothot-Mersch. Paris: 10/18, 1975.

Eleb-Vidal, Monique, and Anne Debarre-Blanchard. *Architectures de la vie privée*. Brussels: Archives d'Architecture Moderne, 1989.

Eliade, Mircea. *Mephistopheles and the Androgyne*. Translated by J. M. Cohen. New York: Sheed and Ward, 1965.

Epheyre, Charles [Charles Richet]. *Possession*. Paris: Ollendorff, 1887.

———. *Soeur Marthe*. *Revue des deux mondes* 93 (15 May 1889): 384–431.

Evans, Martha Noel. *Fits and Starts: A Genealogy of Hysteria in Modern France*. Ithaca: Cornell University Press, 1991.

Ey, Henri. "History and Analysis of the Concept." In *Hysteria*, edited by Alec Roy. New York: John Wiley & Sons, 1982.

Feldman, Jessica. *Gender on the Divide: The Dandy in Modernist Literature*. Ithaca: Cornell University Press, 1993.

Felman, Shoshana. *La Folie et la chose littéraire*. Paris: Seuil, 1978.

Fernier, Robert. *La Vie et l'oeuvre de Gustave Courbet*. 2 vols. Lausanne: Bibliothèque des Arts, 1979.

Ferraro, Fausta, and Adele Nunziante-Cesaro. *L'Espace creux et le corps saturé: La grossesse comme agir entre fusion et séparation*. Translated by Simone Matarasso-Gervais. Paris: des femmes, 1990.

Festa-McCormick, Diana. "Emma Bovary's Masculinization: Conventions of Clothes and Morality of Conventions." In *Gender and Literary Voice*. Edited by Janet Todd. New York: Holmes and Meier, 1980.

Fetterley, Judith. *The Resisting Reader*. Bloomington: Indiana University Press, 1978.

Field, Joanna [Marion Milner]. *On Not Being Able to Paint*. Foreword by Anna Freud. Los Angeles: Jeremy P. Tarcher, 1957.

Fitzpatrick, Thomas B., Arthur Z. Eisen, Klaus Wolff, Irwin M. Freedberg, and K. Frank Austen. *Dermatology in General Medicine*. 2 vols. New York: McGraw-Hill, 1993.

Flaubert, Gustave. *Correspondance*. 9 vols. Paris: Conard, 1926–33.

———. *Correspondance*. Edited by Jean Bruneau. 3 vols. Paris: Gallimard, 1973–91.

———. *Madame Bovary*. Edited by Jacques Suffel. Paris: Garnier Flammarion, 1979. Translated and edited by Paul de Man. New York: Norton, 1965.

———. *Madame Bovary: Ebauches et fragments inédits*. Edited by Gabrielle Leleu. 2 vols. Paris: Conard, 1936.

———. *Oeuvres complètes*. Edited by Jean Bruneau and Bernard Masson. 2 vols. Paris: Seuil, 1964.

Fletcher, Angus. *Allegory: The Theory of a Symbolic Mode*. Ithaca: Cornell University Press, 1964.

Foucault, Michel. "La Bibliothèque fantastique." In *Travail de Flaubert*. Paris: Seuil, 1983.

———. *L'Ordre du discours*. Paris: Gallimard, 1970.

———. *La Volonté de savoir*. Paris: Gallimard, 1976. Translated by Robert Hurley as *The History of Sexuality*, vol. 1. New York: Vintage, 1980.

Fraisse, Geneviève. *Muse de la raison: La démocratie exclusive et la différence des sexes*. Paris: Alinéa, 1989.

France, Anatole. *Jocaste*. Paris: Calmann-Lévy, 1925.

Freeman, Erica. *Insights: Conversations with Theodor Reik*. Englewood Cliffs, N.J.: Prentice-Hall, 1971.

Freud, Sigmund. *The Standard Edition of the Complete Works of Sigmund Freud*. Translated by James Strachey, Anna Freud, Alix Strachey, and Alan Tyson and edited by James Strachey. 24 vols. London: Hogarth Press, 1953–74.

———. "The 'Uncanny.'" In *On Creativity and the Unconscious*. Edited by Benjamin Nelson. New York: Harper and Row, 1958.

Frye, Northrop. *The Anatomy of Criticism*. Princeton: Princeton University Press, 1973.

Fuss, Diana. *Essentially Speaking*. New York: Routledge, 1989.

Gallop, Jane. *The Daughter's Seduction: Feminism and Psychoanalysis*. Ithaca: Cornell University Press, 1982.

———. *Thinking Through the Body*. New York: Columbia University Press, 1988.

Garber, Marjorie. *Vested Interests: Cross-Dressing and Cultural Anxiety*. New York: Routledge, 1992.

BIBLIOGRAPHY

278
•

Gasarian, Gérard. "La Figure du poète hystérique ou l'allégorie chez Baudelaire." *Poétique* 86 (April 1991): 177–91.

Gelfand, Toby. "Medical Nemesis, Paris, 1894: Léon Daudet's *Les Morticules*." *Bulletin of the History of Medicine* 60 (1986): 155–76.

Genette, Gérard. *Figures II*. Paris: Seuil, 1969.

——. *Seuils*. Paris: Seuil, 1987.

Gilbert, Sandra M. "Costumes of the Mind: Transvestism as Metaphor in Modern Literature." *Critical Inquiry* 7 (Winter 1980): 391–417.

Gilbert, Sandra M., and Susan Gubar. *The Madwoman in the Attic*. New Haven: Yale University Press, 1979.

Gilman, Sander L. *Difference and Pathology: Stereotypes of Sexuality, Race, and Madness*. Ithaca: Cornell University Press, 1985.

Goldstein, Jan. *Console and Classify: The French Psychiatric Profession in the Nineteenth Century*. Cambridge: Cambridge University Press, 1987.

——. "The Uses of Male Hysteria: Medical and Literary Discourse in Nineteenth-Century France." *Representations* 34 (Spring 1991): 134–66.

Goncourt, Edmond de. *Les Frères Zemganno*. Paris: Flammarion, 1879.

Goncourt, Edmond and Jules de. *Germinie Lacerteux*. Edited by Enzo Caramaschi. Naples: Edizioni Scientifiche Italiane, 1968.

——. *Journal: Mémoires de la vie littéraire*. Edited by Robert Ricatte. 3 vols. Paris: Laffont, 1956.

——. *Madame Gervaisais*. Edited by Marc Fumaroli. Paris: Gallimard, 1982.

——. *Préfaces et manifestes littéraires*. Paris: Charpentier, 1888.

Gothot-Mersch, Claudine. *La Genèse de Madame Bovary*. Paris: Corti, 1966.

Grasset, Joseph. "Hystérie." In *Dictionnaire encyclopédique des sciences médicales*. Edited by A. Dechambre and L. Lereboullet. Vol. 15. Paris: Asselin & Houzeau/Masson, 1889.

Graves, Robert. *New Collected Poems*. New York: Doubleday, 1977.

Gray, Eugene F. "The Clinical View of Life: Gustave Flaubert's *Madame Bovary*." In *Medicine and Literature*. Edited by Enid Rhodes Peschel. New York: Neale Watson Academic Publications, 1980.

Gray, Francine du Plessix. *Rage and Fire: A Life of Louise Colet, Pioneer Feminist, Literary Star, Flaubert's Muse*. New York: Simon and Schuster, 1994.

Gubar, Susan. "'The Blank Page' and the Issues of Female Creativity." *Critical Inquiry* 8 (Winter 1981): 243–63.

Guillemot, Maurice. "A la Salpêtrière." *Paris illustré* 1 (24 September 1887): 354–56.

——. "A la Salpêtrière." *Paris illustré* 2 (1 October 1887): 371–74.

Hahn, G. "Charcot et son influence sur l'opinion publique." *Revue des questions scientifiques* (July–August 1894): 230–61.

Hamon, Philippe. *Expositions: Littérature et architecture au XIXe siècle*. Paris: **279**
Corti, 1989.

Hawthorne, Melanie. "Rachilde's Paroxysms of Chastity" (unpublished book
manuscript).

——. "The Social Construction of Sexuality in Three Novels by Rachilde."
Michigan Romance Studies 9 (1987): 49–59.

Heath, Stephen. "Difference." *Screen* 19 (Fall 1978): 51–112.

——. *The Sexual Fix*. London: Macmillan, 1982.

Heilbrun, Carolyn. "What Was Penelope Unweaving?" In *Hamlet's Mother and
Other Women*. New York: Columbia University Press, 1990.

——. *Writing a Woman's Life*. New York: Norton, 1984.

Hertz, Neil. "Medusa's Head: Male Hysteria under Political Pressure." In *End of
the Line: Essays on Psychoanalysis and the Sublime*. New York: Columbia University Press, 1985.

Hicks, John, and Robert Tucker. *Revolution and Reaction: The Paris Commune,
1871*. Amherst: University of Massachusetts Press, 1973.

Homans, Margaret. *Bearing the Word*. Chicago: University of Chicago Press, 1986.

Hubert-Matthews, Véronique. "Androgynie et représentation chez quatre auteurs
du dix-neuvième siècle: Balzac, Gautier, Sand, Rachilde." Ph.D. diss., University of Virginia, 1993.

Hunt, Lynn. *Politics, Culture, and Class in the French Revolution*. Berkeley: University of California Press, 1984.

——. "The Unstable Boundaries of the French Revolution." In *A History of Private Life*. Translated by Arthur Goldhammer and edited by Michelle Perrot.
Vol. 4. Cambridge: Harvard University Press, Belknap Press, 1990.

Hunter, Dianne. "Hysteria, Psychoanalysis, and Feminism: The Case of Anna
O." In *The (M)other Tongue: Essays in Feminist Psychoanalytic Interpretation*.
Edited by Shirley Nelson Garner, Claire Kahane, and Madelon Sprengnether.
Ithaca: Cornell University Press, 1985.

Huysmans, Joris-Karl. *En Rade*. Edited by Jean Borie. Paris: Gallimard, 1984.

——. *Là-bas*. Paris: Gallimard, 1985.

Huyssen, Andreas. *After the Great Divide*. Bloomington: Indiana University
Press, 1986.

Ibsen, Henrik. *Ghosts*. Translated by Rolf Fjelde. New York: Signet, 1970.

Irigaray, Luce. "Approche d'une grammaire d'énonciation de l'hystérique et de
l'obsessionnel." *Langages* (March 1967): 99–109.

——. *Speculum of the Other Woman*. Translated by Gillian C. Gill. Ithaca: Cornell University Press, 1985.

——. *This Sex Which Is Not One*. Translated by Catherine Porter with Carolyn
Burke. Ithaca: Cornell University Press, 1985.

280
•
Jardine, Alice. *Gynesis: Configurations of Woman and Modernity*. Ithaca: Cornell University Press, 1985.

Johnson, Barbara. *The Critical Difference: Essays in the Contemporary Rhetoric of Reading*. Baltimore: Johns Hopkins University Press, 1980.

Kafka, Franz. "In the Penal Colony." In *The Complete Stories*. Translated by Willa and Edwin Muir and edited by Nahum N. Glazer. New York: Schocken, 1976.

Kamuf, Peggy. *Fictions of Feminine Desire: Disclosures of Héloïse*. Lincoln: University of Nebraska Press, 1982.

Kaufmann, Vincent. *L'Equivoque épistolaire*. Paris: Minuit, 1991.

Kelly, Dorothy. *Fictional Genders: Role and Representation in Nineteenth-Century French Narrative*. Lincoln: University of Nebraska Press, 1989.

Kessler, Suzanne J., and Wendy McKenna. *Gender: An Ethnomethodological Approach*. Chicago: University of Chicago Press, 1978.

Knibiehler, Yvonne. "Le Discours médical sur la femme: Constantes et ruptures." *Romantisme* 13–14 (1976): 41–55.

Kofman, Sarah. "Séductions, essai sur *La Religieuse* de Diderot." In *Séductions: De Sartre à Héraclite*. Paris: Galilée, 1990.

Kristeva, Julia. *Des Chinoises*. Paris: des femmes, 1974.

——. *Desire in Language*. Translated by Thomas Gora, Alice Jardine, and Leon S. Roudiez; edited by Leon S. Roudiez. New York: Columbia University Press, 1980.

——. *Pouvoirs de l'horreur*. Paris: Seuil, 1980.

——. "Women's Time." Translated by Alice Jardine and Harry Blake. *Signs* 7 (Autumn 1981): 13–35.

Lacan, Jacques. *Ecrits*. 2 vols. Paris: Seuil, 1966.

LaCapra, Dominick. *"Madame Bovary" on Trial*. Ithaca: Cornell University Press, 1982.

Laqueur, Thomas. *Making Sex: Body and Gender from the Greeks to Freud*. Cambridge: Harvard University Press, 1990.

Landouzy, H. *Traité complet de l'hystérie*. Paris: Baillière, 1846.

Laplanche J., and J.-B. Pontalis. *The Language of Psychoanalysis*. Translated by Donald Nicholson-Smith. New York: Norton, 1973.

Laplassotte, François. "Sexualité et névrose avant Freud: Une mise au point." *Psychanalyse à l'université* 3 (1978): 203–26.

Lapp, John C. "Art and Hallucination in Flaubert." *French Studies* 10 (October 1956): 322–34.

Leith, James, ed. *Images of the Commune*. Montreal: McGill University Press, 1978.

Leverenz, David. "The Woman in *Hamlet*: An Interpersonal View." *Signs* 4 (Winter 1978): 291–308.

Lidsky, Paul. *Les Ecrivains contre la Commune*. Paris: Maspero, 1970.

Livi, Jocelyne. *Vapeurs de femmes*. Paris: Navarin, 1984.

Lloyd, Rosemary. *"Madame Bovary."* London: Unwin Hyman, 1990.

Lottman, Herbert. *Flaubert: A Biography*. Boston: Little, Brown, 1989.

Louyer-Villermay, Jean-Baptiste. "Hystérie." In *Dictionnaire des sciences médicales*. Vol. 23. Paris: Panckoucke, 1818.

———. *Traité des maladies nerveuses ou vapeurs, et particulièrement de l'hystérie et de l'hypochondrie*. 2 vols. Paris: Méquignon, 1816.

Lowe, A. M. "Emma Bovary: A Modern Arachne." *French Studies* 26 (January 1972): 30–41.

McClary, Susan. *Feminine Endings: Music, Gender, and Sexuality*. Minneapolis: University of Minnesota Press, 1991.

Mallarmé, Stéphane. *Variations sur un sujet*. In *Oeuvres complètes*. Edited by Henri Mondor and G. Jean-Aubry. Paris: Gallimard, 1945.

Mannoni, Octave. *Clefs pour l'imaginaire ou l'autre scène*. Paris: Seuil, 1969.

Maréchal, Sylvain. *Projet d'une loi portant défense d'apprendre à lire aux femmes*. Paris: Massé, 1801.

Martin, Emily. *The Woman in the Body: A Cultural Analysis of Reproduction*. Boston: Beacon Press, 1987.

Masson, Jeffrey Moussaieff. *A Dark Silence: Women, Sexuality, and Psychiatry in the Nineteenth Century*. New York: Farrar, Straus & Giroux, 1986.

Maupassant, Guy de. "Une Femme." In *Chroniques*. Vol. 2. Paris: 10/18, 1980.

May, Georges. *Le Dilemme du roman au XVIIIe siècle*. New Haven: Yale University Press, 1963.

Mayeur, Françoise. *L'Education des filles en France au XIXe siècle*. Paris: Hachette, 1979.

Mérimée, Prosper. *La Vénus d'Ille*. In *Carmen et autres nouvelles*. Vol. 2. Paris: Livre de Poche, 1983.

Micale, Mark S. "The Salpêtrière in the Age of Charcot: An Institutional Perspective on Medical History in the Late Nineteenth Century." *Journal of Contemporary History* 20 (1985): 703–31.

Michaud, Stéphane. "Esquirol et Esquiros." *Romantisme* 24 (1979): 43–52.

Michel, Louise. *Mémoires*. Paris: Maspero, 1976.

Michelet, Jules. *La Sorcière*. Paris: Garnier Flammarion, 1966.

Miller, D. A. *Narrative and Its Discontents*. Princeton: Princeton University Press, 1981.

———. *The Novel and the Police*. Berkeley: University of California Press, 1988.

Miller, Nancy K. *The Heroine's Text*. New York: Columbia University Press, 1980.

———. *Subject to Change*. New York: Columbia University Press, 1988.

———, ed. *The Poetics of Gender*. New York: Columbia University Press, 1986.

BIBLIOGRAPHY

282
•

Möbius, J. P. "The Physiological Mental Weakness of Women." *Alienist and Neurologist* 22 (1901): 624–42.

Moi, Toril. *Sexual/Textual Politics*. London: Methuen, 1985.

Moreau de Tours, Jacques Joseph. *La Psychologie morbide*. Paris: Victor Masson, 1859.

Morel, Bénédicte Auguste. *Traité des dégénérescences*. Paris: Baillière, 1857.

Moses, Claire Goldberg. *French Feminism in the Nineteenth Century*. Albany: State University of New York Press, 1984.

Nedelsky, Jennifer. "Law, Boundaries, and the Bounded Self." *Representations* 30 (Spring 1990): 162–89.

Neely, Carol Thomas. "Feminist Modes of Shakespearean Criticism." *Women's Studies* 9 (1981): 3–11.

Nelson, Brian. *Zola and the Bourgeoisie*. London: Macmillan, 1983.

Nochlin, Linda. "Courbet's *L'Origine du monde*: The Origin without an Original." *October* 37 (Summer 1986): 77–86.

O'Flaherty, Wendy Doniger. *Women, Androgynes, and Other Mythical Beasts*. Chicago: University of Chicago Press, 1980.

Oliver, Hermia. *Flaubert and an English Governess*. Oxford: Clarendon Press, 1980.

Owen, A. R. G. *Hysteria, Hypnosis, and Healing: The Work of J.-M. Charcot*. London: Dennis Dobson, 1971.

Pascal, Roy. *The Dual Voice: Free Indirect Speech and Its Functioning in the Nineteenth-Century European Novel*. Manchester: Manchester University Press, 1977.

Planté, Christine. "Marceline Desbordes-Valmore: L'autobiographie indéfinie." *Romantisme* 56 (1987): 47–58.

Poe, Edgar Allan. "The Philosophy of Composition." In *Selected Writings of Edgar Allan Poe*. Edited by David Galloway. Harmondsworth: Penguin, 1967.

Pommier, Jean. "Les Maladies de Gustave Flaubert." *Le Progrès médical* 15–16 (10–24 August 1947): 408–16.

Poovey, Mary. *Uneven Developments*. Chicago: University of Chicago Press, 1988.

Postel, Jacques. "Images de la folie au XVIIIe siècle: Quelques différences de sa représentation dans les littératures françaises et britanniques au siècle des lumières." *L'Evolution psychiatrique* 49 (1984): 707–18.

——. "Philippe Pinel et le mythe fondateur de la psychiatrie française." *Psychanalyse à l'université* 4 (March 1979): 197–244.

Poulet, Georges. "Flaubert." In *Etudes sur le temps humain*. Paris: Plon, 1949.

——. "Flaubert." In *Les Métamorphoses du cercle*. Paris: Flammarion, 1979.

——. "Phénoménologie de la conscience critique." In *La Conscience critique*.

Paris: Corti, 1971. Translated as "Criticism and the Experience of Interiority." In *The Structural Controversy*. Edited by Richard Macksey and Eugenio Donato. Baltimore: Johns Hopkins University Press, 1972.

Praz, Mario. *The Romantic Agony*. Translated by Angus Davidson. 1933. Reprint, Oxford: Oxford University Press, 1970.

Prendergast, Christopher. *Balzac: Fiction and Melodrama*. London: Edward Arnold, 1978.

Princeton Encyclopedia of Poetry and Poetics. Edited by Alex Preminger. Princeton: Princeton University Press, 1974.

Queffelec, Lise. "Le Lecteur du roman comme lectrice: Stratégies romanesques et stratégies critiques sous la Monarchie de Juillet." *Romantisme* 53 (1986): 8–21.

Rachilde. *Monsieur Vénus*. Paris: Flammarion, 1977. Translated by Madeleine Boyd. New York: Covici, Friede, 1929.

——. *Monsieur Vénus: Roman matérialiste*. Brussels: Auguste Brancart, 1884.

——. *Pourquoi je ne suis pas féministe*. Paris: Editions de France, 1928.

Radway, Janice. *Reading the Romance: Women, Patriarchy, and Popular Literature*. Chapel Hill: University of North Carolina Press, 1984.

Ramazani, Vaheed. *The Free Indirect Mode: Flaubert and the Poetics of Irony*. Charlottesville: University Press of Virginia, 1988.

Reid, Martine. "Flaubert et Sand en correspondance." *Poétique* 85 (February 1991): 53–68.

Rich, Frank. "The New Blood Culture." *New York Times*, 6 December 1992, "Styles of the Times" section.

Richard, Jean-Pierre. *Stendhal et Flaubert: Littérature et sensation*. Paris: Seuil, 1954.

Richet, Charles. "Les Démoniaques d'aujourd'hui." *Revue des deux mondes* 37 (15 January 1880): 340–72.

Rook, Arthur, F. J. G. Ebling, D. S. Wilkinson, R. H. Champion, and J. L. Burton. *Textbook of Dermatology*. 3 vols. Oxford: Blackwell Scientific Publications, 1986.

Rosolato, Guy. "La Voix: Entre corps et langage." *Revue française de psychanalyse* 37 (1974): 75–94.

Ross, Kristin. *The Emergence of Social Space: Rimbaud and the Paris Commune*. Minneapolis: University of Minnesota Press, 1988.

Rothfield, Lawrence. "From Semiotic to Discursive Intertextuality: The Case of *Madame Bovary*." *Novel* 19 (Fall 1985): 57–81.

Rouy, Hersilie. *Mémoires d'une aliénée*. Edited by Le Normant des Varannes. Paris: Ollendorff, 1883.

The Russia House. Directed by Fred Schepisi. Screenplay by Tom Stoppard. MGM, 1990.

BIBLIOGRAPHY

284 Sarcey, Francisque. *Le Mot et la chose*. Paris: Ollendorff, 1863.

• Sarduy, Severo. "Writing/Transvestism." Translated by Alfred MacAdam. *Review* (Fall 1973): 31–33.

Scarry, Elaine. *The Body in Pain: The Making and Unmaking of the World*. Oxford: Oxford University Press, 1985.

Schapira, Marie-Claude. "Peut-on encore lire *La Servante?*" In *Femmes de lettres au XIXe siècle: Autour de Louise Colet*. Edited by Roger Bellet. Lyon: Presses Universitaires de Lyon, 1982.

Schneider, Monique. *De l'exorcisme à la psychanalyse: Le féminin expurgé*. Paris: Retz, 1979.

Schopenhauer, Arthur. "Essai sur les femmes." Translated by Jean Bourdeau. Paris: Alcan, 1884. Reprint edited by Didier Raymond. Paris: Actes Sud, 1987.

Schor, Naomi. *Breaking the Chain: Women, Theory, and French Realist Fiction*. New York: Columbia University Press, 1985.

——. "Details and Decadence: End-Troping in *Madame Bovary*." *SubStance* 26 (1980): 27–35.

——. *Reading in Detail*. New York: Methuen, 1987.

——. "Sainte-Anne: Capitale du délire." *Cahiers naturalistes* 52 (1978): 97–108.

——. *Zola's Crowds*. Baltimore: Johns Hopkins University Press, 1978.

Sedgwick, Eve. "Privilege of Unknowing." *Genders* 1 (Spring 1988): 102–24.

Segalen, Victor. *Les Cliniciens ès lettres*. Preface by Jean Starobinski. Paris: Fata Morgana, 1980.

Serres, Michel. *Feux et signaux de brume*. Paris: Grasset, 1975.

Shakespeare, William. *Hamlet*. Edited by Edward Hubler. New York: Signet, 1963.

Showalter, Elaine. *The Female Malady: Women, Madness, and English Culture, 1830–1980*. New York: Pantheon, 1985.

——. "Feminist Criticism in the Wilderness." In *The New Feminist Criticism*. Edited by Elaine Showalter. New York: Pantheon, 1985.

——. "Representing Ophelia: Women, Madness, and the Responsibilities of Feminist Criticism." In *Shakespeare and the Question of Theory*. Edited by Patricia Parker and Geoffrey Hartman. London: Methuen, 1985.

Signoret, J. L. "Une Leçon clinique à la Salpêtrière (1887) par André Brouillet." *Revue neurologique* 12 (1983): 687–701.

Silverman, Debora L. *Art Nouveau in Fin-de-Siècle France: Politics, Psychology, and Style*. Berkeley: University of California Press, 1989.

Silverman, Kaja. *The Acoustic Mirror: The Female Voice in Psychoanalysis and Cinema*. Bloomington: Indiana University Press, 1988.

Simon-Dhouailly, Nadine, ed. *La Leçon de Charcot*. Paris: Musée de l'Assistance Publique de Paris, 1986.

Smith-Rosenberg, Carroll. "The Hysterical Woman: Sex Roles and Role Conflict 285
in Nineteenth-Century America." In *Disorderly Conduct: Visions of Gender in* •
Victorian America. New York: Knopf, 1985.

Sollers, Philippe. *Femmes*. Paris: Gallimard, 1983. Translated by Barbara Bray as
Women. New York: Columbia University Press, 1990.

Sonolet, Jacqueline, ed. *Charcot et l'hystérie au 19e siècle*. Paris: La Salpêtrière,
1982.

Sontag, Susan. *AIDS and Its Metaphors*. New York: Farrar, Straus & Giroux,
1988.

——. *Illness as Metaphor*. New York: Farrar, Straus & Giroux, 1977.

Spacks, Patricia Meyer. *Gossip*. Chicago: University of Chicago Press, 1986.

Spelman, Elizabeth. "Colonizing the Language of Suffering." Paper presented at
the University of Virginia, 5 November 1990.

Stallybrass, Peter. "Patriarchal Territories." In *Rewriting the Renaissance*. Edited
by Margaret Ferguson, Maureen Quilligan, and Nancy J. Vickers. Chicago:
University of Chicago Press, 1986.

Stallybrass, Peter, and Allon White. *The Politics and Poetics of Transgression*. Ithaca: Cornell University Press, 1986.

Stevens, Wallace. "Sunday Morning." In *The Palm at the End of the Mind*. Edited
by Holly Stevens. New York: Vintage, 1972.

Stoker, Bram. *Dracula*. New York: Doubleday, 1927.

Swain, Gladys. "L'Ame, la femme, le sexe et le corps: Les métamorphoses de l'hystérie à la fin du XIXe siècle." *Le Débat* 24 (1983): 107–27.

Tanner, Tony. *Adultery in the Novel: Contract and Transgression*. Baltimore:
Johns Hopkins University Press, 1979.

Tastu, Madame A. *Lectures pour les jeunes filles*. Paris: Didier, 1866.

Theweleit, Klaus. *Male Fantasies*. Translated by Stephen Conway. 2 vols. Minneapolis: University of Minnesota Press, 1987.

Thomas, Edith. *Les Pétroleuses*. Paris: Gallimard, 1963.

Ullmann, Stephen. "Reported Speech and Internal Monologue in Flaubert." In
Style.in the French Novel. Oxford: Basil Blackwell, 1964.

Vallois, Marie-Claire. "Les Voi(es) de la sibylle: Aphasie et discours féminin chez
Mme de Staël." *Stanford French Review* 6 (Spring 1982): 35–48.

Vargas Llosa, Mario. *The Perpetual Orgy: Flaubert and "Madame Bovary."* Translated by Helen Lane. New York: Farrar, Straus & Giroux, 1986.

Veith, Ilza. *Hysteria: The History of a Disease*. Chicago: University of Chicago
Press, 1965.

Vest, James M. *The French Face of Ophelia from Belleforest to Baudelaire*. Lanham, N.Y.: University Press of America, 1989.

Wajeman, Gérard. *Le Maître et l'hystérique*. Paris: Navarin/Seuil, 1982.

BIBLIOGRAPHY

286 ——. "Psyché de la femme: Note sur l'hystérique au XIXe siècle." *Romantisme* 13–14 (1976): 57–66.

Walker, Philip. "The Mirror, the Window, and the Eye in Zola's Fiction." *Yale French Studies* 42 (1969): 52–67.

Warner, Marina. *Monuments and Maidens: The Allegory of the Female Form.* New York: Atheneum, 1985.

Wilden, Anthony. "In the Penal Colony: The Body as the Discourse of the Other." *Semiotica* 54 (1985): 33–85.

Williams, Roger. *The Horror of Life.* Chicago: University of Chicago Press, 1980.

Wing, Nathaniel. *The Limits of Narrative.* Cambridge: Cambridge University Press, 1986.

Winnett, Susan. "Coming Unstrung: Women, Men, Narrative, and Principles of Pleasure." *PMLA* 105 (May 1990): 505–17.

Winnicott, D. W. "The Capacity to Be Alone." In *The Maturational Processes and the Facilitating Environment.* New York: International Universities Press, 1965.

——. "Transitional Objects." In *Playing and Reality.* New York: Basic Books, 1971.

Wyatt, Jean. *Reconstructing Desire: The Role of the Unconscious in Women's Reading and Writing.* Chapel Hill: University of North Carolina Press, 1990.

Zola, Emile. *Carnets d'enquêtes.* Edited by Henri Mitterand. Paris: Plon, 1986.

——. "De la moralité dans la littérature." In vol. 45, *Oeuvres complètes, Documents littéraires.* Edited by G. Sigaux. 50 vols. Paris: Fasquelle, 1927–28.

——. *Nana.* Translated by George Holden. Harmondsworth: Penguin, 1972.

——. *Oeuvres complètes.* Edited by Maurice Le Blond. 50 vols. Paris: François Bernouard, 1928.

——. *Pot-Bouille.* Edited by Henri Mitterand. Preface by André Fermigier. Paris: Gallimard [Folio], 1982.

——. *Le Roman expérimental.* Paris: Garnier Flammarion, 1971.

——. *Les Rougon-Macquart.* Edited by Armand Lanoux and Henri Mitterand. 5 vols. Paris: Gallimard, 1960–67.

INDEX

LIBRARY OF CONGRESS CATALOGING-IN-PUBLICATION DATA

Beizer, Janet.
    Ventriloquized bodies : narratives of hysteria in nineteenth-
century France / Janet Beizer.
        p.   cm.
    Includes bibliographical references and index.
    ISBN 0-8014-2914-5 (cloth)   ISBN 0-8014-8142-2 (paper)
        1. French fiction—19th century—History and criticism.
    2. Feminism and literature—France—History—19th century.
    3. Women and literature—France—History—19th century.
    4. French fiction—Men authors—History and criticism.   5. Body,
Human, in literature.   6. Hysteria in literature.   7. Sex role in literature.
    8. Narration   (Rhetoric)   I. Title.
    PQ653.B36   1994
    843'.709352042—dc20   93-41379